Innovation Policy Challenges
for the 21st Century

RIOT! Routledge Studies in Innovation, Organization and Technology

Innovation Policy Challenges for the 21st Century

Edited by Deborah Cox and John Rigby

LONDON AND NEW YORK

First published 2013
by Routledge
Published 2014 by Routledge
711 Third Avenue, New York, NY 10017

Simultaneously published in the UK
by Routledge
2 Park Square, Milton Park, Abingdon, Oxfordshire OX14 4RN

*Routledge is an imprint of the Taylor and Francis Group,
an informa business*

First issued in paperback 2015

Library of Congress Cataloging-in-Publication Data
    Innovation policy challenges for the 21st century / edited by Deborah Cox and John Rigby.
        p. cm. — (Routledge studies in innovation, organization and technology ; 27)
    Includes bibliographical references and index.
    1.   Technological innovations—Government policy.   2.   High technology industries.   3.   Industrial policy.   I. Cox, Deborah.
    II. Rigby, John, 1962–
    HC79.T4I5476 2012
    338'.064—dc23
    2012016471

ISBN 978-0-415-89612-2 (hbk)
ISBN 978-1-138-96059-6 (pbk)
ISBN 978-0-203-08424-3 (ebk)

Typeset in Sabon
by IBT Global.

Contents

PART III
The Labor Force and Human Capital and Societal Issues

PART IV
Broadening and Deepening Innovation Policy

Figures

Acknowledgments

The editors would like to acknowledge Professor Stanley Metcalfe for his valuable comments on the text and for providing the Foreword to this book. We also acknowledge the contribution of Dr Diana Pearson for her assistance in preparing the manuscript. We acknowledge the European Commission, whose funding under grant number 38829 led to the production of some material that was then used as the basis for this book.

Foreword

How can innovation policy be constructed so as to influence the unpredictable, to shape that which cannot be known at the time the policy is put into effect? This is the great dilemma that all innovation policies must struggle and come to terms with. Innovation and the associated acts of enterprise are of uncertain outcome not only because the underlying process of invention is unpredictable but also because innovation requires users and consumers to buy the new device or service at a price that covers the economic costs of supply, and this possibility can never be decided on a priori grounds. It is all too easy to think of innovation policy in terms of the invention process—the conduct of R&D for example—and to forget this elementary fact that innovation depends on creating a market. This double uncertainty is a defining aspect of innovation; good technical ideas may fail because they cannot displace established methods of supply. In a rapidly evolving and increasingly competitive world these uncertainties are compounded.

This book provides a valuable guide to these problems of innovation policy and sets out some of the latest thinking in this most challenging area of public policy. When ideas about market failure dominated policy debate, it was sufficient to think of policy in terms of providing resources to innovate and of enhancing the incentives to innovate through tax breaks or innovation subsidies. New ideas about innovation policy have pointed to the further significance of strengthening the capacity to manage innovation and to create opportunities to innovate in situations where each innovation depends upon the contribution of many distributed actors. These systemic dimensions of the innovation process and the need for connectivity turn out to be of great significance; they point to the policy problem as one of process rather than one of generating specific outcomes. Within the processes involved, factor markets, the supply of finance, skills and intellectual property must be weighed equally with consumer markets, the importance of lead consumers and the role of design as a key to capturing the attention of users. The role of the government as a major consumer of goods and services should be given due prominence and wider questions of innovation cultures need to be addressed. These are the domains covered in this volume of essays; they point to the challenges of innovation policy, its complexity and the irreducible ignorance that every innovator must face in judging whether their business experiment will pay off, and they point to the opportunities that continually emerge to craft new dimensions to innovation policy.

Capitalism is never at rest—this is the great Schumpeterian insight. The system transforms itself incessantly from within, changing structures; new patterns of economic activity, indeed new ways of life, emerge in remarkably short periods of time. Anyone over the age of sixty has witnessed virtually everything that is significant about the information technology revolution. Manufacturing no longer dominates Western economies, the knowledge base for economic activity changes in step with the emerging structures of economic activity, and the growth of productivity means that a given expansion of aggregate output generates fewer jobs; policy inevitably has to respond. Innovation policy must move with the times—it cannot be set in stone, and this is perhaps the strongest of the lessons contained in this set of essays.

JSM, March 2012, Manchester.

Introduction

John Rigby

This book is an exploration of how innovation policy is being developed and implemented as we begin the second decade of the 21st century. The book owes its origins to work carried out for the European Commission to review and examine the scope for innovation policies in a number of areas. Our book takes a number of these enquiries on what we believe are the most important topics and deepens and widens them, critically examining the literature to give an understanding of the policy foundations, the lessons learned from the experience of implementing such policies, and the scope for their further use. Our principle of selection for the book has been to demonstrate the breadth of innovation policies, to show government itself as an innovator, but, like all innovators, finding challenges and difficulties realizing its aims and objectives.

This is not therefore just a book about the EU and its member states. The policies that we consider are diverse and have been applied in a variety of settings and are capable of implementation in many more. Globalization is leading to convergences, not necessarily of wealth perhaps, but of approaches to policy right across the world economy. Trade liberalization such as the GATT/WTO provides new legal frameworks within which government policy must now be developed, while at other levels—for example, in Europe—the process of enlargement of the Union has presented opportunities for the sharing of experiences of good practice in policy-making.

No book on innovation policy should presume that its subject matter, innovation, is without need of description, explication or justification. The increasing and diverse uses of the word innovation recommend that some attention be given to this task. Many things can be said about innovation: it can be seen as too vague a term to be practically or theoretically useful; it is the tedious and insignificant stage producing a product or service for sale in a market that follows the creative act that gives us an invention; conversely it is everything that firms do, from working out what products or services they need to sell to keep ahead of their competitors, from coming up with new product ideas, product design and market testing, from initial concept to the introduction of the product in the marketplace; it is often used to refer to something new and unproblematic and unquestionably desirable;

yet it can also refer to a process and not to an outcome—that is, its sense of how or whether something happens, the means by which something is achieved and not what that actually is. In an age when change in technology and society is so evident, it is perhaps a surprise that we need yet another word to refer to that change.

Those concerned with the more specific meanings of innovation might note that a world in which innovation is central is one that is perpetually changing. For society, there may be a number of implications. Firstly, the changes that we experience, whether we bring them about ourselves or whether they result from outside influences, require us to react in order to survive. That we do so in competition, as well through collaboration, suggests that innovation is a Darwinian process, and one that lacks an ethical dimension.

Secondly, in a society in which innovation is such a clearly dominant political and economic priority, is there not a risk that the future is privileged over the present? This second observation sees innovation no longer in a positive light, as an aspect of a creative and inventive culture, but as a mantra of pro-growth, reckless economic development, or at least as a casual, uncritical 'business as usual' attitude: a slogan to promote or perhaps to disguise a model of society and economy in which perpetual change opens up all areas of human life to the market mechanism, and no stone is left unturned to provide opportunities for capital to maintain its historic compound rate of growth of 3 percent.

There is little doubt that innovation certainly refers to the process of creative destruction by which entrepreneurs and firms seek to realize opportunities for profit. But the term is no longer another name for how solutions to the economic problem of scarcity are found and opportunities for profit are conjured out of thin air. Our contemporary understanding of innovation now involves a connection between our innate creativity on the one hand and our roles in economic life on the other. Through this process of mixing, the act of production is partly rehabilitated through its connection with the creative potential of men, women and children. Innovation therefore becomes the secular creed for modern Western societies.[1] Innovation is seen as an activity that not only provides satisfaction of our material needs but also involves the realization of our potential to create and transform the world, for the better, we hope, but more often than we would like for worse.

But if innovation is an intrinsic part of the world, why should government support it? Where do the justifications for government policy for innovation come from? We innovate to create opportunities and to help us solve problems, but sometimes the innovations cause problems that we need to deal with. Many of our innovations do not give us what we expect—things go wrong. How else can we explain the great financial crisis that began in 2008?

Increasingly government has ceded the power of choice to producers and consumers and its room for action in the economy is much more limited. The promotion of free trade through the reduction of barriers and the limits to government intervention in the economy now in place as a result of the WTO places significant limits on government's role. Traditional industrial policies are no longer possible, although governments have had to find ways of supporting industries and special interests when parts of the economy considered key to the operation of normal life are in danger. Look, for example, at the way in which the financial services industries have been rescued. This new, liberalized world order that privileges markets as the solution to the economic problem produces approaches to economic governance that are generally thinner, more diverse and distributed and rely on the provision of information, the unlocking of potential and coordination of actions on the one hand, or, on the other, large-scale and quite often hurriedly put together attempts to protect the stability of the economic system itself, often involving vast public subsidy.

Our focus here is what can be achieved with this new, thinner form of economic governance. New areas and forms of support are being explored. New concerns are being observed, and policies to support innovation and growth developed in the US are frequently invoked as exemplars. These new policies to support innovation can be found in a variety of areas.

Firstly we consider areas where large-scale government involvement is still needed—the production of public and social goods. We provide a typology for thinking about how the demand for public and social goods is articulated, and how demand is met. We seek to show that it is not always government that has innovated in the area of public goods, and that civil society organizations have had and continue to have an important role to play in meeting the needs of social groups. Very often it has been civil society organizations that have pioneered such activity and it has only been later that government has stepped in to provide such services.

We then look at demand-driven innovation, where demand for goods and services both public and private is framed with the involvement of users. We examine how the innovation process can be redesigned and reoriented towards users and their requirements and how this approach by government to the goods and services that it provides may be used to promote innovation in areas where there has been relatively little in the past. Across Europe, the procurement of innovation by government is being considered as an important policy priority. New approaches to government procurement of innovation were developed in the public procurement directives of 2004, and, following a review during 2010, it is likely that the directives will change again to enable public procurers to call and realize greater innovation from those that provide goods and services to citizens.

A related further chapter within this first section on government driving innovation looks at innovation within the public sector itself in terms of its internal processes of management, priority setting, responsiveness to citizens and the implementation of government services. The use of information technology is an important underpinning for much of the improvement in the way in which governments have delivered their services.

The book then considers how innovation policy has begun to focus on one of the key actors in the innovation process, the entrepreneur, and how support to entrepreneurialism seeks to encourage entrepreneurial behavior across society. We term this section 'the entrepreneurial turn', and within it we include reviews of other policies that seek to give help to smaller firms and to activities often linked to innovation. We look first at a topic of increasing interest, particularly as pressure for a Community Patent grows once again—the role of intellectual property rights and their relationship with open innovation. Open innovation is the practice of relying upon the intellectual property resources outside the firm as much as those inside to innovate and develop new products and processes. There is a view that open innovation is facilitated by a vigorous intellectual property rights regime, but, as we argue, regimes in which property rights proliferate must be those that provide good title, otherwise confusion reigns. The next chapter then looks at the support for high-growth firms in particular, so-called gazelles. In recent years, policymakers in Europe, but also in the US, have paid close attention to smaller firms as evidence has accumulated, particularly in the US, that a small number of these small firms will grow significantly to become major employers. Examples of new information technology and media businesses have been frequently used in discussions, but, as the evidence shows, it is not always the high-technology industries that have the capacity to grow. In practice, firms in traditional sectors are just as likely to increase in size and take on new employees. A further chapter looks at government-supported financing for innovation by small firms, an area of policy-making where the European Union wishes to follow a model developed in the US but that the US has struggled to make work effectively. The section completes with a chapter reviewing the role of microfinance in supporting innovation and its scope and potential.

In part three we present two chapters that examine the issues of skills, older workers and innovation, the linkages between them and the responses of policymakers. The first chapter examines the debate over 'skills and innovation'. The second looks at the links between innovation and older workers and the measures taken to retain those workers in the labor force.

Part three addresses the issue of which skills and competences are required to maintain and improve innovation performance in Europe. The shift, over previous decades, from primarily resource-based to knowledge-based economies has changed and continues to change the kinds of skills and competences required to play their role in maintaining and generating innovation. Recent reports (CEDEFOP 2007/8, INSEAD 2009) indicate that projected skills gaps (or shortages) and skills mismatches present serious challenges to the maintenance of economic growth. European policymakers are confronting these emerging skills gaps in crucial sectors in the contexts of an ageing demographic paradigm and shrinking labor forces. Since the re-launch of the Lisbon Strategy, raising the employment rates of older workers and retaining them in the labor force have become one of the policy priorities aimed at maintaining innovativeness and sustainable economic growth.

The final part of the book seeks to explore the wider context in which innovation policy develops. It is concerned with new areas and new departures in the field and here we explore the broader influences that shape the development of innovations. The first chapter, which focuses on the topic of innovation and creative places, examines the influences on innovation that fall outside of the usual innovation management and policy discussions, namely the 'spatial' and 'organizational dimensions' of culture that have attracted most attention in the context of innovation studies. A second chapter in this section considers 'cultures and innovation'. In this work the authors explore the cultural dimensions of innovation, particularly the ways in which culture shapes and creates the preconditions for creativity, innovation and diffusion.

The third chapter of this final section looks at design as a tool for innovation. It covers key contemporary issues, exploring the concept and relevance of design in innovation including a global perspective, the impact of design for innovation and strategies employed at the firm level. The relevance of these issues to policy is then outlined.

In this new era of innovation policy, where policies of the kind covered in this book have been developed and applied by many governments, state intervention is now justified to some extent by views of the economy that are inspired by the work of Schumpeter. These views see economies not tending towards balance or stability, but as turbulent and dynamic systems, at the center of which is innovation. As our book seeks to show, government policies increasingly seek to promote this dynamism and they do so by supporting innovation wherever it occurs. Our book then seeks to provide some tentative answers to these questions. The concluding chapter reviews the progress that policymakers have achieved in these areas and asks: Do we have the right policies? Is there a consistent approach being followed or is it a more scattergun approach? If innovation is so unpredictable and takes place at so many levels, can effective policies to support it be developed? What policies not covered here could be relevant still?

NOTES

1. In the *Guide to Innovation* in Oxford series of Very Short Introductions, an opening note is made by Philip Pullman, one of the foremost creative writers of the present day.

Part I

Government Driving Innovation

1   Who Drives Innovation?

*John Rigby, Yanuar Nugroho,
Kathryn Morrison and Ian Miles*

INTRODUCTION

The development of new products, processes and services can be organized and led by many different actors in the economy and takes place
at many different levels. After a strong government leadership of economic growth and development through extensive funding of technology
programs during the 1960s and 1970s, the 1980s saw Western governments beginning to withdraw from the innovation process to a significant
degree. During the 1990s, governments increasingly moved to assume
enabling and regulatory roles, emphasizing freedom of choice for consumers in product and factor markets alike. Government has sought to
facilitate innovation rather than leading it or driving it. But a number of
recent policy initiatives arising within the EU suggest that there is now a
wish to reverse this trend by making government once again a key actor in
the innovation process, on the one hand through public procurement, and
on the other hand, through giving government a key role in coordinating
and leading so-called 'social innovation'.

The new emphasis upon government as a central actor results from concern that within the EU economy, insufficient resources are allocated to
R&D, compared with other major economic zones with which the EU is in
competition, and that the current economic crisis may call for increased governmental spending on those areas that may command public support. Both
key research and innovation Directorate Generals (DGs) (DG Research and
Innovation and DG Enterprise and Industry) have been active in this area
of policy. DG Enterprise has explored and continues to examine large-scale
innovations that would have broad social impacts, following the example of
programs that have been run at member state level. DG Research by contrast
has begun to try to find ways of focusing the research systems of member
states on large-scale scientific challenges that are defined at a European level.
Reflecting the larger scale of these new kinds of initiatives in the context of
science, DG Research has begun to use the term 'grand challenges'.

This chapter begins with typology that shows how different actors participate in the innovation process. The typology, which is shown in Figure

1.1, considers which factors determine where the leadership of innovation lies, and we then outline where government typically takes a key role in leading innovation. Our review of the policy literature suggests that the civil society/third sector is often vital, and government often builds upon the work of the third sector. The framework is then used to review and critically assess current EU policy for innovation.

CONCEPTUAL REVIEW OUTLINE OF INNOVATION SYSTEMS ACTORS

Innovation processes vary from place to place and different authors emphasize different drivers and actors in their accounts. The broad trend in innovation studies has reflected increasing awareness, in both theory and policy, of the significance of interconnection between the actors involved in processes of innovation (e.g., Dosi, 1982). There has been a more inclusive view about who and what is involved in innovation, and to realize the importance of interaction between participants. This more inclusive perspective of the innovation and development has also extended to include efforts to grasp the complexity and iterative nature of these processes (e.g., Kline and Rosenberg, 1986). Those specialists focusing on innovation within the firm have also proposed more open models (cf. 'open innovation', Chesbrough, 2003). Major achievements of this debate have been the *system of innovation* approaches, advanced by Freeman (1998), Lundvall (1992) and Nelson (1993), which have formed the basis for policy-making at EU level and among a wide range of governments across the developed and less developed world. Within the EU, the so-called 'Community Broad-Based Innovation Strategy' is an example of such an approach.

Further developments include analyses of the relation between different key actors (Etzkowitz and Leydesdorff, 1998) of the nature of governance questions and the role of scientific knowledge (Gibbons et al., 1994; Nowotny et al., 2001). Attempts to promote engagement between actors include activities like foresight and technology assessment (TA)—particularly constructive technology assessment (CTA) (see Schot and Rip, 1997). Such attempts engage multiple actors to explore possible synergies and conflicts between future social and cultural objectives and opportunities for innovation provided by accumulating knowledge, especially scientific and technological knowledge. Principles emerging from this analysis have gradually informed innovation policy-making in a number of countries.

Analysis of the innovation process has generally focused upon the activity of major groups of actors—firms, government, universities/HEIs and laboratories—and the roles they take in delivering innovations. These groups interact, in various ways, to identify objectives and to produce innovations.

		Responding to Social and Cultural Objectives			
		Citizens	Government	Firms	Universities
Outlining Social and Cultural Objectives	Citizens	Social innovations [Internal Innovation] [Aspects of collective demand = Club Goods]	Regulation; Public Goods; Public Safety; Defence; Laws and Prohibitions, e.g. Stem Cell Research (collectively demanded)	Private Goods (Individually demanded not societally driven); Eco or Social Goods (collectively demanded)	Educational and Knowledge Services
	Government	Merit Goods Health; Education	Reform of Government: Improvement of Processes, including innovation processes [Internal Innovation]	Market Order, Regulation, Public Goods Production	Knowledge for Policy
	Firms	New Technologies, Rules, Forms of Consumption	Market Order	Business to Business Innovation [Internal Innovation] [Aspects of collective demand = Club Goods]	Knowledge for Strategy
	Universities		New Scientific Technology Instrumentalities	New Scientific Technology Instrumentalities	Innovation Knowledge Production [Internal Innovation]

Figure 1.1   Actors of the innovation system and their respective roles.

But the form of interaction and the leadership can vary across cases. Citizens often appear in these analyses only as relatively passive and/or inhibiting actors, thus 'public resistance to new technology' is a common theme, along with calls for increased educational effort aimed at enhancing 'public awareness/understanding'. But there are exceptions, in theory and practice, where a more sophisticated understanding of citizen roles exists. This is one of the central arguments in this chapter.

Indeed, different groups play different roles depending upon the nature of the need, and the type of innovation to satisfy it. Figure 1.1 provides a simple depiction of the relationships between the principal actors in the process of innovation. The figure shows the expression of need and does not explicitly consider resource flows, such as taxation. Expectations that are largely concerned with the innovation performance of the societal group are demands that are formulated within (and often met by) that group. Objectives can be formed individually or collectively. The figure identifies the conventional forms of economic production including private and public markets, but expresses other activities, including innovation by and within classes of actors. The expression of and provision of innovations often involves multiple sets of actors. It is not simply a link between two sets of actors.

The Role of Citizens

Citizens are capable of internal innovation. Their innovations often fall into the category of social innovations. Scholars often refer to social innovation by focusing upon the ways in which the collective processes involved in the definition of needs have been subject to change. This is reflected prominently and particularly in urban studies, policy studies and development studies, which have put more emphasis upon governance questions and the roles and social structures that underpin the definition of societal and individual needs (Moulaert et al., 2005; Swyngedouw, 2005; Davies, 2007; Taylor, 2007). Schumpeter (1980) also addresses innovation processes more directly with 'creative destruction' and defines entrepreneurs as people who combine existing elements in new ways. This idea informs subsequent studies on the importance of social factors affecting adoption and diffusion of technological innovations (e.g., Freeman, 1998). Citizens may organize themselves to articulate their social and cultural objectives, and seek new ways of meeting them. More technological innovation rarely involves more than incremental development, since the major technology advances are typically reliant on specialized knowledge and R&D. But there is much 'user-driven' input into establishing ways of using new technologies, and the malleability of information technology (IT), especially software, means that developments here are common.

Citizens demand external protection and other public goods from government. This may include regulation, which can be applied to any of the actors involved (including firms, universities and other citizens). There are often controversies in this area, with different groups having different views. Stem cell research is a good example of where different positions about ethical and moral dimensions exist. In the US, the Stem-Cell Research Enhancement Act of 2007, which seeks to increase the level of government funding for this form of research, has been opposed by many citizen groups and the presidential veto has been used to prevent the Act becoming law. (The Act was never in fact an act, but a bill, as it never became law.)

Citizens demand private goods and services from firms. This demand is expressed through market choice for those goods and services on offer. But both individually and collectively (e.g., in the form of voluntary organizations, civil society organizations and NGOs), citizens demand that firms provide private goods that may meet certain criteria, such as low environmental impact. These criteria may relate to broader public benefits or the requirements of specific consumers, or even run counter to wider considerations of the public good. Citizens also demand from universities educational and knowledge skills that allow them (or their children) to compete in the workplace or pursue other life goals. Citizens demand training, development, and education from the universities in a similar way to the way in which they demand goods and services from private firms. Information asymmetries are widespread in both instances, and provide a role for government. Generally, expectations on the part of citizens for education and research are not collectively defined. However, there may be times at which these become political issues. In the case of education, the questions of access and standards are often visible. In the case of research, the main concerns have predominantly centered on how it is conducted (e.g., use of animals, embryos) rather than on the goals, although goals can be morally, ethically and politically divisive.

The Role of Government

Government demand for public goods from firms should, in democratic societies, be derivative from the needs of citizens. The payment for the creation of such goods is from taxation. Government creates merit goods, the consumption of which is seen to be in the interests of citizens (reflecting how social needs have been defined). Some of these are produced directly by state-run public services, some are produced by the private sector, but the market is largely one with government purchasing providing the income stream to firms. The production and consumption of such goods are classically said to be driven partly by enlightened citizens and partly by government, which must provide extra supply of some goods and services where some citizens fail to recognize the benefits of making their own market choices to invest in them (e.g., health insurance in many countries). Political economists recognize that government actions often reflect the articulation of interests by organized groups (e.g., politically strategic economic groups (like small farmers), firms regarded as 'national champions' and scientific and professional elites).

Government also innovates internally. Much of its innovation is aimed at achieving greater efficiency in the provision of public goods. A great deal of current activity surrounds e-government, which many commentators see as potentially transforming relationships between the state and its citizens. Government may also have the expectation that firms will be productive and efficient and, by achieving this, will have more resources with which to support its activities, as well as operating in an economic environment that is likely to be more affluent and less prone to problems such as high unemployment. Government seeks information and advice about policy from knowledge-producing activities, and the demand for innovation policy is central to its regulatory role. In formulating innovation policy it will necessarily be required to take into account the expressed (and imputed) needs of other actor groups.

The Role of the Business Sector

Firms seek to promote their innovations to citizens, who will buy them as private goods. The expression of needs through the market is often the result of extensive prior interaction. The market economy provides a set of mechanisms that allocate resources to the satisfaction of private needs. Firms, often acting with other knowledge producers such as universities, define the forms that such products and services take. Firms seek a legal and regulatory system to allow markets to operate effectively. Steps to protect innovation—for example, by intellectual property (IP) regulation—may be urged by firms. Within the context of such private good production, there can be some aspects of the product or service and/or the production process that are regulated. An example might be safety and environmental performance. This form of regulation is society-driven, even when there is no explicit innovation agenda involved. Firms are regulated for the benefit of society through the political process, and regulations may or may not impact innovation processes and trajectories. For instance, regulations about health and safety at work may lead to innovations that increase automation at the workplace, even if this is not the intended impact. In contrast, regulations aimed at reducing use of an environmentally damaging process may simply result in a firm relocating its activities overseas, without damage being mitigated. Firms may also innovate themselves and within/across business sectors. Such innovation may be termed 'internal'.

There is the argument in some schools of thought, however, that regulation-driven innovation might be considered counter to society-driven innovation and that regulation might actually impede the ability to innovate, limit knowledge sharing, particularly through intellectual property rights (IPR), and furthermore, in some cases, prevent societal needs from being met, especially in less developed countries. Some have advocated a 'prize' system instead of IPR to overcome this (see, for example, Stiglitz, 2006). This approach has been practiced with success in California, and in 1999 Sweden launched its own 'Environmental Innovation Competition' for innovations that are 'customer oriented' and have a 'clear environmental objective' (TrendChart website[1]). This type of approach, however, only really works when there is a clear objective and a clear need to be met.

The Role of Universities

Universities, like businesses, face regulation of their activities by government. This arises from the need to provide a measure of standardization for prospective students to be assured of the quality of education available, as well as reflecting policy objectives such as increasing workforce skills and attainment levels and creating a strong science base. Universities demand scientific equipment and techniques from firms, 'instrumentalities', and also may seek to engage with firms—for example, in contractual relationships to carry out research for industry. Such activities meet the needs of firms for new knowledge but also meet the needs of universities for a context in which to test and develop their applied knowledge. Universities are also internal innovators in that they seek to generate new knowledge of which the scholarly community is the main source of legitimacy and validation (e.g., peer review processes). Such basic research is funded by the state.

One famous model that tries to make explicit the links between the actors, particularly universities-industries-governments, is the Triple Helix model (Etzkowitz and Leydesdorff, 1998), which emerged in the mid-1990s. Trying to model the complex system of innovation in the knowledge-based economy, it emphasizes the importance of the relations between university-industry-government. This model starts from the view that any governments, or nation states, share an interest in advancing knowledge-based economic development and this requires a clear mechanism. Therefore central to Triple Helix is that the model not only takes the 'traditional forms of institutional differentiation among universities, industries and government' but also takes account of 'the expanding role of the knowledge sector in relation to the political and economic infrastructure of the larger society' (Leydesdorff and Etzkowitz, 1996, p. 280). Central to this model is the dynamic relationship between government, industry and universities. The proponents of the model argue that without the helix, innovation would go on arbitrarily with many valuable aspects ignored. A more broadly defined system is one that is richer, engages knowledge (academic research) with needs and gives rise to new business models.

Some commentators argue that the Triple Helix model has become more a political rhetoric than a conceptual framework (Shinn, 2002). In the words of Boden et al. (2004), the Triple Helix 'has not delivered on its promise to provide a methodological foundation for the analysis of change that has been occurring in the area of innovation and the links between research, industry and government' (13).

While these critiques have some validity, we would argue from at least two different perspectives. Firstly, the Triple Helix model does not pay enough attention to the problems and contradictions that emerge as research results are commercialized. When research exits laboratories and is scaled up, unforeseen problems often occur, ranging from the changing characteristics of the product when interacting with the outside world, to consumers' concerns towards the impacts of its use and/or application. The big debate of the wide-scale release of GM (genetically modified) crops that sparked controversy in many countries is an example of this. Secondly, taking into account the classical and yet still very much relevant sociological perspective of societal forces in society, it is rather surprising that the Triple Helix model does not include the role of citizen or third sector in the model as third sector organizations also play an important role in the system of innovation, more than just being intermediaries (Howells, 2006).

Some examples can be put forward here, showing how citizens and the third sector play an active role in fostering agendas or putting forward issues that later turn into innovative ideas. The first example that has an obvious link is the open source movement (Raymond, 1999). This movement arguably is a branch from the free software movement beginning in the late 1980s when the GNU/Linux project was launched (Warger, 2002). This movement comes into being to challenge the intellectual property regime in the software industry. Based on his observations of the Linux kernel development process, Raymond examines the struggle between top-down and bottom-up design. The central argument is that 'given enough eyeballs, all bugs are shallow'— that is, the more widely the source code is available for public scrutiny, the more rapidly all forms of bugs will be discovered and the application made much better. Indeed this very central idea is later taken up in 'open innovation' that relates to user innovation, cumulative innovation and distributed innovation (Chesbrough, 2003). This 'open source' arguably also inspires and triggers other innovations that are adopted quite quickly—for example, the establishment of *Wikipedia* and *Wikiversity*, a user-generated online encyclopedia and learning community sharing learning materials; *Project Gutenberg*, which preceded Google Scholar and the first in providing electronic books and a free library. Business and government sectors cannot but respond to this movement. For instance, Google's applications are based primarily on open source software and it continues to do so; Microsoft participates and contributes to the open source community to remain marketable; government agencies and infrastructure are using open source infrastructure, like Linux OS and Apache Web-server (Taft, 2009).

The second example is in the field of energy. The third sector has been very active in driving the issue of energy, fuelled by the quickly growing concern about climate change and environmental destruction and deterioration (Bang, 2010; Florinia and Sovacool, 2009; Müller-Kraenner, 2008).[2] They not only promote civic education in communities but also conduct research and publicize the results so as to balance the information from business and government concerning economic, social and environmental impacts of energy. This can easily be seen in the biofuels case. Many third sector organizations have 'warned' of the environmental impact of the (1st generation of) biofuels produced using palm oil, corn or *jathropa* that is sourced mostly from developing countries, which then escalates the debate on 'car versus human' when it comes to food crop and land conversion. This debate and pressure have somewhat changed the opinion of the public in Western countries about biofuels and are believed to also have fuelled the move towards more efficient and effective 2nd and 3rd generations of biofuel, which should be moving away from consumable crops as the main source. Other citizen groups are actually researching the impact of climate change on regions across the world, including the predicted sea level rises and other possible impacts. All this has also contributed to the emergence and shaping of the so-called 'carbon-economy'. The third sector initiative has promoted partnership with companies to thrive in a carbon-constrained economy. Partners develop greenhouse gas (GHG) inventories, share energy management practices and invest in clean energy technologies. These actions have shaped multi-sectoral policy approaches for a safe climate and sound business future.

The last example is the emergence of ethical labeling and corporate social responsibility (CSR) within the framework of sustainability issues. Within the sustainability discourse, third sector organizations have been active in at least three different directions: (1) to influence consumer behavior in the direction of more sustainable choices; (2) to influence policymakers in sustainability and environmentally related policy decisions and (3) to influence the private sector to act more sustainably and accountably. For example, the campaign for fair-trade products and produce has been around for some time and has been seen as an effective way not only to advocate for a fairer supply chain to help producers but also to shape consumers' preference and consumption patterns (Raynolds, 2000; 2002). Third sector organizations, particularly Non-Governmental Organizations (NGOs), have also been active in influencing public policy, particularly environmental policy.

Above the national level, such organizations even influence international environmental negotiations—for example, in the UN Framework Convention on Climate Change (Betsill and Corell, 2001). With regards to the private sector, quite a number of civil society groups have been trying to influence the behavior of big corporations, be it as 'engagers' (who draw corporations into dialogue in order to persuade them to adopt voluntary codes of conduct) or as 'confronters' (who threaten corporate financial interests through adversarial stance, boycott, labor union protest and 'naming and shaming' strategies) (Winston, 2002). Indeed, there has been pressure from third sector organizations for the corporate world to operate in much more sustainable and accountable ways and to contribute to economic development and better work relationships with employees, local communities and society at large to improve their quality of life (Doh and Guay, 2006). And as it is observed today, CSR has been one of the major organizational innovations adopted worldwide (Enquist, Johnson and Skålén, 2006).

Who Delivers Innovations?

The foregoing discussion indicates how various objectives/needs are identified, emerging from various key societal actors. The 'systems of innovation' literature has much to say about how new needs are met, and how actors integrate their activities to realize needs. The answer to the question 'who delivers innovations' is that to meet socially defined needs, it is often common to involve more than one (and increasingly all four) categories of actors. Much recent policy action seeks to engage multiple contributions to the meeting of societal needs. The EC's Broad-Based Innovation Strategy restates the importance of creating alignments of actors. It is based upon a systems view of the innovation process, with a commitment to engage all actors:

> This broad strategy needs to engage all parties—business, public sector and consumers. This is because the innovation processes involves not only the business sector, but also public authorities at national,

regional and local level, civil society organizations, trade unions and consumers. (COM, 2006)

In the case of public good provision in the area of health, government, universities, firms and citizens may all interact to define a need, and then interact to find a way of satisfying it. By contrast, civil society organizations may define and meet needs that their members alone may experience, and in the business-to-business market, there may be innovations that involve little interaction between groups of actors other than firms. There are also cases of firms and citizens acting together to determine how societal needs should be met, quite independently from government or universities or other knowledge producers.

Societal actors may take a variety of roles in delivering innovations. In order to assess the importance of the contribution that these actors make, it is helpful to consider a typology based on the scale of their involvement and the extent to which their activity leads to the delivery of innovation. A four-fold classification of roles within the delivery process of innovation to meet societal needs distinguishes between: a) initiating action to meet a need; b) creating the network of actors required to meet the need; c) active participation in networks; d) passive participation. Where actors initiate action to meet a need, they are driving innovation. If they are only passive participants, they may not be taking a major role, but their participation may count as endorsement of a form of action and be nevertheless important. Thus the business literature often discusses 'consumer-oriented innovation' rather than 'consumer-driven innovation'—the point being that business may well seek to ascertain consumer requirements and orient new products around these, but that in these cases the ideas for new products rarely flow from citizens themselves.

Government Driving Innovation: Where, How and Why? An EU Perspective

Since the Lisbon Special European Council of 2000, the European Union has given a special emphasis to the promotion of initiatives to support competitiveness, economic growth and employment. It soon became apparent, however, that initiatives developed at the Special Lisbon Council—to increase R&D expenditures across the EU area and to increase competitiveness—had achieved little in the way of immediate increases in R&D expenditures. As a result, the approach of EU policymakers changed significantly. There was some renewed focus on innovation practices and institutions, but more importantly there was significant new emphasis upon demand and upon a range of attempts to 'drive' demand. To some degree this was the only major lever left for government to use to influence the economy as financial support for favored industries through grants and subsidies is no longer legal within new international free trade agreements (including the single market). In this new framework of policy, government and public institutions themselves were the key actors.

The aim of this new policy was to drive innovation in the economies of the EU by changing public procurement practices. Public procurers and their suppliers were given a new legal framework in which to operate. While the new framework was intended to promote the single market, its main objective was to allow public procurers to be more risk-taking and adventurous in what they specified. This, it was hoped, would allow suppliers to innovate, thereby improving or at least maintaining the EU's competitive position globally. Areas or sectors of public procurement where innovation was thought more likely to occur, and where it might be more socially desirable, were deemed 'lead markets'. The EU has developed a number of support actions for the lead markets on specific sectors and overall approaches to procurement, including attempts to understanding barriers to innovative public procurement, especially risk (EC, 2008b).

At the same time that policy was being developed to promote innovation in the areas closer to market, two further major initiatives were launched. The first of these initiatives was an approach to broaden the scope of what kinds of innovation should be considered and to secure public support for them. This policy has been led by DG Enterprise and Industry (DG ENTR). To some extent this was a response to the world economic crisis, to which large-scale public expenditure might have seemed appropriate at the time. The second major response has been an attempt led by DG Research (DG RTD) to encourage a broader view of innovation and to couple the research system of the EU, the so-called European Research Area, to broad societal needs. The former of these two new approaches has a number of candidate sectors. The second of these two approaches suggests a number of examples, but the approach mainly proposes changes to institutional arrangements.

These two approaches to innovation and research policy respectively have a common theme, which is that innovation should be on such a scale as to be able to meet large-scale societal priorities. The DG Research approach labels the kinds of large-scale high-priority innovations that require such large-scale coordination as 'grand challenges'. Such challenges require consensus building to define them and to support the allocation of resources to deliver solutions to them.

> In the tradition of Schumann and Monet, the growth of S&T in Europe becomes legitimate by demonstrating to the public and politicians that they make a key contribution to the problems that society recognizes as central. Our core argument is that to move forward ERA needs to balance its current focus on structure and process with a greater emphasis on content and outputs. (EC, 2008a, 36)

The Expert Group considers in detail the requirements for the development of consensus around particular societal demands termed grand challenges, which the research infrastructure of member states should meet.

Grand Challenges should derive this name from the fact that they are of sufficient scale and scope to capture the public and political imagination, create widespread interest among scientific and business communities and NGOs and inspire younger people. They must be capable of acting as an important tool for percolating attention at all levels of society all the way down to civil society and the public at large. Grand Challenges should be few in number at any moment, although they will be subject, within our ecology approach, to the dynamics of birth and death. It is quite conceivable that not all the Grand Challenges selected will proceed successfully. Where failure becomes apparent and the Challenge does not stop of its own accord, mechanisms must be in place ensuring that the Challenge can be dropped and replaced by another. The introduction of a form of timed support could provide the solution here. (EC, 2008a, 37)

The original use of the term grand challenges comes in the late 1980s and early 1990s, when the term was applied to significant technological challenges faced by researchers in the following areas: engineering; electrical and electronic or computer science; hardware and architecture or mathematics; applied or computer science; artificial intelligence or computer science; software engineering or computer science; and interdisciplinary applications.

The new approach to innovation at the EU level and that of a number of member states sees innovation in the economies of the EU being stimulated through government procurement. But for government to drive demand, institutional change within government procurement practice is necessary because existing procurement procedures have sought to reduce risk and control costs, and this has tended to prevent innovation by suppliers.

While government procurement that focuses on innovation can be seen as a way of increasing the level of innovation in the economy, in practical terms such procurement can deliver improvements in the quality of public services. Furthermore, it may also stimulate innovation more widely by enabling the market to respond to current and future public service needs, that is, a broadening of the range of public services offered. In this regard, more diverse societal demands, voiced by citizen groups or the third sector, are also being recognized by government, accepted as goals to be pursued by government, and considered likely to be sources of innovation.

As briefly discussed in the previous section, the debates surrounding environmental degradation and sustainability, for example, have created a new direction towards innovation in renewable energy. The EU has devised its vision for 2030 in renewable energy (EC, 2006)—much of it now addresses the concern voiced by the third sector. Likewise, concern about impoverishment and fairer supply chain and wealth distribution has played an important role in the emergence of organizational (and product) innovations in the consumer goods industry, as is evident in the labeling innovation. For example, most of the EU companies in this sector now adopt FLO (Fairtrade Labelling Organizations International) standard for fairly traded products. The EU Commission has also actively promoted a European framework for corporate social responsibility (CSR) and pushes companies to go beyond voluntary initiatives (EC, 2001). Promoting CSR, the EU aims to develop guidelines in line with other international initiatives (such as the UN's *Global Compact*, the ILO's tripartite. Declaration of Principles Concerning Multinational Enterprises and Social Policy', and the OECD's 'Guidelines for Multinational Enterprises'). All of this is in order to promote increased transparency, reliability and validity in the private sector.

While the governments of member states currently address a great many societal challenges directly, a review of historical examples reveals that over time, the involvement of governments varies significantly. For example, periods of social unrest are often occasions for previously marginalized voices to be heard and for new needs to be met. In our discussion we focus more on 'business as usual' circumstances. But it is important to be aware that there may be points at which the legitimacy of the 'powers that be' will come under scrutiny, often as a result of the perception that a major crisis has been handled poorly. Such crises can involve innovation and/or technological choices (an example being the BSE 'mad cow disease' affair in the 1990s).

In driving innovation, it is clear that knowledge for policy (evidence-based) has always been required. Governments have always recognized this, as this has been believed to be a prominent strategy to address the 'know-do' gap. This will also make a greater use of research findings and evidence in policy-making. The focus is on the production of feasible and research-informed policy options. The role of third sector and business intermediary organizations can be critical in supporting knowledge brokering. Here there is a need to support and learn the ways to strengthen the links between the research and policy communities. Ultimately this all should aim for a stronger practice of evidence-based policy and policy-relevant research.

Apparently, the formulation of the Grand Challenge (EC, 2008a) reflects how much the EU policy relies on research. The Grand Challenges as formulated are understood to be *the* challenges for the EU in entering the 21st century and therefore have to be addressed. However, we do not think the approach of the Grand Challenges is particularly new. A number of the current challenges have been dealt with by government for many years, with a number of challenges adopted by government first being identified by society/citizen groups. Indeed, such groups have often been the first to develop systematic, large-scale responses to such challenges.

For example, the *economic challenges* as addressed in the GC point out the 'combination of supply-side measures for promotion of RTD and demand-side measures to create innovation-friendly markets' (EC, 2008a,

45). These types of challenges could already be traced back from the mid-1980s, when the role of users and consumers in innovation started to be recognized. The conception of user-led innovation—that is, innovation undertaken by consumers and end users, rather than suppliers/manufacturers (von Hippel, 1986)—was key to understanding this. The formulation of open innovation, which closely relates to user innovation, cumulative innovation and distributed innovation (Chesbrough, 2003) is also important, following the open source movement (Raymond, 1999) and preceding corporate social responsibility initiatives (Doh and Guay, 2006).

Understandably, *social and environmental challenges* also constitute some of the most significant Grand Challenges facing the world. The EU Commission emphasizes that the challenge is to 'deal with the causes and consequences of issues such as climate change, food and energy security and the ageing society' (EC, 2008, p. 45). To the Commission, the initial drive should come from governments, but in fact grassroots initiatives already existed much earlier on several different fronts like climate change (Gough and Shackley, 2001; Gupta, 1997; Raustiala, 1997); food security (Farrington et al., 1993; McCullough, Pingali and Stamoulis, 2008; Riddell and Robinson, 1995); energy security (Bang, 2010; Florinia and Sovacool, 2009; Müller-Kraenner, 2008),[3] and ageing society (Ajala and Olorunsaiye, 2006; Cabrera and Malanowski, 2009; Kreager, 2006; Mann, 2007; Rose, 2008).

The last instance might be the *science and technological challenges* as conceptualized in the Grand Challenge. It involves the 'ability to respond to opportunities in frontier research' (EC, 2008, p. 45, emphasis added). Even here this is not new. Apart from the important question of how we understand 'frontier' here,[4] civil society has been known to be a strategic partner in some areas of frontier research (like Nowotny, 2005), and in a certain field (like agriculture) can be involved upstream in the strategic steering of research initiatives (e.g., Lowe and Phillipson, 2006).

A Grand Challenge?

The implementation of policies to support large-scale, significant and difficult societal challenges is no easy task. New institutional arrangements are often required, and some new institutions may need to be created to coordinate action between member states. In this section we outline the major questions facing those who wish to develop responses to large-scale societal challenges and implement them. We then present a number of examples of such responses and consider what lessons can be learned about government attempts to direct and focus large-scale social innovations. We then present some conclusions.

A Framework for Analysis

While dealing with societal grand challenges would appear to have very obvious merits and to be justifiable on that basis, the development of a systematic program of action to deal with such challenges faces a number of difficult questions to which few answers are self-evident.

Firstly, there are questions relating to how the objectives for grand challenges should be identified. Who should be involved in their definition? What role will there be for civil society organizations, what role for business in deciding which challenges shall be chosen? How important should government itself be? Related to this are questions about where and with whom the benefits of the solution will arise and how each group that contributes will secure a benefit sufficiently large for it to feel justified in participating. Within the EU context, issues about *juste retour* could be highly relevant. Generally, grand challenges that are broad in their scope would appear to be more likely to secure the broad support required for action to be taken. Related to problem definition is the length of time that might be needed to achieve solutions, and the size and scale of the initiative and how many resources to commit. Regarding the problems faced, should action on grand challenges face problems that exist, or problems that are likely to exist in the future? Also connected with the issue of problem definition is the issue of what level of risk grand challenges should entertain.

Questions also arise about the solution to a grand challenge. Technical solutions might be favored by some while others might favor attempts to change behavior. How important is innovation and in particular technological innovation that might increase R&D expenditures to the solution of grand challenges? If society has to agree over which challenges to face, and to fund, it must also agree over what type of solution it wants.

There are also questions about the optimization of resources. At any point in time there is likely to be a need to prioritize one grand challenge over another. Implementation is also a further problem. Should an implementation phase use the same processes and organizations that are responsible for defining a grand challenge? Should implementation be carried out by the state or through more co-production style organization? Should solutions be offered by the private sector?

In the following section we examine examples of broad-scale, government-driven social innovations. Six examples are presented from a variety of fields and countries and these are then analyzed to show how these broad-scale social innovations emerge, find support and are implemented.

Examples of Broad-Scale Social Innovations

Case 1. Sweden 2020 'The World's First Oil-Free Economy'

Driven mainly by environmental concern, in October 2005 the Swedish government announced that Sweden aimed to become the world's first oil-free country by 2020. The implications of the plan were that Sweden would become the first country in the world to stop using oil. Cars were to be environmentally friendly and homes would be heated by renewable energies such as biomass or geothermal sources. The initiative was thought to be prima facie good for the country's environment and for the economy. This initiative came from the government, built upon a citizen consensus and had a strong political mandate, and a scientific case made and presented to the Swedish people by the Royal Swedish Academy of Sciences. The country established the Commission on Oil Independence, and this stimulates innovations by outlining directions and priorities for innovation, R&D and commercialization of new knowledge (Commission on Oil Independence, 2006). There have been developments to promote innovation, improve energy efficiency and develop 'greener' technologies in buildings; industry; transport system technology ('green car' and 'greener aircraft'); technology and plants for biofuels (including *biorefinery*); fuel production in agriculture and forestry, and energy technology (focusing on solar cells, wave power and hydrogen gas). The initiative, despite coming from the government, was built upon a citizen consensus and thus had a strong political mandate.

Case 2. Phasing Out Leaded Petrol in Europe

There has long been concern about the human health risks caused by exposure to high levels of lead and the phase-out of lead-based, octane-enhancing gasoline additives has been widely recognized as a technically feasible measure to reduce ambient environmental lead concentrations. Maximum lead content limits were implemented in 1993 in most of the EU and tax incentives have been used, as have awareness raising measures. Bans on the sale of leaded petrol have also been implemented in many countries and reductions in production and imports of leaded petrol have been witnessed (for example, Hungary and Bulgaria in 2000 and 2003) (COWI, 1998). With action on this scale it has been difficult to set a date for the achievement of the policy target, however, the ECMT Council of Ministers of Transport meeting declared in 1995 that the aim should implement a ban as soon as possible.

Action has been coordinated by the United Nations Economic Commission for Europe (UN/ECE). The 1991 Dobris Ministerial Conference 'Environment for Europe' made an important intervention by calling for a major and "comprehensive assessment of Europe's environment" and ultimately the development of a European environment policy. At the 1993 Lucerne conference, the proposal 'Elements for a Long-Term Environmental Programme for Europe' was endorsed under the UN/ECE framework 'Europe's Environment: The Dobris Assessment', prepared by the European Environment Agency for the 1995 Sofia conference, provided a foundation for the Environmental Programme for Europe. The Third Ministerial Conference 'Environment for Europe' (1995, Sofia) endorsed the Programme prepared within the UN/ECE. The Programme was the first attempt to set long-term environmental priorities at the pan-European level and to make Agenda 21 more operational in the European context, particularly relating to the integration of environmental policy with other policies. It serves as a framework for the better coordination of national and international efforts to improve environmental conditions throughout Europe and to promote convergence of environmental quality and policies. Within the EU, a notable effect of these measures has been 'knock-on' innovations in other areas. Due to lead being phased out, vehicle manufacturers have had to innovate and create new technologies and consumers have been made to change their behavior. Therefore there has been innovation at many different stages.

Case 3. Project UTOPIA (Scotland)

The UTOPIA project (Usable Technology for Older People: Inclusive and Appropriate) aims to address the relationship between older people and technology and is a three-year Scottish Higher Education Funding Council (SHEFC) consortium project between the universities of Dundee, Abertay, Glasgow and Napier. The project was established in recognition of the significant demographic changes that are taking place in Scotland and the rest of the developed world, but that do not appear to have greatly influenced those sectors of industry concerned with mainstream technology. Despite a significantly ageing population these industries have remained focused on designing for young people—a dramatically shrinking market segment (Dickinson et al., 2002).

One of the central foci of the UTOPIA project is the development of methodologies that address the specific difficulties of designing for older people; the software development process is a 'self-conscious' one where methodologies are tested, refined and re-examined through the development of small systems, and users and domain experts play a central role in the development process. A variety of approaches are employed, including discussion groups and individual interviews. This involvement enables a holistic approach to software production, allowing the designer to examine the application in the context of the user's life so as to make it more suitable to that specific user group.

Case 4. CFC Phase-Out (Global)

Scientists linked the use of chlorofluorocarbons (CFCs) and their threat to the ozone layer in the 1970s (Molina and Rowland, 1974). In 1978 the US banned the non-essential use of CFCs as aerosol propellants. Efforts at negotiating an international agreement controlling CFC use began in the 1980s. The Montreal Protocol on Substances That Deplete the Ozone Layer was signed in September 1987 and came into force in 1989. It restricts the use of ozone-depleting substances, including CFCs and HCFCs. The Protocol was the result of years of negotiation by the United Nations Environment Programme (UNEP). In 1988 DuPont called for the phase-out of CFCs and transition to environmentally acceptable alternatives. In the EU, the EC Regulation on ozone depleting substances (EC, 2000) was applied from 1 October 2000. CFC phase-out needed a vast innovation response in terms of the development of alternatives to CFCs and changes to the management of the innovation process itself within industry. Morrisette (1989) cites the Montreal Protocol as an example of how innovative approaches to complicated and contemporary global environmental problems are possible and that such a protocol was seen by industry as providing the necessary economic incentive to develop and market suitable alternatives.

The progress towards phasing out CFCs originally started in the 1970s. New EC regulation came into force in 2000. The complete phase-out of hydrochlorofluorocarbons (HCFCs) is due by 2030. This is a truly international form of initiative with large-scale societal support.

Case 5. Danish National Action Plan against Obesity (Denmark)

The Danish National Action Plan against Obesity aimed 'to contribute to producing awareness and cultural norms in the Danish population that promote normal weight development' (NBH, 2003, p. 15). The plan was stimulated by the fact that obesity is a rapidly increasing problem in Denmark, where 30–40 percent of the population is overweight and 10–13 percent is obese. The causes of obesity are so complex that the health care sector alone cannot solve the problem, so the plan was put together to focus on what the individual can do and how society can support individuals. Obesity is associated with increased morbidity and mortality, poor well-being and social isolation. It also affects the health care budget. In 1999 the Danish National Board of Health (NBH) produced a report on prevalence of overweight in Denmark and in 2000 the World Health Organization (WHO) held a consultation on obesity (WHO, 2000). In 2001 the Danish Society for Obesity Research published a report and in the same year the NBH established an external working group. In 2002 the NBH and the Danish EU presidency held a conference on obesity in Copenhagen.

Responsibility for the plan and its implementation lies with the NBH, and the Danish Nutrition Council has produced a report that forms the basis of the NBH action plan. There are nine ministries involved overall, with a multimillion-euro budget allocated to a number of projects relating to general and childhood obesity. Network meetings took place in 2004 and 2006 saw the launch of the 'Communities on the move' project. 2007 was named 'The year of movement' by the Ministry of Health. There is also ongoing development of a database of projects on the NBH website.[5]

Case 6. Fluoridation of Water Supplies (UK)

The fluoridation of water supplies began in the UK the 1960s when local councils, which took responsibility for public health, became aware that water supplies could be used to improve dental health. Trials carried out on the use of fluoridation showed an improvement in the health of the teeth of young children. In 1976 the Royal College of Physicians published a report called *Fluoride Teeth and Health*, which recommended the fluoridation of water supplies in the UK. In 1985 Members of Parliament passed the Water (Fluoridation) Bill. Under the Water Industry Act (1991) water companies were allowed to implement fluoridation when requested by health authorities, but were not obliged to do so. In 2003 Section 58 amended this legislation so that companies must add fluoride if instructed by a Strategic Health Authority (SHA). The SHA must first complete a local consultation process. The first agents responsible were some local councils in the 1960s. In the late 1980s and early 1990s local councils supported health authorities' proposals for fluoridation. It is supported by the World Health Organisation (WHO), the UK Health Departments, the British Medical Association, the British Dental Association, MENCAP and several NHS bodies, according to the BDA website.

Scientific innovation in this case, is simply the adding of fluoride to water, and is a relatively simple process; further innovations though are required to assess actual levels of fluoride received by end users of the water system. The implementation of fluoridation in water has been a slow process with strong opposition from civil liberties groups and in some areas fluoridation has been discontinued. The policy, which is generally regarded as originating in the US, has been adopted in many countries. Implementation, though, is within national legal systems with responsibility for fluoridation taking place at regional levels on the basis of public consent. The topic of fluoridation is a continuing controversy, with bodies of opinion arguing that this is 'compulsory medication' and that there is already ample opportunity to use fluoridated toothpaste, and raising questions about broader negative health implications, ranging from discoloration of teeth through to bone damage.

Analysis of Examples

What Kinds of Objective Are Chosen?

The societal objectives are generally anticipative, although some are in response to current or recent crises. Initiatives addressing environmental and energy issues are common, suggesting that the impacts of climate change might be a major topic of concern (perhaps the UK Foresight 'flooding' project is an early example of this). Health and age-related themes are also evidently of growing importance. There is also indication that contemporary issues affecting modern social welfare, particularly in employment and access to information, may also be of importance for broad social innovations. Generally speaking, common features of cases that emerge are as follows:

1. Initiatives respond to wider societal needs that are anticipated to grow or emerge in the future.

2. They involve problems where solutions are typically cross-disciplinary and cross-professional and require a range of technological (and
   sometimes social) innovations, drawing on a variety of knowledge
   bases and mobilizing a variety of actors.
3. They require some sort of raised social awareness about the future,
   often on a broad and wide-ranging scale, though not necessarily
   involving a formal Foresight program.

How Are They Defined and Stimulated?

Government intervention plays a major role. This may involve research funding, demonstrator projects, efforts to build lead markets and fostering network
development in support of any of these aims. Action and applied research is
prominent. Research into social innovations is not itself social innovation.

Who Has Responsibility/Who Implements?

In most of these examples, the actors responsible for implementation are
government bodies or other public agencies. This does not necessarily mean
that public/society participation is absent or unimportant. In fact, genuine broad-scale social innovations should involve a wider public to share
responsibility and take part in the implementation of the scheme.

Some innovations can succeed only if they are facilitated by policy in
other areas. Take, for example, the phasing out of leaded petrol. Broader
environmental policies played a critical role in the success of this initiative,
in the form of taxations on vehicles according to their pollution characteristics, so ultimately the coordination of environmental, import and tax
policies was required. Regulation may also need to be changed in order for
innovations to take effect.

What Is the Role of Innovation?

For 'proactive' (and usually visionary and anticipative) broad-scale innovation, innovation can be expected to be a leading element in the execution
of the initiative, in the form of new knowledge. This would give direction
to innovation programs. For 'reactive' social innovation, innovation would
follow the execution of the initiatives. Does this mean that a diffusion process is required, to apply established knowledge? When this kind of social
innovation leads to similar schemes elsewhere, the innovation program may
follow an innovation by emulation trajectory.

What Is the Horizon/Time Span?

This varies from case to case. Although the initiative itself may be short-
or medium-term, the anticipated impact is usually long-term. Conversely,

there are cases of broad-scale social innovation that are more than ten years, though more immediate benefits are often anticipated. This does not always mean that the programs are concerned with future technology breakthroughs, though they may be. Some appear to be as much about promoting more rapid deployment and incremental improvement of existing or near-horizon technologies.

What Is the Scale?

Government-driven innovation can be on a national or even international level. However, there may be regional or city-level initiatives developed or promoted by local governments. These have not traditionally had much influence on innovation policy, but this is changing in the 21st century. (Consider the case of California's promotion of low-emission vehicles, for instance.) The explicit aim often involves mobilizing various territorial actors into a constituency oriented towards solutions for a particular set of societal problems.

Is There Support from Society?

There is high agreement on the need for practical strategy even if there may be debate around certain technological issues, such as particular ways of reducing carbon dependency in energy supplies, as in the controversies surrounding wind power tidal barrages, and nuclear power. Citizen participation in the definition of the need varies.

From our research it is clear that examples of broad-scale innovation are often controversial (e.g., fluoridation) and they are often innovations that are intended to change the innovation process. In some cases innovations may lead to new innovations and changing behavior among different parties all along the process (e.g., in the phasing out of leaded petrol which has led to innovations by petrol and vehicle manufacturers and changes in consumer behavior).

What is apparent, and of some concern, is the fact that there seems to be a distinct lack of information on evaluation methods and indeed on whether evaluation has taken place at all in most cases. Furthermore, where evaluation to gauge social support has been carried out, this has often been met with criticism. To take one example, in the case of fluoridation of water supplies, the public opinion polls carried out were criticized for using biased wording.

Where investigations have taken place, these have also sometimes met with doubt. Again, taking the example of fluoridation, in 2000 an investigation by the University of York Centre for Reviews and Dissemination was carried out and in 2002 (University of York, 2000) the Medical Research Council (MRC) carried out a separate investigation into water fluoridation (MRC, 2002). Both investigations found that much of the research did not meet current standards.

Despite this, in April 2003, the House of Commons All Party Parliamentary Group on Primary Care and Public Health carried out their own investigation, making recommendations that targeted water fluoridation be stated as a legitimate and effective means of tackling dental health inequalities. They also recommend that current legislation be amended to allow the responsible health body to request water companies to fluoridate where there is strong local support for doing so (House of Commons, 2003).

In Which Areas Is Broad-Scale Government Intervention Most Prominent?

Several national Foresight Programmes have fostered projects that look to be close to social innovation. Take, for example, the current UK Foresight Programme. This seeks to have at any one time a pair of projects underway that are more technology-driven, and a pair that are more 'problem-driven', which might be interpreted as 'society-driven'. The latter include topics such as flooding, obesity, drugs and infectious diseases. The intention is to help promote 'joined up' policy across government departments, and stimulate research and innovation to find solutions for these problems. A wide variety of research programs have resulted.

Historically, there have been numerous government-driven innovation programs around more environmentally friendly technologies and industrial systems, especially but not only in the energy field. There is now a large volume of literature dealing with the role of different policy instruments in fostering innovation and adoption of these technologies. Medical and health research and innovation are typically less wide-ranging than the focus on ageing societies noted earlier. They are often limited in terms of typical focus on specific health conditions, and on limited types of biomedical solutions. But many larger programs (and institutions such as medical research sponsors) could be seen as efforts to seed social innovation. Other relatively recent examples might be the use of CCTV in the UK and the introduction of ID cards.

More generally, we find many R&D and innovation programs justified in terms of social objectives, over and above the usual rationales of competitiveness and job and wealth creation. The history of these initiatives may have important lessons for social innovation. There have been many efforts to promote particular IT trajectories as solutions for social problems—for example, extending information society tools to remote communities so as to enhance their social integration, or employing them to support more open and flexible education systems. While many of these efforts have some flavor of technology-push, some might be included within a rigorous definition of broad-scale innovation.

CONCLUSION

Four different kinds of approaches might be seen here: a) *Top down, reactive mode*—defined or guided or implemented by top-down consensus (e.g., dominance of government), which reacts towards certain conditions that may be detrimental to social/environmental and public life; b) *Top down, proactive mode*—comes from the initiative of public authority, which then guides the implementation of the initiative that aims to elevate the societal quality of life; c) *Bottom up, reactive mode*—initiated by a bottom-up process (e.g., public intervention) as a response towards certain concern about a social/environmental circumstance that needs addressing; d) *Bottom up, proactive mode*—the output of bottom-up decision-making or participation that envisages an action to anticipate social/environmental circumstances that will become a concern in the future.

We note that governments have always attempted to support innovation to meet explicit societal needs, particularly in the cases of defense and security. In health, hygiene and sanitation, where there have been major initiatives, societal coherence is important; but in defense, the protection of society from external threats is the goal. Attempts to meet such needs increasingly require steering, management and foresight. In the complex societies in which such needs emerge, policies and initiatives must have greater coherence.

The provision of public goods has a long history. There is general societal acceptance of the important role of government in the provision of certain forms of goods and the need for this to be coordinated and coherent. But there is also a concern that government takes too much of a role in the control of society and that too much consumption is now of public goods. This chapter set out to look at the feasibility of a number of approaches and we have reviewed some cases. The messages emerging are not always clearly defined. Evaluation of these initiatives is often poor and unspecific, as if, because the idea is good and the need a general and public one, this should stand as the sole and unchallenged justification.

Successful development of large-scale, government-driven innovation requires that the innovation is broadly acceptable. It should lack clear large national discrepancies in the outcomes—that is, to avoid obviously advantaging one area over another and to have a relatively unconstrained route to implementation. It should be driven or piloted and will not be successful without an understanding of who the key actors are and the roles they must play.

Within the European context, we believe that such innovation is more likely to be successful if it leads to a more harmonious, balanced and sustainable development of economic activities; if it provides a high level of employment, social protection and equality between men and women; if it leads to sustainable, non-inflationary growth. It should also achieve a high degree of competitiveness and convergence of economic performance. Specific priorities should be protection and improvement of the quality of the environment, the raising of the standard of living and quality of life, economic and social cohesion and solidarity among the member states.

Implementation of broad-scale initiatives is not likely to be successful without an attempt to create coherent networks of actors, to align incentives and to create mutual confidence. This kind of policy, though, carries the risk of free-riding, where governments themselves take the financial risk for large-scale socio-technical changes away from the market and from consumers. The conditions under which this is appropriate are, naturally enough, subject to a heated debate with strong political overtones.

NOTES

1. See online. Available HTTP: http://www.trendchart.org/tc_datasheet. cfm?ID=9101 (accessed 27 February 2012).
2. See Muller-Kraenner, S. (2008) *Energy Security*, Chapter 6, 'Defending the Last Paradise', for case studies.
3. See ibid.
4. The European Commission sponsored EURECIA project studied the impact of European Research Council financial support aimed at funding 'frontier' research.
5. See online. Available HTTP: www.sst.dk (accessed 2 March 2012).

BIBLIOGRAPHY

Ajala, E. M. and Olorunsaiye, D. A. (2006) 'An Evaluative Study of the Impact of Intervention Strategies of Non-Governmental Organizations (NGOs) on Social Well-Being, Economic Empowerment and Health of the Aged in Oyo State, Nigeria'. *International Journal of African and African American Studies* 5 (2): 1–12.

Bang, G. (2010) 'Energy Security and Climate Change Concerns: Triggers for Energy Policy Change in the United States?' *Energy Policy*, 38 (4): 1645-1653.

Betsill, M. M. and Corell, E. (2001) 'NGO Influence in International Environmental Negotiations: A Framework for Analysis'. *Global Environmental Politics* 1 (4): 65–85.

Boden, R., Cox, D., Nedeva, M. and Barker, K. (2004) *Scrutinizing Science: The Changing UK Government of Science*. New York: Palgrave Macmillan.

Cabrera, M. and Malanowski, N. (2009) *Information and Communication Technologies for Active Ageing*. Amsterdam: European Community and IOS Press.

Chesbrough, H. W. (2003) *Open Innovation: The New Imperative for Creating and Profiting from Technology*. Boston: Harvard Business School Press.

COM. (2006) 'Putting Knowledge into Practice: A Broad-Based Innovation Strategy for the EU'. Brussels: Commission of the European Communities.

Commission on Oil Independence. (2006) 'Making Sweden an Oil-Free Society'. Stockholm: Commission on Oil Independence.

COWI. (1998) 'UN/ECE Task Force to Phase Out Leaded Petrol in Europe'. COWI Consulting Engineers and Planners in collaboration with Danish Technological Institute, Danish Environmental Protection Agency. Denmark: Ministry of Environment and Energy.

Davies, A. (2007) 'A Wasted Opportunity? Civil Society and Waste Management in Ireland'. *Environmental Politics* 16 (1): 52–72.

Dickinson, A., Eisma, R., Syme, A. and Gregor, P. (2002) 'UTOPIA: Usable Technology for Older People: Inclusive and Appropriate'. In Brewster, S. and Zajicek,

M. (eds.), *A New Research Agenda for Older Adults*, 38–39. London: BCS HCI. Online. Available HTTP: http://www.computing.dundee.ac.uk/projects/UTOPIA/ (accessed 4 March 2012).

Doh, J. P. and Guay, T. R. (2006) 'Corporate Social Responsibility, Public Policy, and NGO Activism in Europe and the United States: An Institutional-Stakeholder Perspective'. *Journal of Management Studies* 43 (1): 47–73.

Dosi, G. (1982) 'Technological Paradigms and Technological Trajectories: A Suggested Interpretation of the Determinants and Directions of Technical Change'. *Research Policy* 11: 147–162.

EC. (2000) Regulation No. 2037/2000. 'European Parliament and the Council of 29 June on Substances That Deplete the Ozone Layer'. European Commission, Brussels.

EC. (2001) 'Promoting a European Framework for Corporate Social Responsibility'. Com (2001) 366. Brussels: Commission of the European Communities.

EC. (2006) Regulation No. EUR 22066. 'Biofuels in the European Union: A Vision for 2030 and Beyond'. Biofuels Research Advisory Council, Directorate General for Research. European Commission, Brussels.

EC. (2008a) Regulation No. EUR 23326 EN. 'Challenging Europe's Research: Rationales for the European Research Area (ERA)'. Directorate General for Research. European Commission, Brussels.

EC. (2008b) Regulation No. EUR 24229 EN. 'Risk Management in the Procurement of Innovation Concepts and Empirical Evidence in the European Union'. European Union Expert Group on Risk Management, Directorate General for Research. European Commission, Brussels.

Enquist, B., Johnson, M. and Skålén, P. (2006) 'Adoption of Corporate Social Responsibility—Incorporating a Stakeholder Perspective'. *Qualitative Research in Accounting & Management* 3 (3): 188–207.

Etzkowitz, H. and Leydesdorff, L. (1998) 'The Triple Helix of University-Industry-Government Relations: A Laboratory for Knowledge-Based Economic Development'. *EASST Review* 14 (1): 11–19.

Farrington, J., Bebbington, A., Wellard, K. and Lewis, D. J. (1993) *Reluctant Partners?: Non-Governmental Organizations, the State and Sustainable Agricultural Development*. New York: Routledge.

Florinia, A. and Sovacool, B. K. (2009) 'Who Governs Energy? The Challenges Facing Global Energy Governance'. *Energy Policy* 37 (12): 5239–5248.

Freeman, C. (1988) 'Japan: A New National Innovation System?' In Dosi, G., Freeman, C., Nelson, R. R., Silverberg, G. and Soete, L. (eds.), *Technical Change and Economic Theory*, 330–348. London: Pinter.

Gibbons, M., Limoges, C., Nowotny, H., Schwartzman, S., Scott, P. and Trow, M. (1994) *The New Production of Knowledge*. London: Sage.

Gough, C. and Shackley, S. (2001) 'The Respectable Politics of Climate Change: The Epistemic Communities and NGOs'. *International Affairs (Royal Institute of International Affairs 1944–)* 77 (2): 329–345.

Gupta, J. (1997) *The Climate Change Convention and Developing Countries: From Conflict to Consensus?* Dordrecht: Kluwer Academic Publisher.

House of Commons. (2003) 'Primary Care and Public Health, Inquiry into Water Fluoridation'. London: All Party Parliamentary Group (APPG). Online. Available HTTP: http://www.pagb.co.uk/appg/inquiryreports/Inquiry%20into%20water%20fluoridation%20Mar2003.pdf (accessed 5 March 2012).

Howells, J. (2006) 'Intermediation and the Role of Intermediaries in Innovation'. *Research Policy* 35: 715–728.

Kline, S. J. and Rosenberg, N. (1986) 'An Overview of Innovation'. In Landau, R. and Rosenberg, N. (eds.), *The Positive Sum Strategy*, 275–305. Washington, DC: National Academy Press.

Kreager, P. (2006) 'Demography and Civil Society: A Historical Perspective on Contemporary Transitions and Their Implications for Population Ageing'. Working paper no. 306. Oxford Institute of Ageing. Oxford: University of Oxford.

Leydesdorff, L. and Etzkowitz, H. (1996) 'Emergence of a Triple Helix of University-Industry-Government Relations'. *Science and Public Policy* 23 (5): 279–286.

Lowe, P. and Phillipson, J. (2006) 'Reflexive Interdisciplinary Research: The Making of a Research Programme on the Rural Economy and Land Use'. *Journal of Agricultural Economics* 57 (2): 165–184.

Lundvall, B-Å. (ed.) (1992) *National Innovation Systems: Towards a Theory of Innovation and Interactive Learning.* London: Pinter.

Mann, K. (2007) 'Activation, Retirement Planning and Restraining the "Third Age"'. *Social Policy and Society* 6 (3): 279–292.

McCullough, E. B., Pingali, P. L. and Stamoulis, K. G. (eds.) (2008) *The Transformation of Agri-food Systems: Globalization, Supply Chains and Smallholder Farmers.* London: Earthscan.

Molina, M. J. and Rowland, F. S. (1974) 'Stratospheric Sink for Chlorofluoromethanes: Chlorine Atom-Catalysed Destruction of Ozone'. *Nature* 249: 810–812.

Morrisette, P. M. (1989) 'The Evolution of Policy Responses to Stratospheric Ozone Depletion'. *Natural Resources Journal* 29: 793–820.

Moulaert, F., Martinelli, F., Swyngedouw, E. and Gonzalez, S. (2005) 'Towards Alternative Model(s) of Local Innovation'. *Urban Studies* 42 (11): 1969–1990.

MRC. (2002) 'Water Fluoridation and Health'. London: Medical Research Council. Online. Available HTTP: http://www.mrc.ac.uk/Utilities/Documentrecord/index.htm?d=MRC002482 (accessed 5 March 2012).

Müller-Kraenner, S. (2008) *Energy Security: Re-measuring the World.* London: Earthscan.

NBH. (2003) 'National Action Plan against Obesity: Recommendations and Perspectives'. Copenhagen: Center for Health Promotion and Prevention, National Board of Health. Online. Available HTTP: http://www.sst.dk/publ/publ2003/National_action_plan.pdf (accessed 5 March 2012).

Nelson, R. (ed.) (1993) *National Innovation Systems: A Comparative Analysis.* New York: Oxford University Press.

Nowotny H., Scott P., Gibbons M., (2001) *Re-thinking Science: Knowledge and the Public in ad Age of Uncertainty.* Cambridge: Polity Press

Nowotny, H. (2005) 'Science and Society: High- and Low-Cost Realities for Science and Society'. *Science* 308 (5725): 1117–1118.

Raustiala, K. (1997) 'States, NGOs, and International Environmental Institutions'. *International Studies Quarterly* 41 (4): 719–740.

Raymond, E. S. (1999) *The Cathedral & the Bazaar.* Sebastopol: O'Reilly Media.

Raynolds, L. T. (2000) 'Re-embedding Global Agriculture: The International Organic and Fair Trade Movements'. *Agriculture and Human Values* 17 (3): 297–309.

Raynolds, L. T. (2002) 'Consumer/Producer Links in Fair Trade Coffee Networks'. *Sociologia Ruralis* 42 (4): 404–424.

Riddell, R. and Robinson, M. (1995) *Non-governmental Organizations and Rural Poverty Alleviation.* Oxford: Oxford University Press.

Rose, R. (2008) 'Older Europeans in the Aftermath of Transformation: A Bottom-Up Perspective'. Paper presented at AARP-European Centre Expert Meeting on Re-inventing Retirement: Reshaping Health and Financial Security in Europe. Wachau, Austria. 23/24 October.

Schot, J. and Rip, A. (1997) 'The Past and Future of Constructive Technology Assessment'. *Technological Forecasting and Social Change* 54 (2/3): 251–268.

Schumpeter, J. (1980) *Theory of Economic Development* (Social Science Classics Series). Somerset, New Jersey: Transactions Publishers.

Shinn, T. (2002) 'The Triple Helix and New Production of Knowledge: Prepackaged Thinking on Science and Technology'. *Social Studies of Science* 32: 599–614.

Stiglitz, J. E. (2006) *Making Globalization Work*. New York: W.W. Norton.

Swyngedouw, E. (2005) 'Governance Innovation and the Citizen: The Janus Face of Governance-Beyond-the-State'. *Urban Studies* 42 (11): 1991–2006.

Taft, D. K. (2009) 'Microsoft Recommits $100k to Apache Contribution at ApacheCon'. eWeek.com. Online. Available HTTP: http://www.eweek.com/c/a/Linux-and-Open-Source/Microsoft-Recommits-100K-Apache-Contribution-at-ApacheCon-2009–572039/ (accessed 5 March 2012).

Taylor, M. (2007) 'Community Participation in the Real World: Opportunities and Pitfalls in New Governance Spaces'. *Urban Studies* 44 (2): 297–317.

University of York. (2000) *A Systematic Review of Public Water Fluoridation*. NHS Centre for Reviews and Dissemination. York: CRD.

von Hippel, E. (1986) 'Lead Users: A Source of Novel Product Concepts'. *Management Science* 32 (7): 791–805.

Warger, T. (2002) 'The Open-Source Movement, Education Resources Information Center'. Online. Available HTTP: http://net.educause.edu/ir/library/pdf/eqm0233.pdf (accessed 5 March 2012).

WHO. (2000) 'Obesity—Preventing and Managing the Global Epidemic'. Geneva: WHO Consultation on Obesity.

Winston, M. (2002) 'NGO Strategies for Promoting Corporate Social Responsibility'. *Ethics and International Affairs* 16 (2): 71–87.

2 Demand-Led Innovation

Ian Miles and John Rigby

INTRODUCTION

Demand-led innovation (DLI) has become a popular term in recent years—indeed, there has been an explosion of interest in this and a series of related terms. A demand-led innovation process is understood to involve the deliberate design of innovation activity so that it substantially elicits and uses information about user features, requirements and creative ideas in the course of shaping research, development, design and/or other major aspects of the activity.[1]

Demand-led innovation will here be taken to include 'user innovation' (UI) in the von Hippel sense—that is, innovation created by the user of a technology, product or practice, in several circumstances. In particular, user innovation will be included when user innovations are deliberately sought by suppliers in order to improve their products, or seek new product ideas, or when users commercialize or otherwise seek to diffuse their innovation among other practitioners beyond their immediate community. However, UI will *not* be included in this definition of DLI when it is innovation that is employed only by the user individual or organization itself.

DLI policy can refer to one of two quite different things. Firstly, it can refer to policy aimed at promoting DLI processes in general, or in a specific field—for example, policies to improve the utilization of market research tools or user innovation in the management of innovation in commercial firms. We might label this *demand-driven innovation policy*. Secondly, DLI policy can refer to efforts to promote innovation or innovation trajectories of a particular sort, in a particular direction. These might include efforts to stimulate uptake of low-energy light bulbs, so as to encourage more R&D into improving these devices. We might label this *demand-based innovation policy*.

These two meanings of DLI policy reflect a dichotomy in understanding of DLI that is apparent not just in recent discussions of DLI, but also in the analysis of innovation processes more generally.

Much of the current discussion of DLI stems from the second of the policy definitions, from concern with how social objectives, such as sustainability or coping with demographic change, can be the focus of more innovation activity. Grand Challenges are often, perhaps always, problems where technological and other innovations are major parts of the solution. Supply-side initiatives—funding targeted R&D programs, for example—do not seem to be sufficient to mobilize industrial efforts around these problems. Thus attention to DLI initiatives comes to the fore. The issue can be seen as one of articulating demand so as to reflect the problems and thus drive innovation accordingly.

It will still be important to consider the issues implied by the first definition of DLI policy, for several reasons. Perhaps the most important, in the present context, is that we need to understand just how firms recognize and respond to changing market demand, if we are hoping that such change can be used to mobilize innovation to meet Grand Challenges. In the idealized world of introductory economics textbooks this might not seem to be necessary. Firms will respond to market signals by orienting their innovation activities accordingly. In the real world, no actors have perfect information or complete freedom to transform their assets; innovation activities are path-dependent and shaped within national and sectoral systems of innovation. Opportunities for innovation, and opportunities to achieve commercial success for innovation in markets, vary over time and between sectors and firms within sectors. From a policy perspective, better understanding of DLI is required, to enhance competitive advantage and meet Grand Challenges.

Because of the resonance of early discussions of innovation processes with the current debates, it is helpful to begin with an exposition of discussions that were underway several decades ago.

BEYOND PUSH AND PULL

One of the oldest schisms in innovation studies is between *technology push* and *market pull* accounts of innovation. In the former case, the initiative behind innovation is supposed to lie in research and invention, with inventors creating opportunities to satisfy people's needs, regardless of whether these have been expressed, often as a result of striving to understand better how things work. In the latter case, the initiative derives from user needs as expressed through market demand and other channels, with these being posed as problems that could do with innovative solutions. The distinction draws a great deal on the supply-push/demand-pull discussion in economics more generally.

While most commentators would agree that both technology push and market pull can be drivers of innovation, there has been considerable controversy around the precise role of each. In relation to the influence on the innovation outcomes, for example, technology push is supposed to encourage more radical innovation, market pull more incremental ones. In relation to specific cases and conjunctures, for example, does one or another form of driver predominate at particular moments in history?

The classic formulation of technology-push is the much-criticized 'linear model' of innovation. This is often declared dead, and just as often is resuscitated. It portrays the innovation process as a set of stages—beginning with research, often in laboratories, moving on to development, and then to production and marketing. One reason for the continuing vitality of this model is the relative ease of funding research as opposed to closer-to-market stages of the process. Another is the visible origin of some very important innovations in laboratory research-based scientific discoveries— the laser is a well-known case. It is apparent that some basic research does result in new knowledge that engenders capabilities to transform the world in dramatically new ways. In contrast, however, are many consultants, case studies and survey analyses, concluding that successful innovation relies upon identification of customer requirements.

It would be quite possible to consider a reverse linear model, where it is demand that is the leading force, mediated through marketing, with needs for improved products being captured by sales and marketing staff, who feed information back up the firm. If design and development are not enough to meet the requirements that have been expressed, then new research may be invoked. This, however, sounds somewhat artificial, because shortcomings with the product may well be experienced by or expressed to the research department directly. Indeed, linear models tend to imply a single flow of knowledge and action, whereas in practice there are many feedback loops and reiteration of activity across stages of the innovation process. This is why 'chain-link models' and the like have tended to displace the linear model in more serious discussion.

In the late 1970s and early 1980s, when modern innovation studies was first beginning to gather momentum as a vital field of enquiry, the linear model was coming under critical scrutiny. There was lively debate around the major schism—the relevance of technology-push and market-pull approaches to innovation. One classic review of the arguments here, stressing the need for *matching* of technological advance and changes in market demand, but also pointing out how these elements are combined and which takes the lead may vary from case to case, is Mowery and Rosenberg (1979). Another important contribution was made by Freeman (1982), who contrasted the views of Schumpeter and Schmookler, whom he took to be key proponents of technology-push and market-pull approaches. Freeman interpreted their differing emphases as relating to different types of innovation and stages in the macrodynamics of innovation processes.

Joseph Schumpeter (1939) had attributed growth mainly to technological innovation, in which entrepreneurs draw on scientific discoveries and the creative products of inventors. Schumpeter's work had been rediscovered in the 1970s, as one of the few earlier economists to address innovation in a serious and sustained way. Jacob Schmookler (1966), in contrast, was influential in developing the critique of the technology-push, linear model of innovation. He used patent data and historical case studies to support his case for the importance of market-pull. One of his conclusions was that the number of patents in various American industries followed surges of investment in them, rather than preceding investment. Growth seemed to be leading to innovation; markets were pulling innovative efforts. The interpretation was that high levels of demand led to more efforts to solve problems associated with the products in question, resulting in more patentable inventions.

Mowery and Rosenberg (1979) pointed out that Schmookler's account faced problems in addressing radical innovations. It is difficult to discuss market demand when the market knows little or nothing of the new products, their possible utility or their suppliers. Such radical innovations seem to have more to do with technology-push and fundamental advances in science and technology. Thus, Schmookler's account of market-pull innovation seemingly applies to more incremental innovations.

Freeman (1982) pointed out that patents can cover both radical and less dramatic innovations. This may help account for the apparent conflict between Schmookler's claims about the influence of market growth, and Schumpeter's emphasis on creative entrepreneurs and their inventions as the source of new markets and economic growth. Schumpeter addressed innovation's role in the creation of new markets, while Schmookler was looking more at expanding markets. These are not necessarily the same thing: the major expansion of a market may take considerable time to emerge. Schumpeter, too, was tending to emphasize radical innovations, while the distinction between types of innovation was not so important to Schmookler.

The discussion does not stop here, however, since Freeman went on to relate it to analysis of long waves called Kondratieff cycles, major periods of economic growth and stagnation. The discussion of long waves had considerable traction in the 1980s following the economic crises of the 1970s and the rather mechanical reading of a Kondratieff timetable as implying the imminence of a major depression. This discussion may experience a revival in the light of current economic difficulties. Schumpeter related the growth upswings of long waves to major new technologies: the steam engine and textile innovations for the first technological revolution in the late 18th and early 19th centuries; railways and metalworking and mechanical engineering technologies in the second industrial revolution in the mid-19th century; electric power, internal combustion engines and innovations in the chemical industry in the early 20th century. In each case, entrepreneurs were seizing new discoveries and inventions as opportunities for investment, making profits from these innovations, and provoking 'swarms' of imitators to further build upon them. When the innovations are sufficiently numerous and/ or far-reaching, the result is new markets, growth and employment.[2] The debate about technology-push and market-pull takes on a rather different flavor when viewed in the context of debates about 'long waves'.

Freeman argued that the technology-push/market-pull debate needs to be seen in terms of the context of long waves, though even if we suspend judgment on this particular approach, the distinction between more radical and basic innovations, and more routine and incremental ones, remains vital. Radical innovations, especially what came to be known as basic, 'heartland' technologies, are particularly important, opening up many new economic opportunities for products and processes. Typically these require substantial time to be built into products that are usable by large market skills, and sometimes standards, infrastructure and social innovation are required to make effective use of the innovation. In terms of creating new profits and jobs, the economic upswing of the long wave, if we are talking in such terms, the invention or even the initial commercialization of some basic new product is itself unlikely to be very important. It is the diffusion of the innovation, involving the creation of new markets, large-scale investment in the technology from imitators and the like, that is important. Indeed, Freeman's 'swarming' typically involves the emergence of multiple innovations using the capabilities of the new heartland technology. There are multiplier effects (demand for new capital goods, components, supply chains and distribution and market channels, skills and labor, bursts of additional induced innovations) and there is also need for structural adjustment.[3] Freeman points out that the mechanisms being discussed are far different from Keynesian demand management as the source of growth. Schumpeterian investment in technological innovations leads to rapidly growing new industries. This is unlikely to be a smooth process. Such growth reallocates resources across industries, leading to structural changes that can cause problems for some.

The technology-push/market-pull schism may still underpin a good deal of contemporary debate. We could consider some points of view as neo-Schumpeterian, in that they focus on technological breakthroughs that stimulate new demand, while others are neo-Schmooklerian, in that they focus on market demands that stimulate the search for (and achievement of) technological innovations. We could see the first type of DLI policy that was discussed (demand-driven innovation policy, aimed at promoting DLI processes in the economy and economic organizations) as being neo-Schmooklerian, in that it implies an inadequacy in the system that should be supporting market-pull. The second type of DLI policy that was discussed (demand-based innovation policy, aiming to promote innovation or innovation trajectories of a particular sort) has more of a neo-Schumpeterian feel to it, locating the problem in the need to develop new technological trajectories, to create new market demands that can make technological innovation more viable[4] (a point that is discussed in more detail later).

Mowery and Rosenberg spoke of the *matching* of technological capabilities and user requirements, Freeman talks of the two as effectively participating in an elaborate dance (where one or the other partner may take the lead, but coordination is vital). But the technology-push/market-pull schism remains influential. Until recently the role—and especially the evolution—of demand has been rather marginalized in the economics of innovation, even if the rule that an understanding of user requirements is a vital element of successful innovation is widely accepted. Similar points are frequently made in the managerial and marketing literatures.

With the rise of more systemic accounts of innovation shifting the focus of analysis away from the individual firm or innovator to the national or sectoral innovation system, markets and users are, of course, part of systems, though the systems approaches point to the importance of various intermediaries in helping to articulate demand and translate information about user requirements and resources. These relationships vary from system to system. We can expect differences across countries and industries, for example.

DEMAND, USERS AND INNOVATION INTELLIGENCE

How does demand lead innovation in DLI? The answer to this question will have a great bearing on efforts to use demand to influence innovation activities.

Since demand is the expression of consumer requirement through the market, then this can be seen to be signaling about user requirements. These signals can be very hard to interpret, since the purchaser does not face an unlimited array of offers from suppliers, thus being able to select precisely the combination of functions and features that they are prepared to pay the specified amount for, not to mention the existence of information asymmetries and restrictions of the time devoted to making decisions. Sometimes market dynamics are clearly signaling that one design is preferred to another, but often suppliers need to gather additional intelligence to help them determine just what it is that demand is signaling.

Market Research and Market Orientation

Even in the absence of technological innovation, market research may be important in informing suppliers as to what features of their products, marketing and ancillary factors—such as the packaging, delivery channels, aftersales—are valued, and which are the critical features for users. Market research techniques include survey methods often aimed at identifying distinct submarkets, psychogeodemographics and more qualitative approaches, such as focus groups and ethnographic studies of products in use. In B2B markets, use may be made of discussions at trade fairs and exhibitions. Feedback about purchasers from sales and aftersales staff is also widely used as a source of information about user reactions to existing products.

In such ways of gathering intelligence about users, information may be sought about user requirements and about unmet demands that might be satisfied by new or improved products, as well as about possible reactions to innovations. The user may be unaware that she or he is providing such information, or unclear about what organization might be using the information and in what ways. If the information has a substantial impact on the innovation process, or is at least built systematically into the process, so that where there is a change in demand the innovative activity is modified, then we can consider this to be a DLI. It is the sort of activity that firms often refer to as 'customer-orientation' or 'market orientation'.

Some authors distinguish between 'customer orientation' and 'market orientation' (for example, Slater and Narver 1998; 1999). They argue that being 'customer-led' is liable to be a short-term approach, with the organization finding and responding to customer satisfaction and expressed wants, usually in a highly incremental fashion when it comes to innovation. Hazley (2007) suggests that the use of IT-based customer relationship management (CRM) systems is likely to capture and codify the expressed needs of current customers, failing to provide foresight as to latent needs and additional markets. In contrast, Slater and Narver see being market-led as implying a long-term commitment to understanding customer needs, going beyond recognizing needs, to having deep insight into both expressed and latent requirements, and to providing customer value through innovative solutions that can be much more radical. They achieve this by close observation of customers' use of products in specific contexts, working closely with lead users (whose needs may also be leading those of other users), and engaging in mutual learning with innovative and experimental technologies—resulting in new solutions for unexpressed needs.

Agrawal and Pak (2001) reviewed studies of market orientation, broadly supporting the notion that organizational success requires determining and meeting the requirements of target markets more effectively and efficiently than competitors. As compared to what they call *the selling concept* (purchasers can be encouraged to buy more of the company's products; the firm must put its efforts into aggressive selling approaches), the *marketing concept* assumes that purchasers have requirements (needs) that they seek to satisfy through buying or not buying one or another set of products, and should not need intense persuasion to acquire suitable products. Agrawal and Pak note that such a market orientation can provide a unifying focus for employee efforts and projects, leading to superior performance, higher job satisfaction and greater organizational commitment (we would note, however, that a similar sense of mission is often shared by members of an exciting innovative technological project). The studies they reviewed, and their own research, demonstrated some consensus that market orientation influences innovation as well as performance, though few market orientation studies have specifically examined innovation, other than in the guise of successful new product development.[5]

User Engagement

The Alam (2002) study is one of many that explore deeper levels of user engagement in innovation than just the provision of information through market research. Market research may be more or less well understood by users, but essentially places them in a rather passive role: the firm is the active agent in seeking innovation intelligence from users. 'Usability testing' and related design activities engage users (or surrogate users) in working with product prototypes, so as to iron out design flaws and improve user-friendliness of the products and user manuals. But suppliers can also work more intimately with users at earlier stages in product development and, indeed, product development can be initiated by and even partly or extensively undertaken by users.

The lead in developing understanding of such approaches in innovation research is the work of Eric von Hippel (1986; 2005), who has studied both the role of lead users in innovations and users as sources of innovation themselves. He demonstrated the importance of such users in consumer goods markets, such as sports and childcare equipment and games software, and more recently explored the emergence of Internet-based communities where users work together on designing and improving new and/ or existing products. The explosion of interest in this work follows on the shift to 'open innovation' and the involvement of several leading firms in trying to work with and mobilize such communities for their own innovation activities.

There are many ways in which firms can work with their users, and there are several efforts to develop taxonomies of user engagement.[6] A helpful classification scheme has been provided by Emily Wise (Wise and Bisgaard,

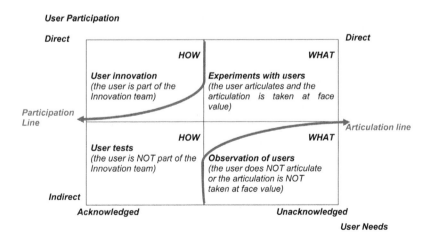

Figure 2.1   Modes of user-led innovation. Source: Wise and Bisgaard (2008).

2008; Wise and Høgenhaven, 2008), who studies user engagement in innovation in Nordic countries. This is based on two main dimensions: how far the consumer needs are acknowledged (acknowledged versus unacknowledged needs) and how far the users are involved in the innovation process (direct or indirect involvement). User-driven processes can be plotted on these two dimensions (Figure 2.1).

The two right-hand quadrants of this 'map' involve what Wise and colleagues term the WHAT phase of innovation—focusing on what to produce (the 'fuzzy front end'), and consisting of four steps: Opportunity Identification, Data Collection, Pattern Recognition and Concept Ideas. The two left-hand quadrants represent the HOW phase—the methods that will be used to produce the innovative product, and again consisting of four steps: Conceptualization, Prototype, Test and Implementation. The *participation line* indicates that in three quadrants companies gain access to user knowledge by asking, observing or experimenting with them. In only one do users innovate by themselves or take part in an innovation team. The *articulation line* indicates that in three quadrants companies use users' articulation of their needs and/or take these at face value, whereas in one quadrant companies gain access to user knowledge without such articulation.

The four quadrants, in more detail, are as follows:

- *Lower-Right Quadrant*: *Observation of users* who are involved indirectly in the process. The users' articulation of their needs is not taken at face value. Typical methods for involving users here are ethnographic methods such as shadowing, user self-observation, guided tours in user homes and workplaces.
- *Upper-Right Quadrant*: *Experiments with users* who are involved directly in the process. Though their articulations are taken at face value, they are not a part of the innovation team. Typical methods for involving users here are personal interviews, role-playing and living labs.
- *Upper-Left Quadrant*: *User innovation* where the users may be company innovators or may participate as members of the company's innovation team (this is the only quadrant where this applies). Their articulation of needs is taken at face value. The typical method for involving the users here is the lead user approach.[7]
- *Lower-Left Quadrant*: *User test* where users are not a part of the innovation team, but their articulation of needs is taken at face value. Typical methods for involving users here are focus groups and different kinds of user/usability tests.

Elizabeth Sanders (2006) presented a similar framework for thinking about the role of users in design processes (Figure 2.2). The design research space here involves four zones of activity. These are represented as large, light-colored areas in the background. Inside these are clusters and smaller bubbles of activity. Clusters are large and professionalized bodies of activity, with specialized journals, methods and traditions of

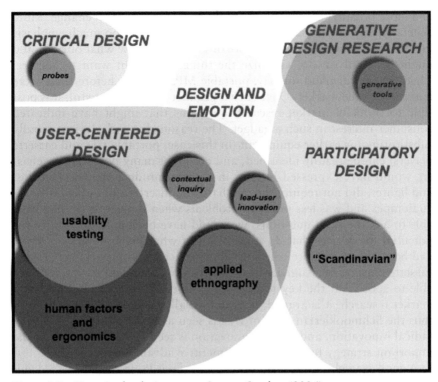

Figure 2.2 Users in the design space. Source: Sanders (2006).

enquiry. Bubbles are smaller than clusters because they are not yet supported by professional organizations.

User-centered design is a large zone, and one that is largely research-led. The expert mindset defines the people as the reactive objects of study. It contains three clusters emanating primarily from the applied social and behavioral sciences and engineering (human factors/ergonomics, applied ethnography and usability testing).[8] It also contains two bubbles—contextual inquiry and lead-user innovation.[9] The latter bubble spans the area of overlap between the user-centered design and the participatory design zones.

The participatory design zone is also large. Participatory design refers to efforts to actively involve the people who are being served through design, throughout the design development process as far as possible, ideally going beyond lead-users to more everyday ones. Typically, participatory design methods use physical artifacts as 'thinking tools', especially in the Scandinavian tradition.[10] Generative tools seek to create a shared design language to enable dialogue between designers/researchers and users.[11]

Arguments against DLI

The 'critical design approach' challenges DLI thinking on the grounds that this is liable merely to reinforce established ways of doing things, and more broadly to overlook possibilities for more radical change. More generally, one of the main arguments against putting too much emphasis on DLI stems from the view that we often do not know what our demand might be, until we can visualize the things we might want to acquire. There was no demand for, say, portable MP3 players, before these were launched on the market. Once such a product proves successful, it is possible to think of market research questions that might have indicated consumer interest in such a gadget. The reasons for such devices rapidly substituting for earlier equipment (in this case, portable CD and cassette players) can be readily identified, and no doubt many potential purchasers would have expressed interest in a cheap product that was smaller and lighter, did not require the purchase and insertion of optical discs or audiotapes and was less prone to problems when shaken. If we had been able to ask the right questions, we would have been able to identify the potential for devices that do some or all of what MP3 players do. If we had been able to explore consumer dissatisfaction with portable CD and cassette players, in a sufficiently evocative way, we might even have been able to spot what the key features of a superior product might be. But market research, it is argued, does not usually provide such intelligence, thus the Schmooklerian view of DLI is seen as inadequate for analyzing radical innovation, and radical innovation is seen in some quarters as the important strategy for sustained competitive advantage.

A good example of this philosophy in practice is Professor Jay Lee's 'dominant innovation' approach. This proposes that innovators need to focus on the new value-added services that they can deliver, not on traditional ideas of product development based on R&D. This can mean more than simply improving current products so that they can reach more users (the 'unserved' group in Figure 2.3), or meet the obvious unmet requirements of existing users (the 'unmet visible needs' group in Figure 2.3). It can mean extending into 'unmet invisible user needs'—in other words, supplying features and functionalities that the user may not have articulated any requirement for, but that will be very welcomed in retrospect. Furthermore, it may involve extending the activity of the firm to providing innovations that meet unexplored requirements of completely new markets. Lee's argument is that by undertaking this sort of innovation, the firm can steal a huge march on its competitors.[12]

But the argument also implies that such innovations are liable to be non-DLI. The innovator here is a visionary, able to visualize how technological capabilities may be applied to generating a completely new product that will be of value in new markets. It is interesting to note that for Lee, many of these innovations are based on a shift from supplying material goods to supplying services ('servicisation').[13] He cites the example of aircraft manufacturers moving from simply selling engines to selling hours of flight time—that is, selling a service that embodies the engine, but also the maintenance and eventual disposal of the engine, whose ownership remains with the manufacturer. Value is added for the customer by continuous improvement

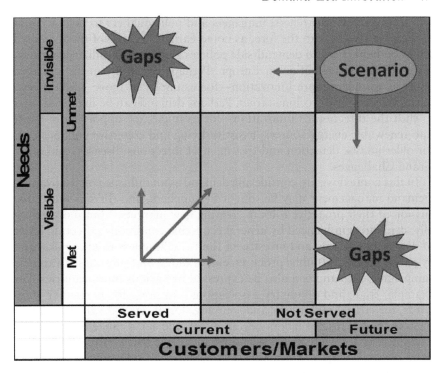

Figure 2.3   Dominant Innovation: Jay Lee, Univ. of Cincinnati. Source: 'The Innovation Matrix' (http://www.slideshare.net/guest7358100/dominant-innovation, accessed 2 March 2012).

of this service, and addition of ancillary services to it, which can involve technological innovation (in-flight monitoring devices), organizational innovation (systems to track the location of engines in real time and dispatch maintenance crews and equipment when problems are detected), and innovation in terms of marketing (how the value proposition is conveyed to the airline companies).[14]

Similar ideas are articulated in various ways by numerous commentators. For example, Slywotzky and Wise (2003) talk about 'demand innovation', rather than DLI. They focus on anticipating the next-generation needs of customers and connecting these with assets such as unique access to customers or window on the market, or specialized technical know-how.

Changing and Articulating Demand

Demand Management and Articulation

The discussion about DLI does not just reflect changes in the industrial innovation process, such as those signified in the term 'open innovation', and the need for researchers, managers and policymakers to take account of these. It also rises to the fore, as noted earlier, because of the increased attention being paid to demand-side policies as efforts to influence innovation, especially innovation in Europe. Perhaps demand can be managed so as to stimulate more innovation—for example, to move R&D investment closer to the Barcelona target. Perhaps demand can be managed so as to shift the direction of innovation—for example, to support more effort into renewable energy sources, assistive living and cognitive enhancement for older adults, detection and treatment of infectious diseases, and other Grand Challenges.

In this context we are considering demand as an influence on innovation. Demand management may be sought by suppliers, and there is much discussion of their proactive roles in creating new markets.[15] But more generally, demand is influenced by general economic conditions (affecting levels of disposable income and investment funds, willingness to take risks) and by policy measures (public procurement, taxation and subsidies, awareness campaigns). Demand can also be expressed by various intermediaries. For example, trade and voluntary associations can press for particular standards, for ethical investment and sourcing, for or against various regimes for testing (e.g., use of laboratory animals), and for a range of social and environmental objectives. In some instances, we can consider this to be more the articulation of demand than demand management. These intermediaries are taking on the role of representative of the purchaser, and are making vocal and explicit criteria that they believe are guiding or should guide purchaser choice.[16] Often this voice is necessary because there are insufficient product alternatives among which the purchasers can choose, or else information about the alternatives leaves a great deal to be desired. The usual case is that alternative choices would be made if product variety or product information was sufficient.

Changing Demand and Shaping Demand

Long-term trends in demand have been studied to a surprisingly limited extent. Business (intermediate) demand has been explored in relation to, for example, the Schumpeterian growth of new sectors and the demand for their products, and the emergence of a more complex industrial division of labor with substantial shifts to use of producer services by businesses across the economy. Such studies frequently explore these issues via input-output analysis.

Consumer demand can be explored via patterns of consumer expenditure, with a very detailed study of US trends over the last two decades of the twentieth century being presented by McCully (2011)—see also Moran and McCully (2001). Personal consumption expenditures (PCE)[17] accounted for over two-thirds of total domestic demand in the USA. From 1959 to 2009, McCully reported 3.4% annual growth in real consumer spending (2.2% on a per capita basis). The share accounted for by services increased from 45.7% in 1959 to 67.7% in 2009, reflecting increased shares of services such as medical care, finance, recreation, and education. In contrast, the share accounted for by nondurable goods decreased from 40.2% to 22.0%, with most categories declining. Durable goods' share only decreased slightly from 14.1% to 10.3%, with declining shares of new cars, household appliances, and furniture and bedding, offsetting increasing shares of "recreational vehicles" and "other durables" (such as consumer electronics). We see a rather different picture when examining growth rates in the quantity of goods and services purchased. Here, the largest annual average growth rate is 5.2% for durable goods, as compared to 3.5% for services, and 2.5% for nondurable goods. Figure 2.4 presents a more detailed breakdown; readers are referred to the original article for greater detail.[18]

While consumer demand trends may be expected to vary across countries, not least because of differences in the structure of public welfare provision, as well as demographic and more general economic factors, this bias toward goods rather than services is interesting, in that it seems to support the

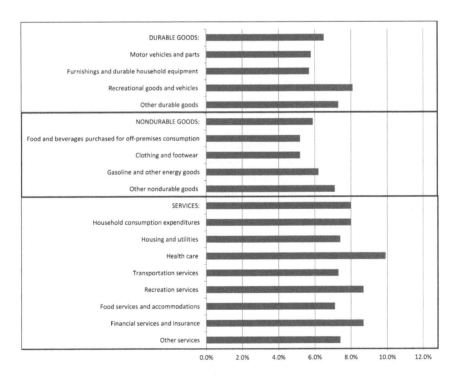

Figure 2.4 Trends in personal consumption expenditures (PCE) in the USA (Average Annual Growth of PCE, 1959-2009, in current dollars. Source: Data from Table 1, in Clinton P. McCully (2011).

"Gershuny hypothesis". More generally, the trends seem to confirm a more elaborate version of Engel's Law, in which we see increasing real incomes as leading to higher spending on discretionary items and higher quality products ("superior goods") relative to spending on basic products and necessities. Moran and McCully (2001) reported that much of the increase in discretionary spending was for home furnishings, motor vehicles, recreation (both in-home entertainment and away-from-home recreation), financial services (reflecting increasing household financial assets), intercity travel (particularly air travel), and electricity (for air conditioning, household appliances, audio and video equipment, and computers). With higher home-ownership rates came higher spending on home furnishings. By 2009, McCully observed that more than two-thirds of the increase in the services share of PCE was accounted for by health care services, financial services and insurance, the two sectors with greatest price increases and ones where consumer expenditure may be rather less "discretionary" than we might wish. Increased expenditure on health services was related by Moran and McCully (2001) to demographic change (higher spending on home health care, nursing homes, and prescription drugs), while they saw technological innovation as important, for example for pharmaceuticals, consumer electronics and communication services. Changes in tastes and lifestyles were reflected in many of the more detailed categories considered, while cheap imports of goods also play a role.

Engel's Law had often been seen as underpinning a shift from goods towards services, and thus the growth of the service economy. Jonathan Gershuny (1978), however, argued that the picture is more complicated. On the one hand, demand does shift away from basic activities such as food and shelter, and towards more sophisticated ones such as education and recreation. On the other hand, within these categories of activity there are alternative modes of provision of the consumer requirement. Mobility can be provided via public or private transport—the purchase of a service (bus journey) or a good (motor car), respectively. Entertainment similarly can be provided via the purchase of a service (theatre or cinema ticket) or a good (TV and DVD system). The Gershuny hypothesis was that technological innovation meant that the prices of goods were tending to decline more sharply than those of services and that in many cases quality improvements were greater for goods than for services. The result would be a shift in demand *within* the activity categories from services to goods. This did appear to be the case for many (if not all) activities across several decades in a number of European countries examined by Gershuny and Miles (1983). The picture will be complicated by service innovation (Gershuny saw great potential in the application of new technologies to services) and by changes in household structure and lifestyle, arguably behind the rise of fast food services. But the long-term trend in consumer demand will be hard to explain simply in terms of a growth in demand for services relative to goods. With this interpretation of the Engel's Law failing, we have little basis on which to go beyond expecting shifts from basic necessities to more discretionary expenditures, whether these are interpreted as indicating more quality, luxury, sophisticated taste, lifestyle fragmentation or, indeed, consumerism.

There have been several lines of analysis that have sought to explore future prospects for consumer demand. Many of these are simple market forecasting exercises, but a few studies go beyond this, with one that is particularly interesting and relevant here being Lührmann's (2005) analysis of long-term implications of population ageing.[19] There are a few studies that seek to address the relationship between demand change and innovation at a macro-level, notably Guerzoni (2007) and Saviotti (2008), but these are highly exploratory approaches.[20] Andersen (2007) reviews the treatment of demand in innovation studies. One interesting feature of his study is the repositioning of the Schumpeter/Schmookler schism in terms of the acquisition of innovations by purchasers. His point is that purchasers need to evaluate an innovation, and in the case of a Schmooklerian innovation they do so in terms of established preferences—that is, the innovation has to meet conventional requirements as well as improving upon performance. A Schumpeterian innovation transcends routine-based decision-making in that it may be so radical that buyers need to be convinced that it will have acceptable functionality and that new characteristics should be taken into account in product selection. The innovative entrepreneur needs to persuade buyers to change their preferences—for example, through good marketing. Lead users have a role to play in establishing new rules for product evaluation.

There are also a few studies of firm strategy that go beyond the nostrums of how managers need to pay attention to consumer demands, to discuss broader changes in innovation and delivery of goods and/or services, notably Howells (2004). Howells highlights the fact that consumption is often not a single event but a sequence of events and activities spread over time. Recognition of this can influence suppliers' decisions as to whether to supply their product as a good or a service. This helps understand the shift towards 'servicization' of products on the part of some manufacturers. In the present context, it can be linked to the discussion of eco-services or 'eco-efficient services', one form of which is aimed at reducing environmental impacts by selling customers a service (which can be repeatedly supplied by the same good) rather than by selling each customer another copy of the same good. Carpooling is a well-known example.[21]

What is lacking is sustained analysis of how to work with changing patterns of demand and more importantly, given interest in Grand Challenges, how these trends might be shaped. There are analyses of the role of marketing and corporate efforts to create markets for new products of one type or another. There are analyses of awareness campaigns and the role of incentives in changing behavior in areas such as food consumption, use of tobacco and alcohol, and a number of environmental technologies (e.g., low-energy light bulbs).[22]

The OECD (2002) study of sustainable consumption drew on Gatersleben and Vlek's (1998) Needs, Opportunities and Abilities (NOA), which relates demand to consumer needs and opportunities, and their abilities to fulfill those needs (objectives of maintaining or improving quality of life or well-being). Opportunities are external facilitating conditions (the availability, accessibility, prices and information of goods and services). Abilities are the capacities of individuals or households to procure goods and services—for example, income, available time, space to store goods, distance to facilities and cognitive and physical status. This approach stresses the multiple drivers of demand and consumption, implying that there are many options for policy to influence consumption patterns, but also that there are likely many points of 'stickiness'.[23]

DLI Policy and Policy Issues

Two Types of DLI Policy

The general arguments for public policies to promote innovation—market failure and system failure arguments—need not be rehearsed here. Why should there be interest in DLI policy? The argument in this chapter and the policy literature more generally has been that without better understanding of the role of demand in innovation processes and systems, policies are likely to overemphasize the supply side, and thus fall short on various grounds.

Earlier, we noted that DLI policy might refer to two rather different things. One was policy aimed at promoting DLI processes in general, or in a specific sector or technology. This demand-driven innovation policy is aimed at overcoming Schmooklerian failures of firms to take sufficient account of demand signals. We see such thinking in several policy initiatives—for instance, in the Finnish Ministry of Employment and the Economy's (2009) promotion of 'user-driven innovation policy'. Tools to support better linkages with demanding users may be emphasized—support with development and use of new web-based tools, and the sorts of user-centered and participative design process discussed before. More basic support for the utilization of market research information and tools may be part of such a strategy, and government support for statistical and other analysis of broad market trends can be seen in this context.

This sort of neo-Schmooklerian, demand-driven policy approach can be justified as a reaction to the perceived failure of much R&D and other supply-side innovation policy, which has not always resulted in commercialized or socially adopted innovations. There has been a perception that such policy is too readily 'captured' by interested parties on the supply side, who promote the technology development that suits their own commercial or research organizations, and tack on claims about market demand for their ambitions only as a legitimating ploy.

The neo-Schumpeterian argument about DLI policy, which we suggested might be called demand-based innovation policy, is not incompatible with the foregoing. It is possible to promote closer engagement with users *and* to seek to promote innovation or innovation trajectories of a particular sort, in a particular direction. Indeed, 'lead users' are often seen as vital in the location and/or creation of the niche markets that are often seen to precede development of new mass markets and technological regimes. However, the flavor of policy here is quite different in that it seeks to shift demand in order to induce technological innovation. Whereas most neo-Schumpeterian analysis sees demand shifts as triggered by technological innovation, this version of the approach sees new demand conditions as creating the stimulus for technological innovation that will hopefully reinforce these demand shifts and reproduce them on a wider scale.

Influencing Demand and Influencing Innovation

DLI policies of the neo-Schumpeterian kind are aimed at influencing demand, so as to effect innovation of various sorts. A Schmooklerian strategy, aimed at achieving similar effects, would be one that focused on achieving or enhancing linkages between users of particular types of innovation and the suppliers and potential suppliers of such products.

These strategies come to the fore when innovation is positioned in terms of Grand Challenges, as one of the leading ways of addressing major problems that confront our societies. Technological innovation will be only one of the approaches needed here; there may be requirements for social innovations (new types of care for older adults?) or organizational and institutional ones (improved environmental taxation schemes?). Demand management of the classic kind can play a role. But shaping demand and demand links to innovation will have a critical role to play.

'Creating an Innovative Europe' (Aho et al., 2006) argued that low levels of business investment in research and innovation in Europe resulted to a great extent from the lack of an innovation-friendly market in which new products could be launched. To create such a market required harmonized regulation, ambitious use of standards, a competitive intellectual property rights regime and demand-side measures. In particular, they stressed public procurement as such a measure and called for large-scale strategic actions to create innovation-friendly demand that could be complemented by supply-side measures for research and innovation around what came to be known as Grand Challenges.

The Aho report stressed public procurement, but this is only one of a range of policies that can be used to seek to influence innovation from the demand side. Edler (2010) presents a comprehensive framework for examining such methods. A range of approaches to influencing private demand are listed, alongside those influencing public demand and those with a more systemic orientation. Note that there are many discussions of how to influence demand that do not have a specific focus on innovation impacts. This is indeed true for most of the literature on 'sustainable consumption'.

During the period 2001–2011, there has been increasing recognition of and increasing attempts to promote the government's role as a procurer as a stimulus to innovation in the economy (EC, 2007a; 2010). In the European context, a number of member states have introduced measures to promote the procurement of innovation by public authorities, while at the level of European Union itself there have been a number of important developments with the same aim. Policy initiatives can be seen to fall into two main groups: establishment of measures and schemes that promote R&D procurement (by government); and the creation of a culture and set of practices that facilitate the procurement of actual products and services that are more innovative.

R&D procurement, which is the first of these approaches, is not in fact a procurement of goods and services as such but the procurement of R&D that may, ultimately, lead to the purchase of actual goods and services. The technique has been widely discussed, but is not widely used. By 2012, R&D-style procurement schemes had been established by four European countries: the UK (for an early evaluation, see Bound, 2010), Flanders, the Netherlands and Hungary, although Hungary's was at a pilot stage. The R&D procurement approach, from which all European-based approaches derive, is that of the US SBIR, the Small Business Innovation Research program, established in 1982, although the conditions under which the US scheme operates are rather different.

R&D procurements in the EU legal order exist in two forms: procurement of R&D services under the article 16f exemption from the Procurement Directives, and the so-called PCP (pre-commercial procurement) approach developed by the European Union (EC, 2007b; National IST Research Directors Forum Working Group, 2006) that is based on the article 16f exemption but is more specific as to its application. Both approaches have a number of aspects that make them attractive to governments seeking to promote procurement of innovation. Firstly, the procurement of R&D services, although complex, is itself likely to lead to innovation. Secondly, the approach can be conducted outside the procurement directives (the so-called public sector directives) that, according to article 16f, allow contracting authorities to procure innovation where the benefits do not accrue exclusively to themselves and the full costs are not borne by the contracting authority.

The European Union's development of a detailed procedure to take account of the 16f exemption for R&D services includes further conditions that ensure compliance with the Union's Treaty principles of equal treatment and fair competition. This procedure, known as the PCP procedure, is more restrictive than a procedure that is merely compliant with the article 16f exemption. The UK Netherland and Flanders schemes are based on this approach and have been moderately successful. As the research study notes (P3ITS Consortium, 2011), however, the procedure is one that is used by governments and the EC rather than by individual contracting authorities. The PCP procedure, because of its adherence to Treaty principles, cannot favor SMEs, a contrast with the US SBIR program, which, by federal law, requires government departments to allocate a certain proportion of their budgets to SMEs.

All the PCP schemes in operation in the EU (UK, Flanders, Netherlands and Hungary) use a centralized, national agency body to undertake the R&D procurements on behalf of public sector clients, or occasionally clients where there is a public sector interest. While such schemes have the advantage of using a well-developed capability to carry out the procurement, they may not always involve end users to the degree that would lead to a truly effective solution and one that would be widely purchased.

Such has been the recent attention given in Europe to the PCP procedure that the impression might now have been given that the European Union's procurement directives—which apply to the procurement of goods and services by public authorities (contracting authorities in the terminology of the directives)—fail to provide opportunities for public authorities to conduct procurements of innovative goods and services. In fact, the current directives, established in law in 2004, provide significant scope for contracting authorities to undertake the procurement of innovation through a range of provisions that involve market testing, interaction with suppliers, design contests, and use of standards and specifications that are performance-based (Apostol, 2010). Within the existing legal framework therefore there have been significant opportunities for the procurement of innovation and the development of practices, such as First Commercial Procurement or Forward Commitment Procurement (FCP), under which there have been convincing examples of procurement of innovative goods and services.

A main policy challenge within the European context is to encourage the wider implementation of these options (R&D procurements and actual procurements under the directives) and to ensure that these two forms (PCP and PPI) of procurement are more firmly connected together without undermining competition and value for money. At present, they are legally alternatives, and for that reason, promising technological concepts and prototypes that result from a PCP must be subject to further, and therefore separate, tender under the procurement directives. The fact that the procurement directives require this further tendering for the actual goods and services is a strong disincentive to both contracting authorities and to suppliers, preventing them from engaging more widely in pre-commercial procurement. As the report on the feasibility of introducing support to the procurement of innovation by the European Union notes, 'According to various studies commissioned by the European Commission, contracting authorities throughout the EU consider the fact that they are not allowed by legislation to purchase the products/services developed through a PCP procedure as an important disincentive to the application of PCP' (Rigby et al., 2012, p. 74).

During 2011, the European Commission conducted a consultation on the modernization of the procurement directives and this has led to proposals for significant changes. In particular, it has been suggested that the new directives should include a procedure termed 'innovation partnerships' to provide the necessary demand-side pull to bring forward truly groundbreaking innovations:

> Innovation partnerships would provide research oriented economic operators with a structured long-term partnership with CAEs enabling them to understand the specific needs of CAEs and to develop new personalized innovative solutions to be delivered to agreed performance levels and costs. The framework of the innovation partnership would guarantee a sufficient degree of competition during the innovation partner selection phases and should provide for the necessary IPR transfer and protection arrangements depending on the individual circumstances. The structure of the innovation partnership and the possible participation of multiple contracting authorities and entities (CAEs) should provide the necessary 'market pull' for innovative solutions enabling the economic operators to reach the thresholds of economic profitability without foreclosing the market. (EC, 2011, p. 61)

The European Commission clearly wishes to promote the demand-side, user-oriented and user-led innovation in the area of public procurement, but such changes are often difficult to implement and institutions, especially contracting authorities, are slow to adapt to the opportunities that such changes provide. How successful such initiatives will be in the long term, only time will tell.

Another helpful account has been provided by the Finnish Ministry of Employment and the Economy (2009) of what it terms 'demand-driven innovation policy'. Such policy is seen as being justified both by its potential contribution to meeting Grand Challenges and by the scope for enhancing the competitiveness of firms—in other words, in both neo-Schumpeterian and neo-Schmooklerian terms. Rather than use public/private demand as the structuring framework, policies are here classified into the following:

- Knowledge and capability development;
- Development of incentives;
- Infrastructure improvements; and
- Regulatory reform.

Knowledge and capability development is highlighted because DLI requires greater knowledge and competence on the part of suppliers and the users that they engage with. Competence development is equally required in public procurement. Suppliers require networking skills and the ability to identify opportunities to create value for the end user, and users need skills to be demanding, responsible and participative stimuli for innovation. This highlights the role of new design approaches and ways of managing intellectual property in open innovation arrangements. Foresight approaches are suggested as helping to identify market trends (including potential for creating lead markets), and raising awareness about innovative solutions. New web-based tools may play roles in foresight and networking.

Development of incentives necessarily includes financial incentives (including tax-related ones) that can be used to support and steer user-driven research, development and innovation activity. Public procurement is another source of incentives to innovators, with the public sector acting as lead market or demonstrator for specific types of products or production processes. The European Union's Lead Market Initiative for Europe selected six areas in which to create lead markets in Europe: eHealth, protective textiles, sustainable construction, recycling, bio-based products and renewable energy.

Infrastructure improvements relevant here include those to do with the information technology infrastructure, where compatible systems are stressed by the Finnish policymakers (along with the quality, openness and the trustworthiness associated with the system and its users). Innovation platforms and development environments that permit networking across traditional sectoral boundaries are another area for effort—for example, with 'Living Labs' initiatives and public/private partnerships.

Regulatory reform (and standards issues) also loom large—for example, the issues involved in the terms of the utilization of data held by the public sector, so as to make it more readily available for user-driven innovation activities and more efficient for users of information and for commercial actors. In many cases, DLI requires collaboration between various service providers, which may also call for regulatory change to promote partnerships between service providers. Intellectual property rights and related issues of valuing and assessing intangible assets need to be addressed, especially where open and user innovation are involved, raising questions of stakeholder rights, returns and responsibilities. Regulation is a familiar driver of demand and innovation in areas such as environment and health, but these innovation impacts need to be taken into account when drafting regulation—for instance, by setting challenging targets for the market actors involved. 'Softer' forms of steering, such as recommendations and labeling, should also be considered, as enabling better-informed purchaser choices.

We noted earlier the multiplicity of factors influencing demand, and the theme of this chapter has been the complex relationships that interrelate demand and innovation. This necessitates 'joined-up' DLI policy and evaluation of such policies and learning about what their success (or otherwise) tells us about the DLI system. Edler (2010) similarly concludes that demand-based innovation policy will call for a high level of commitment on the part of policymakers. Strategic intelligence will need to be developed and applied at different levels and in different forms, with substantial networking and coordination of governance across institutions and levels of policy. Equally, DLI *policies* need to be 'joined up' with supply-side measures, since it is quite possible that Schumpeterian breakthroughs connected with some of the Grand Challenges will come from the major technological opportunities offered by information technologies, biotechnologies, and nanotechnologies, if the incentives are right. DLI *policies* are manifold but DLI policy needs to have a comprehensive approach.

CONCLUSIONS

Demand-led innovation is attracting a great deal of attention and a sophisticated discussion has already emerged about the relevant policy instruments here. There has been some discussion of how policies have been pursued in different countries (e.g., Edler, 2010) but there is still a shortage of evaluation of such policies. This means that the main arguments for them must rest on the underpinning case for the importance of DLI, and such limited evidence as we have been able to muster from Innobarometer and related sources about the importance of DLI and demand elements of public innovation policy. It is also apparent that there is some confusion engendered by the lack of clarity about basic terminology here, and this chapter has sought to clarify the main terms used.

Despite the fuzziness of some of the key concepts—or at least, the varying ways in which they have been employed—it is clear that the topic of DLI is a very important one. Regardless of whether a Schmookler or a Schumpeter perspective is adopted, or what sort of synthesis of the two is articulated, the need to take demand into account in fostering successful industrial innovation, and in helping innovation confront the Grand Challenges of our time, is inescapable. We cannot wait for scholarly clarification of the complex and evolving links between demand and innovation before policies are formulated. Indeed, policymakers have not waited, and have already developed a large palette of actual and potential policy instruments. The major challenge may be one of coordination of the application of different DLI tools and integrating such tools with more conventional supply-side measures.

Policy evaluation will be difficult, because of this necessary intertwining of numerous instruments and strategies. It should be given very serious attention, because it offers opportunities to learn about what does and does not work effectively, and how to better orient innovation to meet Grand Challenges. It will also almost inevitably lead to learning about how DLI processes operate in practice, even as it contributes to reshaping such processes. The likelihood is that in a decade's time, a review of the DLI literature could be much more extensive than that provided in this chapter. It is also likely that DLI practice will have been transformed, both by endogenous changes in management philosophy and strategy, and by policy interventions that aim to accomplish this.

NOTES

1. We reserve judgment as to whether marketing is included among these features of the innovation process. We would not consider market research that is merely directed to how to advertise or brand a product that has already been created with little exploration of demand side to be DLI.
2. Freeman also discusses the work of Gerhard Mensch (1979), who had claimed that economic depression induces bursts of basic innovations and that his empirical data supported this idea.
3. The classic study of such structural adjustments and one that did much to clarify what it takes to qualify as a heartland technology is Perez (1983).
4. This approach diverges from a great deal of neo-Schumpeterian analysis in that it does not begin with a technology-led heartland technology development, but rather looks for a series of socioeconomic conditions that can lead to a shift in technological regime to one based on a new heartland technology or set of technologies (see Green and Miles, 1996).
5. For a review of studies on how R&D and marketing may be integrated, see Griffin and Hauser (1995).
6. For example, Gristock's (2008) *user-led innovation typology* differentiates between (a) Users driving ideas (b) Users changing products (c) Users changing services (d) Users changing processes (e) Users changing systems and (f) Users interacting via open systems.
7. The classic definition, from von Hippel (1986, 791), is that 'Lead users are users whose present strong needs will become general in a market-place months or years in the future. Since lead users are familiar with conditions that lie in the future for most others, they can serve as a need-forecasting laboratory for marketing research. Moreover, since lead users often attempt to fill the need they experience, they can provide new product concept and design data as well'.
8. Sanders defines these thus: *Human factors/ergonomics*: The study of how humans behave physically and psychologically in relation to particular environments, products or services (which borrows from physiology, psychology and engineering). *Applied ethnography*: The qualitative description of cultures and cultural practices, which is based on observational research (and borrows from anthropology). *Usability testing*: Measures how well people can use something for its intended purpose (which borrows from cognitive psychology and cognitive engineering). She notes some overlap of people, methods and tools between the human factors/ergonomics cluster and the usability testing cluster.
9. Contextual inquiry is, according to Sanders, most often used in the software development process. It is a user-centered design method, employed early in the software development life cycle, comprising preparation, evaluation, analysis and design phases. It involves discussion sessions and more recently design-led methods such as visioning and storyboarding to explicate users' daily routines or processes and enable the product to be designed to either work effectively with, help shorten or eliminate these processes.
10. See, for example, Bødker et al., 2000.
11. The critical design zone is said to have emerged more recently and is interpreted by Sanders as a reaction against the user-centered approaches' focus on usability and utility. It is a more design-led approach, with the designer in the role of the expert, asking about alternatives to the prevailing situation through designs that embody alternative social, cultural, technical or economic values. The 'probes' mentioned here are ambiguous stimuli that

designers send to people who then respond to them, providing insights for the design process. No attempt is made to understand or to empathize with the people probed; the objective is design inspiration. The materials used in probes research and in generative tools approach can be quite similar—for example, disposable cameras with instructions for use, diaries, daily activity logs and open-ended postcards to write. But with probes, these materials are sent to people who fill them out and send them back to inspire the designers, who do not meet the respondents and explore what they were thinking when they filled out the probes. In generative tools, such 'probes' in this case serve to prepare people for creative sessions.

12. For explication, see Lee and AbuAli (2011)
13. Also described as 'servitisation' and 'servation'.
14. This discussion is informed by conversations with Professor Lee, and material at the IMS Center website. Online. Available HTTP: http://www.imscenter.net/ (accessed 1 March 2012).
15. A pivotal study here is Dougherty (1990).
16. An interesting case study of the intermediary role played by the Dutch Steering Committee on Orphan Drugs is presented by Boon et al. (2007).
17. PCE here consists of expenditures on goods and services by individuals and by the nonprofit organizations that serve them, in this study being those resident in the US or US civilian and military personnel stationed abroad and residents travelling or working temporarily abroad. PCE consists primarily of market transactions and includes purchases from private business, from government enterprises and from government agencies (consisting mainly of tuition payments for higher education and charges for medical care and water and sanitary services). PCE includes expenditures financed through certain government programs; primarily those that provide medical care to the elderly, poor, military dependents and retirees; aid to students; and assistance for purchases of food and fuel.
18. See also Redmond (2001), who explores the trend over this period towards spending rather than saving consumer income.
19. The study examines Germany, forecasting developments from 2000 to 2040. Age structure and the intergenerational distribution of spending power were shown to have significant effects on aggregate demand (given the assumptions of the model used), while decreasing average household size and number of households do not. Design of the pension system has only a minor impact on the distribution of incomes and total expenditures and on aggregate demand.
20. Guerzoni provides a helpful review of the treatment of demand in innovation studies, and adds to the Schmooklerian account of market size as a driver of innovation by considering how more sophisticated markets provide information to innovators about user requirements. Saviotti explores sophistication and the increasing variety of products that become available.
21. Behrendt et al. (2003) and Bartolome (2003) focus on eco-efficient producer services.
22. An annotated bibliography of relevant material in the passenger transport field has been prepared by the UK Energy Research Centre's Technology and Policy Assessment team in its project on policy strategy for carbon emissions reduction in this sector. Online. Available HTTP: http://wwwukerc.ac.uk/Downloads/PDF/09/0904TransAwarenessMktg.pdf (accessed 1 March 2012). Also, for work on the 'rebound effect', see http://www.ukerc.ac.uk/support/tiki-read_article.php?articleId=1187&highlight=rebound%20effect (accessed 2 March 2012).
23. See Jackson and Michaelis (2003) for a review of approaches to consumption and sustainability policies.

BIBLIOGRAPHY

Agrawal, M. K. and Pak, M. H. (2001) 'Getting Smart about Supply Chain Management'. *McKinsey Quarterly Special Edition* 2: 22–26.

Aho, E., Cornu, J., Georghiou, L. (rapporteur) and Subira, A. (2006) 'Creating an Innovative Europe'. Independent Expert Group on R&D and Innovation appointed following the Hampton Court Summit. European Commission. Online. Available HTTP: http://ec.europa.eu/invest-in-research/pdf/download_en/aho_report.pdf (accessed 1 March 2012).

Alam, I. (2002) 'An Exploratory Investigation of User Involvement in New Service Development'. *Journal of the Academy of Marketing Sciences* 30 (3): 250–261.

Andersen, E. S. (2007) 'Innovation and Demand'. In Hanusch, H. and Pyka, A. (eds.), *The Elgar Companion to Neo-Schumpeterian Economics*, 754–765. Cheltenham, UK: Edward Elgar.

Apostol, R. (2010) 'Formal European Standards in Public Procurement: A Strategic Tool to Support Innovation'. *Public Procurement Law Review* 2: 57–64.

Bartolome, M. (2003) 'Eco-efficient Producer Services—What Are They, How Do They Benefit Customers and the Environment and How Likely Are They to Develop and Be Extensively Utilised?' *Journal of Cleaner Production* 11 (8): 829–837.

Behrendt, S., Jasch, C., Kortman, J., Hrauda, G., Pfitzner, R. and Velt, D. (2003) *Eco-service Development: Reinventing Supply and Demand in the European Union*. London: Greenleaf Publishing.

Bødker, S., Ehn, P., Sjögren, D. and Sundblad, Y. (2000) 'Co-operative Design—Perspectives on 20 Years with the Scandinavian IT Design Model'. Keynote presentation at Proc. NordiCHI 2000, Stockholm, 23–25 October. Online. Available HTTP: http://www.irit.fr/SIGCHI/old/docs/debat/Utopia.pdf (accessed 1 March 2012).

Boon, W. P. C., Moors, E. H. M., Kuhlmann, S. and Smits, R. E. H. M. (2007) 'Demand Articulation in Intermediary Organizations: The Case of Orphan Drugs in the Netherlands'. *Technological Forecasting & Social Change* 75: 644–671.

Bound, K. and Puttick, R. (2010) *Buying Power: Is the Small Business Research Initiative for Procuring R&D Driving Innovation in the UK?* London: NESTA.

Corvers, S. F. M. and Bos, L. (2006) 'Pre-commercial Procurement'. *Tijdschrift Aanbestedingsrecht (Procurement Magazine)* 5.

Dougherty, D. (1990) 'Understanding New Markets for New Products'. *Strategic Management Journal* 11: 59–78.

EC. (2007a) 'Guide on Dealing with Innovative Solutions in Public Procurement: 10 Elements of Good Practice'. SEC(2007) 280. Brussels: European Commission.

EC. (2007b) 'Pre-commercial Procurement: Driving Innovation to Ensure Sustainable High-Quality Public Services in Europe'. SEC(2007) 1668. Communication from the Commission to the European Parliament, the Council, the European Economic and Social Committee and the Committee of the Regions. COM (2007) 799 Final. Brussels: European Commission.

EC. (2010) 'Europe 2020 Flagship Initiative Innovation Union'. COM(2010) 546 Final. Brussels: European Commission.

EC. (2011) 'Commission Staff Working Paper: Impact Assessment'. Accompanying the document 'Proposal for a Directive of the European Parliament and of the Council on Public Procurement' and the 'Proposal for a Directive of the European Parliament and of the Council on procurement by entities operating in the water, energy, transport and postal sectors'. SEC (2011) 1585 Final. Brussels: European Commission.

Edler, J. (2010) 'Demand-Based Innovation Policy'. In Smits, R., Kuhlmann, S. and Shapira, P. (eds.), *The Theory And Practice Of Innovation Policy*, 275–302. Cheltenham: Edward Elgar.

Finnish Ministry of Employment and the Economy. (2009) 'Demand-Driven Innovation Policy'. Online. Available HTTP: http://www.tem.fi/index.phtml?l=en&s=2853 (accessed 1 March 2012).

Freeman, C. (1982) 'Schumpeter or Schmookler?' In Freeman C., Clark, J. and Soete, L. (eds.), *Unemployment and Technical Innovation*, 35–43. London: Pinter.

Gatersleben, B. and Vlek, C. (1998) 'Household Consumption, Quality of Life, and Environmental Impacts: A Psychological Perspective and Empirical Study'. In Noorman, K. and Uiterkamp, T. (eds.), *Green Households? Domestic Consumers, Environment, and Sustainability*, 141–183. London: Earthscan.

Gershuny, J. I. (1978) *After Industrial Society?* London: Macmillan.

Gershuny, J. I. and Miles, I. D. (1983) *The New Service Economy*. London: Pinter.

Green, K. and Miles, I. (1996) 'A Clean Break? From Corporate R&D to Sustainable Technological Regimes'. In Welford, R. and Starkey, R. (eds.), *The Earthscan Reader in Business and the Environment*, 129–144. London: Earthscan.

Griffin, A. and Hauser, J. R. (1995) 'Integrating R&D and Marketing: A Review and Analysis of the Literature'. WP No. 112–94. Sloan working paper no. 3735. Sloan School of Management, Massachusetts Institute of Technology.

Gristock, J. (2008) 'A Typology of User-Led Innovation: The Case of "Anything Left-Handed", the World's First Real and Virtual Shop for Left-Handed Goods'. Working paper. Department of Biology and Environmental Sciences, University of Sussex. Online. Available HTTP: http://eprints.sussex.ac.uk/1741/ (accessed 1 March 2012).

Guerzoni, M. (2007) 'Size and Sophistication: The Two Faces of Demand'. Working paper no. 197. CESPRI (Centro di Ricerca sui Processi di Innovazione e Internazionalizzazione), Università Commerciale 'Luigi Bocconi', Milan.

Hazley, C. (2007) 'Knowledge Management Interactions for a Customer Centric Strategy: The Role of Human and IT Based Interactions in Understanding Customers' Needs'. PhD diss. PREST, University of Manchester.

Howells, J. (2004) 'Innovation, Consumption and Services: Encapsulation and the Combinatorial Role of Services'. *Service Industries Journal* 24 (1): 19–36.

Jackson, T. and Michaelis, L. (2003) *Policies for Sustainable Consumption*. London: Sustainable Development Commission.

Lee, J. and AbuAli, M. (2011) Innovative Product Advanced Service Systems (I-PASS): methodology, tools, and applications for dominant service design. *The International Journal of Advanced Manufacturing Technology*, 52 (9–12): 1161–1173.

Lührmann, M. (2005) 'Population Aging and the Demand for Goods & Services'. MEA discussion paper series 05095. Mannheim Research Institute for the Economics of Aging (MEA), University of Mannheim. Online. Available HTTP: http://ideas.repec.org/e/plu132.html (accessed 2 March 2012).

McCully, C. P. (2011) 'Trends in Consumer Spending and Personal Saving, 1959–2009'. *Survey Of Current Business* June: 14-25. Online. Available HTTP: http://www.bea.gov/scb/pdf/2011/06%20June/0611_pce.pdf (accessed 14 August 2012).

Mensch, G. (1979) *Stalemate in Technology*. New York: Ballinger.

Moran, L. R. and McCully, C. P. (2001) 'Trends in Consumer Spending, 1959–2000'. *Survey of Current Business* March: 15–21. Online. Available HTTP: http://www.bea.gov/scb/pdf/national/nipa/2001/0301pce.pdf (accessed 1 March 2012).

Mowery, D. and Rosenberg, N. (1979) 'The Influence of Market Demand upon Innovation'. *Research Policy* 8: 103–153.

National IST Research Directors Forum Working Group. (2006) 'Pre-commercial Procurement of Innovation: A Missing Link in the European Innovation Cycle'. European Commission, Brussels.

OECD. (2002) 'Policies to Promote Sustainable Consumption: An Overview'. Paris: OECD. Online. Available HTTP: http://www.oecd.org/dataoecd/1/59/40317373.pdf (accessed 2 March 2012).

P3ITS Consortium. (2011) 'Pre-commercial Public Procurement for ITS Innovation and Deployment, WP2 Analysis of Public Pre-commercial Procurement Models and Mechanisms'. Online. Available HTTP: http://www.ertico.com/assets/Activities/P3ITS/P3ITS-D2.1-Analysis-of-public-Pre-Commercial-Procurementv1.8.pdf (accessed 27 June 2012).

Perez, C. (1983) 'Structural Change and Assimilation of New Technologies'. *Futures* 15 (5): 357–375.

Redmond, W. H. (2001) 'Exploring Limits to Material Desire: The Influence of Preferences vs. Plans on Consumption Spending'. *Journal of Economic Issues* 35 (3): 575–589.

Rigby, J., Boekholt, P., Semple, A., Deuten, J., Apostol, R., Corvers, S. and Edler, J. (2012) 'Feasibility Study on Future EU Support to Public Procurement of Innovative Solutions: Obtaining Evidence for a Full Scheme'. Final report. European Commission. Online. Available HTTP: http://ec.europa.eu/enterprise/policies/innovation/policy/lead-market-initiative/files/meeting-procurement-feb2012/study-eu-support-public-procurement-innovative-solutions_en.pdf (accessed 6 March 2012).

Sanders, E. B. N. (2006) 'Design Research in 2006'. *Design Research Quarterly* 1 (1): 1–8.

Saviotti, P. P. (2008) 'Structural Change and Economic Development: The Role of Consumption'. Paper presented at The Role of Consumption for Structural Change in the Economy. Max Planck Institute for Economic Research. Jena. 16–18 July.

Schmookler, J. (1966) *Invention and Economic Growth*. Cambridge: Harvard University Press.

Schumpeter, J. A. (1939) *Business Cycles*. New York: McGraw-Hill.

Slater, F. and Narver, J. C. (1998) 'Customer-Led and Market-Oriented: Let's Not Confuse the Two'. *Strategic Management Journal* 19 (10): 1001–1006.

Slater, F. and Narver, J. C. (1999) 'Market-Oriented Is More Than Being Customer-Led'. *Strategic Management Journal* 20 (12): 1165–1168.

Slywotzky, A. and Wise, R. (2003) 'Three Keys to Groundbreaking Growth: A Demand Innovation Strategy, Nurturing Practices, and a Chief Growth Officer'. *Strategy & Leadership* 31 (5):12–19.

von Hippel, E. (1986) 'Lead Users: A Source of Novel Product Concepts'. *Management Science* 32 (7): 791–805.

von Hippel, E. (2005) *Democratizing Innovation*. Cambridge, MA: MIT Press. Online. Available HTTP: http://web.mit.edu/evhippel/www/books.htm (accessed 1 March 2012).

Wise, E. and Bisgaard, T. (2008) 'User-Driven Innovation: Context and Cases in the Nordic Region'. Presentation of final report. NICe/Winnoway meeting. Karlstad. 9 September. Online. Available HTTP: http://www.imi.tkk.fi/files/news/Final_Report_UDI_Context_and_Cases.pdf (accessed 2 March 2012).

Wise, E. and Høgenhaven, C. (2008) 'User-Driven Innovation Context and Cases in the Nordic Region'. Written for the Nordic Innovation Centre. June.

3 Innovation in the Public Sector

Hugo Thénint and Ian Miles

INTRODUCTION

If Europe seeks to be a dynamic and innovative knowledge-based economy, this will not simply be a matter of transforming high-technology sectors. Public services are among the most knowledge-intensive of all sectors, as indicated by the high share of graduates in the public service workforce (especially, but not only, education and health). They contribute to welfare, quality of life and overall economic performance. Public services and public administration represent a significant part of the European socioeconomic activity. Government spending in the EU amounted on average to 47 percent of GDP (Eurostat, 2008) compared to 32 percent in the US or 26 percent in Japan, and public employment represents more than 15 percent of the total employment in the EU. Thus, public services also need to be part of this mobilization towards a knowledge economy.

Public services have important roles as demonstrators, as setters of standards, as lead markets and procurers, all of which make their contribution to innovation and their role in innovation in other sectors extremely significant. Hence, public services could become a comparative advantage for European competitiveness, by creating innovation-conducive environments. Global grand challenges—such as demographic change, pollution and security concerns—are creating new demands for public services, and the public sector may be a strong driver for EU leadership in these domains too.

Demand for public services in many advanced countries is growing faster than the rest of the economy, even before the onset of the recent economic crisis. As the GDP is increasing more slowly than public expenditure, the public sector is subject to major budget constraints. The economic crisis exacerbates this. Meanwhile public services are facing higher expectations from their users. Consequently, innovation is vital for increasing public sector efficiency in terms of value for money, more for less and for delivering new and better quality services. Some of these services affect the whole economy or key sectors within it, as well as being important for quality of life more generally.

With these considerations in mind, this chapter aims to explore mechanisms that generate or introduce and help encourage innovation in the public sector, and to identify potential EU actions supporting these mechanisms across European countries.

Grasping the Specifics of Innovation in the Public Sector

Traditionally, the public sector has been perceived as less innovative than the private sector. Is this view factually correct? Or is it rather that public sector innovation is less perceptible because it is not sufficiently celebrated or adequately measured?

The Intangible Nature of Innovation

Firstly, it is important to notice that the idea of innovation in the public sector has evolved alongside a more nuanced understanding of innovation, which now encompasses non-technological processes and the service industry in addition to its more traditional meaning.

Government organizations typically have multiple objectives that can be vague compared to clear business objectives, such as clients or profits. Often the issues faced by public authorities are complex, and the wrong policy mix can have adverse effects. When public authorities tackle social or environmental challenges, effectiveness depends not only on direct policy action but also on society overall. Innovation in the public sector is closely linked to social attitudes towards innovation and change.

In this regard, identifying and measuring innovation and its effects, an area that is already fraught with methodological problems as regards the private sector, are even more difficult in the case of public organizations. As in the private sector, innovation cannot be understood solely as a way of improving cost or efficiency—there are other objectives, such as greater market reach, improved and original goods and services, regulatory compliance and more. The appropriate criteria for appraising public sector innovation need to be examined.

Risk-Taking and Political Issues

Governments provide goods and (especially) services, very often by definition affecting all of society. Thus, the implications of changes as to how governments provide these goods and services have to be thought through carefully. Unlike private companies, governments usually do not have niche markets in which to test things (though there is growing interest in various ways of engineering experimental designs with which to explore policy impacts).

A great responsibility is taken on by policymakers, especially by elected representatives. Political push, a top-down process, is considered as a major driver of innovation—and may be compared to the influence that market changes have in the private sector. But politicians who are multiplying ambitious objectives are taking considerable risks; they are exposed to criticism from opponents and the media, which prefer to celebrate failure (Manley, 2001).

The intrinsic political dimension of the public sector brings up a time horizon issue. Electoral cycles may not be long enough to fulfill a project's objectives and thus for the initiators to benefit from its impact. For this reason, short-term political horizons, underpinned by public polling, can hinder longer-term innovation processes.[1]

Needs-led innovation is rarely driven by a major crisis but rather mostly by internal problems, such as budget constraints, which lead to dynamic incremental innovation processes. Top-down innovations are less frequent than bottom-up innovation, though more radical; they seem to be more driven by changes in the agencies' organization or pressure from the civil society than from legislative or electoral processes.

Organizational Structure and Management

The public sector consists of a complex, open system of organizations with various tasks. As a consequence, decision-making can be slower than in the private sector—there are large chains of command, and many sources of relevant intelligence (and potential delay). Innovations here will often have an impact across this complex organizational structure, and thus must be supported by a robust strategy. It is possible for innovations of some types to be 'rolled out' and distributed within the large systems, in a top-down way.

However, these particular large systems are typically not an effective environment for the diffusion of innovation. Each of these systems is rather compartmentalized—for example, by policy field and geographical coverage; and even less exchange exists between nation-states. As a consequence, the diffusion of innovation (and the learning of lessons from innovative efforts) can be complex and takes more time than in a private sector evolving in an international environment.

Another important factor of differentiation between the two sectors is customer relationship management. Conventionally, relations with end users have been unilateral in the public sector, where civil servants were managed and evaluated by policymakers, and not by citizens, whereas innovation in the private sector depends more on market feedback.

Knowledge Sources and Supply Chain

The public sector is among the most knowledge-intensive of all sectors and has a great role in innovation processes as both procurer and diffuser.

Innovation in the public sector can be divided into several types, for instance:

- A new or improved service
- Process innovation
- Administrative innovation
- System innovation (a new system or a fundamental change of an entire existing system)
- Conceptual innovation or radical change of rationality (e.g. change in paradigm, political priorities)

The first two types of innovation can be subsumed under product innovation. The innovations can be labelled in the following ways:

- Incremental innovations / radical innovations (denoting the degree of novelty, in industry most innovations can be considered incremental improvements of already existing products, processes or services)

- Top-down innovations / bottom-up innovations (denoting who has initiated the process leading to behavioural changes)

- Needs-led innovations and efficiency-led innovation (denoting whether the innovation process has been initiated to solve a specific problem or in order to make existing products or procedures more efficient)

Figure 3.1 Types of innovation in the public sector. Source: PUBLIN report D9 (Halvorsen et al., 2005).

Technology procurement is important for the public sector because it can introduce better technologies in the production of public services and goods. But the public sector has a broader range of sources of technologies and knowledge, some of which are more open than the private sector and do not require procurement procedure. Cooperation with other public organizations, universities, unions and NGOs is a major driver for innovation and represents a great complement to private goods and services providers. Figure 3.1 provides a listing of types of innovation in public services.

Main Innovation Trends in the Public Sector

A Historical Perspective

As opposed to the general prejudice, there has always been substantial innovation in the public sector, notably since the middle of the 20th century. The postwar period has been prolific in building strong centralized administrations and a wide range of public services in many countries, especially in Europe, including the UK, France and Germany. Political push was a particularly important driver for innovation as the development of effective welfare states was considered a way to curb communism expansion. However, the lack of flexibility of these systems and increasing resource constraints in the late 1970s underlined the limits of these models (Rosanvallon, 1981; Mishra, 1984; Esping-Andersen, Rainwater and Rein, 1987).

During the early 1980s, political shifts in many countries, most notably in England and the US, reinforced the call for change in the model of governance of the public sector. These arguments were underpinned by neoliberal economics and theories of new public management, which promote the introduction of organizational and management approaches modeled on those of the private sector: markets, quasi-markets and competition among units, outsourcing of functions, application of extensive systems of performance management, and the like. The assumption was that such approaches would stimulate innovation, as well as generally encourage greater efficiency.

In the late 1980s, new political arrangements in local governments and decentralization pushed towards a better organization of public sector systems. Decentralization and public management approaches have been considered complementary processes. Nonetheless, full decentralization without a certain degree of coordination at a central level may have impeded cooperation and increased inequity. It also became apparent that the implementation of new public management practices and other reform strategies have not necessarily resulted in more innovative activities, structures and outcomes. Detractors have even argued that eliding the differences between private and public sectors in a 'one size fits all' view is having adverse effects.

Asserting that this approach was misjudged, public value theory emerged in the mid-1990s. It refers to the value created by government through services, regulation and other actions. In simple terms, public value poses three central questions to public managers (Coats and Passmore, 2008), which form the backbone of the approach: What is this organization for? To whom are we accountable? How do we know if we have been successful?

The 1990s saw considerable extension of ICT-influenced innovation in the public sector, which has often been a leader in IT use. However, the adoption and diffusion of these technologies have often been beset by problems and have been slow to replace some more conventional and formal communication procedures. IT systems in government are large and expensive. The larger the development, the more likely it is that it will be unsuccessful. It has been argued that 20 to 30 percent of all developments are total failures, in which projects are abandoned, and 30 to 60 percent are partial failures, in which there are time and cost overruns or other problems (Goldfinch, 2007). Explanations include data inadequacies, technical problems, management/process/technical skill shortages, cultural clashes, political infighting and external environmental factors (Heeks, 1999).

Beyond the strict technological aspect of innovation, IT should be considered more as an innovation driver rather than an innovation in itself. New information systems may be the impetus for new organizational models, cross-sector institutional cooperation and knowledge exchange. In addition,

	Traditional public administration	Public management	Networked governance
Context	Stable with homogenous population	Competitive, atomized population	Continuously changing with diverse population
Needs/issues	Straightforward, defined by professionals	Expressed through the market	Complex, volatile and prone to risk
Governance	Hierarchies within public servants	Markets (purchasers, providers and contractors)	Networks and partnerships
Key concept	Public good	Public choice	Public value
Innovation type	Large-scale, radical	Organizational innovation more than content	Innovation at both central and local levels
Improvement	Large step-change but little adaptation capabilities	Managerial processes, some cost-effectiveness improvements	Transformational and continuous improvement (especially front line)
Policy-makers	Commanders	Commissioners	Leaders & interpreters
Public managers	'Clerks & Martyrs'	Efficiency	Explorers
Population	Citizens	Customers	Co-producers

Figure 3.2 Different models of governance and public management. Source: Hartley (2005).

the emergence of e-government and online services has substantially facilitated empowerment and bottom-up innovation. Recently, networked governance and the search for public value have found new impetus through the development of pilot initiatives, innovation labs and living labs.

Figure 3.2 represents a helpful attempt to summarize the characteristics of different models of governance in the public sector. Though the demarcations between the three models may be made more sharply than is always the case in real-life situations, they capture some major ways in which public service organization and philosophy can vary and to some extent how they have evolved.

Some Recent Developments in European Countries

Recent debate and associated initiatives dealing with public sector innovation have mainly aimed at improving the effectiveness and efficiency of the delivery of public services and improved transparency and user friendliness.

Beyond typical administrative reforms, innovation is expected to help address societal challenges such as the ageing population, inclusion, health care, education, public safety, environment and greenhouse gas emissions reduction.

A survey led by the INNO-Policy Trendchart project and covering 40 countries has identified six major types of national initiatives (classified in order of incidence):

- E-Government: introduction of new information systems, 'electronification' of public services to raise quality and speed,
- Administrative simplification: ranging from simplification of regulations to the restructuring of the public sector or its programs and/or processes;
- Public procurement: innovation in public procurement, green public procurement, e-procurement;
- Dissemination: disseminating innovation culture and good practices in the public sector;
- Public sector performance/workplace innovation: improvement of the performance of individuals or organizations;
- Public involvement and/or cooperation: engaging the public, private companies in public services or in the improvement of public services.

This survey underlines the statement that while academics and policy-makers in a small number of countries—for example, the UK, Denmark, Netherlands and Finland—have moved beyond ICT and administrative reform–related issues, there are still a significant number of countries that are focusing their effort on these features. Some countries have implemented e-government initiatives but without pursuing the objective of administrative simplification. All this indicates that there might be a substantial and growing gap between EU member states, maybe even more than innovation in the private sector, where international diffusion is much less constrained.

It is important to remember that new innovation processes such as networked governance are mostly occurring at the regional or local levels and these innovations are often not recognized at the national level. If such initiatives can be identified in small countries such as Denmark, Belgium or Ireland, more precise investigation should be launched in larger countries, especially if they are federal or largely decentralized (Spain, Italy and Germany). Even in historically centralized countries such as the UK (more specifically England) or France, local initiatives are being encouraged. Recent decentralization processes in France have created new opportunities to experiment with pilot initiatives, even though this can challenge the principle of equity and territorial continuity. In France, regional councils and new communities of municipalities (grouping of local authorities) are the best areas for creating public value.

A final issue that should be closely examined is the current economic downturn and more specifically the growing public debts. The impact on public sector innovation may be important in the coming years as the current budgetary stimulus will be rapidly followed by a shortage of public finance. This specific context will call for an improved quality of financial forecasting and financial management, in order to avoid resource disruption. People are liable to call for greater transparency in budget spending and will ask to stop policy initiatives that have failed to deliver results, as well as internal projects that do not benefit the users of services. Hence, the understanding and appraisal of innovation in the public sector are likely to become an important matter in the next few years.

Attempts at Measuring Public Sector Innovation

The majority of studies addressing innovation in the private sector have led to a widely used, standard classification scheme capturing major types of innovation, which are: product and service innovation; process innovation;

Inputs	Precondition and support instruments
Resources and spending (dedicated innovation budgets; R&D spend)	Existence of a strategy (guidelines and objectives)
Staff capabilities (dedicated staff, qualifications)	New organizational settings such as trial-and-error testing or systematic procedures
Demand for innovation (procurement and commissioning to incentivize innovative solutions)	Existence of a monitoring and reporting system
Responsiveness and ability to incentivize innovation (from citizens, frontline workers or suppliers)	Mechanisms for sharing learning and encouraging adoption across and between organizations
Acquisition of new equipment (ICT) and contracting external services (consulting, design)	Specific publications
	Awards & rewards schemes
Outputs	*Outcomes*
Number of new products and services implemented	Assessment of whether innovation has achieved the intended outcomes
Number of novel processes, procedures, delivery models introduced	Cost-benefit analysis and assessments of 'value added' of innovation
New global organizational model/ information system	Quality measures
New methods of communication	Customer satisfaction measures, staff satisfaction (working conditions, shirking, turnover)
Patents, copyrights, other intangible assets	Public sector performance impact measures (realization of public service agreements/ assignments)

Figure 3.3   Criteria for appraising innovation in the public sector.

and organizational and marketing innovations (Oslo Manual, Community Innovation Surveys, Eurostat[2]). The inclusion of non-technological innovation and a specific focus on services have allowed for more examination of the role of organizational innovation. Innovation in the public sector is more difficult to appraise than in the private sector. Even the Oslo Manual is still biased towards manufacturing innovations based on technological development. These methods have failed to capture all of the innovation in services sectors and creative industries (see Miles and Green, 2008)—and most of all in delivery of public services.

Several initiatives have recently set out to develop appraisal tools for public sector innovation, such as the *DIUS/NESTA Index*[3] or the *Network for Measuring Public Innovation*[4] project initiated by the Danish Ministry of Science, Technology and Innovation. This project tries for the first time to collect systematic information about innovation in the Nordic countries' public sectors. Eventually, the project will lead to the development of a 'Copenhagen Manual' to allow for better statistical capturing of such activity. Figure 3.3 synthesizes some elements considered by these projects for appraising innovation in the public sector.

A first issue to consider is the scope of observation. The public sector can consist of large national organizations as well as small local agencies. The large organizations may have numerous small establishments—for example, the health service will contain numerous hospitals and they themselves may be constituted of several specialist establishments. In order to measure and compare innovation processes in this sector, it is important to look for some form of standard unit and level impact.

Information may be difficult to collect and eventually should be objective and verifiable. This means that the methodology cannot be confined to a survey addressed to public sector staff. Innovation is not the objective itself but improvement of public administration and services; in a democracy this value is ultimately defined by the public themselves. Value is determined by citizens' preferences, expressed through a variety of means and refracted through the decisions of elected politicians. As a rule, the key things that citizens value tend to fall into three categories: outcomes, services and trust.

Identifying Existing Barriers and Possible Drivers

By comparing the differential between public and private sector and the results from several studies and surveys (Halvorsen et al., 2005), it is possible to distinguish various types of barriers for innovation—that is, social, financial and technical phenomena that hinder innovation activities in institutions. Figure 3.4 reports these results.

Figure 3.5 shows the results from a survey on barriers to innovation of over 300 government reformers in the US and Commonwealth countries.

Professional resistance and heritage	- Horizontal or vertical lack of dialogue - Professional groups pressure
Absence or inadequacy of resources	- Lack of financial support - Limited human resource or not well allocated - Shortages in relevant skills
Public resistance to change	- Habits disturbances - Lack of information about the benefit of the changes or communication towards those directly affected
Pace and scale of change	- Excessive number of radical changes/ reforms (innovation fatigued) - Unstable environment with no medium- and long-term visibility - Little opportunity to reflect upon and assess the impact of the innovations introduced
Risk aversion and accountability	- Political cycles and reluctances - Tendency towards a blame culture and high levels of accountability - Difficulties in obtaining a clear picture of the benefits
Technical barriers	- New uses/services that push the technology to the limits of its capabilities, or - Too much emphasis put on the technical aspects of the implementation process
Absence of capacity for organizational learning	- Frequent reorganizations and staff turnover - Tradition of secrecy and rigid top-down command chains

Figure 3.4　Main barriers.

It shows various actions to overcome the obstacles to innovation used in both the US and Commonwealth samples (the sign + means that the considered tactic is used to overcome a specific barrier). The tactics most commonly used can be categorized into two broad groups. The first is persuasion, which is achieved by showing the benefits of an innovation, establishing demonstration projects and social marketing. The second is accommodation, which takes the form of consultations with affected parties or involving them in the innovation process, providing training for staff, compensating losers and ensuring that a program is culturally or linguistically sensitive.

Overall, the responses to the obstacles raised show innovators should not necessarily view opposition to change as an invitation to conflict but consider this as an opportunity to better communicate, respond to objectors and improve the design of programs.

This set of actions, however, is composed mainly of short-term enablers and therefore cannot support sustainable innovation systems in the public sector. Recent research activities show that few countries are tentatively putting in place more sophisticated sets of devices to promote innovation in the public; although these can vary considerably, the schemes typically contain many of the same elements.

Barriers \ Tactics	Bureaucratic	Coordination	Technology	Inadequate Resources	Political opposition	Ext. doubts	Reaching Target Gr.	Affected interests	Public opposition
Show benefits	++				+++	++		++	
Social Marketing						++	+++	+	+
Demonstration Project	+				+	+			++
Training	++	+	++				+		
Consultation	++	+++				+++		+	++
Co-optation (with opponents)	+++	++				++		++	+
Resources Finding				+++					
Persistence					++	+	+		
Alliance					++				+
Modify Technology		+	+++						
Change Regulation	+							+	
Program Culturally sensitive							+		
Compensation	+							+	

Figure 3.5 Tactics used to overcome innovation barriers. Source: Borins (2006).

Innovation Pushes and Goal Settings

While leaders should support the conditions for innovation, specific innovations usually start with specific 'pushes' or 'pulls'. The pushes may come from a political leadership that seeks to promote new ideas, or from crisis, financial necessity or technology breakthroughs. But, increasingly, the drive to innovate is coming as much from pulls as from pushes (Mulgan, 2007). Accordingly, public innovators should be good at listening to what it is that people really want or need.

At the delivery level, political goals may be reflected through the imposition of performance targets. Behn (1999) argues that goals can redefine the meaning of success, start everyone thinking and behaving innovatively, foster leaders at all levels and encourage organizations to reach out to other institutions whose work is useful in achieving these goals. Some have pointed out that simply specifying goals and targets is not enough to convert unimaginative people into innovators, and it can tend to bring rigidity back. There is actually much discussion about the ways in which indicators and targets expressed in terms of indicators can distort the behavior of actors within the system in unanticipated and possibly undesirable ways, notably through 'gaming' (Holmstrom and Milgrom, 1991; Propper and Wilson, 2003). Indicators inevitably capture only particular features of the phenomena and outcomes in which we are interested, and unreflective reliance upon them has its dangers.

Culture and Leadership

Political and official leaders can establish a culture in which innovation is seen as natural. Several writers thus see leadership as a key link between individual creativity and knowledge and organizational innovation (Amabile et al., 1996; Glor, 2001). Leadership influences motivation and should come from the highest level, but middle management can also be very important. Leaders should also protect innovative employees from internal and external critics and at the same time convince politicians of the need for innovation.

Experimentation

The public sector entails more formality and precaution, and so innovation processes often need to rely on prototyping and testing in secure, controlled environments, such as pilots. It has been pointed out (Mulgan, 2007) that the standard cycle of prototyping–piloting–broadening may be too slow as regards political cycles, and many innovations freeze at the pilot stage and are considered only as scientific experiment. As an alternative, governments can use more iterative methods, such as pathfinders and trials that are persistently evolving and foster learning by doing.

These methods require strong risk management. Governments should also be honest about the chance of success of experimentation and give users choice (pluralism) so they can perform an arbitration role. Innovations are often managed by external organizations such as subsidiary agencies, NGOs and businesses, so that if things go wrong they can take the blame.

Empowerment and Co-creation

In order to address societal challenges, innovative thinking and operation require a strong, user-centered approach and involve a wide range of knowledge and expertise. Experience suggests that innovative teams generally work best with a mix of skills, backgrounds and contacts. Teams should combine civil servants from various concerned agencies, social entrepreneurs, researchers, designers, engineers and practitioners. These working teams may need a specific, more neutral space to better collaborate, making innovation units or laboratories an interesting option as a first step towards greater innovation in the public sector. Several of these labs can be identified in the European Union, such as the NESTA lab in the UK, MindLab in Denmark or la 27ième region in France.

Citizens' empowerment is also a key aspect for ensuring *ex ante* the most value-driven and acceptable solutions. This point is further elaborated in the chapter.

Scaling and Diffusion

If numerous pilots or prototypes have shown success, an even greater challenge lies ahead. This is the challenge of launching the innovation on a larger scale. Scaling up is widely seen as a major problem in many services, where the success of innovations may be closely related to the people engaged in the service production and delivery. For the public sector as a whole, the adoption and diffusion of innovation are extremely vital. Successful experiences can be discounted because of a perceived lack of connectivity and relevance to the rest of the organization; this may lead to their added value being overlooked, and to failure to adequately emulate the practices necessary for success. Here again, innovation processes face problems of horizontal and vertical silos; even strong networking is not always a sufficient solution.

Reflexivity and Learning Processes

Innovating organizations need a high degree of reflexivity, understanding the impact of their own actions on a broader social structure. In terms of popular jargon, this essentially involves an ability to demonstrate organizational learning. Quite often these processes are carried out directly by insiders, so that the learning is not diffused more widely in the organization, though sometimes there are efforts to ensure that learning is a feature of the broader system. This is not just a matter of better knowledge management systems, let alone audit-like evaluation processes. Reflection and appraisal should occur at all levels, be continuous and reflect a widespread culture of review and the willingness of partners to take part in learning processes. A high degree of responsiveness is important here, as there is little point in monitoring activity if it does not prompt reaction.

PATTERNS FOR THE DEVELOPMENT
OF PUBLIC INVOLVEMENT

Public organizations in democratic societies are expected to live up to the ideal of democratic principles. They can do so in many ways—for example, by promoting and implementing the following:

- Transparency to support public scrutiny
- Accountability for the exercise of power by public officers
- The dissemination of information to encourage awareness and facilitate citizens' access to government
- Consultation to improve quality and responsiveness
- Participation to ensure greater buy-in and support for government initiatives

These principles and related measures constitute what the OECD calls 'open and inclusive government'. In this respect public authorities in many countries over the last 20 years have shown some similarities in paying more attention to service delivery and user satisfaction. This has led to the exploration of how the public sector may work with citizens as value creators and as active agents to produce public results of high quality and high value. More specifically, government organizations seek out innovative ideas, which could then develop into new services and programs, from a diverse network of citizens, volunteer researchers and nonprofit organizations.

But citizens can also initiate such processes. Because of the limited expected impact on policy development and implementation through the political party process, citizens interested in policy are looking for other routes to provide input to government (Bourgon, 2008).

The approach of the Canadian government in 2000 suggests that public involvement can take place on five levels. Level one is informing or educating the public; level two is gathering information or views from the public; level three is discussing with or involving the public; level four is engaging; and level five is partnering with the public. Level five includes empowerment of citizens and groups to manage the process, the government being ready to assume the role of enabler and an agreement to diffuse the solutions generated. At this level, policy and programs are developed in partnership.

Empowerment, Sharing Power and Responsibility

When looking at current practices across countries, empowerment often remains merely a matter of consultation processes, generally to obtain feedback (or simply approval) from citizens for policies that have already been largely preselected. Consultation with stakeholders does not necessarily lead to citizens' full support as had been expected by elected officials and the public servants responsible for the consultations. This is not really participation, as it tends to define citizens as objects rather than subjects in the consultation process. Subjects should be able to decide on the level and content of participation, and be informed about the follow-up.

There are relatively few examples of genuine collaborative processes in which citizens play an active role in initiating an innovation. Though public services and governments say that they want to stimulate citizen empowerment, there is a failure to reliably implement appropriate programs.

The first reason for this is the difference between citizen empowerment and customer or user involvement. This confusion between citizen and customer creates a permanent state of tension. Governments' objectives usually consider citizens strictly as customers and are looking for feedback about implementation and buy-in. Many countries have a strong tradition of bureaucratic relationships in which citizens experience asymmetrical and hierarchical relationships with civil servants. On the other hand, citizens are often more interested in sharing decision-making power about policy.

If they are not consulted about objectives, priorities and decisions, they feel like objects, disempowered in terms of their ability both to have an impact and to be heard.

Another important aspect of this distinction between customer and citizen is the extent to which collecting user's expectations is an adequate and democratic process. There may be a tendency to hear the claims and satisfy the demands only of those who better voice their needs, at the risk of excluding other citizens. Direct democracy should not hinder more fundamental objectives such as universal suffrage and equitable representation (e.g., population, geographic). Trust and transparency are very important here. For example, while participation in setting objectives and priorities is important, empowering and relationships should result in significant action, not only intention. Customer or citizen recommendations should be implemented and monitored, and if not, the failure to do so explained.

Difficulties do not arise only from the public sector side. While citizens may want public authorities to hear them, they do not always take the initiative in assuming responsibility and self-governance. This implies that the public sector needs first to establish the internal infrastructure to establish, facilitate and build on sustainable and long-term relationships with the public. As most private companies have discovered, embracing external innovative ideas and converting them into new products and services often require changes in consumers and the internal organizational culture, structure and processes (Nambisan, 2008).

The Role of ICT in Empowerment

The development of ICT and the information society has created a vast variety of potential applications for the public sector. The resulting notion of e-government encompasses applications that aim at (i) better informing and communicating between public agencies, businesses and citizens, (ii) conducting transactions and registration, (iii) improving interaction with policymakers and direct democracy including online consultation, petitioning, voting and campaigning.

The spread of Web 2.0 technologies based on social networking allows us to create genuinely new kinds of connections between citizens and the public sector. Government 2.0 goes far beyond merely adopting Web 2.0 tools for the public sector, as it is a philosophy and culture that reflect society's radically new way of interacting and communicating. The resources required for Web 2.0–type policy- and decision-making are often underestimated, particularly in terms of the facilitation, tailoring of information, monitoring, moderation or feedback to participating citizens and stakeholders.

Globally, the population is progressively experiencing and adopting such a culture and a growing number of people are developing skills of information analysis, knowledge production, team working and so forth.

A potential promising use of this new way of interacting consists of creating a local community of users/citizens by using new ICT tools in order to share needs, co-create and experiment with related solutions. This concept is called Living Labs[5] and often focuses on citizen/user empowerment and user experience in actual settings or in (semi) realistic demonstrations through the use of ICT.

Another possible way of using ICT to foster innovation in the public sector is to make government information easily accessible to third parties. This can stimulate new non-governmental networks that share advice, provide mutual support and allege governmental changes. This transparency revolution consists in ensuring the information held by public administrations is more available for re-use by citizens and civic organizations while obviously protecting citizens' data security and privacy.

Networks, NGOs and the Third Sector

Not-for-profit organizations, charities and voluntary organizations—the third sector—play a very important role in driving and diffusing innovation in public services. It is often argued that the third sector is agile and flexible and that voluntary organizations provide a climate for entrepreneurship and creativity. While these organizations do not have the same democratic legitimacy or government resources as public authorities, they nevertheless represent interests that are committed to public causes. In some cases, they respond to citizens' needs that are not met by the public sector, such as the National Trust in the UK.

Third sector organizations may also have access to additional financial resources, especially private funds, that are not strictly dedicated to running costs and can more easily be allocated to the research, evaluation or piloting of an innovation. Examples even show private charitable funds that function as 'venture capital' for development projects in third sector organizations (Halvorsen et al., 2005; Martin and Dror, 2004; Letts, Ryan and Grossman, 1997). Some financial organizations such as *clearlyso* in the UK or *Credit coopératif* in France are interesting examples of private funding for the development of innovative public services.

New Perspectives for Public-Private Cooperation

'Public-private partnership' (PPP) is a widely used term in the lexicon of government policy in recent years and refers to a broad range of interactions between governments and the private sector. (Note that the terminology has quite different use in different parts of the world: we here consider mainly the European use of the term). In the 1990s, PPP was adopted by governments as a 'softer' alternative to privatization. Initially, this term included concession contracts and private finance initiatives, in the UK mostly, and progressively included joint ventures and service procurement.

According to a Siemens survey, PPPs account for only four percent of all public sector investment. As a matter of fact, many public organizations still have negative attitudes towards PPPs after several bad experiences in the 1990s. Notably competitive tendering processes, aimed at achieving cost reduction and efficiency savings, have sometimes driven service quality down. In some areas contracting-out has led to private monopolies (which are not necessarily better than public ones); to underinvestment in shared infrastructure; to requirements on public authorities to subsidize the risk sharing with the private sector (Hall, 2008). Concessions of water management in France or railway transport in the UK—Metronet has often been used as a case study—are particularly illustrative of the limits of privatization and outsourcing.

Considering these elements, the public sector is now willing to collaborate with private companies when relevant and with a more mature strategy. Instead of merely supplying the public sector with products and services demanded (outsourcing), companies have started working together with the public sector to deliver innovative solutions. In most advanced economies the biggest sectors today are health care and education, which require longer-term partnerships. Companies can innovate for the public sector, while for political, cultural or economic reasons, the public sector continues to have the responsibilities for the services offered (FORA, 2009).

Innovation in PPPs often consists in using technologies or services developed elsewhere. To correctly commission and make use of these technologies or services, public sector organizations cannot rely solely on the supplier and need a minimum of competence to define their needs and check the quality of the services supplied. PPPs are not linear processes and require interaction and learning processes in which both parties contribute to achieve the innovative end product (Koch, 2006).

Public-private partnerships increasingly need to be based on this interactive process to better anticipate and respond to the issues faced by public services (Parker and Parker, 2007). The need to develop new technologies, processes and services has, in some cases, led to new forms of partnership between the state and private companies. This issue is underlined in a guide published by the UK DTI (2004), which draws attention to innovation from the beginning of a policy process to the following procurement strategy. The key recommendations notably underline the importance of embedding long-term dialogue with markets and suppliers, allowing the market to propose innovative solutions (openness) and improving the skills of procurement officers.

More flexible and iterative relationships between the public and private sectors would involve more risk for all players, which cannot merely hide behind conventional complex contracts. For example, the business sector can participate with the third sector in open, multi-partner initiatives such as the pilots or laboratories presented earlier. Some companies, specialized in service design, are particularly relevant in providing expertise to these initiatives. The British Public Services by Design[6] initiative argues that design methodologies can notably improve public service delivery in five keys ways:

- Developing more personalized services
- Harnessing the knowledge of frontline staff
- Managing risk by prototyping new ideas
- Improving efficiency and value for money
- Giving service users more control

Developing these capacities through public-private partnerships can help public sector organizations manage their creative processes and find innovative solutions for service delivery. In this respect, service design agencies have applied design tools, techniques and thinking to support the public sector in providing new facilities and services within hospitals, post offices, library or schools.

According to a survey led by the Design Council (UK), small innovative design agencies felt strongly that government procurement processes were an obstacle to working with public sector clients. Public procurement processes appear better suited to products than services delivery and may hinder small early-stage projects where ideas can be tested before larger initiatives are launched.

Policy Actions for Instigating and Spreading Innovation

The scope for policy action can be explored by relating together the barriers and drivers to change and the relevant policy frameworks.

Political Push and Goal Setting

As regards the public sector, it appears that merely focusing on innovation as the means to objectives is probably not the most appropriate approach. The starting point should be to emphasize the challenges addressed, and the improvements that are expected, in terms of clear objectives and appropriate political support. Societal and environmental issues need to be tackled at the adequate political level; public sectors have a great responsibility in leading innovation to develop common answers to challenges that are effectively communal ones. Policymakers must ensure, through clear policy objectives, that the public sector and the civil society (including private companies) are striving towards shared goals, with efficient allocation of financial and human resources.

Higher expectations in terms of quality and cost effectiveness of public services can be (partly) achieved at the legislative level, where setting standards can be an important tool. Action also needs to be taken in order to ensure high public value and the harmonization (or at least interoperability) of certain public services standards between regional/national public sectors. Regulations can be used to push forward more innovative practices within public sectors and encourage certification, such as by means of labels or certification by the International Organization for Standardization management standards. In addition, a 'citizen involvement charter' could be developed that would detail features such as consultation versus decision, and modes of consultation.

At the beginning of this chapter, we pointed out that public services can be provided by the private or the public sector. Services of general economic interest are mainly provided by large firms (the public services industry—cf. Julius, 2008), which are subject to a degree of competition and market regulation (e.g., the directive on services in the internal market). Innovation in the provision of these services is similar to innovation processes in oligopolistic sectors; public authorities have various types of policy instruments at their disposal (standards, public procurement, contract specifications, state aid) where innovation objectives can be taken into account.

Capacity Building and Knowledge Exchange

At the 'technical/operational level', the creation and diffusion of innovative practices throughout the public sector can be supported. In order to reach this level, for which front staff and middle managers are directly accountable, policymakers need to facilitate cross-sectoral/institutional initiatives. Support programs for co-creation and scaling up already exist in much diversified policy areas but may benefit from transversal approaches.

Whereas issues related to skills and human capital are a major issue for the public sector, training is often not seen as a priority in view of budget constraints and the solicitation of private expertise is still not considered enough. Skills for service design could be enhanced through the development of innovation credits and/or vouchers to favor consultation of relevant intermediaries by public services, public or private research organizations, consulting companies as well as for professional mobility. Specific public services innovation-oriented venture capital funds could be launched to support activities that regular/functioning budget allocations do not finance because of high risk and uncertainty.

Finally, actions such as awareness activities, competitions and indicators would provide all-level actors with the necessary competences and information and to enable self-measurement and impact assessment. Sharing success stories but also experience of failures would certainly reinforce capitalization and help reduce fruitless initiatives. Friendly competitions and value-driven acknowledgment are also a way to raise awareness.

Governance & Institutional Issues

Finally, it is important to identify, and work at, the adequate geographical and institutional scale when tackling societal/public policy challenges.

This scope for action relates to innovation between national/regional/local institutions. The aim is to improve multi-layer governance within a country or at a broader scale and to minimize systemic failures. Such an approach would notably enable the better mainstreaming of grand policy issues and orient policies more towards citizens. Depending on the public authority's level (geographical/institutional), one or several of these scopes are to be privileged. If local or regional authorities can be very active at the operational or political level, it is less likely to be effective at the legal or institutional level for which national authorities are better endowed.

International cooperation can also provide interesting drivers. At first, the role of the European Union may appear limited, because of institutional arrangements and state prerogatives.[7] Beyond legal considerations, EU action may also be limited by the widely varying heritages of public sectors in different EU countries, which render simple harmonization or integration of practices very problematic. However, there is still a basis for EU-level action regarding the public sector, especially through the specific focus of innovation support policies. Firstly, subsidiarity means that some issues can be better faced at the EU level. For instance, some societal and environmental challenges are best addressed at the EU level and the role of public sectors is quite often central to these kinds of challenges.

In addition, this diversity of models can be an advantage, since it can enable parallel experimentation of different models or solutions. This European specificity could form a real asset for developing public sector innovation. But it can play this role only if knowledge of practices, results and requirements is shared and explicated across Europe. We also have to take into account the problem that diversity can obstruct EU enterprises and citizen mobility. This suggests emphasis on the 'interoperability' of, for instance, regulations and professional standards and accreditations.

CONCLUSIONS

The public sector has a great potential for innovation, and for stimulating innovation more widely, but this is still not sufficiently recognized. The limits of public management theory and practice, mixed experiences with privatization, and growing socioeconomic and environmental concerns have all highlighted the need to better understand the role of the public sector in our society and in innovation processes.

With increasing budget constraints, European countries need both better and cheaper public services. Innovation in the public sector can make a profound difference in improving service to the public and creating public value.

For these reasons, innovation in the public sector is liable to be particularly significant when addressing grand challenges, fostering a more democratic society, and championing social equity. It is time to give it due attention.

NOTES

1. Some could argue though that the current weight of stock markets and the power gained by companies' boards of direction (which are elected) and control management play a similar role.
2. The Community Innovation Statistics are the main data source for measuring innovation in Europe. Aggregated data are disseminated on the Eurostat webpage under CIS data. The tables cover the basic information of the enterprise, product and process innovation, innovation activity and expenditure, effects of innovation, innovation co-operation, public finding of innovation, source of information for innovation patents, etc. Further details can be found on the Eurostat website http://epp.eurostat.ec.europa.eu/portal/page/portal/microdata/cis (accessed 12 June 2012)
3. Online. Available HTTP: http://www.nesta.org.uk/library/documents/innovation-index.pdf (accessed 7 February 2012).
4. Online. Available HTTP: http://www.mepin.eu/ (accessed 7 February 2012).
5. For example: *Lahti Living Lab* in Finland or *Normandy Living-lab*. Online. Available HTTP: http://www.openlivinglabs.eu/ (accessed 7 February 2012).
6. Online. Available HTTP: http://www.designingbusinessexcellence.org.uk/Design-Council/1/What-we-do/Our-activities/Public-services-by-design/ (accessed 7 February 2012).
7. Framework on General-Interest Services, principles of Subsidiarity and Proportionality.

BIBLIOGRAPHY

Amabile, T. M., Conti, R., Coon, H., Lazenby, J. and Herron, M. (1996) 'Assessing the Work Environment for Creativity'. *Academy of Management Journal* 39: 1154–1184.
Behn, R. D. (1999) 'Do Goals Help to Create Innovative Organizations?' In Frederickson, H. G. and Johnston, J. M. (eds.), *Public Management Reform and Innovation*. Tuscaloosa, AL: University of Alabama Press.
Borins, S. (2006) 'The Challenge of Innovating in Government'. Innovation series. IBM Center for Business of Government.
Bourgon, J. (2008) 'Citizen at the Heart of Public Administration Reform'. *IGPDE Newsletter*. Research Studies Intelligence Watch, No. 25. December.
Coats, D. and Passmore, E. (2008) 'Public Value: The Next Steps in Public Service Reform'. London: The Work Foundation.
DTI. (2004) 'Capturing Innovation: Nurturing Suppliers' Ideas in the Public Sector'. Office of Government Commerce (OGC). Online. Available HTTP: http://webarchive.nationalarchives.gov.uk/20100503135839/http://www.ogc.gov.uk/documents/capturing_innovation.pdf (accessed 13 June 2012).
Esping-Andersen, G., Rainwater, L. and Rein, M. (eds.) (1987) *Stagnation and Renewal: The Rise and Fall of Social Policy Regimes*. New York: M. E. Sharpe.
Eurostat. (2008) 'Europe in Figures'. Eurostat Yearbook. Online. Available HTTP: http://epp.eurostat.ec.europa.eu/cache/ITY_OFFPUB/KS-CD-07–001/EN/KS-CD-07–001-EN.PDF (accessed 22 February 2012).
FORA. (2009) 'New Nature of Innovation'. FORA/OECD. Online. Available HTTP: http://www.newnatureofinnovation.org/full_report.pdf (accessed 8 February 2012).

Glor, E. D. (2001) 'Key Factors Influencing Innovation in Governments'. *The Innovation Journal* 6: 2.

Goldfinch, S. (2007) 'Pessimism, Computer Failure, and Information Systems Development in the Public Sector'. *Public Administration Review* 67 (5): 917–929.

Hall, D. (2008) 'PPPs in the EU: A Critical Appraisal'. Public Services International Research Unit (PSIRU). Paper presented at ASPE conference. St. Petersburg, October 31st–November 1st. Online. Available HTTP: http://gala.gre. ac.uk/2880/1/2008–11-PPPs-crit.pdf (accessed 12 June 2012).

Halvorsen, T., Hauknes, J., Miles, I. and Røste, R. (2005) *On the Differences between Public and Private Sector Innovation*. PUBLIN Project, report D9. Oslo: NIFU STEP. Online. Available HTTP: http://www.nifu.no/Norway/Publications/2006/d9differences.pdf (accessed 8 February 2012).

Hartley, J. (2005) 'Innovation in Governance and Public Services: Past and Present'. *Public Money & Management* 25 (1): 27–34.

Heeks, R. (1999) *Reinventing Government in the Information Age: International Practice in IT-Enabled Public Sector Reform.* London: Routledge.

Holmstrom, B. and Milgrom, P. (1991) 'Multitask Principal-Agent Analyses: Incentive Contracts, Asset Ownership, and Job Design'. *The Journal of Law, Economics, and Organization* 7: 24–52.

Julius, D. (2008) *Public Services Industry Review.* Department for Business Enterprise & Regulatory Reform (BERR). London: HMSO.

Koch P M (2006) *Interact—innovation in the public sector and public-private interaction,* NORDEN. Online. Available HTTP: http://nordicinnovation. org/Global/_Publications/Reports/2007/Interact%20-%20innovation%20 in%20the%20public%20sector%20and%20public-private%20interaction.pdf (accessed 12 June 2012).

Letts, C. W., Ryan, W. and Grossman, A. (1997) 'Virtuous Capital: What Foundations Can Learn from Venture Capitalists'. *Harvard Business Review* March–April: 36–44.

Manley, K. (2001) *Innovation in the Public Sector.* Brisbane: Queensland Innovation Council/Queensland University of Technology

Martin, M. and Dror, D. (2004) 'Entrepreneurial Solutions for Social Challenges: Leverage Social Entrepreneurship and High-Impact Philanthropy'. Working paper. University of Geneva, Department of Economics.

Miles, I. and Green, L. (2008) 'Hidden Innovation in the Creative Industries'. NESTA Research report HICI/13. Online. Available HTTP: http://www.nesta.org.uk/library/documents/Report%2013%20-%20HICI%20v7. pdf (accessed 8 February 2012).

Mishra, R. (1984) *The Welfare State in Crisis: Social Thought and Social Change.* Brighton: Wheatsheaf Books.

Mulgan, G. (2007) 'Ready or Not? Taking Innovation in the Public Sector Seriously'. London: NESTA.

Nambisan, S. (2008) 'Transforming Government through Collaborative Innovation'. Innovation series, IBM Center for Business of Government.

Parker, S. and Parker, S. (2007) *Unlocking Innovation: Why Citizens Hold the Key to Public Service Reform.* London: DEMOS.

Propper, C. and Wilson, D. (2003) 'The Use and Usefulness of Performance Measures in the Public Sector'. CMPO working paper series, no. 03/073. Centre for Market and Public Organizations, University of Bristol.

Rosanvallon, P. (1981) *La Crise de l'État-providence.* Paris: Le Seuil.

Part II
Policy to Support Innovation
The Entrepreneurial Turn

Part II

4 Are IPR and Open Innovation Good For Each Other
Surely an Open and Shut Case?

John Rigby and Jennifer Hayden

INTRODUCTION

This chapter considers the relationship between intellectual property rights (IPR) frameworks and open innovation. The chapter focuses on how intellectual property frameworks might support 'open innovation', the increasingly common practice of profiting from a company's IPR by using external links to source and develop it.

IPR frameworks are a key aspect of the innovation process; they constitute rules that innovation actors can make use of and that guide and shape their conduct in developing and selling products and services. In the context of innovation, rules not only apply to known and settled states of affairs, but also give rise to incentives that relate to future behavior. These incentives can render strategy-making difficult for firms and regulators involved in innovation processes. Such strategy-making remains, in many cases, under-researched (David and Shapiro, 2008).

There has been a considerable accumulation of certain types of evidence about the implications of the IPR system for innovative behavior. But there is concern that patent data and, in particular, simple counts of patents can be a very misleading guide to the role that patents play in the innovation process (Bessant and Tidd, 2007; Cameron, 2009; Etzkowitz, 2009). In this chapter, we are concerned with patents but also to a lesser extent with other forms of IPR. We note that, while the research on patents may well be difficult, for a variety of reasons, to translate into clear conclusions for policy purposes, research conducted on other forms of IPR may be more problematic still in terms of its ability to inform policy. While we need to be aware of the wider context of IPR frameworks, for much of this chapter our focus will be on patents rather than the host of other IPRs, but more because these are a particularly consequential IPR mechanism in open innovation systems. The other consequential tools here tend to be more informal approaches such as confidentiality agreements, rather than instruments like copyrights, design rights and trademarks—though the role of the latter may change over time.

There has been much argument in recent years concerning how the current IPR framework is impacting on the innovation process (and thus on economic development and welfare). As well as controversies about 'patenting life' (to do with IPR associated with genomic information and the new biotechnologies), there has been much argument about IPR in the digital industries—for example, software, where extensions of patent law to cover more software activities have been met with controversy and polarized responses. There are features of digital industries (for example, the ease of copying and distributing digital products) that mean that the impacts of the IPR framework may be different, and of more immediate concern, than in traditional industries such as pharmaceuticals. It is also important to note that some forms of 'open innovation', especially those connected with open source software, are closely associated with these industries, though not only with these. The online availability of information from the Human Genome Programme means that even pharmaceutical companies may be involved in bioinformatics-related innovation.

In this chapter, we consider a number of questions concerning open innovation and its relationship with the IPR framework. We wish to shed more light on the widely shared assumption that the practices of creating, trading and using intellectual property are enabled by open innovation. We wish to investigate the limits to this relationship and to comment on the emphasis on interaction and information-sharing between actors in the process of innovation, which has a complex, if not ambiguous, relationship with the current IPR framework. Is the IPR regime a stimulus for, a hindrance to, or some other influence on open modes and practices of open innovation? Addressing such questions necessitates consideration of differences between sectors in terms of IPR use, since technologies, knowledge bases and innovation processes are different across them. A more balanced view of the role of IPRs in innovation and in open innovation in particular appears to us justified by the evidence.

Our approach in preparing this chapter has been to focus on the EU context. However, it would be imprudent not to take account of the IPR frameworks of the US because these, rather than those of the EU and its member states, to a very significant degree are driving IPR systems in many areas of the world. We therefore refer at a number of points to developments outside the EU, notably the US, where the development of IPRs and IPR-related policy has important implications for the EU.

A NEW WORLD OF KNOWLEDGE PRODUCTION?

In the last twenty years it has become increasingly clear that actors in the innovation process, including firms and other knowledge producers, have been in closer interaction. The source for new ideas that become product and process innovations has come less from the work of a single organization or individual. Increasing interaction has come about for a variety of reasons. Firstly, knowledge production has changed, particularly in the fields of science; secondly, innovation has become more combinatorial and embedded, partly by the way technologies have been developed and through human ingenuity, but also through economic incentives and global markets. Economic pressure has created more organizations that are engaged in innovation. Closer linking of private and public within innovation activities may also have arisen from attempts by business to gain control over public institutions and because governments tried to protect the public organizations by increasing the dependence of the private sector upon the public.

The production of knowledge has become more routinized and now occurs on a larger scale. By way of this systematization, more has become known about the process of knowledge generation. Collaboration for knowledge production has been increasingly perceived as central to the generation of variety and, through this, knowledge. On this assumption, more collaboration has been funded and, because of the opportunities that flow from collaboration, new scientific fields have emerged based on interdisciplinarity.

RISE OF COLLABORATION AND THE NEW KNOWLEDGE

One of the most important of the novel perspectives on knowledge generation, which is perhaps typical of the trend, is that of Professor Michael Gibbons' Mode 2 (Gibbons et al., 1994). Here, in Mode 2 (also the related common research area), and in the European Research Area promoted by the European Commission, there is a new type of knowledge creation that is multi-disciplinary and application-oriented. Gibbons' work on Mode 2 in the New Production of Knowledge did not address the implications of IPR regimes upon this new form of knowledge generation, and indeed it seems that it has been left behind by events because the most important developments in recent years in this area have been the growing use of and strengthening of IPR, under pressure from US pro-patent interests. The Mode 2–type discourses propose and support the use of collaborative research, but this leads to the conclusion that there is no easy way to distinguish which parts of Mode 2 knowledge generation should be subject to IPR protection and which should not.

In this context, all actors involved in research and technological development look to others for ideas and inspiration. The 'collaborative turn' in innovation very much reflects the linguistic turn in philosophy and the collectivist turn in political science, developments that emphasize interdependence, inclusion and the co-production of material and social products including knowledge and regulatory systems. At the micro-level, collaboration is seen as a superior form of research collaboration (Katz and Martin, 1997), while above the micro-level, the promotion of collaboration within research and technology is seen as a means to emphasize national and international identities and interests and as central in achieving economic and social well-being.

COMBINATORIAL INNOVATION

Interdisciplinarity outputs flow through into the area of products and processes, where the combination of innovations is now far more common. Combinatorial innovations, linked to de-materialization of technology and its miniaturization, are powerful and central aspects of the new context in which firms operate to provide products and services.

ECONOMIC PRESSURES—LEADING TO SPECIALIZATION

Economic pressures, particularly the short-term pressure from investors, have led larger firms to take an ever more short-term view. In most economic sectors, it has become very difficult to take a long-term perspective with the effect that some firms have begun to regard the government as the R&D funder of the last resort, and have sought out government resources to fund their own R&D priorities. As larger firms have cut back on all of their R&D activities, a new range of service firms has emerged. R&D services and research are increasingly being provided by smaller, specialized firms. To some extent, larger firms have tried to adopt or 'farm' the innovation processes of smaller firms, developing intrepreneurship and corporate venturing activities with some success (e.g., Lockheed Martin, 3M and Philips). The overall trend, though, is for innovation to involve more organizations now than in the immediate post–Second World War period.

WAKING UP TO OPEN INNOVATION?

These various developments have led a number of scholars in the field of innovation studies to apply the sobriquet 'open innovation' to these new practices, the first to do so being Henry Chesbrough (2003). The coining of the term 'open innovation' explicitly recognizes that changes in the practice of firm-level innovation are taking place, that new opportunities exist and that new strategies are required for firms to survive. There is, however, a view that Chesbrough's approach overstates the novelty of the position (Gann, 2004) by ignoring the historical record and overlooking earlier scholarship on distributed innovation practices that saw firms looking outside themselves for the source of ideas (for example, user innovation—see Von Hippel, 1988; Rothwell, 1992). Material presented by Hargadon (2003) offers Edison's research laboratory at Menlo Park (est.

1876) as an exemplifier of early open innovation as it embodied many of the characteristics Chesbrough discusses.

Nevertheless, Chesbrough's vision that a new form of innovation practice and strategy is becoming important and more widespread appears valid. In this context, firms are more aware of what is happening elsewhere because they need to be able to source ideas from outside the firm. Furthermore, firms can now export, or sell, their ideas to other firms that might make better use of the knowledge than could the firm that created it.

While the open innovation paradigm was seen to be one in which IPR would matter more than in the past, in that firms would trade their ideas ('valorization' being the term given to denote the practice), there was, at the outset, no explicit recognition of the interplay between the IPR system and innovation practices in particular areas. It has been later writings that have focused upon this issue, notably in the software industry (Bessen and Meurer, 2008; de Jong et al., 2008).

In the next section of the chapter we consider this interaction, which has become the key area of concern at the crossroads of IPR and innovation policy in recent years and what steps have been taken to promote it.

OPEN INNOVATION AND THE ROLE OF THE IPR SYSTEM

This next section examines the link between innovation and IPR frameworks and specifically answers the question, how does open innovation make use of IPR and what should the IPR framework look like to assist open innovation?

Rigby and Zook (2002) were the first formally to propose that a link existed between the IPR framework and the rise of open innovation. Their analysis identifies five main trends that have given rise to the increase in open innovation:

1) Venture capital is now more plentiful than ever (although in the current economic downturn, this is no longer the case) and the availability of this capital is a source that allows innovation in small companies in particular to take place.
2) Interdependencies of product are far more common now than previously, and this is particularly noticeable in the area of digital technology. The need for specialization is partly behind this and certainly is a feature of the IT sector and those industries, which are increasing in number, that rely upon the IT sector for technologies.
3) Innovation exchanges are increasing in number. One of the best known was TechEx, which emerged from Harvard University. This technology exchange system allowed firms to locate and ultimately source licensable technologies.

4) Innovation agents operate in a similar manner to innovation exchanges, except where individuals or firms, funded with venture capital, perform the task of matching the needs of those who wish to acquire or sell IPR of various kinds.
5) Accessible innovation databases provide online sources of registered IPR, giving firms that are facing innovation challenges the information they need about whether to innovate themselves or whether to go into the market and acquire innovations.

Their analysis suggested that there was some positive feedback effect between the IPR framework and the development of the software industry. The work of de Jong and colleagues (2008) and West (2006), which has focused on specific cases and firm strategy, supports this view. The major question for policymakers and firms is whether this synergy or positive feedback does indeed exist, and for which industries. There is, in fact, strong evidence that the scope provided by the IPR framework as it has been developed in the US in particular has increased costs in the software sector, although it has not affected chemicals and pharmaceuticals very much.

FREE TRADE—WTO AND TRIPS AND
EU IMPLEMENTATION

The development of the positive relationship between open innovation and IPR frameworks has taken place within a period of important international action on IPR through the gradual implementation of the Agreement on Trade-Related Aspects of Intellectual Property Rights (TRIPS). The changes imposed by TRIPS mark a growing acknowledgment by nation states of the importance of IPR within the system of international trade. Signatory bodies, including the European Union, are now required to establish policies and procedures for the implementation of intellectual property rights. As Dixon and Greenhalgh (2002) have noted in discussing the extent and depth of their impact, TRIPS has been of immense importance. Maskus (2000) regards TRIPS 'as the most significant international undertaking on IPR in history' (quoted by Dixon and Greenhalgh, 2002, p. 47). Changes to incentives and national practice ushered in by TRIPS took place initially in such technology areas as pharmaceuticals. In the area of software, the consequences of TRIPS have been far more unclear.

TRIPS has led nation states and the EU to develop more extensive and systematic IPR policies. Recognizing the IPR as an indicator of value and industrial and commercial productivity, the EU Commission has promoted the use of IPR for the purposes of increasing innovation and economic growth in the context of industry science relations. Recently, in COM (2008)1329, the Commission noted:

An effort should be made to better convert knowledge into socio-economic benefits. Therefore, public research organizations need to disseminate and to more effectively exploit publicly-funded research results with a view to translating them into new products and services. Means to realize this include in particular academia-industry collaborations—collaborative or contract research conducted or funded jointly with the private sector–, licensing and the creation of spin-offs.

The EU Commission as well as most of the larger and more economically developed member states of the EU have taken the view that policies for the management of IPR and associated resources and valorization are a prime responsibility that needs to be tackled at the highest levels of government. The following statement could have emanated from any of the European governments, but is in fact from the EC:

> Effectively exploiting publicly-funded research results depends on the proper management of intellectual property (i.e. knowledge in the broadest sense, encompassing e.g. inventions, software, databases and micro-organisms, whether or not they are protected by legal instruments such as patents), on the development of an entrepreneurial culture and associated skills within public research organizations, as well as on better communication and interaction between the public and private sector.
>
> Support the development of knowledge transfer capacity and skills in public research organizations, as well as measures to raise the awareness and skills of students—in particular in the area of science and technology—regarding intellectual property, knowledge transfer and entrepreneurship.

The EU's broader approach to IPR has included, in addition to the promotion of IPRs within science industry interactions, an attempt to create a form of patent enforceable across the whole EU, and support for software patents. Neither of these initiatives has been entirely successful, and a common patent for the EU is still some distance away. However, in regard to software, the objectives of the EU have been to some extent realized with changes to European patent law and national case law now deeming that inventions implemented wholly or partly in software are no longer an excluded category.

FURTHER INSTITUTIONAL DEVELOPMENT

A range of institutional developments above and beyond the policy response of governments has taken place to promote the development of IPR through collaboration and to enhance mechanisms for its exchange. These developments further emphasize the role of IPR as the principal asset that gives firms their key strategic and tactical advantages. IPR takes the form of input and output measure, being, as 'background', an input to collaboration activities within supply chains and, as 'foreground', the result of a collaborative production process.

RIGHTS VALORIZATION AND MARKETS
FOR IPR—TOWARDS INNOVATION

It is the referential character of patent data (in that patents often cite other patents and other scientific work), and the fact of its being able to be stored and analyzed, that allows for the production of a wealth of indicators for a variety of purposes. Common measures produced from such analysis are: cites per patent, which gives the impact of a firm's patents; the current impact index (CII), which adds the number of cites in the current year achieved by a firm's patents from the whole of the previous five-year period and divides this by the global average number of cites, giving insight into the strength of a firm's patent portfolio. Other measures link the patenting activity of a firm or country to the science base. This so-called Science Linkage (SL) measure indicates, for a set of patents, the average number of citations to scientific chapters.

Tech Ex:

'Technology Exchange is the world's leading source for locating licensable technologies for use by intellectual property, licensing, and business development departments. Sourced from hundreds of Universities and Research Institutes from around the world, Tech Ex provides the most comprehensive and up-to-date access to breakthrough innovations and global technologies. If your goal is to stay on top of the latest in new innovations, then you need Tech Ex.

Features include:

Access to tens of thousands of currently available licensable technologies from universities and research institutes around the world. Technology coverage includes all functional areas in the life and physical sciences. Fully searchable database that is updated every week. Weekly email alert keeps you informed automatically. New technologies are sourced continuously, and unavailable technologies are removed promptly'.

Figure 4.1   Tech Ex features.

Among these institutional developments that rely upon these characteristics of patent databases and more fully exploit the technology-related information present in patent databases is the well-known TRIZ system developed by Genrich, which allows firms to examine the patents in a technology area with a view to identifying those they need to take account of in their innovation process. Related services like Tech Ex also provide information on patents that can be used to access new technologies. Cohendet et al. (2009) and Jeon et al. (2011) have recently documented the development of these methods that help collaborators locate the most appropriate partner organizations and technologies. They show that methods for determining with whom to seek collaboration have moved from the ad hoc and small-scale to more large-scale scanning that uses computer algorithms to locate those working in similar technology areas. Jeon et al. (2011) note a key distinction between brokerage in which searching is a third-party activity and the open market activities operated by such organizations as Ocean Tomo and Innocentive.

IPR REGIMES AND OPEN INNOVATION— A CASE TO ANSWER?

In this section we consider the details of the relationship between IPR regimes and open innovation. We look at some of the difficulties that have emerged from the extension of IPR that pose specific challenges for innovation generally and open innovation in particular.

PROLIFERATION OF IPR THICKETS

Heller (1998; 2008) is one of a number of writers who has argued that a central and dysfunctional characteristic of modern westernized market systems is the superabundance of property rights. This superabundance of property rights makes two tasks difficult to carry out, which leads in turn to the creation of new forms of market failure that patents were intended originally to remove. Firstly, the task of identifying those patents that can create a new technology is rendered too complex because there are too many patents. But large and complex webs of rights (patent thickets) also act to prevent firms from attempting to find solutions to the problem of securing a return upon their property.

The related activity of creating patent stockpiles—which creates 'intentional thickets'—that can be used as a means of raising revenue by firms is one that has attracted the attention of some commentators. Stockpiles can, although not necessarily, constitute a less efficient way of rewarding property.

GAMING

The use of patents as resources that can be traded is, of itself, a useful development. However, while the trading of IPR in markets may in theory increase its availability, the interrelatedness of patents, which, it should be emphasized, are very far from being discrete atoms of information, can give rise to gaming behavior. Indeed, gaming behavior is already an essential feature of the IPR landscape and has given rise to a new category of innovation actor, the non-practicing entities (NPEs) or patent troll. The principal strategy of such actors is to create blocks of patents that can prevent other firms from developing their innovations, or to develop or acquire such blocking patents, perhaps involving some secrecy, which are then used to ambush other innovation actors who are actively selling products or services. Trolls use the legal system to obtain injunctions that prevent the ambushed firms from trading. Injunctions (or the threat of legal action) are lifted only when satisfactory compensation is paid.

Gaming behavior can also take place within contracts (ex post) where patents that were previously undisclosed are revealed at some later date following the agreement of a contract. Solutions are difficult to specify, although integration of the firms concerned has been proposed by Williamson (1979). This practice is particularly problematic when it occurs in the context of government standard setting, whereby a standard is agreed without knowledge that a patented technology is included. Once the standard is set, the patent holder reveals its IPR and all those affected by the standard are obligated to comply (Cameron, 2009). IPR in standards will be further explored later.

TROLLS—INNOVATION ARBITRAGEURS OR A TAX ON INNOVATION

The role of trolls is highly contentious and is often seen solely in the context of gaming. However, the evidence that trolls are the sole cause of inefficiency in the economic system is not as strong as many have suggested. There is evidence that the activities of trolls, in seeking out and realizing the value of patents that would conceivably lie unused, could be valuable. It is our view that trolls can lead to economic efficiency; but uncertainty of patent definition, coupled with troll-like behavior, is likely to be what gives rise to inefficiency.

LEGAL SYSTEM COSTS

The increasing awareness of companies of the importance of IP as a source of value, as means of trading and interacting with other firms, including as a way of blocking and disrupting competitors, has led to a far greater requirement for legal services, and to delays in the process of patent regis-tration, award and litigation. Such services have been provided within firms and through the market for legal services. Barton (2000) has noted this increase over the last three decades and has concluded that the costs of liti-gation are now so large that the resources available to firms for producing IPR are being put under strain. While there is no evidence presented here that the increase in the number of professionals involved in the area has risen beyond what firms need reasonably to protect themselves, it is clear that the costs of protection and IPR strategy-making have risen significantly.

CRUCIAL ROLE OF STANDARDS

The possession of IPR gives firms a range of options that span collabora-tion on the one hand and conflict on the other, the choice between which depends upon the most economically advantageous outcomes. Within the context of standard setting, firms often find that the most effective option is that of going on the offensive. The European Commission report (EC, 2007) has considered how the culture of conflict can arise and what might encourage a more collaborative approach to the use of IPR. The authors consider two main recommendations: (a) that an attempt be made 'to create "good practice" rules and procedures to prevent "ambushes" by IPR own-ers that sit quiet while the standard is being defined' and (b) 'changes to the "undeniable" nature of the ownership of an IPR for ICT related items in order to prevent "ambushes" in a definitive way' (p. 109). The authors further note, referring to the comments of Kahin (2007):

The authors examine a range of difficulties which are examined in detail by Kahin (Kahin, 2011). His exposition suggests fundamental changes are occurring in the way the innovation system now works.

Indeed in the US, the innovation system appears to have been overtaken by attorneys and patent holders:

> Today, we have a system where patent holders have all the cards, while those invested in standards face unknown and practically unforesee-able "land mines" in the form of patents. Standards, too, deserve pro-tection by virtue of the great investment that is needed to make IT products, systems and infrastructure work efficiently. If patent holders are going to threaten investments on this scale, they should be obliged to make their rights known in a timely manner—or lose them against those who do no more than implement an open standard. It is far more efficient to put patentees on notice of a relatively small number of open standards than to put multitudes of standards adopters and users on notice of multitudes of patents.
>
> This should not place an undue burden on patent holders. At least initially, the credentialing and advertising of standards efforts should

be limited to standards that are open in the strongest sense of the word i.e. non-proprietary or royalty-free.

This recognizes the special vulnerability of non-proprietary standards while it circumscribes the universe that patent holders are responsible for knowing. This narrow scope will provide an opportunity to work out any problems in a formal clearance process. (p. 111)

AN IPR PARADOX DOUBLED

The IPR paradox, which we noted earlier, is, in our view, a far more serious threat to the innovation activity of firms in certain areas, notably that of software. While commentators have indicated that software innovation is more 'open', we believe that this openness is the result partly of the way in which patents have been drawn up and the consequence of this in terms of the strategies that software firms, most of them small, must follow.

Clear and unambiguous text in patent notifications could make it easier for IPR owners to defend existing IPR and to guard against infringement. Contrary to this stance, a new development to reduce the risks faced by patent holders has been the use of greater abstraction in patent definition. Related to this, the trend towards abstraction has led to the patenting of business methods and software, a process now in question as a result of the Bilski case. Abstraction, while apparently extending patent protection to new areas, cuts and risks reducing clarity of patent definitions, thereby increasing uncertainty for other innovators, which can then cause problems for owners. The Gowers Review of Intellectual Property (HM Treasury, 2006), which attempts to move the UK IPR regime, shows awareness on the part of the UK government of these dangers.

The use of greater abstraction is, in a sense, a logical approach to the needs of innovators who hold patents already. However, its implications for those seeking to collaborate and engage in innovation outside their firm (through open innovation) are serious in that abstraction makes it hugely difficult to identify collaborators and innovation potential.

Abstraction, whether in software or in other technical areas, creates a blanket that could cover or encompass new forms of innovation. It is possible that the principle of abstraction has been followed not only to enhance the rights of those who have IPR, but also to simplify the patent system by making the definition of any one patent more extensive. The number of potential patents is thus reduced. Differences in the way different patent systems define property have important implications for quality and the resulting costs and benefits of those who use them, as van Pottelsberghe, B. & de Saint-Georges (2011) have noted.

An often cited example of a patent that the US courts have taken to be broad in its implications is US Patent 4528643 (the Freeny patent), which expired in 2003 in the US and 2005 in Europe. This single patent had

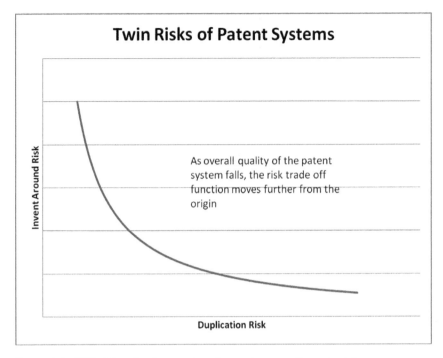

Figure 4.2 IPR risk reduction—using abstraction as policy principle.

considerable applicability into the area of web-based business transactions, and such an extension of its remit could not have been remotely foreseeable in 1983, the date of filing. The patent owner (a group of savvy businessmen, not the original inventor) was able to successfully enforce its IPR through either litigation or settlements with many corporations, including the likes of IBM and HMV (Shulman, 1999).

A further issue that makes the registration of a new idea more difficult is the increasing prevalence of patents that have been granted to 'inventions' that are obvious and that do not represent any true inventive step. This, coupled with the increasing use of abstract patents, has made it increasingly more difficult to develop new products and processes outside the remit of existing IPR. Thus, the scope for innovation is reduced both through obviousness and through abstraction, by which existing patents cover more potential innovations than might have been in the mind of the original inventor and indeed thought of at the time of registration.

INFORMATION PROBLEMS NOT SOLVED

Leydesdorff and Meyer (2010) provide evidence that the rate of university patenting generally is beginning to fall and conclude that this is the result of changes to the incentive systems under which universities in most countries operate. One exception to this is the University of Tokyo, which sees a continually increasing rate of patenting, but this is also likely to be the result of its particular national incentive system. We may observe that the changes in the activities of universities and their relation to commercial and other interests have not occurred as Gibbons and colleagues suggested they would have to in their work on Mode 2 (Gibbons et al., 1994). Decline in patenting is also likely to result from firms changing their behavior as they begin to understand how to develop their patenting strategies, and now, rather than churning out indiscriminately large numbers of patents that have little economic value, they are focusing on how to obtain intellectual property protection for inventions that collectively—that is, as a portfolio—will lead to an economic return.

COSTS AND BENEFITS—A BALANCING ACT

As we noted earlier, the IPR system provides benefits to its users in terms of the revenues generated from the use of products and services that are based on IPR, but it also gives rise to costs, which in part stem from registration and litigation. The balancing of costs and benefits can take place at the firm, sector or industry level and also at the level of the economy as a whole.

Research on the US carried out in Bessen and Meurer's (2008) sectoral level approach suggests that, in the case of some industries, the cost benefit is satisfactory in that the cost to the industry of the IPR system is less than the revenues generated. However, in other industries (the software industry, for instance) this balance is negative. In the following figures, two main industry groups are compared.

As their data shows, in the case of chemicals and pharmaceuticals, the cost of IPR protection is far lower than the profits to the industry; but in the case of all other industries, in which software is included, the picture is wholly different. Their research shows clearly that the costs of IPR protection to most sectors are significantly higher than profits and leads to the claim that 'the average public firm outside chemicals and pharmaceuticals would be better off without the patent system' (Bessen and Meurer, 2008, p. 16).

STRATEGY-MAKING FOR FIRMS

IPR in Firms

Harryson (2008) views innovation processes within the firm as taking three distinct forms: 'creativity networks, transformation networks and process networks' (p. 290). These different types of networks allow the firm both to in-source and export ideas for innovation. Harryson's view, which is based on a series of case studies, is that the integration of ideas from outside the firm requires various forms of capabilities inside the firm and that these capabilities change over time. The task of managing these various processes is one of significant difficulty. Howells (2008), for example, argues that firms should beware the costs of maintenance of these links and networks, noting that firms 'need to review constantly the benefits and costs of R&D collaboration and networking; it may not always be as good as it seems' (p. 242).

We do, however, consider that the existence of patents generally is important in both allowing firms to begin collaboration and later on in deriving benefit from their collaborations when those collaborations produce results. However, the extent to which the collaborative activities of firms and other research actors working singly or together (as discussed earlier) is supported by an IPR regime depends upon the clarity of the rules covering the definition of patentable subject matter, and the number and stringency of the tests that are applied to patent applications, and other administrative aspects of the application process—for example, the language or costs of patent applications. Cohendet et al. (2009) have argued in favor of IPR as a means to enable collaboration. For those industries involved in combinatorial technologies, patents provide a platform for a level and fair collaborative playing field, ensuring that intellectual exchange can take place without risk of breach of faith. In this context, patents are also seen as a goal of collaboration.

The Larger Firm

In this short section we consider the main priorities for larger firms that are operating within an open innovation framework. The characteristics of these firms are that they are usually well resourced, they have good access to existing innovations and innovation actors, and their business success depends upon a range of IPR. Larger firms are well placed to collaborate or to work alone, depending upon the perceived business advantage at a particular time or for a particular project. Their IPR portfolio and innovation capabilities are often diverse and heterogeneous; some parts of the firm contain major assets, while others are limited in their scope. We indicate specific strategies that larger firms will adopt in terms of innovation policy and IPR:

- A global reach for their innovation efforts.
- Collaboration will take place across a range of areas and will include all areas of IPR including freely available IPR—open innovation and open source. The creation of technology parks, university industry links and participation in R&D will be a priority.
- Engagement with user-driven and open innovation as a priority; but innovation within the firm and of the traditional type may also be valuable.

- Existing IPR will be vigorously defended.
- The firm will engage in the trading of IPR.
- The use of trade secrets is less likely than the use of IPR.
- The link between existing IPR and other capital assets and revenue streams will be established and closely monitored.

The Smaller Firm

The strategies of the small firm innovating in the area of open innovation are limited by a number of factors, the most significant of which is the resources it may have available to secure the protection of its IPR. However, innovation, whether of the open variety or the more traditional closed kind, usually involves external organizations, either as partners or as clients. It is with these organizations, through collaboration, that new ideas come into being, achieve a commercializable form and can then be marketed. It is at this point of collaboration that innovation begins and to which strategy formulation must be addressed. The following offers strategies typical to small, innovative firms:

- Innovations may represent a valuable asset; but the asset does not always take the form of IPR.
- Protection of assets by trade secrets—agreements within the workplace that prevent disclosure.
- Within collaboration and open innovation, the contribution of users to innovation can be secured through compensation deals.
- Avoidance of patents due to high costs involved.
- High patenting costs necessitate collaboration through open innovation or 'open source' routes.
- Small firms can sell out to large firms, making a one-time profit for their owners.

Some Further Observations

For both large and small firms, open innovation represents a fundamental change to the way in which business is done. The range of possible strategies increases dramatically, with a number of major management challenges emerging. Here we note a number of key issues that firms of whatever size must take account of.

Strategies for the acquisition and use of individual technologies may vary even within the same firm and even where the collaborators are the same. The strategies of other firms and in particular the market opportunities that they possess, will affect a firm's own strategy.

Strategies for the entire company portfolio of technologies should be considered together, however, teal options approaches may be a viable way of considering how to decide whether to invest in particular technologies.

Recognition of alternative incentive systems will be required. These may be reputational, as is often the case within open source, semi-reputational (academic), financial or indeed a combination of these. As Voss (2009) notes, academic collaborators will wish to publish their findings as soon as possible, while industrial partners will wish to file a patent application, or indeed to achieve secrecy for their invention.

As we implied earlier, firms have to be active in markets for technology as suppliers and customers, which places upon them often wholly new roles and responsibilities. Additionally, and again as we noted earlier, markets for technology provide further information to firms about the forms of technology available and their price and this can be a basis for further invention.

SUMMARY AND CONCLUSIONS

Why Is Open Innovation Happening?

Collaboration in the innovation process is a long-standing phenomenon, and one that has been promoted extensively through the collaborative R&D programs of national governments and other funding bodies, notably the European Union. The new emphases on cluster policies and public-private partnerships are further factors here. But there are several phenomena that may be reinforcing open innovation developments further. The other 'push' factors are as follows:

- The increased complexity of technological innovation, as manifest in convergent technologies and digital convergence, for example, means that much knowledge is required outside of the core knowledge base of many organizations.
- Likewise markets are often turbulent and fragmented, and wider bodies of knowledge about the nature of users and user demands also prove challenging for innovators.
- At the same time, firms have been attempting to 'downsize', focus on core competences, 'de-layer' and so on.

There are also other 'pull' factors:

- The growth of willingness to collaborate among other firms subject to push factors such as those earlier.
- The development of contract R&D, design and other knowledge-intensive business services assisting in the innovation process, with specialized capabilities and relatively high flexibility.
- New tools supporting collaboration and innovation management, and the demonstration effect of developments on new platforms as applied, for example, to open source software.

Do Weaknesses in the IPR System Provoke 'Open Innovation'?

The IPR system may influence open innovation in a number of ways:

- In some cases, belief in the ability to protect innovations may promote openness rather than secrecy.
- In some cases, the perception that potential partners will be seeking to restrict access to knowledge may reduce the willingness of partners to engage in collaboration with them, or promote some modes of collaboration (such as patent clubs) rather than others.
- In some cases, open innovation is used as a strategy to offset the power of dominant or oligopolistic producers, or the threat of such actors arising. This seems to be a major factor in many software firms' adoption of open source approaches. In this case, it is one party's exploitation of the IPR system that drives others to open innovation.
- IPR may be used to signal capabilities to potential collaborators and anecdotal evidence points to the role of 'patent clubs' and the like, but the importance of this signaling role is not clear.

What Other Reasons Are There for 'Open Innovation'?

In addition to the factors noted earlier, it is possible that there are broader social and economic factors involved. The shift of economic activity from manufacturing to services, and from lower-tech to higher-tech, is liable to give greater prominence to digital innovation and perhaps to innovations that are hard to patent (many service innovations) or effectively protect (much digital material). Younger generations may have different attitudes to intellectual property. On the one hand, efforts at stimulating entrepreneurial attitudes and IPR awareness might support more attention to IPR. On the other hand, the success of 'piracy' in digital media may indicate that many younger people are coming to see IPR as a needless obstacle. Controversies and general opposition to corporate 'patenting of life' articulated by environmental and developmental NGOs may support these latter perspectives.

Where Is Open Innovation More Prevalent and Why?

As noted earlier, the relevant information on this theme is very partial. Geographically, Northern Europe would appear to be the region where cooperation in support of innovation is most common—though we do not know of any analyses that would allow for US/EU comparisons. Possible analysis of collaboration in patent data would be a way of examining this, at least until innovation surveys become more prevalent in the US. Larger firms, and those in more high-technology related sectors, also seem to engage in more collaboration and with a wider range of collaborators, though not all studies agree on this. User innovation seems to be important in some high-tech areas and also in some highly specialized fields, even involving consumers. Motives for various types of collaboration and, by extension, open innovation seem to vary across sectors, and there is also evidence that cross-national differences are important here.

What Are the Significant Forms of IP (Other Than Patents) in Open Innovation Decisions?

There is still much need for further research on this theme. Empirical results suggest that the picture may not be clear-cut. One starting point, however, is to note the consistent finding that 'informal' approaches to IPR, confidentiality agreements, lead-time advantage and the like, are repeatedly stressed as being more important to most innovators, including those engaged in collaborative arrangements, than are formal instruments such as patents and copyrights. Given that the importance of formal instruments varies across sectors, it is quite possible that there will not be simple correlations between use of particular instruments and open innovation approaches. Even within high-tech and knowledge-intensive sectors we might find variations—for example, design rights are important to architects. We might assume that instruments such as trademarks, which carry little by way of information about the nature and functioning of the product, might be fairly unimportant in open innovation, though even here it might be that in some instances association with a prestigious trademark would be seen as advantageous to collaborators.

In some open innovation approaches, knowledge and insight are freely shared and benefits arise from others' application of this knowledge. Monetary compensation is the rule, not the exception. This is the case, for instance, for many of von Hippel's user-innovators. They provide manufacturers with ideas that will result, they hope, in equipment that will fulfill their own requirements. In some other circumstances, collaborators are brought together by the need to pool knowledge and capabilities and in these conditions IP may be used in a barter-like arrangement. The interesting issues arise where new knowledge is generated through the collaboration—when there is a significant innovation. While this may be made subject to various IP arrangements, how this happens will represent an interaction between the strategies of the different partners and the cooperation frameworks (both formal contracts and tacit agreements) that they are working within. Case studies of how these interactions have proceeded in a range of different types of collaboration would be valuable here.

BIBLIOGRAPHY

Barton, J. H. (2000) 'Reforming the Patent System'. *Science* 287: 1933–1934.
Bessant, J. and Tidd, J. (2007) *Innovation and Entrepreneurship*. Chichester: John Wiley Ltd.

Bessen, J. and Meurer, M. J. (2008) *Patent Failure: How Judges, Bureaucrats, and Lawyers Put Innovators at Risk*. Princeton: Princeton University Press.

Cameron, H. (2009) 'Reflections on Intellectual Property and Innovation'. Chapter presented at the INNO-GRIPS Early Career Researcher Workshop on Open Innovation and IPR. Manchester. 26–27 January.

Chesbrough, H. (2003) *Open Innovation: The New Imperative for Creating and Profiting from Technology*. Boston: Harvard Business School Press.

Cohendet, P., Farcot, M. and Pénin, J. (2009) 'Intellectual Property in a Knowledge-Based Economy: Patents to Include vs. Patents to Exclude'. BETA Working Chapter, Document de Travail No. 2009—15.

COM. (2008) 1329. 'Commission recommendation on the management of intellectual property in knowledge transfer activities and Code of Practice for universities and other public research organizations.' Page 2. The Commission of the European Communities.

David, P. A. and Shapiro, J. S. (2008) 'Community-Based Production of Open-Source Software: What Do We Know about the Developers Who Participate?' Special Issue, *Information Economics and Policy* 20 (4): 364–398.

de Jong, J. P. J., Vanhaverbeke, W., Kalvet T. and Chesbrough H. (2008) 'Policies for Open Innovation: Theory, Framework and Cases'. Research project funded by VISION Era-Net. Helsinki, Finland.

Dixon, P. and Greenhalgh, C. (2002) 'The Economics of Intellectual Property: A Review to Identify Themes for Future Research'. Paper for Intellectual Property Advisory Committee (IPAC), UK Patent Office.

EC. (2007) 'EU Study on the Specific Policy Needs for ICT Standardization'. Final report by DLA Piper, Universidade Nova de Lisboa and T. U. Delft. Brussels: European Commission. Online. Available HTTP: http://ec.europa.eu/enterprise/ict/policy/standards/piper/full_report.pdf (accessed 21 February 2012).

Etzkowitz, H. (2009) 'Beyond the Science Park: A Triple Helix Response to the Economic Crisis'. Lecture at Manchester Institute of Innovation Research (MIoIR), 23 February.

Gann, D. (2004) 'Book Review of Open Innovation: The New Imperative For Creating And Profiting From Technology'. *Research Policy* 34 (1): 122–123.

Gibbons, M., Limoges, C., Nowotny, H., Schwartzman, Scott, P. and Trow, M. (1994) *The New Production of Knowledge: The Dynamics of Science and Research in Contemporary Societies*. London: Sage.

Hargadon, A. (2003) *How Breakthroughs Happen*. Boston, MA: Harvard Business School Press.

Harryson, S. J. (2008) 'Entrepreneurship through Relationships—Navigating from Creativity to Commercialization'. *R & D Management* 38 (3): 290–310.

Heller, M. (1998) 'The Tragedy of the Anticommons: Property in the Transition from Marx to Markets'. *Harvard Law Review* 111 (3): 621–688.

Heller, M. (2008) *The Gridlock Economy: How Too Much Ownership Wrecks Markets, Stops Innovation, and Costs Lives*. New York: Basic Books.

HM Treasury. (2006) 'The Gowers Review of Intellectual Property'. London: HMSO.

Howells, J. (2008) 'New Directions in R&D: Current and Prospective Challenges'. *R & D Management* 38 (3): 241–252.

Jeon, J., Lee, C. and Park, Y. (2011) 'How to Use Patent Information to Search Potential Technology Partners in Open Innovation'. *Journal of Intellectual Property Rights* 16 (5): 385–393.

Kahin, B. (2007) 'Common and Uncommon Knowledge: Reducing Conflict between Standards and Patents'. In Bolin, S. (ed.), *The Standards Edge: Golden Mean*, 85–92. Ann Arbor, MI: Sheridan Books.

Katz, J. and Martin, B. (1997) 'What Is Research Collaboration?' *Research Policy* 26: 1–18.

Kahin, B. (2011) 'Common and uncommon knowledge: Reducing Conflict between Standards and Patents'. In DeNardis, L. (ed.) Opening Standards: The Global Politics of Interoperability (The Information Society Series), 177–190. MIT Press.

Leydesdorff, L. and Meyer, M. (2010) 'The Decline of University Patenting and the End of the Bayh-Dole Effect'. *Scientometrics* 83 (2): 355–362.

Maskus, K. E. (2000) *Intellectual Property Rights in the Global Economy*. Washington, DC: Institute for International Economics.

Rigby, D. and Zook, C. (2002) 'Open-Market Innovation'. *Harvard Business Review* 80 (10): 80–89.

Rothwell, R. (1992) 'Developments towards the Fifth Generation Model of Innovation'. *Technology Analysis & Strategic Management* 4 (1): 73–75.

Shulman, S. (1999) 'Patent Absurdities'. *The Sciences* 39 (1): 30–33.

Van Pottelsberghe, B. & de Saint-Georges, M. (2011) 'A quality index for patent systems'. Working Papers ECARES, ECARES 2011–010, Universite Libre de Bruxelles.

Von Hippel, E. (1988) *The Sources of Innovation*. New York: Oxford University Press.

Voss, G. (2009) 'Tension between Actors: An Examination of IP in Open Innovation'. Paper presented at the INNO-GRIPS Early Career Researcher Workshop on Open Innovation and IPR. University of Manchester. 26–27 January.

West, J. (2006) 'Does Appropriability Enable or Retard Open Innovation?' In Chesbrough, H., Vanhaverbeke, W. and West, J. (eds.), *Open Innovation: Researching A New Paradigm*. 109–133. New York: Oxford University Press.

Williamson, O. E. (1979) 'Transaction-Cost Economics: The Governance of Contractual Relations'. Journal of Law and Economics 22: 233–262.

5 The Role and Importance of Gazelles and Other Growth Firms for Innovation and Competitiveness

Mercedes Bleda, Kathryn Morrison and John Rigby

INTRODUCTION

This chapter focuses on the study of the role and importance of small, high-growth firms for innovation and competitiveness, and the way in which policy support can stimulate their further development and growth. The chapter begins with a discussion of how these firms (usually known as gazelles) have become a policy priority area. Gazelles are placed in the policy context and rationales for policy support are examined. The issue of what definitions are used in this area is a key one. By varying size and growth criteria in the definition of a gazelle firm, it is possible to define various sets of growth firms, each of which have fundamentally different characteristics and policy requirements. We examine these definitional issues and consider the ways in which policymakers should address support for gazelle firms. We put forward the difficulties of defining precise and effective policies and illustrate the different measures used so far in a variety of countries.

GAZELLES IN THE POLICY CONTEXT

An increasing level of interest in the characteristics of high growth in small firms has recently arisen among economists and policymakers as a result of the significant influence that these firms have had in the creation and transformation of whole economic sectors. A new generation of firms (e.g., Apple Computer, Chiron, Compaq and Intel) has emerged, attaining a size and level of dominance that were wholly unexpected. In the US, for instance, some of the most successful enterprises in terms of growth, profitability and employment are new firms that thirty years ago were simply small-scale SMEs in need of support from government to survive and grow. Given the contribution of small, high-growth firms to national economies, government initiatives aimed at encouraging their further growth have been a noticeable feature of economic policies in many developed and developing countries. These initiatives have included differentiated methods of support across the economy, comprising a broad policy mix of measures (including taxation, grants, awards and competitions, and legislation training) as well as more specific programs.

In the US, for example, the Small Business Innovation Research (SBIR) program was created in 1982 with the purpose of reducing the decline in the competitiveness of SMEs. In a number of other countries, major initiatives focusing on small firms have also been implemented; for instance, in the UK, a Small Business Research Initiative (SBRI) working on preferential procurement for smaller firms has been operating since 2001.

The European Union's Lisbon Agenda has defined goals for economic growth, employment, enterprise and productivity and provides the overall policy context, including that for SMEs. In addition, the Competitiveness and Innovation Framework Programme (CIP) for 2007–2013 (CEC, 2005) has sought to support growth with initiatives that focus on SMEs. Under the re-launched agenda of March 2005, member states have been seeking to achieve more in the area of sustainable long-term growth and high levels of employment through their own national reform programs. The UK, for example, has an 80 percent target rate for employment.

Notwithstanding these initiatives, it is still somewhat difficult to establish a rationale for policy support of small, high-growth firms. Such firms are considered the most successful SMEs in an economy with high growth and, often, further high growth potential. Gazelles are, by definition (albeit an ex post definition), successful, able to handle the risk that growth and expansion bring far better than other firms, and thus could be considered as having no need of policy assistance. There are, however, some arguments that provide a sound rationale to support gazelles.

First, the broader social benefits, such as jobs and earnings, that small, high-growth firms generate for the economy as a whole are often quite significant. In addition, the risk of market failures that arise when gazelles are considering investment may be just as significant as for other small and slower-growing firms, precisely because they engage in higher-risk activities. Despite this, it is generally not easy to determine a clear strategy for policy support. A difficulty is related to the establishment of the appropriate moment in time to provide support in order to avoid any potential waste of public money and resources. This presents a significant challenge to policymakers: since gazelles are highly dynamic firms in a constant state of change, static SME sector policies that do not discriminate in terms of rate of growth will not be effective. It is even possible that such policies may put a brake on growth, particularly on the most successful firms since policies designed to work for the majority of firms are not necessarily appropriate for the most dynamic and fastest growing.[1]

Empirical evidence has suggested that the rate of growth of a firm is independent of its size, and so a large firm is just as likely to grow as a small firm (Gibrat, 1931; Sutton, 1997). On the other hand, work by Birch (1979;

1987) on small firms with fewer than twenty employees has proposed a different relationship between the rate of growth and the size of firms, showing that smaller firms are more likely to experience faster growth than larger firms. While Birch's work has been criticized for defining growth as gross—rather than net—job creation, many studies have built on it and have led to the generally accepted idea that that small firms do grow more quickly than larger ones.

The occurrence of differential growth in gazelles in different countries and/or business systems constitutes an additional challenge in terms of articulation of policy for their support, and some controversies still remain about the contribution of gazelles to the economy as a whole. Evidence from the US shows how rapid this growth can be. In 1999, just four firms (Microsoft, Dell, MCI and Cisco Systems) had a combined market valuation of 13 percent of US Gross Value Added (GVA). All had been in business for only less than twenty years (Jovanovic, 2001). A major concern for European policymakers is how to achieve or encourage this level of growth in the EU (Hölzl, 2006).

Finally, a further difficulty in the determination of a strategy of policy support for gazelles is related to the variety of definitions applied to them. This is a fundamental issue since by varying size and growth criteria it is possible to define various sets of 'growth' firms, each of which has essentially different characteristics and policy requirements. The next section examines these definitional issues and explores the ways in which governments should address policy support according to the different definitions.

DEFINITION OF GAZELLE FIRMS

The aforementioned analysis by Birch (1979; 1987) on firm size and growth constitutes the initial work that led to the coining of the term 'gazelle'. While a diversity of factors have been discussed in the literature, the main features usually employed to characterize gazelles are small size and rapid growth sustained over time.[2] In general, differences exist across countries in relation to the definitions of gazelles based on these two factors (Autio, Arenius and Wallenius, 2000). For instance, the definitions of threshold growth to characterize an SME might differ significantly among countries. Since different studies use varying categorizations, so the evidence base for policy and investment is heterogeneous. In the threefold SME definition of the EU (EC, 2002), SMEs are split into three categories according to size band and either their annual turnover or their annual balance sheet total.

The criterion of growth has also been measured in a number of ways: in terms of increases in employment/sales, in terms of the net assets of the company, or as a combination of all three. The acknowledgment of the use of different criteria in order to quantify growth is a key issue since these will, to a great extent, determine the results and policy conclusions in analyses of national growth and economic performance (Heshmati, 2001). The need to settle on a single measure that allows for comparison between countries has resulted in a preference for defining firm growth by employment. This definition works effectively across countries, and is relevant from a policy perspective since much of the interest in the provision of support for gazelles has been centered on employment and employment growth.

According to this definition, the rate of growth has been measured as proportional growth, absolute growth or as a combination of measures including both. This latter method to quantify growth was the one employed by Birch (1981; 1987) and Schreyer (2000); it is also the measure used by Europe's 500 and recommended by Hölzl (2006) in the approach of the Europe INNOVA network. This growth measure, known as 'm', allows the creation of a ranked list of small and medium firms, from which, through the use of additional criteria, firms are selected as gazelles. These criteria allow the selection of firms on an absolute basis—that is, firms that have a growth factor above a certain threshold level; or on a relative basis—for example, firms in the top 5 percent are considered to be gazelles. As before, selection procedures following this approach vary significantly across countries.

An additional feature that is usually considered to characterize firms as gazelles is related to their strategic management. In particular, for firms to be considered as 'true gazelles', they must also have plans for further growth. This criterion is based in the idea that only firms with a strategy for long-term growth will be able to respond well to the stimulus of policy or investment support. As Parker et al. (2005) have shown, the quality of management in a small firm can have a significant impact upon its future performance. Supporting firms that are small and have a track record of growth but lack a plan to grow further may lead to the inefficient use of government resources.

In general, there are a variety of different criteria and specifications to define gazelles, depending on policy aims and institutional and national contexts. As we have noted, small firms are diverse, and a number of alternative classifications are viable that emphasize different aspects of growth. This has contributed to difficulties in defining and understanding the behavior of gazelles. In addition, since gazelles are small firms, they are often unnoticed in empirical analyses, which often do not take into account so-called micro firms that have fewer than ten employees. As Autio et al. (2000) indicate, there are a number of other problems that make it difficult to identify and track small firms and their rates of growth. These include, for example, changes to the firm's registered name; modifications to the kinds of activities carried out; and changes to location and ownership. Firms may also cease to trade for some time, perhaps failing to file accounts, and then resume business. To exacerbate the situation, small firms may do several of these things, increasing the difficulty of identification and tracking. All the foregoing generally leads to a systematic bias for small firms not to be included in samples of data.

Furthermore, since gazelles grow quickly, it is possible that they are gazelles only for a short period of time. Some continue to grow to become larger firms. These are the success stories. But other gazelle firms grow for a while and then go into a decline, becoming what we might call ordinary SMEs again, and, of course, some firms will fail altogether, disappearing from view. While we know from the work of Parker et al. (2005) that the growth rate of a small firm in one year is positively related to its growth rate the following year, eventually, most fast-growing small firms will experience a reduction in their growth rate. Only a relatively small number achieve long-term, high levels of growth. However, it is difficult to ascertain how many gazelles become really big and successful. Parker et al. (2005), based on their research of 'dynamic management strategy', suggest that there are certain factors that can explain why some gazelle firms continue to grow while others do not. They suggest that successful gazelles—ones that continue to grow beyond an early phase of fast growth—have certain characteristics and a key feature of their approach is that they adapt to the challenges they face as they grow. This means that as they grow, they—sometimes continuously—re-evaluate and change their growth strategy. Work by Sims and O'Regan (2006) endorses this notion identifying 'agility' as a key survival and success characteristic of a gazelle firm.

Although, as we have indicated, gazelles are difficult to identify, they are present in many economic sectors: in those that are declining (e.g., textiles) as well as in those that are experiencing significant growth (e.g., biotechnology and computing). The extent to which gazelles are spread out across economic sectors can also lead to problems for policymakers. Buss makes the point that 'policy makers chase high-tech firms as a priority when other sectors might pose better opportunities' (2002, p. 18). As the work of Autio et al. (2000) highlights, in Finland, although there has been spectacular growth in the high technology sector with Nokia, there are surprisingly very few high technology gazelles. Most are actually found in trade or service companies. When Autio et al. (2000) compared the actual number of gazelles in various sectors with the expected number, they found a lower than anticipated representation of gazelles in a number of sectors including health services and real estate agencies. The study also identified that, in Finland, sectors that are less likely to be represented by gazelles include advertising, framing, repairs, publishing, printing and reproducing of recorded media. The wide distribution of gazelle firms across sectors and the lack of a link between high technology sectors and growth are also true in other parts of the world. In South Korea, for instance, high-growth firms are not found exclusively in the high technology sectors (Hill, 2005) and in some cases are in fact found within the lower technology sectors. It is clear from the literature that the existence of gazelles within different sectors varies hugely from country to country.

Indeed, there is little evidence suggesting that the sector has a large impact on the emergence of gazelles. However, the growth of the industry plays a more significant role. One of the factors affecting the scope for growth in a company is the stage of technological development of the industry to which the company belongs (see Utterback, 1994). In general, young firms that are new to an industry at an initial stage of technological development (e.g., the industry of potential applications of graphene) are likely to be able to present a higher and more rapid growth than those in other industries. Overall, although gazelles can be found in all industries, a recent study by Mitusch and Schimke (2010) examined the results of industry life cycles and concluded that gazelles tend to emerge in growing industries.

In summary, because the study of high-growth firms is relatively new for many researchers and policymakers, there are, as has been highlighted, problems of definition, both conceptual and practical, and in the use of terminology relating to gazelle firms. Furthermore, the fact that much of the data on high-growth firms is often held 'in the hands of private investment companies' and 'not readily shared because of their value to investors', and the fact that existing databases are very small, can mean that data is sometimes insufficient to form viable conclusions (Buss, 2002, p. 18).

ECONOMIC CONTRIBUTION OF GAZELLES TO INNOVATION AND COMPETITIVENESS

Employment generation abilities are usually the focus of attention when assessing the economic importance of gazelles. However, this is not their most important contribution to the generation of wealth and economic growth. In fact, it is their role as innovators that gives gazelles their main economic relevance, and places them at the center of public policy decisions (EC Europe INNOVA, 2006a). Gazelles consistently outperform the industry average as a result of their distinctive role as innovators. They are entrepreneurial in a Schumpeterian sense—that is, they are the expression of the dynamic nature of entrepreneurial capitalism, in which competition is dynamic, based not on prices but on product differentiation and on doing things in a novel way (Nelson and Winter, 1982). Indeed, Joseph Schumpeter was one of the earliest economists to argue that entrepreneurs were one of the key mechanisms of wealth creation and redistribution for a capitalist society. Creative entrepreneurs—by bringing innovations to the market—'creatively' destroy existing markets, redistribute wealth, and create new products, processes and services (Metcalfe, 1998). This view constitutes a fundamental departure from the mainstream neoclassical vision of industries formed by homogenous 'representative' firms competing merely in terms of price.[3] In this perspective, the competitive advantage and economic performance of gazelles arise from their firm-specific and idiosyncratic knowledge capabilities, such as their capability of delivering products quickly, their flexibility to adapt to anticipated changes, their ability to provide high-performance products and apply updated technology, and their capability of mastering financial management

(Barès et al., 2006). These dynamic capabilities, which allow the efficient use of knowledge and technology, are a key determinant in the rapid growth that characterizes gazelles.

Innovation as a critical source of entrepreneurial economic rents does not rely solely on the introduction of new products, markets and technologies, but also on new types of organizational arrangements.[4] For instance, the research of Barès et al. (2006) in their study of high-growth business in the Lorraine region in France shows that high growth is more related to new applications of resources and organizational processes than to the generation of new technologies. In addition, since the development of radical innovations generally requires great resources, very often small, high-growth businesses do not have enough of these to invest in radical changes in their products or processes, and thus develop mainly incremental, rather than radical, innovations.

As stated earlier, contrary to popular perception, gazelles are not systematically found in high technological sectors. In eight OECD countries, only around one-third of gazelles were defined as 'high-tech' companies (OECD, 1998). Fast-growing firms whose success comes from innovative approaches to marketing, organization or distribution can be found across a wide range of activities (some examples are Wal-Mart, Starbucks, Office Depot and Amazon). Franchising has also provided a way for firms to grow quickly and exploit good ideas, while sharing the risks and reducing the capital the firm would otherwise require in financing expansion (OECD, 1998, p. 248). Gazelles are also very often responsible for the creation of new markets and industries (for example, Federal Express and UPS, the frozen potato industry and the personal computer and software industries). They also often enter existing markets with a significant innovation, either technological or organizational, which provides them with a key competitive advantage and enables them to compete on a basis other than price, thereby creating value for the firm and attracting the resources necessary to fuel growth (Slaughter, 1996; Revenga, 2006).

In general, gazelles are quick in detecting and exploring new market opportunities, improving their productivity and efficiency in a continuous manner. They are adaptable to changes in their environment once a market opportunity is detected, and have the organizational capacity to explore it and reduce the time between detection and exploitation. Successful gazelles know that opportunities are found where discontinuities exist in the marketplace or where they can create a unique product. Taking advantage of these opportunities allows them to impact upon both supply and demand— and therefore prices—and gives them their unique role in the generation of wealth creation and growth.

Alongside the innovation-related contribution to welfare growth and expansion is, of course, the aforementioned creation of new and sustainable jobs that gazelles may bring. A great deal of empirical evidence both in Europe and the US supports the idea that small businesses are significant drivers of employment expansion in economies (Hölzl, 2006; Autio, 2003; Audretsch, 2003). Works by Birch (1981; 1987) in the US, Westhead and Cowling (1995) and Konings (1995) in the UK, Autio and Yli-Renko (1998) in Finland, Heshmati (2001) in Sweden, and GrowthPlus (2002)—a study of Europe's 500 fastest growing companies—provide empirical evidence demonstrating the significant role that small businesses have in employment generation. The relationship between employer size and job generation can be traced back to the work of Birch (1987), who emphasized the disproportionate contribution of small businesses to the creation of jobs. Since Birch's research, the job-creating process of small businesses has been a polemic issue, the controversy of which hinges on a methodological issue. Results from different methodologies and more recent work by Birch and other authors[5] show that it is the small number of fast-growing firms that accounts for the considerable amount of employment gains in the economy. These studies suggest that while not any small firm can generate high levels of employment, it is the small, high-growth firms that raise the average employment levels in an economy.

The main idea put forward by these studies is that job creation is a consequence of the entrepreneurial ability and creativity of gazelles in making a new idea succeed in the marketplace. For instance, according to the Hölzl (2006) study, fast-growing firms affect productivity and employment almost by definition (see also Slaughter, 1996). The work by the OECD (1998) supports the same argument. In the eight countries covered by the study, small businesses exhibited much quicker net employment growth compared with larger ones as they accounted for most of the net employment growth over the period (1984–1992), and their performance was extraordinary in comparison to firms of other sizes. According to this study, it is not possible to draw definite conclusions on whether the SMEs sector is indeed responsible for a disproportionate share of net job creation. What is clear, however, is that the bulk of new jobs created are in a small number of fast-growth firms—both SMEs and large firms. In the US, these fast-growing firms account for only 3 percent of all firms but are responsible for 70 percent of gross job growth (Birch and Haggerty, 1997). The study also shows that the same holds true for the UK and Australia, where it is estimated that about 5 to 20 percent of firms are responsible for as much as 70 to 80 percent of gross job creation (Hall, 1995).

ECONOMIC ENVIRONMENT FACTORS DRIVING INNOVATION AND GROWTH IN GAZELLES

In addition to the aforementioned 'internal' dynamic capabilities of gazelles to innovate and generate employment, the economic environment in which these firms operate is a fundamental determinant for their economic performance and high growth. In this context, economic environment can be defined as the broad set of specific environmental variables or factors that influence the activities of gazelles (Barès et al., 2006), such as economic stability and growth, legal systems, cost of production factors, level of specialized research and educational institutions, the protection of intellectual property rights, tax burdens and the shared values in the society and cognitive programs that affect the way people notice, categorize and interpret stimuli from their environment. In a context of Schumpeterian dynamic competition, this environment is not a passive placement of strategies and actors but is formed by the changing characteristic of its specific participants and their dynamic interactions[6] that create a socioeconomic space in which institutional and economic structures are articulated and regulated. This space of integration in which business transactions take place possesses its own characteristics, and is of crucial importance for the high growth of gazelle firms. In particular, evidence from the Barès et al. (2006) study shows that successful gazelles are characterized by a clear differentiation strategy that privileges their customers' needs, and by a 'smart' use of the resources and opportunities available in their environment, in particular those that allow the reduction of risk and uncertainty, and support the generation and dissemination of knowledge and innovation. Small businesses in general will have more opportunities to grow in an environment that fosters the development of resources, and nurtures an interaction space for their operation and innovation activities. In this respect, clusters acquire a key role in driving innovation and growth. They provide new firms with an ideal breeding ground, by offering them the proximity to other companies, investors, educational institutions and research centers.

According to Hölzl (2006), however, while the existence of networks and clusters is highly significant for small firms in decentralized innovation systems, their importance regarding gazelle firms' policy is less clear. This analysis argues that the integration into vertical networks (i.e., into supply chains) is of central importance for gazelles, so that they do not experience delays in their expansion phase. However, the implication of a firm's integration into horizontal clusters—that is, networks of firms producing goods with similar characteristics—is less clear-cut. Available research suggests that the survival rate of such cluster firms is higher, and that at the same time growth potentials are exploited by both the individual firms and the cluster as a whole (ibid., p. 30).

Environmental conditions that facilitate access to finance are also key for making possible and driving the growth gazelles, as well as for fostering entrepreneurship, competition and innovation in general. Angel investors, or simply 'angels' (i.e., high-net-worth individuals who provide money for start-up firms with growth potential), are crucial in this respect. According to Marianne Hudson (2007), from the Ewing Marion Kauffman Foundation in the US, angels, who are often former entrepreneurs themselves, can bring value to new firms through both mentoring and industry connections. In particular, angels invest in innovative entrepreneurs at the crucial stages when ventures are just getting off the ground. In fact it is estimated that angels in the US are responsible for up to 90 percent of outside equity (i.e., money not from friends or family) in start-up and early-stage firms. In addition, while their investing has long been carried out in an informal, isolated way, it is now becoming more systematic and organized, achieving higher quality and more effective results particularly in the US. According to EC Europe INNOVA (2006b), business angels provide both financing and managerial experience, which increase the likelihood of start-up enterprises surviving. In the case of Europe, in comparison to the US, the European venture capital market has some serious weaknesses in relation to seed and early stage finance due to market fragmentation and different national regulatory and taxation systems. Thus, in a particularly difficult market environment, the capability of business angels to continue investing is a highly valuable feature (EC, 2002). It has to be noted, however, that despite the growing importance of the angel investing community in relation to the financing of gazelles, this source of funding also has its limitations. Most individual angels are very private, which contributes to the inefficiencies of early-stage equity markets. In addition, some angels, despite their own entrepreneurial experience, may not be very sophisticated investors, and this clearly limits their usefulness and may even hinder the acquisition of additional funding. Often an entrepreneur has not been able to attract venture capital or other growth financing because an angel investor has proceeded in ways that made the firm unattractive to follow-on funders.

Another environmental economic factor that may influence the ability of a gazelle firm to grow and innovate is the proximity to universities and research centers.[7] In the context of university-based incubators, a 2001 United Nations report challenged the perception that most universities have technology for commercialization, on the grounds that university research results are rarely of commercial value. In addition, universities normally prefer to work with larger firms rather than with small businesses. In general, overcoming existing cultural barriers to a successful long-term interaction between businesses and universities requires making university staff more aware of industrial enterprise, and allowing prospective academic entrepreneurs an actual view of the range of available useful business skills (UN, 2001, p. 17).

Corporate venturing, which commonly, though not exclusively, involves a relationship between a larger company and a smaller independent one, is another factor that can influence the growth of gazelles. The most direct way a large company can assist a gazelle is by providing an alternative or supplementary source of finance. It may also be able to provide particular skills or knowledge (for example, in technical or management areas) that a smaller company might otherwise not have access to, and may also open doors to established marketing and distribution channels (HM Revenues & Customs, 2007). Although some disagreements prevail in the literature, corporate venturing can be more effective in providing support than general venture capital because of the potentially superior knowledge of markets and technologies that these investing corporations hold, alongside access to their own resources and branding (Rasila, 2004).

There are, however, dangers and limitations of corporate venturing, as might be encountered with venture capital and business angels, in terms of attracting future investors, if there is already a corporate venture investor on board. There is also the danger that the proximity to a corporation might in fact hinder the innovation capabilities of a gazelle, and in turn actually disadvantage the investor. In practice, in the US, corporate venturing is an established growth strategy, but in the UK, for example, its use is more limited. Recently the Corporate Venturing Scheme (CVS) as outlined in the UK 2007 budget is intended to encourage corporate venturing involving equity investment in the UK.

Finally, high levels of entrepreneurial activity and growth have been ascribed to cultural attributes (Shane, 1993; OECD, 2001).[8] According to the OECD (1998) a near unanimous view held by analysts of entrepreneurship is that culture plays a critical role in determining the level of entrepreneurship. Other things being the same, an environment in which entrepreneurship is esteemed, where legitimate business failure is not stigmatized, will almost certainly be conducive to entrepreneurial success. However, partly because 'culture' is a broad and diffuse concept there has been little systematic assessment of this issue and its policy implications. The issue of 'culture' and gazelles is complicated, not least because of the multidimensional nature of culture. The term can refer to psychological variables, such as attitudes to risk-taking, achievement motivation (McClelland, 1961),[9] 'learned helplessness' (Peterson, Maier and Seligman, 1995) and 'locus of control' (Rotter, 1966; Lefcourt, 1966), and these propensities may apply significantly not only to (potential) entrepreneurs, but also to key individuals in their environments: teachers, family members, local and national authorities, business leaders, employers and financiers. Culture can also refer to social and economic variables, such as the existence of business networks, the extent of institutionalization of support organizations for SMEs and the integration of higher education and research bodies into the local economy. It can also refer to the 'self-image' of societies as depicted through the media.

Typically, different aspects of this multidimensional phenomenon have been studied by different social research disciplines, and there is limited development of a more holistic and integrated view. Clearly cultural differences do play a role but these are numerous and complex, and while some are clearly institutional and thus can be targeted by policy, some are more intangible, and are to do with attitudes.[10] There is evidence to show that some psychological variables are important, and there is limited evidence to suggest that entrepreneurial training including these variables can be valuable but is probably more effective if it includes mentoring/apprenticeship approaches (as suggested by Birch, 2004). There are also more diffuse attitudes held by other parties that need to be considered—for example, teachers who do/do not encourage students, parents and media promotion of role models. There is no simple fix, but it might be suggested that a concerted effort with many local partners involved may be effective. One may also extend the cultural issue to sources of support for innovation. For example, to give a very generalist picture, European attitudes to business failure are often negative and may discourage venture capitalists and other agents from investment, while in the US business failure may be viewed as an experiential and learning process that contributes to the future likelihood of success.

SUPPORTING GAZELLES: POLICY IN PRACTICE

Despite the increasing interest in gazelle firms in the academic and policy arenas, there are no systematic, large-scale studies that examine the role of policy in fostering their economic growth. In general, policies that have had some influence upon gazelles have been targeted at SMEs. The difficulties to design specific policies and programs for gazelles partly emerge from the features outlined earlier—that is, definitional issues of the concept of gazelle, and the diversity in the methods and data sets used for their study. The lack of specific associations to represent their interests (they are in a sense unrepresentative of other small firms) and the fact that they are often 'gazelles' only for a relatively short period of time constitute added difficulties in the design of policy support. Indeed, the dynamism and innovative behavior characteristic of gazelles make their study and the development of effective policies highly challenging. Different policies may need to be implemented and/or modified at different stages in a gazelle's life, and so traditional public policies are unlikely to be suitable (OECD, 2001). In addition, public support for gazelles is not easily justifiable, due to either the lack of a clear policy rationale, or the existence of conflicts between policy aims—for example, differential government support among companies belonging to the same industry with different rates of growth, and policy priorities (e.g., job creation and innovation) (Chittenden, 2007).

The market and systemic failure arguments together with the risks normally entailed by growth processes that generally justify policy intervention are not so compelling either when applied to gazelle firms. It is generally difficult to define a policy as 'gazelle-specific' using these arguments since they apply to all firms in a sector or a location to varying degrees. For instance, in the case of information asymmetry failures, information support targeted to gazelles could also be useful to other small firms that may not have the potential for growth. Since information policies are open to all companies on the basis of need, it would be difficult to withhold such a policy from all firms in a sector, or a geographical location, simply on the basis of firm size. Regarding the risk involved in expansion processes, as we have already indicated, the fact that gazelles often face levels of risk that may be greater than those faced by other SMEs, and the presence of greater wider social or welfare benefits in relation to the scale of this risk could justify public support. However, there are increasingly other means open to gazelles to minimize risk, such as the use of advice and support from a business angel, equity from venture capitalists and/or other support from a corporate venturing activity at a lower cost of finance.

There are also different and conflicting views regarding the type of support that is required to encourage growth in gazelles. Some authors (e.g., Levie, 1994; Lohmann, 1998) advocate a relatively passive role of government, and no specialized assistance to a specific industry or firm, while most policymakers are more inclined to an active governmental role involving the implementation of targeted policies and programs (Collinson, 2000; Hallberg, 1999). Findings from a study carried out by Fischer and Reuber (2002) have shown that the opinion of 'what a gazelle requires from policy' differs substantially among external resource providers, policymakers and gazelle firm owners. Policy advisers see the role of governments as critical, firm owners consider public support could be useful but is not necessary and can be unreliable, and external providers generally doubt the role of government entirely. A think tank on gazelles held in 1997, attended by entrepreneurs, venture capital firms, bankers, consultants, academics and government executives, suggested that gazelles might not actually want to be targeted by policy. They want services to be available to them, but they want to be able to 'tap into' these when they are ready (Fulcrum Partners, 1997, p. 1). This might be because they do not want to attract the attention of their competitors or they are just too busy at one time or another, or they want a high degree of autonomy both to be in control of the kind of help they receive and the time at which they receive it.

Gazelles themselves, and supporting agencies and governments, have endeavored to provide 'checklists' of what they consider high-growth firms want in terms of support. These checklists normally depend on the country and sector characteristics as well as on the firms' individual stages of growth. In general, the existing literature on the subject usually highlights measures aimed at (i) removing barriers to expansion, such as encouraging more flexible labor markets and greater freedom in working time arrangements (CroissancePlus, 2006; Betbèze and Saint-Étienne, 2006), and developing better regulation and policy (CBI, 2006); (ii) encouraging innovation and entrepreneurship—for example, by increasing the SME threshold and reducing the need for capital holding from 75 percent to 25 percent, through the creation of 'virtuous circles' endorsing the notion of 'clusters' through increased implementation of 'competitiveness poles', with the idea of giving more autonomy to the actors in these 'poles', especially universities and research centers (CroissancePlus, 2006). Also providing more capital and better partnerships to help develop new technologies, reducing turnaround times for IP patents, which can hinder fast growth, and encouraging corporations to place a greater emphasis on working in alliances with SMEs (Meyers, 2006); (iii) improving access to finance for small businesses (CBI, 2006), and creating financial markets to fund growth (Stam et al., 2006). In this respect decreasing income tax (Carroll et al., 2000) and reducing capital gains taxes constitute key measures to stimulate venture capital markets (Poterba, 1989; Jeng and Wells, 2000) that can provide necessary financial support. Another method is direct, government-created venture capital, where the government works alongside private venture capitalists (Lerner, 2002). Policy measures to make it easier for venture capital investments might include easing reporting requirements and lowering hold periods for publicly listed companies and, again, lowering tax rates (Cumming, 2007). Networking, education, training and sharing of skills have also recently emerged as key issues to support ambitious individuals with entrepreneurial ideas or potential. In particular, strong backing for training and knowledge has been highlighted as beneficial for a gazelle firm, more so than for average SMEs. In addition, gazelles invest more in employee training in comparison to other companies and greater employee involvement can lead to greater efficiency, better quality and greater innovation, resulting in greater diversification and internationalization (Oliveras, 2003).

Generally, policies for gazelles normally take two forms: direct support to the firm to increase their internal capabilities, and indirect support aimed at creating the external environmental and institutional conditions conducive to growth. Policies are usually targeted at (both or either) internal and external growth factors. Internal factors include managerial capabilities, networking, personal attributes of the entrepreneur and education. The personal qualities of the entrepreneur are perceived to be of great importance in gazelles. It is the vision and drive of the entrepreneur that are often instrumental in facilitating high growth. Thus it is often questioned whether policies should allow entrepreneurs some degree of autonomy to use their skills to drive the business. In general SME policy, this passivity might not be the best form of support. According to EIM (2006) high-growth firms are more likely to call for and utilize external help; therefore some kind of external public support service can assist. Because of their entrepreneurial nature, encouraging education and networking may also assist firms/people with the potential to become gazelles/entrepreneurs. For instance, the Netherlands has been particularly active in this respect, in setting up entrepreneurship centers based on the US model. In Finland, a more proactive policy approach has been implemented. The Growth Firm Service approaches potential high-growth firms to tailor support packages to their specific needs (Autio, Kronlund and Kovalainen, 2007). This is often said to be in contrast to traditional SME policy, whereby an SME usually does the approaching. Indirect support is related to the reduction of barriers to growth and regulation, capital and market situation, location and access to resources aimed at the promotion of healthy competition, adequate legislation, the reduction of administrative burdens and the creation of a productive climate (EIM, 2006).

Direct support can be given at different stages of company formation and development, including to entrepreneurs who may not yet have founded the firm (Autio, Kronlund and Kovalainen, 2007). Research has shown that policy aimed at providing assistance before entrepreneurs create their firms is valuable in that it creates firms that grow more quickly (Baum and Silverman, 2004). In this respect, the career histories of entrepreneurs are also an important factor in the success of ventures (Shane and Khurana, 2003). Providing different support at different stages of the firm's life cycle is key as firms have different goals as they move through each phase—awareness, idea, start-up and growth stages (EIM, 2006). Firms may need assistance to invest/restructure/innovate/increase production at different stages of growth, and policy needs to be targeted towards these goals.[11]

Indirect support aimed at influencing the dynamic context in which firms operate—including framework conditions—is generally focused on fostering innovation. According to EC Europe INNOVA Report (2006a) if Europe is to keep up with the US and China, it must provide a better environment: removing obstacles and barriers to innovation—for example, with improved intellectual property systems and increased R&D resources, a priority identified by the Lisbon target. In this respect, it is important to distinguish between policies with the aim of promoting high-growth firms and general SME policies: ' . . . *dedicated gazelle policies are likely not equivalent to SME policies, as gazelles are not typical SMEs. Gazelle policy is actually more than entrepreneurship policy, if fostering entrepreneurship is understood solely as fostering self-employment. Gazelle policy is entrepreneurship policy that is concerned with reducing barriers to growth and fostering innovative growth*' (EC Europe INNOVA, 2006b, p. 3).

In a similar vein, the EC (2006) highlights the lack of an innovation-friendly environment as the main barrier to investment in R&D and innovation, suggesting that policy actions should be taken in relation to regulation, standards, public procurement, intellectual property and entrepreneurial culture in order to encourage innovation. Some authors (e.g., Audretsch and Lehmann, 2005) have claimed that policies targeted specifically at gazelles should place emphasis on the knowledge base of a society. In the US, access to government R&D funds and changes to the patent and copyright laws are said to have been effective in enhancing IP protection for entrepreneurial innovations (Stam et al., 2006) even if this effectiveness is often dependent upon sector. Gazelles may face difficulties in areas that typical SMEs might not; therefore policies need to be targeted specifically at these problems. For example, they may have trouble in hiring suitably qualified staff able to deal with a dynamic environment; and they may find it difficult to acquire finance on reasonable terms, because of the increased risk perceived in financing a high-growth firm (Dutch Ministry of Economic Affairs, 2007). Gazelles are also quite different to ordinary SMEs in terms of management needs. Gazelle managers need to be able to pursue their entrepreneurial visions and grab opportunities. Active policies aimed at SMEs, it could be argued, may hinder this ability to some extent. However, this is a contested issue.

As we have already indicated, it is normally difficult to differentiate between policies designed for SMEs in general and those designed to target gazelles specifically, since some policies have a marked effect on a particular type of firm unintentionally. Indeed, policies focused exclusively on high-growth firms are in general quite rare (Autio, Kronlund and Kovalainen, 2007).[12] Since gazelles are located across the economy in a wide range of sectors, the variety of challenges that they face usually requires more specific and diverse policy measures (Autio, 2003). The type of support required will be determined by the industry sector within which the firm operates, and the critical success factors (CSFs) identified in this sector.[13] A policy that strengthens intellectual property rights might favor gazelles in a new sector, whereas in a more traditional one, it is more likely to benefit a larger, more established firm because they are more likely to win patent disputes. As a report by EIM (2005) indicates, firm growth may actually be penalized by policies in some sectors. Policy to encourage entrepreneurship may support all entrepreneurial activity per se, without adequately considering how the business will progress. Thus, many start-ups and ventures may be supported, which may be adequate for SMEs if the general aim of SME policy is to create more entrepreneurial firms, but this may be at the expense of gazelles (Autio, Kronlund and Kovalainen, 2007). For instance, Morris et al. (1996) cited the US as an example where tax and regulation costs are disproportionately heavy on high-growth firms, making it an incentive to actually stay 'small'. Subsidizing entrepreneurs and small new firms in general might also bring about substitution and deadweight effects (Santarelli and Vivarelli, 2002; Vivarelli, 2004). Subsidies might also work to the advantage of ordinary SMEs, in that less efficient or less ambitious entrepreneurs are given financial assistance that they use to remain in the market longer than they might have been able to without such support, to the disadvantage of 'genuine' high-growth firms.

According to Autio et al. (2007) policy support to high-growth firms should be horizontal and highly selective; it should be proactive; have the participation of private sector actors; should address managerial motivation and skills; and should involve highly customized and tailored management development activities. Policies require broad-based measures that address multiple aspects of policy design, implementation and monitoring, at the level of the individual, firm, sector and society (ibid., p. 3).

While gazelle policy has traditionally been somewhat fragmented, particularly in Europe, support for high-growth firms has been moving up the

Country	Examples of gazelle policy and networks set up to support gazelles*
The Netherlands	Growth Facility Mastering Growth Program Enterprise Zones Growth Plus and Fast Growth Master classes for entrepreneurs Biopartner Technopartner
France	Gazelles programme (1 of 5 'SMEs' growth programmes') – Ministry of SMEs, Trade, Small-Scale Industry and the Professions (2006) France Gazelles investment fund (2006)
Finland	Growth Firm Service (2005) INTRO
Spain	Contest of Ideas for the Creation of Technological or Science-Based Industries Embryo Project – Program for University Entrepreneurs Prestecs Participatius del CIDEM – Participative Loans
US	Competitive Technology Act SBIR (Small Business Innovation & Research scheme) SBIC (Small Business Investment Companies) program
Australia	Innovation Investment Fund (IIF) Commercializing Emerging Technologies (COMET) Co-operative Research Centres Commercial Ready Program
UK	The Enterprise Initiative Business Links Business Birth Rate Strategy (Scotland, 1990s) Entrepreneurship Action Plan (Wales, 1990s) Enterprise Allowance Scheme (1990s) Small Business Service (2000) Gateway2Investment (g2i) (2005) The High Growth Programme (2010)

Figure 5.1 Examples of policies that have supported gazelles in selected countries.
* *Includes those not specifically targeted at—but have had an impact on—gazelles.*
Sources: Dutch Ministry of Economic Affairs (2004);EIM (2006); Stam et al. (2006); Van Stel and Storey (2004, p. 2); Chesbrough (1999) Lerner (1999); Autio et al. (2007). http://www.gazelles.pme.gouv.fr/partenaires.htm; http://www.pme.gouv.fr/.

agenda of policymakers at all levels in the last decade (Pages, Freedman and Von Bargen, 2003). The final section of this chapter provides some examples of programs and schemes aimed at supporting gazelles in a selection of countries (see Figure 5.1).[14]

As Figure 5.1 shows, in the Netherlands, for instance, the government has pledged its commitment to creating more entrepreneurs and encouraging start-ups (Dutch Ministry of Economic Affairs, 2004), and an increasing prominence of the importance of education and skills is echoed in the Dutch emphasis on the training of individuals, particularly through master classes. In addition, some programs in the country have been the result of policy mix–for example, technology policy and high-growth policy, in the case of Biopartner and Technopartner (Stam et al., 2006, p. 11). In

Catalonia (Spain) there is a similar rising interest in education and training, but seemingly more geared towards the employees of high-growth firms (see Oliveras, 2003). Most existing policies in the country are fairly new and tend to originate in universities.

The US is often put forward by many as a 'role model' in terms of support to high-growth companies (Stam et al., 2006). By 'creating and opening markets; providing R&D and intellectual property protection and investing in technically talented people' (Von Bargen, Freedman and Pages, 2003, p. 316) the US seems to have made it relatively easy for gazelles to flourish. Policy measures have, to this end, been designed to change securities, tax, pension, patent and copyright laws and enhance intellectual property (IP) protection for entrepreneurial innovations; utilize government R&D funds and change the knowledge base; allow the effective use of technically trained immigrants; create flexible labor markets (see Chesbrough, 1999) and deregulate leading industries (particularly in the 1980s). In Australia, the Innovation Investment Fund (IIF) program, established in 1997, has been likened to the US SBIC and works on the basis of partnership with private venture capitalists to stimulate investment in developing economies. The program, it was claimed, had several advantages over similar governmental programs implemented in Canada and the UK in this respect (Cumming, 2007).

Finally, in the UK, a variety of policies were prevalent in the 1990s, which, while not necessarily specifically targeted at gazelles, undoubtedly influenced them. During this period increasing employment was said to be the underpinning of all business support policies in the UK, and their effectiveness in achieving this aim was often called into question.[15]

Currently the UK government, in common with other governments of the European Union and other governments around the world, has developed a broader range of policies that seek to support the small firm sector. In keeping with the need to further develop and support the small companies sector, and in light of research[16] and policy development on the importance of coaching undertaken in the UK, the chancellor of the exchequer in his December 2004 pre-budget statement proposed that all regional development agencies (RDAs) should develop schemes to support high-growth companies in their own respective areas through 'tailored coaching and support' (HM Treasury, 2004). The chancellor's statement was followed by a series of trials or pilots of high-growth programs by all RDAs. The subsequent full-scale schemes are now in their final stages or at completion.

The overall aim of the High Growth Programme is to raise the number of growth and high-growth SMEs in the UK regions through a 'structured programme of coaching'. The projects are targeted towards businesses from all sectors with high-growth potential, whether at pre-start, start-up or existing stage. It is aimed to help businesses that would not grow or would not grow as fast without the specialist help that they are not able to find in the market mainly due to information failures. Each regional development agency is implementing the program according to a general design and in response to the HM Treasury proposal. However, the program recognizes that in different places, a different approach to the design of the scheme should be followed to take account of regional variations in the economic growth conditions, types of business, sectoral distributions of companies, support networks, business cultures and existing policy mix and priorities.[17]

The program employs a range of interventions including consultancy, mentoring, business diagnostics and business advice, usually through the use of private sector intermediaries (such as accountants, sales and marketing specialists). The funding element of the program does not involve grant aid. Instead it is focused on assisting companies to become viable and attractive investment opportunities for external investors. This is based on the idea that the problem underlying the 'finance gap' for growing businesses (HM Treasury, 2003) is not the lack of sources of finance but the knowledge and skills of how to access the finance available. Indeed, a considerable part of the program is aimed at improving companies' management skills, the readiness and robustness of their business plan and their organization in general to make the growth business more attractive for potential investors.

The regional development agencies were established under the Regional Development Agencies Act 1998, and were formally launched in 1999 and 2000. The government has recently announced that these regional agencies will close at the end of March 2012, and by then all the activities linked to the High Growth Programme will be finalized. Regional economic development and regeneration initiatives will in future be led by local enterprise partnerships and other successor bodies.

CONCLUSIONS

In this chapter we have provided an analysis of the role and relevance of small, high-growth firms (or gazelles) in terms of innovation and competitiveness. The significant contribution of these firms to national economies via their innovation and employment generation abilities has led to a broad spectrum of policy initiatives to support their further growth in many developed and developing countries.

Defining specific and effective policy support for gazelles is, however, a problematical issue. The definitional issues of the 'gazelle' concept previously discussed and the variety of methods and data sets employed for their analysis have made it challenging for governments to design specific policy actions and programs. The difficulty to develop policies that are effective at the different stages in the life cycle of a gazelle's life cycle is exarcerbated by their characteristic highly dynamic and innovative behavior. In addition, public support for gazelles is generally not easily justifiable, due to either the lack of a clear policy rationale, or the existence of conflicts between the 'standard' policy aims and priorities, as well as conflicting views regarding the type of support that will encourage their growth.

As a result of these difficulties, specific policies focused exclusively on high-growth firms are generally quite rare, and gazelle policy has traditionally been somewhat fragmented. Notwithstanding this, support for high-growth firms has been rapidly moving up the agenda of policymakers at all levels in the last decade, with now clearly identifiable specific programs and schemes aimed at supporting the continued growth of gazelles in a variety of countries.

NOTES

1. This could be related to the adequacy of the type and scale of support, and the rate at which this support is delivered. For instance, according to coaches working within the UK High Growth Programme, the application, processing and evaluation time for SMEs' innovation support grants currently provided in the UK is often proven to be too lengthy for the development and exploitation of unique ideas in rapidly innovating companies.
2. The Europe INNOVA Working Paper (Hölzl, 2006), for instance, has proposed the consideration of other relevant aspects such as the age of the firm— that is, how long the firm has been in business.
3. This idea of dynamic competition is in line with the competence and resource-based views of the firm—within the management and organizational literature—and the evolutionary approaches to the firm in economics (cf. Dosi and Marengo, 1994; Langlois and Robertson, 1995; and Teece, Pisano and Shuen, 1997, among many others).
4. In this context, innovation is understood in a broad sense as encompassing managerial, organizational and technological changes (Nelson and Winter, 1982).
5. For a discussion of methodological issues and the results from more recent studies see Slaughter (1996); Davis et al. (1996); Birch and Haggerty (1997); OECD (1998); Kirchhoff and Greene (1998); Davidsson et al. (1998); Schreyer (2000); Audretsch (2003) and Hölzl (2006).
6. These are specific interactions regarding the organization of production factors; the strategic relationships between the firm, its partners, suppliers and clients; and the relations with political and financial agents.
7. From a commercial firm's view, proximity to industrially oriented R&D facilities is generally considered to be more important than access to a university's educational facilities.
8. For a more detailed analysis of this argument and a review of the relevant literature see Suddle et al. (2006).
9. Despite having come under much criticism, McClelland's early work (1961) on the 'need for achievement' paved the way for many studies on the *characteristics* of entrepreneurs. McClelland related the concept of 'achievement motivation' to economic development and growth, and provided evidence that it is possible to increase this motivation through training programs aimed at increasing business performance (Mirron and McClelland, 1979).
10. For a detailed discussion of the institutional expression of culture and the complex interaction between culture and innovation, see Chapter 10,

'Innovation and Creative Places' (Miles, I. and Gee, S.) and Chapter 11, 'Cultures and Innovation' (Gee, S. and Miles, I.), this volume.
11. See Autio et al. (2007) for a more detailed discussion of what policies should be implemented at what growth stage.
12. The incipiency and relatively small number of policies clearly targeted at supporting gazelles have implied the existence of very little research on their evaluation and the determination of their additionality (Autio, Kronlund and Kovalainen, 2007).
13. See, for example, Feindt et al. (2002) on CSFs in the e-commerce industry.
14. This list is for illustrative purposes and thus by no means exhaustive.
15. See also Roper and Hart (2005) for a discussion on the effects of the *Business Links* policy.
16. See NESTA (2009) for a recent UK review of high-growth firms and their contribution to growth.
17. Online. Available HTTP: http://www.highgrowthprogramme.co.uk/ (accessed 10 November 2011).

BIBLIOGRAPHY

Audretsch, D. B. (2003) 'Entrepreneurship: A Survey of the Literature'. Enterprise Papers, No 14. Enterprise Directorate-General European Commission.
Audretsch, D. B. and Lehmann, E. E. (2005) 'Mansfield's Missing Link: The Impact of Knowledge Spillovers on Firm Growth'. *Journal of Technology Transfer* 30 (1–2): 207–210.
Autio, E. (2003) 'High potential entrepreneurship'. In The Entrepreneurial Advantage of Nations: First Annual Global Entrepreneurship Symposium. United Nations, April, pp. 1–17.
Autio, E., Arenius, P. and Wallenius, H. (2000) 'Economic Impact of Gazelle Firms on Finland, Helsinki University of Technology'. Working paper series 2000/3. Espoo, Finland.
Autio, E., Kronlund, M. and Kovalainen, A. (2007) 'High Growth SME Support Initiatives in Nine Countries: Analysis, Categorization, and Recommendations'. Report prepared for the Finnish Ministry of Trade and Industry. Edita, Finland: Edita Publishing Ltd.
Autio, E. and Yli-Renko, H. (1998) 'New, Technology-Based Firms in Small Open Economies—An Analysis Based on the Finnish Experience'. *Research Policy* 26 (9): 973–987.
Barès, F., Boiteux, S., Clerc-Girard, M-F. and Janczak, S. (2006) 'Entrepreneurship and the High Growth Companies: The Evolution of the Gazelles and Their Ties to the Territory'. ICN working paper written within the framework of the International Chair 'Haut Potentiel de Croissance', ICN Business School.
Baum, J. A. C. and Silverman, B. S. (2004) 'Picking Winners or Building Them? Alliance, Intellectual, and Human Capital as Selection Criteria in Venture Financing and Performance of Biotechnology Startups'. *Journal of Business Venturing* 19: 411–436.
Betbèze, J-P. and Saint-Étienne, C. (2006) 'Une stratégie PME pour la France.' Paris: Conseil d'Analyse Économique. . Online. Available HTTP: http://www.cae.gouv.fr/IMG/pdf/061.pdf (accessed 13 June 12)
Birch, D. (1979) 'The Job Generation Process'. MIT Program on Neighborhood and Regional Change, unpublished paper. Online. Available HTTP: http://ssrn.com/abstract=1510007 (accessed 10 November 2011).
Birch, D. L. (1981) 'Who Creates Jobs?' *The Public Interest* 65 (Fall): 3–14.

Birch, D. (1987) *Job Creation in America: How Our Smallest Companies Put the Most People to Work*. New York: Free Press.

Birch, D. (2004) 'Education Matters—But Does Entrepreneurship Education?' By M. Aronsson. *Academy of Management Learning and Education* 3 (3): 289–292.

Birch, D. and Haggerty, A. (1997) *Who's Creating Jobs?* Cambridge, MA: Cognetics, Inc.

Buss, T. F. (2002) 'Emerging High Growth Firms and Economic Development Policy'. *Economic Development Quarterly* 16: 17.

Carroll, R., Holtz-Eakin, D., Rider, M. and Rosen, H. S. (2000) 'Personal Income Taxes and the Growth of Small Firms'. NBER working paper 7980. National Bureau of Economic Research.

CBI. (2006) 'Encouraging Small Business Growth. Enabling the Enterprise Revolution'. Enterprise brief 7, September.

CEC (Commission of the European Communities). (2005) 'More Research and Innovation—Investing for Growth and Employment: A Common Approach'. Implementing the Community Lisbon Programme: Communication from the Commission to the Council, the European Parliament, the European Economic and Social Committee and the Committee of the Regions. Online. Available HTTP: http://www.era.gv.at/attach/MoreResearchandInnovation_2005.pdf (accessed 2 February 2012).

Chesbrough, H. (1999) 'The Organizational Impact of Technological Change: A Comparative Theory of National Institutional Factors'. *Industrial and Corporate Change* 8: 447–485.

Chittenden, F. (2007) Interview performed by Dr John Rigby, Kathryn Morrison and Deborah Cox. 6 March. The University of Manchester [transcript in possession of authors].

Collinson, S. (2000) 'Knowledge Networks for Innovation in Small Scottish Software Firms'. *Entrepreneurship & Regional Development* 12 (3): 217–244.

CroissancePlus. (2006) Laissons courir les gazelles ('Let the gazelles run free'). Online. Available HTTP: http://www.thomas-legrain.com/wp-content/uploads/2007/01/lancement-laissons-courir-gazelles.pdf (accessed 10 November 2011).

Cumming, D. (2007) 'Government Policy towards Entrepreneurial Finance: Innovation Investment Funds'. *Journal of Business Venturing* 22: 193–235.

Davidsson, P., Lindmark, L. and Olofsson, C. (1998) 'The Extent of Overestimation of Small Firm Job Creation—An Empirical Examination of the Regression Bias'. *Small Business Economics* 11: 87–100.

Davis, S. J., Haltiwanger, J. C. and Schuh, S. (1996) 'Small Business and Job Creation: Dissecting the Myth and Reassessing the Facts'. *Small Business Economics* 8 (4): 297–315.

Dosi, G. and Marengo, L. (1994) 'Toward a Theory of Organizational Competences'. In England, R. W. (ed.), *Evolutionary Concepts in Contemporary Economics*, 157–178. Ann Arbor: The University of Michigan Press.

Dutch Ministry of Economic Affairs. (2004) 'Action for Entrepreneurs: Entrepreneurship Policy in the Netherlands'. Enterprise Directorate of the Ministry of Economic Affairs, The. Hague, The Netherlands: Ministry of Economic Affairs. In OECD SME And Entrepreneurship Outlook 2005.

EC (European Commission). (2002) 'Observatory of European SMEs 2002 / No 5 Business Demography in Europe'.

EC (European Commission). (2006) 'Creating an Innovative Europe: Report of the Independent Expert Group on R&D and Innovation Appointed Following the Hampton Court Summit and Chaired by Mr. Esko Aho'. January. Online. Available HTTP: http://www.eua.be/Libraries/Page_files/aho_report.sflb.ashx (accessed 10 November 2011).

EC Europe INNOVA. (2006a) 'Executive Summary of the First Session of the Gazelles Innovation Panel'. 29 March. Brussels.

EC Europe INNOVA. (2006b) Gazelles Scoping Paper 31.05.06.

EIM. (2005) *Entrepreneurship in the Netherlands: Business Transfer: A New Start.* EIM Business & Policy Research. December.

EIM. (2006) *Entrepreneurship in the Netherlands: High Growth Enterprises: Running Fast But Still Keeping Control.* EIM Business & Policy Research. December.

Feindt, S., Jeffcoate, J. and Chappell, C. (2002) 'Identifying Success Factors for Rapid Growth in SME E-commerce'. *Small Business Economics* 19: 51–62.

Fischer, E. and Reuber, A. R. (2003) 'Support for Rapid Growth Firms: A Comparison of the Views of Founders, Government Policy Makers and Private Sector Resource Providers'. *Journal of Small Business Management* 41(4): 346–365.

Fulcrum Partners. (1997) 'Report of a Think Tank on Rapid Growth Firms' Fulcrum Partners (1997) Report of a Think Tank on Rapid Growth Firms organised by Fulcrum Partners,19 Nov 1997. Online. Available HTTP: http://www.fulcrum-partners.com/ (accessed 14 June 2012).

Gibrat, R. (1931) *Les inégalités économiques.* Paris: Librairie du Recueil Sirey.

GrowthPlus. (2002) Growth Plus Europe's 500. Online. Available HTTP: http://www.growthplus.org (accessed 10 November 2011).

Hall, C. (1995) 'Entrepreneurial Engine'. Paper presented at the OECD 'High-Level Workshop on SMEs: Employment, Innovation and Growth'. Washington DC. 16–17 June. Mimeograph.

Hallberg, K. (1999) 'Small and Medium Scale Enterprises: A Framework for Intervention'. Washington, DC: Small Enterprise Unit, Private Sector Development Department, The World Bank.

Heshmati, A. (2001) 'On the Growth of Micro and Small Firms: Evidence from Sweden'. *Small Business Economics* 17: 213–228.

Hill, J. (2005) 'Financing Technology Based High Growth Company'. TAFTIE Annual Seminar. Online. Available HTTP: www.taftie.org/Events/Events/TAFTIE_Annual_Seminar_2005.html (accessed 10 November 2011).

HM Revenues & Customs. (2007) Online. Available HTTP: http://www.hmrc.gov.uk/guidance/cvs.htm (accessed 10 November 2011).

HM Treasury. (2003) 'Bridging the Finance Gap: Next Steps in Improving Access to Growth Capital for Small Businesses'. Report. London: HMSO.

HM Treasury. (2004) 'Devolving Decision Making: 2—Meeting the Regional Economic Challenge: Increasing Regional and Local Flexibility'. Report. London: HMSO.

Hölzl, W. (2006) 'Gazelles Scoping Paper'. Europe INNOVA publication.

Hudson, M. (2007) 'Why Entrepreneurs Need Angels—and How Angels Are Improving'. Ewing Marion Kauffman Foundation. Online. Available HTTP: http://www.kauffman.org/entrepreneurship/why-entrepreneurs-need-angels.aspx (accessed 10 November 2011).

Jeng, L. A. and Wells, P. C. (2000) 'The Determinants of Venture Capital Funding: Evidence across Countries'. *Journal of Corporate Finance* 6: 241–289.

Jovanovic, B. (2001) 'New Technology and the Small Firm'. *Small Business Economics* 16: 53–55.

Kirchhoff, B. and Greene, P. (1998) 'Understanding the Theoretical and Empirical Content of Critiques of US Job Creation Research'. *Small Business Economics* 10: 153–169.

Konings, J. (1995) 'Job Creation and Job Destruction in the U.K. Manufacturing Sector'. *Oxford Bulletin of Economics and Statistics* 57: 5–24.

Langlois, R. and Robertson, P. (1995) *Firms, Markets, and Economic Change: A Dynamic Theory of Business Institutions.* London: Routledge.

Lefcourt, H. M. (1966) 'Internal versus External Control of Reinforcement: A Review'. *Psychological Bulletin* 65: 206–220.

Lerner, J. (1999) 'The Government as Venture Capitalist: The Long-Run Effects of the SBIR Program'. *Journal of Business* 72: 285–318.

Lerner, J. (2002) 'When Bureaucrats Meet Entrepreneurs: The Design of Effective "Public Venture Capital" Programmes'. *The Economic Journal* 112: F73–F84.

Levie, J. (1994) 'Can Governments Nurture Young Growing Firms? Qualitative Evidence from a Three-Nation Study, Frontiers of Entrepreneurship Research'. Wellesley, MA: Arthur M. Blank Centre for Entrepreneurship, Babson College.

Lohmann, D. (1998) 'Strategies of High Growth Firms in Adverse Public Policy and Economic Environments, Frontiers of Entrepreneurship Research'. Wellesley, MA: Arthur M. Blank Centre for Entrepreneurship, Babson College.

McClelland, D. C. (1961) *The Achieving Society*. Princeton, NJ: Van Nostrand Co.

Metcalfe, J. S. (1998) *Evolutionary Economics and Creative Destruction*. London: Routledge.

Meyers, N. P. (2006) 'Financing Global Gazelles'. Submitted to Small Business Policy Branch, Industry Canada. 31 March.

Mirron, D. and McClelland, D. C. (1979) 'The Impact of Achievement Motivation Training on Small Businesses'. *California Management Review* 21 (4): 13–18.

Mitusch, K. and Schimke, A. (2010) *Gazelles: High-Growth Companies*. Consortium Europe INNOVA Sectoral Innovation Watch. Final report. December. Available Online HTTP: http://www.europe-innova.eu/c/document_library/get_file?folderId=330868&name=DLFE-13607.pdf. (accessed 13 June 2012).

Morris, M. H., Schindehutte, M. and Pitt, L. F. (1996) *Sustaining the Entrepreneurial Society*. Washington, DC: Small Business Foundation of America.

Nelson, R. and Winter, S. G. (1982) *An Evolutionary Theory of Economic Change*. Cambridge: Belknap Press.

NESTA. (2009) 'The Vital 6 Per Cent: How High Growth Innovative Businesses Generate Prosperity and Jobs'. Report. National Endowment for Science, Technology and the Arts. October.

OECD. (1998) 'Fostering Entrepreneurship'. Paris: OECD Publications.

OECD. (2001) 'Enhancing SMEs Competitiveness'. OECD Bologna Ministerial Conference.

Oliveras, E. (2003) 'The Balance Scorecard. Driver of Business Growth'. *International Accountant* September: 32–35.

Pages, E. R., Freedman, D. and Von Bargen, P. (2003) 'Entrepreneurship as a State and Local Economic Development Strategy'. In Hart, D. (ed.), *Entrepreneurship Policy*, 240–259. Cambridge: Cambridge University Press.

Parker, S., Storey, D. J. and van Witteloostuijn, A. (2005) 'What Happens to Gazelles? The Importance of Dynamic Management Strategy'. Paper. Durham Business School.

Peterson, C., Maier, S. F. and Seligman, M. E. P. (1995) *Learned Helplessness: A Theory for the Age of Personal Control*. New York: Oxford University Press.

Poterba, J. (1989) 'Capital Gains Tax Policy towards Entrepreneurship'. *National Tax Journal* 42: 375–389.

Rasila, T. (2004) 'Venture-to-Capital—A New Framework for Growth Venturing and Professional Ownership'. PhD diss. Tampere University of Technology.

Revenga, B. (2006) 'Factores Conditionantes del Tamaño y del Crecimiento Empresarial: Mice, Gophers, Gazelles and Elephants'. Publicaciones de la Direcion General de la PYME, Ministerio de Industria, Turismo y Comercio.

Roper, S. and Hart, M. (2005) 'Small Firm Growth and Public Policy in the UK: What Exactly Are the Connections?' Aston Business School, UK.

Rotter, J. B. (1966) 'Generalized Expectancies of Internal versus External Control of Reinforcements'. *Psychological Monographs* 80 (5): 1–28.

Santarelli, E. and Vivarelli, M. (2002) 'Is Subsidizing Entry an Optimal Policy?' *Industrial and Corporate Change* 11 (1): 39–52.

Schreyer, P. (2000) 'High Growth Firms and Employment'. OECD STI Working Paper 2000/3.

Shane, S. (1993) 'Cultural Influences on National Rates of Innovation'. *Journal of Business Venturing* 8: 59–73.

Shane, S. and Khurana, R. (2003) 'Bringing Individuals Back In: The Effects of Career Experience on New Firm Founding'. *Industrial and Corporate Change* 12 (3): 519–543.

Sims, M. A. and O'Regan, N. (2006) 'In Search of Gazelles Using a Research DNA Model'. *Technovation* 26: 943–954.

Slaughter, M. P. (1996) 'Entrepreneurship: Economic Impact and Public Policy Implications. An Overview of the Field'. Kauffman Center for Entrepreneurial Leadership Publications.

Stam, E., Suddle, K., Hessels, S. J. A. and van Stel, A. (2006) 'High Growth Firms, Public Policies and Economic Growth'. Working paper. SCALES-initiative, EIM Business and Policy Research.

Suddle, K., Beugelsdijk, S. and Wennekers, S. (2006) 'Entrepreneurial Culture as Determinant of Nascent Intrepreneurship. SCALES (Scientific Analysis of Entrepreneurship and SMEs, Netherlands)'. Paper N200519.

Sutton, J. (1997) 'Gilbrat's Legacy'. *Journal of Economic Literature* March 35 (1): 40–59.

Teece, D., Pisano, G. and Shuen, A. (1997) 'Dynamic Capabilities and Strategic Management'. *Strategic Management Journal* 18: 509–533.

UN. (2001) 'Technology Capacity-Building Initiatives for the Twenty-First Century in the ESCWA Member Countries'. United Nations Publications.

Utterback, J. M. (1994) *Mastering the Dynamics of Innovation*. Cambridge, MA: Harvard Business School Press.

Van Stel, A. J. and Storey D. J. (2004) 'The Link between Firm Births and Job Creation: Is There a Upas Tree Effect?' *Regional Studies* 38: 893–909.

Vivarelli, M. (2004) 'Are All the Potential Entrepreneurs So Good?' *Small Business Economics* 23 (1): 41–49.

Von Bargen, P., Freedman, D. and Pages, E. R. (2003) 'The Rise of the Entrepreneurial Society'. *Economic Development Quarterly* 17 (4): 315–324.

Westhead, P. and Cowling, M. (1995) 'Employment Change in Independent Owner-Managed High-Technology Firms in Great Britain'. *Small Business Economics* 7: 111–140.

6 Financing Europe's Innovative SMEs with Public-Private Partnerships

John Rigby and Jennifer Hayden

INTRODUCTION

A starting assumption for those making policy to grow innovative smaller firms is that small to medium-sized enterprises (SMEs) with the potential for high growth are often unable to access sufficient capital from the private sector to fund their development, especially at the early stages. The provision of greater and better targeted financial support through government-supported but partly private schemes (hybrid venture capital) to these firms would be beneficial for their development and ultimately for the economy and society at large. Public-private partnerships in innovation financing are seen by policymakers to combine public resources with private financial resources and private expertise in the targeting and management of funds. On the face of it, this looks like the best of both worlds, but the consensus is that while this is a policy that can work, it is difficult to get it right.

By reviewing the literature on this interdisciplinary subject, we reflect on the current approaches to hybrid venture capital with a particular focus on the trans-European approaches that have been taken and how they can be improved or altered. The first section examines the basis and rationales underlying policy action in this area. This is followed by an overview of the general mechanism of hybrid venture capital funding, including examples from a variety of countries. In the final sections some emergent issues are highlighted and potential opportunities for new policy directions are anticipated. The chapter is concluded with suggestions for much needed future research.

RATIONALES FOR PUBLIC-PRIVATE PARTNERING IN FINANCE

Given the bewilderment that the term public-private partnership (PPP) can induce (Weihe, 2006), perhaps it is unhelpful to add yet another instance of PPP to an already long list of such activities. However, a number of various writers on policy have busily applied the term to the financing of start-up firms by way of financial vehicles such as hybrid venture capital funds (e.g., Bascha and Walz, 2007), so we must now recognize the existence of a sixth family of PPP: public-private partnerships in finance.

The PPP model is regarded as a policy tool that enables government to capture private sector efficiencies in the pursuit of its public policy goals (EIB, 2004) and by its (problematic) perception of offering improved value for money (IMF, 2004; Morallos and Amekudzi, 2008; Yescombe, 2007; see also Shaoul, 2005). In this chapter, we look at the rationales particular to PPP for financing innovative SMEs, and we review the evidence of how PPP has performed.

FOSTERING SOCIAL GOODS RATIONALE

Regardless of title or categorization, the role of partnering with the private sector to increase access to finance for SMEs is thought to be justified by governments, at least in part, owing to its perceived ability to aid in fulfilling policy goals such as increasing jobs and innovation in the economy at large. In addition, SMEs may also give rise to positive externalities that benefit the environment or other social goods through the development of clean technologies or tele-health solutions, for example. Given the positive public goods that can be generated through SME activity, governments can rationalize involvement in this arena, especially if the private sector is seen to not be providing the necessary capital for enterprises to have the best chance of succeeding.

SME Barriers to Access (Market Failures) Rationale

Small and medium-sized enterprises report greater barriers to accessing finance than large firms, and these barriers have a significant effect on the ability of an SME to realize its growth potential (Beck and De La Torre, 2007; Beck, Demirg and Honohan, 2009). It is widely agreed that there is a need for the subsidization of early-stage entrepreneurship, a rationale that arises from the often cited market failures in financing high-tech and innovative SMEs (Takalo and Tanayama, 2008).

As the OECD (2004) has noted in its work on the causes of the market failures affecting innovation financing of innovative SMEs, see Figure 6.1, there is significant uncertainty in returns with only a small number of investments providing any return, although a very small number will provide very significant returns; there are asymmetries of information affecting both entrepreneurs who do not understand the financing arrangements under which they may have to work and potential financiers who may not know all the relevant knowledge about the innovation in which they are about to invest; innovations, even when they exist in the form of a patent or are a trade secret, are difficult to price.

Causes of the Market Failure in Financing Innovative SMEs
• The returns to innovative activities are often skewed and highly uncertain.   • Entrepreneurs may possess more information about the nature and characteristics of their products and processes than potential financiers.   • Innovative activities are usually intangible thereby making the assessment of their monetary values difficult before they become commercially successful.

Figure 6.1 Causes of the market failure in financing innovative SMEs. Source: OECD (2004).

Since financing innovative SMEs is perceived as being too risky by many private investors, governments have stepped in to address the issue, which has led to 'a proliferation of government programmes to close perceived financing gaps faced by innovative SMEs' (OECD, 2004). The European Union, for its part, has recognized that many member states offer exemplary financing environments; as such, it has actively recommended the uptake of these practices across all member states. Likewise, the EU has taken steps towards ensuring more hospitable financial conditions for SMEs across Europe in accordance with the Lisbon Strategy (EC, 2006a).

A recent analysis concerning Canadian SMEs begins by stating, 'there is a substantial body of research . . . suggesting that problems arising from asymmetric information can lead to market failures in the financing of early-stage entrepreneurial ventures—much more than in other parts of the financial sector', and adds that the situation is further complicated by positive social externalities that the government may wish to foster but that the market cannot bring to bear in its financing decisions (Brander et al., 2008, p. 11). In Europe, this financing constraint on innovative early-stage businesses is claimed to be acute in the equity finance market in particular; European venture capitalists continue to focus on later-stage deals (EC, 2007b).

While the existence of such market failures are commonly cited, it must be said that the issue is controversial, especially when applied to all SMEs (rather than the specific group of innovative start-ups under consideration here) or all forms of finance (it has been argued that SME debt financing constraints are not as prevalent or severe as some suggest) (Gibb, 2000; OECD, 2006; Parker, 2002; Vos et al., 2007).

Signaling or Leveraging Rationale

Government partnering to finance SMEs can have the effect of certifying an entrepreneur by acting as a signal for private partners to enter into a new financing relationship (Takalo and Tanayama, 2008). The European Investment Fund (EIF), which is charged with the support of SMEs in particular, is now perceived to act often in this vein; its involvement in a venture capital fund is nearly mandatory for that fund to attract other investors. This signaling or de facto certification role manifests from the perception that the EIF (as a hybrid public institution) has a certain legitimacy coupled with the expertise to screen its investments with due diligence, thereby addressing the information asymmetries that may restrict private investments for innovative SMEs.

Public-Private Venture Capital

While goals have been identified and some progress has been made (see, for instance, EC, 2007a; NORDEN, 2009), the programs currently available within the EU have not yet created the best possible trans-border financing environment in support of high-technology start-ups and other fast-growing innovative firms. In light of this, the EU has expressed the desire to improve the position by shaping the host of public and public-private financing programs that give innovative European SMEs access to capital.

A panel of European business representatives was recently convened to provide their perspective on priorities for future European innovation policy. The panel concluded that 'the existing support for smaller or innovative companies (grants, seed or venture capital, loan guarantees) is fragmented', which leads to the suboptimal mobilization of private sector investment (Innovation Unlimited, 2009, p. 4). The hope is therefore to find appropriate policy solutions that will enable a better functioning and freer EU-wide investment environment in support of innovative SMEs.

The solution to the fragmentation problem can be dealt with by two policies that are compatible but that reflect different approaches and philosophies of intervention. On the one hand, extension of the single market for capital investment could increase the availability of capital; on the other, support schemes using hybrid capital could also enhance access to capital.

Joint Provision of Equity Funds

Venture capital investment that combines public and private money to provide equity financing is often called the hybrid fund(s) approach and is widespread in OECD economies. Hybrid venture capital funds take a number of forms and some have proved very beneficial to the economies in which they operate (e.g., Israel's Yozma (Avnimelech, Schwartz and Bar-El, 2007)).

Hybrid venture capital, in common with many policy instruments that might at first appear to be novel, is not new. The first example of this approach was the Small Business Investment Company (SBIC) fund in the US, which was created over half a century ago (Kennedy, 1961).

Examples of this policy approach are not uniformly successful by any means—for instance, an evaluation of all such UK funds has suggested a largely negative result, apart from one instance (Arnold, 2009). However, they are a popular prospect in the EU context for boosting what many see as a somewhat immature venture capital market.

Hybrid funds typically target the equity gap that affects small firms that have growth aspirations but that have difficulty in accessing capital to finance their expansion. Hybrid funds use government money to leverage private money; this is in contrast to purely public venture capital, such as France's ANVAR funds (now defunct), where the investment is solely public and acts more as a form of repayable grant[1] (Le Bas and Picard, 2006). The provision of public money in hybrid ventures provides a form of risk reduction for private investors that is held to act as an inducement for private firms to invest.

Goals of Government-Backed VC

Policy in this area is predicated upon the notion of market failures. As mentioned previously, while this is a commonly used concept, it is controversial when applied to SMEs in general or to points in a firm's life cycle other than the start-up and early stages. It is in the public's interest to correct the market failure because innovative SMEs create positive externalities in terms of employment, taxation and other public benefits, such as an increase in innovation and competitiveness in the society at large.

Policymakers believe that hybrid funds can deal with the market failure and thin market[2] aspects of the equity gap in the short term. Hybrid funds can help small firms grow that might be termed the rectification of a market failure. In the longer term such interventions may encourage structural changes to remedy the failure by creating new institutional capabilities and actors. PPP intervention, according to the rationale for government action, removes information asymmetries, allowing investors to locate growth firms in need of finance while also reducing the risk of ex post opportunistic behavior by firms or investors. Government policy should be clearly articulated in respect of whether it seeks to rectify market failures or to remedy them; often, however, this is not the case.

Most government schemes and indeed venture capital funds are clear about what types of firms they are seeking to invest in. However, there is sometimes confusion about whether the firms are high-growth in general or high-growth technology firms. Recent research on high-growth firms suggests that high technology firms are no more likely than low-tech firms to grow significantly. Even if this is so, it should not be policy to fund both types of firms if there is not a clear objective to do so, either in terms of welfare benefits or of market failures. The effectiveness of funds with multiple goals has been disputed (Pierrakis and Westlake, 2009).

The development of the EU venture capital industry suggests that there might well be a tendency for investors to focus on the later, more profitable stages of venture capital funding (i.e., acquisition, mergers, strategic alliances, and second offerings) because of the high costs and risks in making early stage investments work. Consequently, it may be possible to argue that the early stage of the financing life cycle will always be characterized by market failures. From this point of view it will be interesting to see how the Israeli venture capital market develops following the closure of the government hybrid fund equity provider Yozma,[3] as this scheme was seen to have corrected the failure. Unfortunately as yet, there are no studies that report on this question.

IMPLEMENTATION STRATEGIES

The design of a venture capital fund establishes the nature of the commitment of investors, the expectations of relative benefit and loss, and how risk will be shared. Design also involves deciding how to allocate tasks within the fund, including the all-important tasks of choosing firms in which to invest, the amounts to be invested and monitoring.

GIF: A (quasi) Fund of Funds at the EU Level
The High Growth Innovative Companies Financing Scheme (GIF) is an investment programme managed by the EIF in partnership with the Commission. It forms part of the SME support under the Competitiveness and Innovation Framework Programme (CIP).

GIF1 – EARLY STAGE
Innovative SMEs with high growth potential in their establishment or early stages < 10 years
Between 10% and 25% of total commitments.

GIF2 – EXPANSION STAGE
Innovative SMEs with high growth potential in their expansion stage
Between 7.5% and 15% of total commitments.

- Private-public partnership
- Commercially oriented/best market practices
- Minimum 50% of private investors
- Pari passu with private investors, catalytic effect (added value)
- Equity or quasi-equity investments in Intermediaries
- EIF operates as investor on behalf of the EC
- Fund agreements can be signed until 31 December 2013
- 5- to 12-year positions in Intermediaries
- Support for eco-innovation

Figure 6.2 A (quasi) fund-of-funds at the EU level. Source: Online. Available HTTP: www.eif.org (accessed 13 February 2012).

A design of particular interest to government investors is the funds-of-funds approach (such as GIF—see Figure 6.2), which typically employs one or more private sector contractors to invest the government's money on at least a *pari passu* (matching) basis with private investors in venture capital funds rather than directly in firms themselves. Funds-of-funds may be more desirable for government venture capital participation because individual firms are obscured in favor of supporting certain technologies, sectors or life-cycle stages.

In any fund, the general partner takes the role of investment manager, arranging the fund and making the investment decisions on the behalf of the other investors or limited partners. General partners may also take a stake in the fund, although this is normally small. The task of fund management is left to private sector specialists because they have specific experience and training and exceed government officials in their capabilities in this regard, and because the process of investment is thought to need to be politically independent.

For governments, there are two main areas of concern that affect the success of their hybrid fund investments. The first concern regards the policy goal to which the fund is addressed. At its simplest, the goal can be to increase the amount of capital available to finance constrained SMEs. But hybrid funds can be created to focus on particular areas or sectors that are seen to have social merit as well, such as eco-innovation, or to bolster innovation and competitiveness or even to support the venture capital market itself. The second area of concern is the risk the government wishes to run with its investment and what payoffs it demands for itself and will allow for the other partners. Specifically, what is the cushion that the government wishes to provide to the private investors? This concern is not easily separable from the first issue of the fund's policy goal, which may well affect its financial returns and therefore the ability to attract private investment partners.

A common principle widely promoted in the design of hybrid funds is *pari passu* or 'like risk, like reward'. The *pari passu* principle can be variously interpreted, but essentially it requires that government seeks equal investment from the private sector. While the principle is intended to ensure equality of treatment for both public and private investors and is a good working principle for the division of gains (Maula, Murray and Jääskeläinen, 2007), it can stand in the way of encouraging private sector investment when the prospect of a return is low, which would be the case where there is market failure, such as in the support of early-stage innovative SMEs. As has been argued (Jääskeläinen, Maula and Murray, 2007) if significant market failures are identified, it may be difficult for government to engage private investment partners at all unless return expectations are tempered and substantial risk reduction is offered by the public partner to the private partner.

In addition, when funds are targeted at low-quality investments, which are where market failures are most often located, high-quality investors and fund managers are hard to attract. Without significant cushioning in the form of risk reduction and higher rates of return, private investors are unlikely to invest. Where investment opportunities are likely to create social and environmental benefits, but where there is no regulatory requirement, private investors will invest only where there is significant asymmetry of payoff that favors their interests.

These issues suggest that the investing government, if pursuing a public policy goal that is foremost socially motivated, may be induced to accept greater risk and less reward in order to facilitate a hybrid fund's creation and survival. However, disregarding the *pari passu* principle may be a difficult position for policymakers to defend in the name of 'public' interest, especially in the case of negative financial returns for the government—for instance, the performance of US SBICs shows that for every dollar invested over the lifetime of the SBIC, the government had a retained interest of 78 cents, while private investors saw 130 cents (SBA, 2004).

Perhaps of even greater concern than the *pari passu* issue, the foundation of the hybrid model itself may be unworkable in the long run. As NESTA recently reported in the UK case, government 'subsidies weaken the exposure of fund managers to poor investment choices' while 'guarantees nullify the aim of demonstrating that institutional investors can make money in the equity gap' (Nightingale et al., 2009, p. 15). It appears that entrepreneurs who may seek such finance are aware of the weaker stance that hybrid and other constrained funds may have; they prefer to work with private, autonomous investment fund managers because they are perceived to take a more active role in their portfolio firms to create, through their expertise and guidance, larger returns (Bengtsson and Wang, 2010).

PATENT EXPLOITATION FUNDS

A novel form of venture capital fund, the patent exploitation fund or IPR fund, has begun to attract the interest of policymakers recently. It has been suggested that such funds will play an important role for the future of innovation in Europe (Innovation Unlimited, 2009). But will this new mechanism be a boon for innovative SMEs seeking finance?

In 2006, the EC considered the question by convening a workshop specifically to review the potential for leveraging IP rights to enable SMEs' access to finance. The discussion hinged on the premise that innovative firms, and especially high technology innovative firms, often have little in the way of tangible assets in the early stages of development and that the sale, or loan, of their IP rights could be a novel means to attract debt and equity finance.

A key issue here is in the valuation of IP; commercial valuation methodologies are not yet standardized and are thought to be less than objective (EC, 2006b). This is a significant problem that leads to the unwillingness of banks to accept this form of risk as collateral (Harhoff, 2009). Given the current concerns about the need to reduce systemic risk in the banking system, this proposal looks misguided at best and irresponsible at worst, unless safeguards can be found to reduce the risk. Another, perhaps more glaring issue, is that most SMEs do not hold patents at all (Barrell, 2009; EC, 2004; Leiponen and Byma, 2009; Rogers, Helmers and Greenhalgh, 2007); even if they do have a greater propensity than larger firms to patent, the validity of the proposals made for firms to access finance through their IPR is called seriously into question.

A uniform IP ratings model is needed to provide an objective metric for buyers; this would provide a means of quickly identifying and assessing an SME's technologies. Recognizing this need, the Initiative Finanzstandort Deutschland (IFD) has been creating a patent valuation guideline for German banks as a means to make them more willing to accept intellectual property as assets for securing loans for small innovative firms. At the same time, the French development bank Caisse des dépôts (CDC) is also addressing the issue of IPR valuation, but with a view to a Europe-wide standard system. It has recently partnered with Ocean Tomo, the foremost US merchant bank specializing in IP trading, to establish an EU patent rating platform that would be linked to the one operating in the US. CDC has also been working to create a Europe-wide IP trading market to support such funds.

Germany, being the major patenting member state in Europe, has already developed patent exploitation funds. There are now several such active funds, offered by the likes of Credit Suisse and Deutsche Bank. By mid-2008, these funds had been very successful, attracting over €300 million in investments. However, there is some doubt that the funds will be able to produce the kinds of returns necessary to keep investors interested, given the relatively small pool of patents that are available each year in Germany; it would be hard to diversify enough to ensure a suitable rate of return (Kollner, 2008).

In the active US and German examples, IP funds operate by purchasing patents outright and then bundling and licensing or selling them to offer returns to investors. The original patent holder may or may not be involved in commercializing the knowledge. This means of finance may therefore be less attractive to innovative SMEs but may serve to boost innovation in the society at large. As far as the financial merits of the model, the returns to investors have not yet been proven as the funds are too new (Wild, 2008).

It is envisaged that European IP funds, the kind that CDC is involved in supporting, will be foremost concerned with university patent valorization. Because researchers in university settings are necessarily more concerned with the academic merit of their work than with the potential to commercialize new findings, this approach to find value in latent IP appears sensible, although, as with science parks, expectations are likely to be unrealistically high. In the new approach to university-created IP, IPR fund managers would 'rent' university-generated patents, agglomerate them with related patents and license these out to user firms for commercialization. It must be said that in this instance the small to medium-sized enterprise, and certainly those struggling to find finance, will not be part of the equation— at least in the early stages of these new funds and markets. SMEs may be able to license in needed IP from these funds. However, most SMEs do not participate in patenting their own IP nor would they have the financial resources to acquire outside IP.

The role of government, and government-linked or backed bodies such as CDC, is important for creating the valuation standards that this realm of initiatives depends on. It is a complex arena in which to create policy, not least because the role of IP within innovation is complex and contested (Rigby and Miles, 2009). Furthermore, a recent gathering of experts on the topic suggested that there is a sizeable gap in our knowledge about the relationship between SMEs, patents and policy (IPO, 2009). While patent exploitation funds and markets may benefit innovation in the society at large, their role in supporting innovative SMEs looks to be very limited.

SUPPORT FROM THE WIDER INSTITUTIONAL FRAMEWORK

Sufficient venture capital funding in any economy and in any sector depends upon the possibility of a reasonable rate of return for private investors, if not also for the government. A variety of changes at institutional level can increase this rate of return, and therefore the flow of funds. For example, the development of stock exchanges that specialize in the shares of small firms can help, although in Europe, there have been few successes and a number of exchanges have had to close. The problems are well understood within the EU, which has diagnosed a number of problems and is working to rectify them (EC, 2007b). Action on taxation and on investment regulation (through mutual recognition of national schemes and also private placement regimes) offers some promise. The ongoing work to address structural issues of venture capital flow across borders is much needed. In particular there are taxation issues that hinder private investments as well as geographically focused mandates on public investments.

Finland, Sweden, Norway and Denmark offer a good example of the financial support that can be created by working together across borders. Their example also provides evidence of the considerable hindrances of moving this model of hybrid venture capital forward in the cross-border context (NORDEN, 2009). However, the main policy recommendations to achieve this goal, which were identified in 2006–2007, remain as yet unfulfilled. They included: ensuring fund investors are taxed only in their country of residence; ensuring VAT is not charged on fund management services; and explicitly disallowing taxation of foreign funds.

An example of the kind of legal and taxation issues faced can be found in Sweden's case, where there is perceived to be an inadequate link between the perceived acceptability of the kinds of venture capital arrangements allowed under the law (a limited liability company would provide the most attractive tax structure) and that which is deemed acceptable, or trustworthy, to the majority of international venture capital investors (who are accustomed to and prefer a limited partnership arrangement). This has caused a publicity issue for the venture capital industry in Sweden because many funds are located in tax havens as a result. The legal issues to solve this are being worked on.

While problems remain across the region, the operation of the Nordic venture capital industry is improving. Geographically restrictive barriers have been removed from most of the region's public and hybrid funds, and there are now discussions as to whether some funds should actually have a mandate for international cross-Nordic investment (NORDEN, 2009). In a similar vein, the nascent UK Innovation Fund also allows for international investment, though with a remit to retain the majority of the fund's benefits for its home country (Capital for Enterprise Ltd., 2008). The EU has been working to identify and suggest corrections to barriers for trans-border venture capital across the member states since at least 2007, including the adjustment of state aid rules to allow for freer investment in innovative SMEs as well as the continued monitoring and enforcement of free capital movement (EC, 2007a).

REFLECTION

There remain significant challenges for equity financing of SMEs in Europe, with or without a public element. This challenge has arisen, at least in part, because many of the key institutional players that would provide expertise in the allocation of equity financing are absent. Financially and socially profitable opportunities may not be exploited because small firms with the potential for high growth that could benefit from venture capital support are not necessarily receiving it.

A Paradox of EIF Success

Progress has been made by government institutions in filling the SME equity gap both in terms of money spent and expertise offered. The role of the quasi-governmental European Investment Fund (EIF) in supporting certain venture capital funds in Europe looks to have been positive. At the same time, the institution has not been able to create a robust pan-Europe venture capital market and some would see this as a failure.

EIF often acts as a cornerstone investor; its involvement as a limited partner in a range of funds acts as a signal to private investors to co-invest.

However, the EIF is involved as a limited partner in a significant number of funds, which may be reducing the signaling effect of such investments. The signaling effect falls as the proportion of schemes in which it is involved rises. In this way, the EIF may be seen to now play the role of an expensive certification mechanism; its involvement is becoming necessary as a minimum, rather than as specific stimulus to attract private investors. A challenge then is how to ensure that other investors of scale and quality are drawn in, particularly when general partners are in short supply and more profit for private investors can be made elsewhere in the venture funding cycle (i.e., not in early-stage financing needed by innovative SMEs but rather in buyouts).

While the current EIF approach has involved this corner-stoning and is likely to continue to do so, corner-stoning and signaling are practices not without risk. When investments are made by one party on the basis of the perceived reputation of other investing parties (i.e., signaling), the decision to invest is based substantially upon trust, and less upon diligent research to understand the investment's risk and reward possibilities. Much financial investment has taken place in this way in the past but it has not always had a successful conclusion; a number of unfortunate examples exist. As such, emphasis should be placed on the importance of all partners fully examining the investment prospect with due diligence, thus necessitating (and promoting) a minimum level of expertise by fund managers.

A Shortage of Capital or Expertise?

It is argued that venture capital may be available in sufficient quantities to finance small, high-growth firms that might need it; but there may not be enough expertise within the investment industry itself to identify these firms, carry out the due diligence, structure the deals and channel the funds to promising firms. While investment returns remain low, new capabilities will not be developed among fund managers, nor will new human capital be attracted to this field. Hence, the major challenge, which is an opportunity, is to re-develop expertise in this area.

While many believe that the sufficient condition for the health and growth of innovative SMEs is the availability of venture capital, this is in fact only one condition for success of Europe's innovative SMEs. Of equal importance is the provision of management expertise to these firms from proactive venture capital fund managers (Bengtsson and Wang, 2010).

Generally, successful venture capital investors generate profit when their portfolio comprises investments at different levels of maturity and when they are able to work with one firm longitudinally through to exit. Only when venture capital investors can hold portfolios that span the whole range of investment opportunities will firms at the early stage receive the capital and the expertise they require. Therefore, government venture financing that focuses solely on the finance gap at the early stage for innovative SMEs may be unhelpful for developing the venture capital industry itself and subsequently detrimental.

A further point for consideration is the geographic variation in the availability of investment opportunities for early-stage venture capital in high-growth SMEs. There are some regions where there are many opportunities and some where there are few. Increasing the level of venture capital through PPPs specifically in areas where there are few opportunities is not likely to have a significant impact upon the problem.

Schemes that allocate resources regionally have had a poor record in the US and UK. In their recent report, the UK National Audit Office found that regionally constrained funds had performed very poorly indeed: all nine such funds had a negative pooled return rate, with over a third of the public investment going towards management fees (NAO, 2009). Clearly this does not represent value for money on behalf of the taxpayers, nor does it serve to entice private investors. If the goal is to create a viable European venture capital industry, bolstered by public funding for early-stage innovative SMEs, placing geographic restraints on the government funding is counterproductive.

Investment Readiness

Discussion of innovation financing policy often centers on the lack of suitable investor expertise and the insufficiency of the private sources of finance. Policy interventions have in fact been almost exclusively on this 'supply' side of the SME finance equation (Mason, 2009). However, some policymakers have begun to focus on the skills and capabilities of innovating firms themselves. While innovating firms may have a technological lead, they often face a shortage of expertise in knowing where to look for innovation financing, in business strategy and marketing, leadership skills and employee development.

Conventionally, entrepreneurs of early-stage firms rely on business angels and on venture capital investors for these forms of expertise. But when suitable opportunities are not available, firms may stagnate. To assist firms in this predicament, governments have begun to provide business coaching and other investment readiness programs.

Business coaching programs are both complementary and an alternative measure to innovation financing. They are thought largely to be supportive of financing innovative SMEs under the policy umbrella of creating 'investment readiness.' The use of these schemes could be hugely beneficial to SMEs, particularly given the absence of suitable skills within investor firms.

Investment readiness programs speak to the demand-side issues inherent in the equity finance arena in the EU. While many initiatives to bolster the supply of venture capital for early-stage SMEs have been deployed, the

---

LINC Scotland: Investment Facilitation Grant
This government-run grant scheme enables investors to cost-effectively pursue opportunities that they might otherwise have rejected. Potential investee companies apply in response to the feedback they received from potential investors on what issues need to be resolved to make them investable (e.g., costs relating to market analysis and access, technology validation, legal due diligence). The grant, which is limited to a maximum of £15,000 of eligible costs, becomes convertible into LINC Scotland equity if the investment goes ahead.

Figure 6.3   LINC Scotland: Investment Facilitation Grant. Source: Mason and Harrison (2004).

firms seeking capital must first be worthy of it, be able to find it and also willing to accept it in the form of an outsider having a stake in their nascent firm. Entrepreneurs who are new to the venture capital game may be fearful of sharing control of their company while also being unprepared to present their business in a way that best displays their investment worthiness (EC, 2006b). One such government program to facilitate private or hybrid investment readiness in firms that were initially rejected by venture capital investors has been deployed in Scotland (see Figure 6.3).

Business angel networks have been actively identifying the issues inherent in investment readiness in an effort to create robust programs at both regional and pan-European levels. A recent review by the European Business Angel Network identified eighteen investment readiness programs across six European countries (Mason and Harrison, 2004). However, many of these programs focus on the easiest to fix problems—finding finance opportunities, presentation skills and business plan writing, while the issues concerning 'diagnostics and business support' are left unaddressed (Mason, 2009).

Policy Approaches

Here we suggest new policy approaches that may support the financing of innovative SMEs in partnership with private actors with the public goal of increasing innovation across Europe.

As discussed here, policies to support innovative SMEs' access to equity finance should be constructed to better entice high-quality private investment partners and better provide SMEs with independent, active management expertise. In addition, if government wishes to pursue hybrid venture funding, it may prove best to focus on the funds-of-funds approach rather than traditional, individual firm-based venture funds.

Returns to Private Partners Must Be Attractive

The *pari passu* principle, while regarded as a sensible basis on which to share investment returns, is likely to be regarded as unacceptable to private finance partners in government-supported, early-stage innovation-focused venture capital funds because of the generally low historical returns here. There are two immediate implications; firstly, the most discriminating investors will not be attracted to government partnering because of low returns; secondly, hybrid portfolio SMEs will not be in receipt of the best managerial skills available. SMEs perceive this qualitative difference in hybrid funds versus pure funds and it is the latter that they most desire to work with because the benefits to their firm are thought to be greater. The expertise and human capital component of venture fund involvement in an SME should not be underestimated. As such, it seems necessary that *pari passu* clauses in hybrid funds should be rethought. Schemes to promote, or leverage, high-quality, knowledgeable private sector investors and managers will work only when attractive returns are available to them. Deals could be structured to direct the monetary returns in favor of the private partner while the public partner continues to reap the social benefits.

However, as the recent UK National Audit Office report (Arnold, 2009; NAO, 2009) points out, such uneven return structures may further erode any value for money arguments that are put forward as justification for this type of business support. They point especially to the case of the very poorly performing Regional Venture Capital Funds, where the UK government will see an investment return only if the funds outperform the preferential 10 percent return to other investors. It is clearly difficult to justify such investment in a traditional manner focused on monetary returns.

In view of this, it is doubly important that the goals of any such fund include not only a positive rate of return for at least the private investor but also the greater social/business goals of the government partner (such as creating a robust venture capital market; supporting innovation). Such elucidation from the outset will enable better evaluation of the fund, especially on behalf of the public investor.

Rethinking Arm's-Length Investing

Whichever forms the EU decides to take to promote venture capital investment in European SMEs, policymakers should consider the issue of keeping investments 'at arm's length.' While it is politically undesirable for government or quasi-government programs to have a stake in the success or failure of any one particular private firm, it is equally undesirable to have venture fund management that is unwilling to get personally engaged in the management and direction of its portfolio firms (Bengtsson and Wang, 2010).

The human capital element of venture fund investment is a determinant of a receiving firm's success. Fund managers who have personal entrepreneurial and business management experience as well as a track record of venture investments are best suited to guiding a nascent SME to a successful IPO, thus reaping monetary rewards for themselves and providing the best possible platform for the SME to continue to grow, creating jobs and deploying innovation in society at large.

Arm's-length investments are not appropriate for the SMEs themselves, nor does this approach aid in the creation of competent fund managers. Therefore, the EU should support private venture funds foremost; vehicles such as funds-of-funds would then be the best strategy for government involvement in venture capital.

An EU Fund-of-Funds for Innovation

An EU-wide fund-of-funds for innovation, perhaps expanding on the CIP's GIF initiative, may prove to be beneficial to both innovative SMEs and the underdeveloped EU venture capital market. While the GIF mechanism under the CIP acts as a quasi-fund-of-funds, there is potentially room to expand this or create a new EU fund-of-funds specifically focused on innovation. The fund could be developed by the Commission in partnership with the EIF, with attention paid to harnessing the best sectoral knowledge available from each organization to design the fundamental investment strategy. The fund would need to be managed by EIF investment management professionals or an independent third party with EC oversight. The danger of such direct oversight of fund managers by governmental departments has been highlighted in the UK case (Arnold, 2009; NAO, 2009).

In the creation and deployment of such a fund, the time scale under investment consideration would be important. On the one hand, the commercialization of innovations, especially high technology ones, will need perhaps a decade or longer to realize returns; and early-stage venture capital funds are thought to take at least eight years to see investment returns (NAO, 2009). On the other hand, it would be ideal to draw on the example of Israel's Yozma fund, whereby the fund has—as a goal from the outset—the correction of market gaps or failures, and once this goal is realized the fund is shut down to allow for the private sector to establish the relevant institutions and improve information quality.

Given the public-private partnership nature of such a program, great care must be taken to establish the financial case for the investments and which form of market failures the fund-of-funds policy addresses. While there would be scope to operate the fund-of-funds with a view towards supporting innovations that address social challenges, there is the additional challenge of supporting the creation of an EU-wide venture capital market. These two goals may be in conflict and the balance between them is an important consideration in the design of such a policy. In addition, full transparency must be embedded in the process of creating and running the funds (NAO, 2009, p. 8).

Further Research Directions

As mentioned earlier, the issue of whether innovative SMEs do in fact face market failures in procuring financial support remains controversial. Therefore, all policy predicated on the existence of a finance gap would benefit greatly from a better understanding of, if and where this gap exists.

The OECD (OECD, 2006) states that there is no systematic market failure in the area of the provision of finance for SMEs generally, although problems may exist in the area of innovative small firms. Considering this smaller set of firms that seek to grow and that might experience greater risk in doing so, evidence of their experiencing market failure could be said to exist if support schemes had led to higher levels of performance among them. As Nightingale et al. (2009) argue (for NESTA), in the case of the UK, where such policies have been widely tried, there is no evidence as yet at all:

> UK government support for equity investment has been justified in terms of a market failure. Specifically a market failure in the provision of equity finance within the funding gap. Policy has been based on the assumption that if funding is provided then high potential firms being held back by (only) a lack of funding will be able to achieve their full potential. The current solutions on offer have not (to date) produced the disproportionately higher performance firms seen in US VCs' early-stage investment portfolios. Whatever problems UK firms have, they are more complex than a lack of funding alone. (Nightingale et al., 2009, p.20)

We conclude by noting the skeptical views of Murray (2008), who reminds policymakers that 'Market failure (is) often used as a justification for public policy without rigorous empirical or theoretical support'. (Murray, 2008, p. 1) Could it be that the supply side of the presumed equity gap may be much less of an issue than the demand side? Might it be the case that small firms need investment readiness programs, good advice and other non-monetary support more than financiers need extra capital to invest or a better venture capital infrastructure? Clearly, more research is required.

NOTES

1. 'In the case under observation [ANVAR] the form of the financial support is in the form of a grant that (normally) must be reimbursed by the applicant. This form of financial support does not match precisely the usual definition of venture capital. But the ventures are risky and uncertain, the developments are in their early stages, and the grants are clearly not one of the other

forms of equity investment. Thus, we will follow Lerner (2002) who first suggested that public agencies may act as public venture capitalists' (Le Bas and Picard, 2006, p. 187).
2. Thin markets are held to exist where there are insufficient participants to ensure the costs of trading are low enough and the frequency of trading is sufficient for effective price disclosure.
3. Yozma effectively created the Israeli venture capital market in 1993 through the formation of its first venture fund, Yozma I. Originating from a government program aimed at prompting venture investments in Israel, Yozma I has transformed the domestic landscape of private equity investments. Over a period of three years, the Group established ten drop-down funds, each capitalized with more than $20 million. In parallel Yozma started making direct investments in start-up companies. This marked the beginning of a professionally managed venture capital market in Israel. Online. Available HTTP: www.yozma.com (accessed 13 February 2012).

BIBLIOGRAPHY

Arnold, M. (2009) 'Watchdog Lists Flaws in Venture Spending'. *Financial Times.* 10 December.

Avnimelech, G., Schwartz, D. and Bar-El, R. (2007) 'Entrepreneurial High-Tech Cluster Development: Israel's Experience with Venture Capital and Technological Incubators'. *European Planning Studies* 15 (9): 1181–1198.

Barrell, R. (2009) 'Fiscal Stimulus—How Do We Get Ourselves Out of Recession?' Everyday Economics Seminar. National Audit Office, National Institute of Economic and Social Research. London. 18 February.

Bascha, A. and Walz, U. (2007) 'Financing Practices in German Venture Capital Industry: An Empirical Study'. In Gregoriou, G., Kooli, M. and Kraussl, R. (eds.), *Venture Capital in Europe*, 217–232 Oxford: Elsevier Science & Technology.

Beck, T. and De La Torre, A. (2007) 'The Basic Analytics of Access to Financial Services'. *Financial Markets, Institutions and Instruments* 16 (2): 79–117.

Beck, T., Demirg, K. A. and Honohan, P. (2009) 'Access to Financial Services: Measurement, Impact, and Policies'. *World Bank Research Observer* 24 (1): 119–145.

Bengtsson, L. and Wang, F. (2010) 'What Matters in Venture Capital: Evidence from Entrepreneurs' Stated Preferences'. *Financial Management* 39 (4): 1367–1401.

Capital for Enterprise Ltd. (2008) 'Enterprise Capital Funds: Guidance for Applicants'. April. London: BERR.

Brander, J. A. ., Egan, E., Hellmann, T. F. (2008) Government Sponsored Versus Private Venture Capital:Canadian Evidence, NBER Working Paper Series Working Paper 14029. Online. Available: HTTP http://www.nber.org/papers/w14029 (accessed 4 July 2012)

EC. (2004) Innobarometer. Online. Available HTTP: http://www.proinno-europe.eu/page/admin/uploaded_documents/Innobarometer_2004.pdf

EC. (2006a) 'Financing SME Growth—Adding European Value'. Communication from the Commission to the Council, the European Parliament, the European Economic and Social Committee and the Committee of the Regions Implementing the Community Lisbon Programme.

EC. (2006b) 'Intellectual Property and Access to Finance for High-Growth SMEs'. Summary report of the workshop. Brussels. 14 November. Brussels: Directorate-General for Enterprise and Industry.

EC. (2007a) 'Removing Obstacles to Cross-Border Investments by Venture Capital Funds'. COM (2007) 853 final. Brussels: Commission of the European Communities.

EC. (2007b) 'Removing Obstacles to Cross-Border Investment by Venture Capital Funds'. SEC(2007)1719.

EIB. (2004) 'The EIBs Role in Public-Private Partnerships (PPPs)'. Luxembourg: European Investment Bank.

Gibb, A. A. (2000) 'SME Policy, Academic Research and the Growth of Ignorance, Mythical Concepts, Myths, Assumptions, Rituals and Confusions'. *International Small Business Journal* 18 (3): 13–35. doi: 10.1177/0266242600183001.

Harhoff, D. (2011) 'The Role of Patents and Licenses in Securing External Finance for Innovation', In Audretsch, D. B., Falck, O., Heblich, S. and Lederer, A. (eds), Handbook of Research Innovation and Entrepreneurship, 55–73. Massachusetts: Edward Elgar.

IMF. (2004) 'Public-Private Partnerships'. Prepared by the Fiscal Affairs Department in consultation with other departments, the World Bank, and the Inter-American Development Bank. Washington, DC: International Monetary Fund.

Innovation Unlimited. (2009) 'Reinventing Europe through Innovation: From a Knowledge Society to an Innovation Society'. Business panel report on future EU innovation policy consultation. Online. Available HTTP: http://ec.europa.eu/enterprise/policies/innovation/files/panel_report_en.pdf (accessed 14 February 2012).

IPO. (2009) 'The Economic Value of Intellectual Property: An Agenda for Policy Relevant Research'. UK Intellectual Property Office.

Jääskeläinen, M., Maula, M. and Murray, G. (2007) 'Profit Distribution and Compensation Structures in Publicly and Privately Funded Hybrid Venture Capital Funds'. *Research Policy* 36 (7): 913–929.

Kennedy, R. (1961) 'The SBIC—A New Concept in Finance'. *The Southwestern Social Science Quarterly* 42 (3): 240–249.

Kollner, M. (2008) 'Patent Party'. *Intellectual Asset Management* June/July: 56.

Le Bas, C. and Picard, F. (2006) 'Models for Allocating Public Venture Capital to Innovation Projects: Lessons from a French Public Agency'. *International Journal of Technology Management* 34: 1–2: 185–198.

Leiponen, A. and Byma, J. (2009) 'If You Cannot Block, You Better Run: Small Firms, Cooperative Innovation, and Appropriation Strategies'. *Research Policy* 38 (9): 1478–1488.

Lerner, J. (2002) 'When Bureaucrats Meet Entrepreneurs: The Design of Effective "Public Venture Capital" Programmes'. *Economic Journal* 112 (477): 73–84.

Mason, C. and Harrison, R. T. (2004) 'Improving Access to Early Stage Venture Capital in Regional Economies: A New Approach to Investment Readiness'. *Local Economy* 19: 18.

Mason, G. (2009) 'Public Policy Support for the Informal Venture Capital Market in Europe: A Critical Review'. *International Small Business Journal* 27 (5): 536–556. doi: 10.1177/0266242609338754.

Maula, M., Murray, G. and Jääskeläinen, M. (2007) 'Public Financing of Young Innovative Companies in Finland'. Helsinki: Ministry of Trade and Industry.

Morallos, D. and Amekudzi, A. (2008) 'The State of the Practice of Value for Money Analysis in Comparing Public Private Partnerships to Traditional Procurements'. *Public Works Management Policy* 13 (2): 114–125. doi:10.1177/1087724x08326176.

Murray, G. (2008) 'Market Failure: The Last Refuge of a Scoundrel?' Southwest of England Regional Development Agency.

NAO. (2009) 'Venture Capital Support to Small Businesses'. National Audit Office.

Nightingale, P., Murray, G., Cowling, M., Baden-Fuller, C., Mason, C., Siepel, J., Hopkins, M. and Dannrether, C. (2009) 'From Funding Gaps to Thin Markets: UK Government Support for Early-Stage Venture Capital'. Research report from BVCA and NESTA. London: NESTA.

NORDEN. (2009) 'Obstacles to Nordic Venture Capital Funds'. Nordic Innovation Center.

OECD. (2004) 'Financing Innovative SMEs in a Global Economy'. Promoting Entrepreneurship and Innovative SMEs in a Global Economy: Towards a More Responsible and Inclusive Globalization. Paris: OECD (Organization for Economic Co-operation and Development). Online. Available HTTP: http://www.oecd.org/dataoecd/6/11/31919231.pdf (accessed 20 June 2012).

OECD. (2006) 'The SME Financing Gap: Volume 1: Theory and Evidence'. Paris: Organization for Economic Cooperation and Development.

Parker, S. (2002) 'Do Banks Ration Credit to New Enterprises? And Should Governments Intervene?' *Scottish Journal of Political Economy* 49 (2): 162–195.

Pierrakis, Y. and Westlake, S. (2009) 'Reshaping the UK Economy: The Role of Public Investment in Financing Growth'. Research report. NESTA.

Rigby, J. and Miles, I. (2009) 'IPR and Innovation Are Good for Each Other—An Open or Shut Case?' Paper presented at the PATINNOVA Conference, Prague. 28–30 April.

Rogers, M., Helmers, C. and Greenhalgh, C. (2007) 'An Analysis of the Characteristics of Small and Medium Enterprises That Use Intellectual Property'. Online. Available HTTP: http://84.12.207.146/ipresearch-characteristics-200710.pdf (accessed 14 February 2012).

SBA. (2004) 'Small Business Investment Company Program Financial Performance Report for Cohorts 1994–2004'. Washington, DC: Small Business Administration.

Shaoul, J. (2005) 'Megaprojects and Risk: An Anatomy of Ambition'. *Housing Studies* 20 (1): 169–171.

Takalo, T. and Tanayama, T. (2008) 'Adverse Selection and Financing of Innovation: Is There a Need for R&D Subsidies?' Research discussion papers. Helsinki: Bank of Finland.

Vos, E., Yeh, A. J.-Y., Carter, S. and Tagg, S. (2007) 'The Happy Story of Small Business Financing'. *Journal of Banking & Finance* 31 (9): 2648–2672.

Weihe, G. (2006) 'Public-Private Partnerships: Addressing a Nebulous Concept'. WP No. 16. International Center for Business and Politics, Copenhagen Business School.

Wild, J. (2008) 'Mixed Views on German Patent Investment Funds'. *IAM Magazine* blog. 27 May. Online. Available HTTP: http://www.iam-magazine.com/blog/Default.aspx?archive=May+2008&pn=1 (accessed 22 June 2012).

Yescombe, E. R. (2007) *Public-Private Partnerships: Principles of Policy and Finance*. Oxford: Elsevier/Butterworth-Heinemann.

7 Microfinance and Innovation

Ian Miles and Yanuar Nugroho

INTRODUCTION

Financing innovation has been a long-standing concern. It has been prominent in the EU, where there is a widespread view that raising such finance is more difficult than in the US. Lack of finance regularly appears as a major issue in media debates, and this is supported empirically. It is cited as a major obstacle to innovation by firms responding to the Community Innovation Survey (CIS) (Canepa and Stoneman, 2002; 2008; Hölzl and Janger, 2011). At the time of the 'dot com bubble', venture capital became a major source of R&D and other innovation funding. Many small firms raised funds from this source for pursuing their (sometimes) new ideas. The 'dot com crash' led to less emphasis on venture capital's innovation-supporting role of venture capital. It may well return to prominence in the future, but the economic crisis from 2008 and beyond has posed questions about the future role of all types of financing instruments, and many firms—even large and established ones—have been experiencing difficulty in raising finance.

Microfinance has proven resilient during previous financial crises,[1] and there are high hopes that microfinance will prove to be robust and even become more vital in the present economic crisis. It is hoped that microfinance will remain a viable tool for development and that it will support the financing of innovation both in developing and developed economies. This chapter explores the prospects for the role of microfinance in innovation.

Microfinance has long been proposed as providing instruments for stimulating entrepreneurship in developing and economically deprived countries and regions. The original motivation for this interest was mainly the alleviation of poverty. Even before the current economic crisis, microfinance had attracted attention from investment companies, given evidence that it could deliver impressive returns.

Policymakers, too, have given attention to microfinance, not just in the context of development, but also in terms of possible solutions to the problems small firms face in more industrialized countries. Most attention has been focused on issues such as support for peripheral and deprived regions and for socially excluded groups. Despite some rhetoric, relatively little analysis has dealt with microfinance as an alternative route to financing innovation.

This chapter reviews the relevant available material, focusing on empirical studies of microfinance, rather than on prescriptive arguments and proposals for sophisticated new designs for instruments. Microfinance *for* innovation has attracted little analysis to date, although there are streams of work on (a) microfinance *as* innovation itself—examining the blockages, barriers, success factors and agents of change, and (b) innovation *for* microfinance—the role of technological and organizational innovation in supporting microfinance. These can tell us things about the orientation to innovation of those involved in microfinance, and about the sort of innovation required for microfinance instruments to be able to support innovation more generally.

MICROFINANCE

What Is Microfinance?

The World Bank defines 'microfinance' as financial services provision to low-income clients, including consumers and the self-employed (Ledger-wood, 2000). These clients are usually borrowers who are considered 'unbankable' by conventional financial services, and who, though they may well be experiencing financial difficulties, may have loan repayment rates as high as 97 percent (Callaghan et al., 2007).[2]

Microfinance can include small-scale financial services—loans, remittances, insurance and savings—that reflect the heterogeneity of their clients' financial needs. In practice, the term is often used more narrowly to refer to '*microcredit*'[3] services, provided by microfinance institutions (MFIs), to deliver loans to unsalaried borrowers with little or no collateral. In most cases, MFIs make small loans to clients in developing countries. Such loans may be as little as $50. In contrast, in the EU context, and reflecting the higher costs and incomes encountered, microcredit was defined (in 2003) as loans below €25,000 (EC, 2003b) that could help microenterprises—that is, businesses with fewer than ten employees including small entrepreneurs, and with turnovers (or balance sheet totals) less than €2 million (EC, 2003a).

Other financial products targeted at poor and low-income people are often included within the scope of microfinance. These include savings, insurance, money transfers and other similar instruments. MFIs provide various financial products and services, such as insurance and provision for deposits, as well as business training and networking opportunities, tailored to the needs of their specific client set.

Most of the relevant literature and discussion focuses on a fairly narrow set of instruments, especially microcredit. It remains to be seen how far the arguments and results that are presented in this literature might apply to deal with these different instruments. The shared characteristic of these services relates to their size—that is, they are *microfinancing*. Features such as the legal status of client enterprises, their collateral requirements, method of delivery, geographical context, funding institution or the use of services are a secondary matter in definitional terms (Callaghan et al., 2007).

A size-based definition reflects the general assumption that lower-income groups and those with restricted access to finance tend to use smaller-scale financial services. As microfinance is designed to help those excluded from access to formal financial services to fund their income-producing activities, build assets, provide stability and protect against risks, such services are not limited to credit and can include savings (deposit), insurance and money transfers. Microcredit and saving (deposit) services are most commonly researched. Microfinance has gained recent attention as an important new financial service. For example, the UN declared 2005 the 'International Year of Micro-Credit', and the 2006 Nobel Peace Prize was awarded to Muhammad Yunus, the founder of Grameen Bank in Bangladesh (Callaghan et al., 2007).

How Does Microfinance Work?

Microfinance services include loans, saving and money transfers—involving small amounts of money for clients that traditional financial institutions would not deem creditworthy. Typically, to acquire credit from an MFI, loans are secured against the 'honor' of a peer group of clients—that is, social collateral, rather than against personal collateral. If a client fails to make repayments, others in the lending circle will be denied future credit. Thus, the peer group takes on joint liability and acts to ensure loan repayment. Peer pressure encourages borrowers to be selective about their group members and to repay loans completely and on time. Hence, high repayment rates are common, but there are suggestions that, for various reasons, group lending mechanisms may not work well in Europe, or certain parts of Europe.

In terms of financing for innovation, it remains unclear just how far such financing encourages or discourages novel types of risk and enterprise. Social psychologists, for example, talk of 'risky shift' behavior when groups take riskier decisions than would their members do as individuals. A concise summary of 156 references on this topic was presented by Myers and Lamm as long ago as 1976.

Microfinance loans usually demonstrate shorter cycles than traditional commercial loans—for example, 6–12 months of payments and interest due weekly. Such shorter loan and payment cycles help the borrowers stay current, preventing them from being overwhelmed by large payments. This is the rationale for MFIs to charge interest rates that are relatively high (e.g., around 35 percent per year), in part because these cycles make running microfinance schemes expensive.

MFIs' main sources of finance are usually charities, governments and international organizations. Donor and subsidy capital is not unlimited; the microfinance industry may need to become more self-sufficient in financing if it is to grow enough to serve its potential market. Recently, structured financing for microfinance institutions, offering returns to investors at market rates that are commensurate with risk, have been developed. Such transactions may increase the access of microfinance institutions to public financing markets.

ACTORS IN MICROFINANCE AND MAJOR TYPES OF MICROFINANCE INSTITUTIONS

Helms identifies *four categories of microfinance providers* (Helms, 2006, p. 35–57). He argues that each requires a proactive strategy of engagement to help providers achieve the goals of the microfinance movement:

- *Informal financial service providers.* Moneylenders, pawnbrokers, savings collectors, money-guards, Rotating Savings and Credit Associations (ROSCAs), Accumulating Savings and Credit Associations (ASCAs) and input supply shops. As they share the same community, they understand each other's financial circumstances and can offer flexible, convenient and quick services. These services can also be costly, with the choice of financial products limited and short-term. Informal services that involve savings are also relatively risky.
- *Member-owned organizations.* Self-help groups, credit unions and hybrid organizations, such as 'financial service associations' and CVECAs (from the French *Caisse Villageoise d'Epargne et de Crédit Autogérée*, a self-reliant village savings and credit bank). They are generally small and local, with good knowledge about each other's financial circumstances; they offer convenience and flexibility. Although the costs of operation are low, these providers may have little financial skill, and can run into trouble in an economic downturn or dealing with complex operations.
- *NGOs (non-governmental organizations).* By the end of 2005, there were 3,133 microcredit NGOs lending to about 113 million clients.[4] These NGOs have spread around the developing world in the past three decades and proven innovative in developing banking techniques such as solidarity lending, village banking and mobile banking, which are claimed to have overcome barriers to serving poor populations.
- *Formal financial institutions.* Commercial banks, state banks, agricultural development banks, savings banks, rural banks and non-bank financial institutions. These are regulated and supervised bodies offering a wide range of financial services, usually controlling branch networks that can extend nationally and internationally.

Typical microfinance clients are low-income individuals, especially in the developing world, who do not have access to formal financial institutions. Microfinance is often used to support or start small-scale entrepreneurial or self-employed ventures, often household-based. With appropriate regulation and policy, MFIs can assist in solving the main problem of microfinance from the financial perspective of lenders ensuring that clients will repay loans and interest.

Major types of MFI are as follows:

- *The cooperative model.* Inspired by the success of cooperatives in Europe and North America at the end of the 19th century, this was the first model for microfinance in developing countries. The cooperative members are the owners, contributing to the equity capital through shares, and loans are granted only to them. Cooperative MFIs focus solely on the provision of financial services.
- *Solidarity credit groups.* Here, three to ten clients join a group to receive access to financial services (primarily credit), on the condition that they will have saved some money before being able to receive a loan. In addition, non-financial services are offered to group members, such as training or access to market information. Group members collectively guarantee loan repayment, and access to subsequent loans is given only once previous loans are paid in full.
- *Village banks.* The village bank is effectively a mix between the cooperative and solidarity group models, seeking to capitalize on the advantages of each. The village bank usually has fewer members than a cooperative, and is less formalized and complex in structure. Some international NGOs promote the establishment of village banks. Their main form of credit guarantee relies on peer pressure among members, as is the case in solidarity credit groups.
- *The linkage model.* This model builds on existing informal self-help groups, such as rotating credit and savings associations (Sika and Strasser, 2000). A self-help promoting institution (SHPI, usually an NGO) helps groups of 10–15 individuals through an incubation period after which the bank lends to the groups in a single or multi-period. Once the link is established, the SHPI supervises the loan portfolio. There is no particular incentive for the SHPI, however.
- *Microbanks with individual financial contracts.* There are other MFIs that are member-based, with members contributing to their management, ownership and control of the MFI. Microbanks (e.g., BancoSol in Bolivia) are a case in point, relying on individual contracts between the institution and its client. Although this type of MFI is closest to the conventional banks, the loan collateral approaches are usually non-conventional.

CAPITAL STRUCTURE AND THE EXPANSION OF MICROFINANCE

Most MFIs employ high leverage, and finance their operations with long-term, as opposed to short-term, debt. Highly leveraged microfinance institutions perform better by reaching out to a wider clientele, enjoying economies of scale, and thus being better able to deal with moral hazard and adverse selection, enhancing their ability to deal with risk (Kyereboah-Coleman, 2007).

Various factors other than stage in the life cycle seem to be associated with the performance of MFIs. Bogan (2008), for example, finds MFIs' size of assets and capital structure to relate to their performance. Asset size is important for sustainability and outreach. A measure of grants received by MFIs from donors such as charities, governments and international organizations as a percentage of assets is significantly and negatively related to sustainability, and is positively related to MFI cost per borrower. Bogan also finds evidence indicating that the use of grants drives down MFI's operational self-sufficiency. Bogan suggests that long-term use of grants means less of the competitive pressures associated with attracting market funding, and this may lead to less efficient operations. Since the results do not demonstrate that grants are related to greater or more costly outreach, it may be that (in some real-life circumstances) dependence on grants can hinder MFIs' development into competitive, efficient, sustainable operations (Bogan, 2008).

A few years ago, one estimate determined that more than 67 million households were served by microfinance programs (Armendáriz de Aghion and Morduch, 2005, p. 3); but an earlier benchmark in 2004, established through an analysis of 'alternative financial institutions' in the developing world (Christen, Rosenberg and Jayadeva, 2004), counted approximately 665 million client accounts. These used over three thousand institutions who were serving clients poorer than those served by the commercial banks. Of these accounts, 120 million were with institutions normally understood to practice microfinance. Gonzalez (2007) analyzed data from 2,207 MFIs—representing 77 million borrowers in one hundred countries—and concluded that most MFIs are concentrated in South Asia and sub-Saharan Africa, while most borrowers are concentrated in South Asia and East Asia/Pacific region.[5]

MICROFINANCE IN EUROPE

Though credit unions and similar instruments have already been in existence for many decades, European microfinance is often traced to the introduction of microcredit in Central and Eastern Europe after the fall of the Berlin Wall. With the banking sector unable to respond to emerging needs, microcredit filled the gap by providing transitional support for people needing to enhance their livelihoods. In a relatively short time, MFIs in Central and Eastern Europe and in the newly independent states had attracted more than 1.7 million borrowers and 2.3 million depositors, with an average client growth rate of 30 percent, per year. In addition to MFIs, NGOs are also involved in the provision of microfinance in Eastern Europe. Commercial banks, too, are increasingly interested. They downscale in order to provide microloans for the poor. It is not clear from the published accounts if, and to what extent, small companies are explicitly included. The microfinance sector thereby continues to expand and become more structured.[6]

In Western Europe, microfinance remains a fairly recent phenomenon, despite some historical background through institutions such as the Raiffeisen Bank (Germany), lending charities (England) and the cooperative model of the 'Casse rurali' (Italy). The growth of MFIs has been more limited, although interest in their potential seems to be increasing. In the Netherlands, for example, the *Committee for Microfinancing* sees microfinance as having great potential in encouraging entrepreneurship, boosting economic growth and helping to integrate disadvantaged groups and reduce unemployment. This can be done through various local initiatives to help target groups access simple funding models and coaching networks (Committee for Microfinancing, 2007). Further, the Dutch government takes the position that 'micro-credits must become available for individuals wishing to start their own business, with extra attention being paid to entrepreneurs in the . . . disadvantaged neighbourhoods' (p. 5).

In other countries such as Spain, France, UK and Finland, too, microfinance has been supported as encouraging small and medium enterprises (SMEs). This is closely related to the tendency, in the EU, to see microfinance as primarily being a tool for *economic growth* and *social cohesion* (EMN/MFC/cdfa, 2007). SMEs are seen as drivers of job creation and economic growth—often as the only bright hopes for private sector employment in many disadvantaged regions. The argument that they can be important innovators is usually at best secondary. Although microfinance was initially viewed as an economic issue—promoting entrepreneurship—the correlation between lack of access to finance and social exclusion has been increasingly acknowledged. Many small and medium enterprises (SMEs) and families lack access to financial services despite the existing banking network, and financial exclusion is concentrated among those suffering from poverty and social marginalization. This has economic as well as social impacts. The ability of the banking system to reach and serve such small entities is crucial for the achievement of general socioeconomic improvement. Exclusion from banking services often constitutes a major obstacle to the launch of new business activities (Evers, 2007; Evers and Lahn, 2006). Microfinance services can fill this gap, since microcredit can help foster entrepreneurship by facilitating business start-ups, and granting microloans to unemployed and marginalized people can make them economically independent players, able to participate more fully in a financial society. Hence, microcredit should play an important role in strategies for growth, employment and social cohesion (such as the European Union's Lisbon Strategy).

Micro and small enterprises form the core of the Western European economic system, representing 99 percent of the two million start-up enterprises that are created every year. One-third of these enterprises are launched by unemployed people.[7] In the EU context, some recent research has studied influences on the capital structure of European SMEs (Viviani et al., 2008). Since nearly all (99.8 percent) of European companies (over twenty million firms) can be classified as SMEs, the EC defines these as 'the real giants of the European economy[8]' (Euractiv, 2006a; 2006b). The issue of the financing of SMEs is thus very important in the European context.[9] Viviani et al. (2008) suggest that debt is generally the most important funding source for SMEs, as it represents 60 percent of total assets. The major part of the debt is composed of short-term loans, access to which may be less a strategic choice than an instantaneous and uncontrolled necessity. It seems that generally small European firms are likely to prefer internal finance to external capital. This means that they prefer to take loans than to receive investments that may reduce their ownership and control.

In the EU, the role of microfinance in regional cohesion policy has been reinforced through the programs *Joint European Resources for Micro to Medium Enterprises* (JEREMIE)[10] and *Joint Action to Support Microfinance Institutions in Europe* (JASMINE).[11] These do emphasize supporting the Lisbon growth and jobs agenda, supporting technology transfer, start-ups, technology and innovation funds and microcredit; but there is little documentation of intentions, let alone results, in terms of the relationship between innovation and microfinance.

Though these programs were launched with innovation on their agenda, the anticipated contribution does not yet feature extensively in their documentation. It is hoped that as experience grows, evidence of the scope of these MFIs to contribute to SME innovation will accumulate.

TWO SIDES OF MICROFINANCE AND INNOVATION

Although some of the core ideas of microfinance have been around for a long time, we are seeing new actors emerging, and established actors behaving in new ways. Thus, *microfinance can be seen as an innovation in financial services*, but *microfinance can also be used as an alternate means to finance innovation*. It may support adoption of innovation, funding acquisition of basic equipment, and can facilitate larger investments by lengthening loans' term structures. It can support improvement of the companies' business practices by encouraging firms to elaborate improved business plans and models and to value their resources adequately.

MICROFINANCE AS ITSELF INNOVATION

Providing financial services to clients that are considered 'unbankable' by the conventional financial institution, MFIs also develop new techniques and methods to ensure that the services reach the targeted clients while yielding profits. MFIs innovate in terms of rules and procedures to ensure clients' repayment. This includes training policies and human resource management practices that aim at modifying financial facilities and structuring the working units to provide services. This resembles accounts of incremental innovation. The impact of the new microfinance service can be major, especially in the developing world, where many microfinance schemes and services bring new products to markets and provoke strategic changes in financial services, and impact upon clients by pressing them to undertake new business processes in order to achieve creditworthiness.

Among the innovative features of microfinance are the following:

- New methods of providing credit to the borrowers—for example, the usage of social collateral such as group guarantee instead of personal physical collateral, progressive lending approaches, peer pressure and peer monitoring.
- Approaches to mobilization of savings from the clients and linking credit provision to savings.
- Emphasis on social mobilization processes, involving awareness building and formation of self-help groups.
- Provision of other services, such as insurance, to cover risks and distress faced by the clients.

Microcredit is probably the most prominent of the financial service innovations covered by the term 'microfinance'. This reflects the universality of credit[12] and its importance in many development contexts. Other services that the term covers include microsavings, money transfer vehicles and microinsurance. These services have become diversified and attract not only small family businesses and other SMEs in developing economies, but also fast-growing small companies in developed countries. (For Spain see Estapé-Dubreuil and Torreguitart-Mirada, 2011; for summary of grey literature see Mersland, 2005).

INNOVATION FOR MICROFINANCE

Technological innovation, especially involving new information technology (IT), can be, and has been, exploited to improve the efficiency, scale and quality of microfinance services. Six technologies are catalogued by the Microfinance Gateway (CGAP) as having been adopted by MFIs:[13]

1. *Automated teller machines (ATMs)* facilitate transactions that would otherwise require staff attention—for example, retrieving account information, accepting deposits, drawing down on pre-approved loans and transferring funds. ATMs are most effective for MFIs that

accept savings and want to serve customers in multiple locations and/
or during non-business hours.

2. *Interactive voice response (IVR) technology.* This helps MFIs clients
   to quickly receive information via telephone rather than by travelling
   to a MFI office and requesting the service in person.

3. *Smart cards.* The use of smart cards can help MFIs deliver services in
   managing savings accounts, disbursing loans or making transfers.

4. *Personal digital assistants (PDAs) and smart phones.* MFI staff can
   benefit from the use of PDAs, which can be customized to run specific
   programs to manage MFIs and clients' data and perform financial
   calculations. PDAs can help officers who are away in the field provide
   electronic data concerning clients/borrowers, which can be useful for
   loan applications and review and approval.

5. *Biometrics technology.* New biometric methods of measuring individuals' unique physical characteristics, for purposes of identification, are being adopted by MFIs who have become alerted to the
   importance of data security. Some MFIs find low-cost biometric
   technology to be preferable to passwords and PINs to access the
   clients' financial data.

6. *Credit scoring.* Credit scoring systems analyze the pattern of clients'
   historical data to predict how they will act in the future, and can help
   MFIs make more reliable decisions on loan applications, collections
   strategies, marketing and client retention. The scoring technology can
   also be used in more advanced ways, such as pricing loans in relation
   to individual client risks, and for provision against loan losses.

We can anticipate that innovative uses of IT will proliferate around MFIs.
Microfinance in general has already benefited from the Internet, which has
meant that people from across the world are now able to take part in the
microfinance movement. One example of how this new technology is being
implemented is in the creation of microfinance websites, such as www.kiv-
aB4B.org, which acts as an online broker connecting donors and recipients (who can be individuals, SMEs or MFIs).[14] Another example is www.
microplace.com, a for-profit subsidiary of eBay, which facilitates online
peer-to-peer micro lending, enabling people to invest in microbusiness.
A recent case is www.myc4.com (My Care For), which similarly enables
investors to invest in African microbusiness and SMEs.[15] The term 'crowd-
funding' has been coined to capture the spirit of this development. Some of
the lenders here are explicit about their desire to fund innovations.[16]

As increasing numbers of people have access to the Internet, the Web or
social networking technologies can be used to promote the microfinance
movement and to provide funds for investment in microbusinesses. Websites can link individuals and small businesses, including allowing lenders
to review the profiles of SMEs seeking financing. Models such as Kiva,
MicroPlace and MYC4 aim to attract social investors who want a personal

connection as well as a return on investments (social and/or financial). Here, strategic use of Internet technologies (Web 2.0 and social networking) can be crucial. While more donors may be engaged, with more information resources, there are some concerns that online models are liable to be more distant and inflexible than conventional peer-to-peer lending, and that the use of the Internet will not only popularize microfinance among lenders, but also move it into closer rapprochement with established, corporate financial institutions. Such institutions, acting on a profit-driven model, may be less concerned with social benefits of microfinance, which is liable to be reflected in the sorts of project financed. Speculatively, this might have implications for the types of innovations fostered through microfinance. For example, innovations with quick yields might be favored as opposed to those that are ultimately more sustainable or more broadly socially beneficial.

MICROFINANCE FOR INNOVATION

While microfinance is widely celebrated as a possible solution to the financing problems of smaller firms and microbusinesses, there is remarkably little examination of the connection between microfinance and innovation. Whereas microfinance has been discussed overwhelmingly in terms of rationales other than boosting innovation, some of these aims are liable to be associated with innovative products, processes and practices. Reducing the cost of access to financial services, for example, should benefit companies directly, and facilitate their innovative efforts. The possibility of making larger investments improves the income and economic capacity of clients, and better valuation processes facilitate larger loans to existing clients and engage clients who would not be served otherwise. The possible links between microfinance and innovation mean that we need to consider the rationales for microfinance in more depth, and then consider different sorts of innovations and the role of finance in innovation.

THE FINANCING OF INNOVATIVE AND TECHNOLOGICAL FIRMS

Innovation in the private sector is often a response to competitive pressures and is intended to enhance competitiveness. Innovation activities can be hindered by financial constraints, though these will be experienced in different ways across various types of firm and innovative activities. There is strong evidence to support the idea that finance is among the most important factors hindering innovation. Canepa and Stoneman (2002) analyzed CIS2 data, concluding that financial constraints are the most important of the internal and external factors constraining innovation. Financial constraints mean that projects did not start, or were delayed or postponed. These authors suggested that cross-national differences were in part explained by differences in financing across countries. Finance appeared to be more of a constraint in market-based systems than it was in bank-based systems, for instance. Reviewing results from the CIS3, Eurostat noted the following:

> Among the economic factors that are listed as part of CIS3 . . . innovation costs appear to be the most often cited reason why innovation activity is hampered, followed by a lack of appropriate sources of finance and excessive perceived economic risks. Within the EU, almost one quarter (24 per cent) of enterprises with innovation activity cited the cost of innovation as a hampering factor, while 19 per cent cited a lack of appropriate sources of finance and 17 per cent excessive perceived economic risks. (Eurostat, 2004, p. 33)

Using more recent CIS data, Hölzl and Janger (2011) find that only skills shortages were more frequently mentioned as a barrier to innovation than financial obstacles, with skills and finance being respectively more important in technologically leading and lagging countries. Their detailed results are complex, but poorer development of financial markets also emerges as a source of more financial problems.

WHO FACES FINANCIAL CONSTRAINTS ON INNOVATION?

The obstacles cited by Eurostat (2004)—cost of innovation, lack of appropriate sources of finance, excessive perceived economic risks—all have financial dimensions, and all tended to be more prevalent among service firms than those in the manufacturing industry. This could be related to the typically smaller size of service enterprises, but if one looks more closely at the results (Eurostat, 2004) it emerges that the high-tech services—computer and engineering business services, for example—report outstandingly high levels of finance-related problems. This is not to say that firm size was unimportant. The Eurostat report went on to note the following:

> As a general rule, the proportion of enterprises that regarded selected hampering factors as highly important decreased somewhat as the enterprise size-class increased. In other words, hampering factors affect proportionally more small enterprises than large ones. One of the most typical hampering factors faced by SMEs was a lack of appropriate sources of finance . . . Indeed, this category had the largest difference between the proportion of small and large enterprises citing it as highly important (6 percentage points), as 16 per cent of small enterprises reported a lack of appropriate sources of finance compared to 10 per

cent of large enterprises. Other factors that were ranked relatively highly by SMEs were the high cost of innovation and the excessive perceived economic risks associated with innovation. (Eurostat, 2004, p. 49)

Figure 7.1 displays CIS3 results. Though smaller firms do report financing and related problems more often, these are problems that are widely experienced and while they are the most frequently cited, they are not the only problems encountered.

Innovation costs and lack of sources of finance generally emerge as more important for smaller firms in these sectors in CIS analyses, sometimes strikingly so, though not so much in the Netherlands. In some other studies, such as the 'Innovation Benchmarking Survey' conducted in the UK and US, this was less evident (see Figure 7.2). The reasons are not entirely clear, but may be to do with the survey samples being structured in different ways. The CIS surveys, which aim to be nationally representative, do depict a great deal of variation between EU countries, so we may need to be cautious about the Innovation Benchmarking results failing to show any dramatic difference in the incidence of finance-related problems in similar firms in the UK and US. Other dynamics may also affect just how and when finance is seen to be a problem.

SMEs have constrained funds of their own to use and may often be in a weaker position regarding the appropriability of the results of their innovation activities. Funding innovation through their cash flows, SMEs may find it hard to achieve sustained and high levels of commitment as required by some long-term innovation programs. Using R&D as a proxy for innovation, one study (Bond, Harhoff and van-Reenen, 2003) found real constraints in both the UK and Germany facing companies investing in innovation. Those companies who fund their innovation programs from their own resources prefer to use available funds, usually cash flows, which are typically very limited. Despite the well-developed financial and capital markets in the UK, there was more volatility and lower overall investment in innovation development there than in Germany, though how far this can be attributed to the financial system alone is debatable.

Generally, SMEs face considerable problems in seeking the funds necessary to innovate. Intangible activities such as R&D or innovation are considered riskier, so that SMEs face a higher cost of capital. Intangible assets may be undervalued when being used as collateral for credit, reducing the amount of capital debt that can be raised. Considering this, SMEs investing in technology and innovation are more likely to find difficulties in accessing credit than are those other SMEs that focus on more traditional businesses! High transaction costs, the risks connected with their business and limited capacity to appropriate innovations combine with the difficulties of lenders understanding the real value of innovative projects, to limit the capability of innovative SMEs to raise external funds (Stiglitz, 1993).

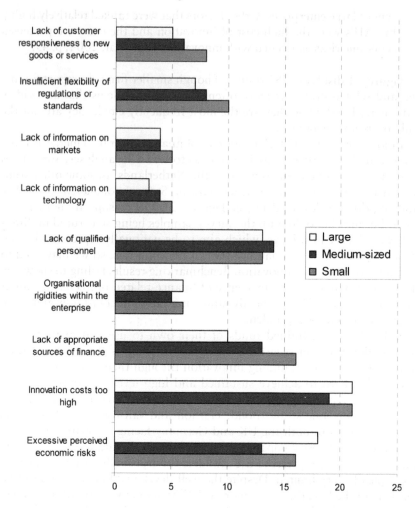

Figure 7.1 Obstacles to innovation across different types of firms. (Percentage of enterprises that regarded selected hampering factors that they had experienced as highly important, EU, 1998–2000). Source: Based on data in Eurostat (2004).

Indeed, a large share of SMEs report barriers to innovation in the access to external sources of financing (Hoffman et al., 1998). These difficulties are mostly caused by the fact that intangible assets are specific to each company and are hard for banks and other creditors to deploy in the case of bankruptcy. The banks judge this as a risky investment, and impose a higher interest rate (Brewer et al., 1996). This affects the capital structure of innovative and technological SMEs, which show some distinctive features compared to that of other firms (Viviani et al., 2008). It is understandable that innovative SMEs operating in new sectors and thus having a high risk level will face difficulties in finding financial support. Sau (2007) argues that this is due to the failure of the market to develop mechanisms

Business Services, 2000

Total sample

Size class	Belgium	Germany	Italy	Netherlands	Portugal	Finland	UK	UK_IB	US_IB
No innovation activity due to costs of innovation									
10-249	6.1%	32.1%	12.1%	3.7%	22.6%	11.9%	19.4%	30.8%	29.5%
≥250	0.0%	19.6%	5.5%	14.5%	0.0%	8.3%	10.3%	33.0%	33.3%
No innovation activity due to lack of sources of finance									
10-249	12.8%	29.8%	14.0%	8.0%	31.1%	7.7%	22.4%	24.1%	21.9%
≥250	0.0%	12.8%	2.4%	6.2%	0.0%	4.1%	5.3%	26.6%	37.5%

Manufacturing, 2000

Sample: Innovation active

Size class	Belgium	Germany	Italy	Netherlands	Portugal	Finland	UK	UK_IB	US_IB
No innovation activity due to costs of innovation									
10-249	12.0%	31.9%	19.3%	5.3%	32.8%	4.9%	25.3%	24.1%	27.1%
≥250	10.2%	21.9%	14.0%	8.7%	28.2%	7.3%	21.4%	31.6%	25.9%
No innovation activity due to lack of sources of finance									
10-249	11.3%	23.0%	14.8%	6.6%	27.0%	3.8%	16.8%	24.7%	24.0%
≥250	11.0%	7.9%	9.1%	5.6%	16.2%	2.2%	13.8%	25.9%	29.1%

Figure 7.2   Results from Community Innovation Benchmarking Survey. Source: Cosh et al. (2005).

to screen and monitor applicants, reducing the informational opacity and the risk connected with financing. A study of an SME sector in Ireland (Hogan and Hutson, 2005) showed that when innovative SMEs are forced to find external funds, they tend to look for equity rather than capital debt. For this reason, in their early life, innovative SMEs tend to prefer financial instruments that can better manage risk.

However, with banks often relying on collateral as protection for loans, there is a difficult situation for innovative SMEs. For these companies, a great proportion of the firm's value is about future activities or the 'value of growth opportunities' as Myers (2001) terms it. As these activities are intangible, banks are less willing to accept them as collateral. This suggests that there could well be opportunities to use microfinance to reduce the financing difficulties confronting and disabling innovative SMEs.

SMALLER FIRMS AND INNOVATION

Small firms can be innovative. In the US, SMEs were found to have more than double the innovations per employee than larger ones (Eurostat, 2004), but small firms often report problems raising financing. Bogan (2008) and Viviani et al. (2008) have carried out studies that may shed some light on the extent to which SMEs can benefit from microfinance schemes, especially with regards to their innovativeness. What is more important is that nearly half of the two million European industrial SMEs are market innovators, who excel in developing new product concepts and whose innovative impact is produced by a new combination of existing technologies. This makes SMEs crucial to Europe's innovation and diffusion of innovation, and quite possibly to some of its technological breakthroughs (Euractiv, 2006b). EC research reveals, however, that Europe continues to fall behind the US in R&D investment, which is vital for innovativeness, and that this is mainly due to decreasing R&D investment by European SMEs. Helping SMEs to invest more could help Europe to achieve its targets of increasing research spending as a share of GDP (Butler et al., 2006) .

Small firms report facing finance-related obstacles to innovation more frequently than larger firms, and it is smaller firms for whom we might expect microfinance to be most relevant. The challenges of innovation might differ between larger and smaller firms:

> While the failure of an innovation project may jeopardize the very survival of a small enterprise, it is less likely to do so for larger structures, where there are generally more diversified activities that can compensate for the loss of a failed project. (Eurostat, 2004, p. 49)

This might be one factor making smaller firms less likely to embark upon more radical and large-scale innovation projects. Tether et al. (1997) are among several researchers who have demonstrated that smaller firms are *less* likely to be sources of more radical innovations, and analyses of CIS and other surveys indicate that their shares of expenditure and turnover on innovative activities (R&D and other activities) also tend to be smaller. Nevertheless, with the huge number of SMEs, the cumulative activity can be considerable and there are always many exceptions that defy the average.

Not all innovations are radical and large-scale and there is much scope for smaller firms to adopt small-scale innovations. Larger firms may typically be pioneering innovators, but then there is scope for imitation, catch-up and diffusion. Sometimes the costs of adopting innovation do not descend rapidly, so the uptake of innovations by smaller firms might be expected to be delayed. Sometimes, as in the case of many recent IT-based innovations, for example, costs do fall rapidly. There may be a rapid takeoff with little lag between early and later adopters. Relatively small amounts of finance might be required to purchase equipment, technical support and such computer services as databases and web design tools. Finance might also assist other innovation activities: protecting intellectual property, developing markets, preparing business plans and scanning the competitive environment.

Small firms' financial barriers may involve relatively small amounts of money for relatively small-scale innovation activities. These might be adoption of fairly routine process innovations, but there can also be relatively inexpensive aspects of product innovations such as testing markets, checking conformance with standards or requirements for environmental or service quality. Financial needs could relate to consultancy or other advice, establishment of websites, and many other innovation-supporting activities. In some cases, microfinance could be a solution. Even if such innovation financing would only rarely be significant in terms of pioneering major innovations, it could play an important role in enabling smaller firms to keep abreast of technology developments undertaken by larger firms and, of course, some small enterprises are liable to be highly innovative. Sometimes their new ideas will be very expensive to commercialize, but not always. Many 'gazelles' have pioneered new business models that required relatively little by way of start-up costs. The bigger challenge is often to ward off the advances, or imitation efforts, from larger firms, as they discover that they face new competition, and allocate resources to meeting the challenge.

FINANCING FOR INNOVATION

Canepa and Stoneman (2002) suggested from their CIS2 analysis that 'riskier', newer industries are more constrained by financial difficulties. Canepa and Stoneman (2008) went on to suggest, from analyses of UK CIS2 and CIS3 data, that the impact of financial constraints upon innovative activity is more severe in higher tech sectors, as well as for smaller enterprises. Similarly, Bugamelli et al. (2003), focusing on innovation advancing 'the new economy', concluded that financing the new economy has more to do with traditional firms investing in IT than with the creation of new IT-producing firms. Thus they discounted the view that finance is a major obstacle to the development of the new economy in Europe in general, though there could be specific difficulties in countries like Italy, where firms tend to be small on average. But perhaps we want to encourage small firms, and perhaps small innovators do not all wish to be absorbed by bigger firms.

More generally, Rivaud-Danset (2001) used a range of approaches to explore whether financial institutions are biased against innovators. The evidence from CIS2 and elsewhere seemed to indicate that innovators can actually access more long-term credit than non-innovators. She concluded that there was no such bias. Her thinking, then, was that the importance accorded to finance in preventing innovative projects is due to financial directors considering that these are too risky and thus refusing financial support, while delays in completion of innovative projects are more likely to reflect issues such as human resources and organizational rigidity, though the picture varies across countries, with finance being important in the UK.[17] Later still, problems may be associated more with lack of market responsiveness. Rivaud-Danset (2001) did note the importance of venture capital as a key financing mechanism for high-tech firms with high growth potential.

The preceding discussion has argued for the relevance of considering microfinance as a response to the financial constraints faced by small companies, when it comes to innovation as well as to other aspects of the business. The current financial crisis, and the increased difficulties many firms are confronting where it comes to raising money, makes this response appear ever more relevant. However, microfinance schemes have their own limits, too. Expectations of microfinance should be realistic and the general financial crisis may well mean that some expectations have to be trimmed for MFIs, as well as for mainstream banks.

The current financial crisis is unlike the crises of the 1990s, when microfinance was largely a closed system only loosely attached to the currency market. Now microfinance is far from isolated from the banking system that suffers from the crisis. It is at least possible that the global recession will in the longer term also impact the microfinance system. This is a topic that requires close monitoring. It is also important to recognize that microfinance is not a panacea, and that misjudged microfinance schemes can cause as much pain as any other inappropriate use of financial instruments. *The Guardian* reports that microfinance schemes 'devastate the lives of millions of poor people and reveal the dark side of India's economic boom'. What happened was that the microfinance scheme was inappropriately executed by aggressive selling of loans to illiterate villagers, followed by aggressive debt collection (Burke, 2011). A strong, but not uncritical, defense of microfinance is made by Hulme and Arun (2011).

Microfinance can often be a first step towards formal or even legal work. 'Moonlight workers' and people working outside of the formal economy often do not have access to formal financing. MFI can work with them and help them build credit history so that gradually they can improve their financial profiles. In order to do this, the loan scheme that microfinance offers must be small and flexible, with easy and affordable administrative requirements,[18] and effective advice services.

There might also be a link between microfinancing and innovation vouchers.[19] Both of these ideas deal with small amounts, involving minimal bureaucracy and maximum accessibility. In the case of innovation vouchers, the public reimbursement for innovation support is paid directly to the service provider that the SME has chosen, rather than to the SME itself. There is scope for coordinating the loan part of microfinance with support services, which could be publicly reimbursed through vouchers or other schemes.

POLICY IMPLICATIONS

Key Stakeholders

Orienting microfinance to support innovation requires support from the business sector as well as from the public sector and government. There are commercial interests from mainstream financial institutions in microfinance, which should support concerted activities from such bodies (and relevant intermediaries such as accountancy and standards organizations) to demonstrate that microfinance constitutes a body of transparent business practices that can be conducted on a sound and accountable footing. Businesses could also be encouraged to include support for MFI among the aims and applications of their much-trumpeted commitment to corporate social responsibility (CSR). Bodies involved in promoting and developing guidelines for CSR—including business schools, social audit organizations, and bodies such as the European Association for Business in Society (EABIS)—can foster this.

Community development and NGO services can also play important roles in ensuring the positive development of microenterprises supported by microfinance. They may provide such support as working with volunteers—for example, retired business managers from other regions or sectors providing mentoring and basic infrastructure. These non-financial services may support microfinance's growth, outreach to more clients and contributions to the innovation agenda. European initiatives in developing support for microfinance may be usefully extended to other parts of the world and lessons from other regions should also be transferred back to Europe.

Governments, as already indicated, have a critical role to play. Bodies such as the World Bank and IMF stress the need for sound policies and legal frameworks, as well as macroeconomic stability, in microfinance as well as in other financial affairs and economic development strategies. The attractiveness of microfinance to the private sector and to NGOs can be reduced, however, by interventions such as direct service provision and caps on interest rates. Until recently, governments generally believed that the generation of development finance was largely their own responsibility, including, for example, credit programs for the disadvantaged. There has been much criticism of excessive and often ill-informed government intervention in social and economic affairs (though some of the neoconservative agenda here has been undermined by the current financial crisis, which has exposed some of the limits of private sector management and deregulation strategies). There has been much argument that a primary (let alone exclusive) role for government in development financing is inappropriate. State aid is depressingly often highly political—and politicized—so that resources are liable to flow away from those areas where there is greatest convergence of socioeconomic needs and opportunities, to those where political needs and opportunities are prominent.

Pressure should be put on governments, then, to make them focus on putting the basic economic, social and physical infrastructure in place and to support more effective microfinance. With microfinance becoming popular, governments are tempted to promote their own microcredit schemes, employing savings banks, development banks, postal savings banks and agricultural banks for this end. Many governments have set up facilities that channel funds from multilateral agencies to MFIs. This can be quite complicated. There are few successful examples in microfinance, where effective organizations tend to be built on the backs of successful MFIs and not the other way around.

Government can also fund MFIs (Curran, 2005), but it is widely agreed that government funding should not be the only resource. A multiplicity of sources will be more resilient to shifts in policy or economic circumstances. It could also bring more transparency and a wider range of experience with monitoring and evaluation, making the system less likely to be inefficient or corrupt. MFIs should, then, look to mobilizing other resources like concessional loans, commercial and multilateral loans, term deposits, savings accounts and bond issues—these points apply especially to the more developed MFIs. Concerns like cost, maturity, volume and continuity of access have to be taken into account in the MFIs' liability structure, in order to ensure growth and stability in its lending. This is not to argue against government initiatives in this field; these could play a vital role in enhancing and dynamizing MFI performance. The point is simply to caution against heavy-handed government action that might stifle initiatives emerging from NGOs of various kinds, and even from commercial financial institutions.

Regulation and Supervision

Governments can choose to support microfinance by means of regulatory frameworks that empower a wide range of financial actors to offer financial services to poor or small clients. Financial regulators can support microfinance through modifying their rules. In most cases, the level of microfinance development does not currently necessitate the licensing of separate financial institutions to serve small clients, but in some countries, including EU member states, alternative institutional frameworks may be set up to allow organizations (NGOs, credit unions, community-based intermediaries) to obtain a license to offer deposit services to the general public and obtain funds. The Microfinance Gateway website[20] suggests some ways in which regulators can work with microfinance, including cooperation on such issues as the following:

- Modifying limits on usury, to allow appropriate levels of interest to be set for loans.
- Enabling credit information clearinghouses to share information on defaulting borrowers so as to limit their ability to go from one MFI to another.
- Working with civil authorities to ensure that private loan contracts can be recognized by courts (especially in those transition economies that lack even basic legislative infrastructure).
- Reporting requirements that will prepare MFIs to eventually become regulated.[21]

Financial regulators can also examine the laws and other related regulations that limit the ability of traditional banking institutions to offer microfinance schemes.[22] Banking regulators may need to look at the ways in which they would evaluate microloan portfolios within large banks.

In order to reach large numbers of clients, microfinance must eventually be institutionalized, in the sense that services will need to be licensed and supervised by a country's financial authorities. Licensed institutions can offer saving services to their clients, and increase their own equity capital by acquiring deposits. As outlined by the World Bank (CGAP, 2003), microfinance's differences from conventional banking mean that the banking laws and regulations in many countries need adjusting to accommodate licensed microfinance. Microfinance needs different treatment, as compared to normal banking, primarily because microfinance assets consist of many small, uncollateralized—that is, unguaranteed—loans. The rules applied to microfinance, and the systems of supervision that can enforce compliance with these rules, are thus unlikely to be precisely those put in place for other financial institutions and arrangements. Areas of regulation that typically require adjustment include unsecured lending limits, capital-adequacy ratios, rules for provisioning loan-losses and minimum capital requirements (CGAP, 2003). Microfinance providers that take deposits need 'prudential' regulation, which protects their financial soundness to prevent them from losing depositors' money and further damaging confidence in the financial system (CGAP, 2003).

In the present financial crisis, where trust in financial bodies is at a low level—including among those working for these bodies themselves[23]—this is particularly important. Regulators will need considerable reassurance that they are not running further risks in enabling MFI expansion. Politicians will need to be convinced that microfinance is part of the solution to the financing problems of small firms that have been exacerbated in the current crisis, so that they will encourage regulators to support MFIs. Innovation is part of the answer to the structural problems that underlie the current crisis. The message that microfinance could support such innovation could be influential here, at least for policymakers that are not preoccupied with short-term damage limitation.

CONCLUSIONS

Microfinance is an important social innovation. It is playing a significant role in promoting social and economic development in many deprived areas and among many socially excluded groups. Discussions of microfinance very rarely touch on the potential contribution that these instruments can make to the innovative activities of the clients of microfinance. This is despite wide awareness of the financial problems encountered by small firms, in particular, when it comes to their pursuing innovative products and processes. Innovation projects require more or less extensive funding, both in terms of the time scale involved and the amount of money required, and not all small firms are pursuing particularly innovative projects. Some firms' needs for finance concern are simply maintaining or growing established activities, but microfinance appears to be highly applicable to some types of innovation financing issues encountered by small firms.

These issues are liable to vary considerably across regions, sectors and types of enterprise. The CIS results could be explored in more depth so as to examine some of these details. This applies even though this survey asks only very basic questions about the barriers that are encountered, and such large-scale surveys can really only scratch the surface of innovation financing problems. However, more probing may be required. It is quite possible that many small firms will have articulated their needs only to a limited extent. Thus more detailed consultation may be required to help them think through the ways in which finance inputs, of one kind or another, could contribute to their innovation-related activities. Often several types of financing might be needed to facilitate a combination of related innovation activities. In-depth case study research is the obvious way to improve understanding here.

Which types of innovation-related activity could benefit from microfinance? It is likely that microfinance will be more relevant to incremental innovations and those that are less technologically demanding. This does not rule out the scope for potentially significant developments in, especially, service and software innovation, and in innovation that can help to configure and add value to existing complex socio-technical systems. Microfinance can support diffusion and adoption of innovations, including smaller enterprises' acquisition and implementation of products and processes that are well established in larger firms (and/or other sectors or regions). It may contribute to other innovation-related activities—for instance, those connected with IPR and market development (including development of B2B markets). It may be that the learning processes involved in engaging with MFIs—preparing business plans, establishing monitoring and reporting systems, instituting more formalized accounting regimes—will be as important to supporting innovation as will the provision of finance directly to enable innovation-related activities.

In conclusion, the role of microfinance in innovation is a topic that urgently demands further exploration and analysis. Practically, the implication of the discussion is that innovation should be included among the rationales for microfinance services. Innovation should not displace other criteria used by MFIs. Microfinance already helps promote extremely worthy developmental goals. But innovation needs to be mainstreamed in microfinance policy as in other policy areas. This includes microfinance strategy as articulated by development agencies and financial institutions. Some case studies of how microfinance has contributed to innovation on the part of its clients could help raise the profile of this area. Innovations that support MFIs are also worth fostering, which means raising awareness of microfinance as a social innovation. Neither innovation nor microfinance is a panacea for the grand challenges of sustainable social and economic development, but together they can make greater contributions to resolving the urgent problems of the 21st century.

NOTES

1. The World Bank Group president, Robert B. Zoellick, has made this case. Online. Available HTTP: http://web.worldbank.org/WBSITE/EXTERNAL/NEWS/0,,contentMDK:23046760~pagePK:34370~piPK:42770~theSitePK:4607,00.html (accessed 18 January 2012).
2. The rates associated with various illicit loan schemes may be much higher than this.
3. Microcredit is defined as very small loans, typically provided by legally registered institutions, to unsalaried borrowers with little or no collateral by the Microfinance Gateway website. Online. Available HTTP: http://www.microfinancegateway.com/section/faq#1 (accessed 18 January 2012). Consumer credit provided to salaried workers, based on automated credit scoring, is usually not included in this definition, although this is contentious, and may be subject to change in the future.
4. Online. Available HTTP: http://www.microcreditsummit.org/pubs/reports/socr/2007.html (accessed 18 January 2012). State of the Microcredit Summit Campaign Report 2007, Microcredit Summit Campaign, Washington, 2007.
5. The MicroBanking Bulletin #15, Microfinance Information eXchange, 2007, pp. 30–31.
6. Online. Available HTTP: http://www.european-microfinance.org/europe-microfinance_en.php (accessed 18 January 2012).
7. Online. Available HTTP: http://www.european-microfinance.org/europe-microfinance_en.php (accessed 18 January 2012).
8. http://ec.europa.eu/regional_policy/archive/themes/business/index_en.htm (accessed June 20 2012)
9. While many studies concentrate on the capital structure and the financial policy decisions of SMEs, few consider international differences in capital structures of SMEs and their determinants. Viviani et al. (2008) investigate this issue, and the relation between the capital structure and the innovation level, using a sample of European SMEs and analyzing the determinants of their capital structure, asking how innovativeness, growth and risk affect it. Data from AMADEUS (a pan-European database that contains information on about nine million firms in more than forty countries) is also used to explore the impact of the country on the European SMEs' capital structure.
10. Online. Available HTTP: http://www.european-microfinance.org/jeremie_en.php (accessed 18 January 2012).
11. Online. Available HTTP: http://www.european-microfinance.org/jasmine_en.php and see also http://ec.europa.eu/regional_policy/sources/docgener/presenta/jasmine/microcredit2010_en.pdf (both accessed 18 January 2012).
12. The Nobel-Laureate Yunus even believes that 'right to credit' should be recognized as a human right. Online. Available HTTP: http://www.voanews.com/bangla/archive/2006–11/2006–11–17-voa11.cfm (accessed 18 January 2012).

13. Online. Available HTTP: http://www.cgap.org/p/site/c/tech/ (accessed 18 January 2012).
14. Kiva is a nonprofit charity that allows donors to choose individuals to donate to. Kiva bridges the donors and the recipients, and the donors can use an Internet application like PayPal to send money to Kiva, which will then send the money to the local MFI coordinating the transaction.
15. MYC4 has been in beta since May 2007, and the first 150 loans in Uganda have been funded by more than eight hundred investors/investor groups from thirty-five countries. Ivory Coast will join MYC4 as the second country in Africa and another fifty-one will follow step-by-step.
16. A wiki that documents this development, providing links to many firms active here, is online. Available HTTP: http://crowdfunding.pbworks.com/w/page/10402176/Crowdfunding and the Wikipedia page http://en.wikipedia.org/wiki/Crowd_funding (both accessed 11 July 2011).
17. She suggests that the UK may have had particular problems of linkages between finance and innovation in the 1990s. Whether this remains the case was beyond her scope.
18. See, for example, French initiative. Online. Available HTTP: http://www.lautoentrepreneur.fr/ (accessed 18 January 2012).
19. Innovation vouchers are small grants that can be spent on improving links between SMEs and sources of innovative knowledge such as consultants and universities. See the UK report 'Innovation Nation' for a definition used in UK regions. Online. Available HTTP: http://www.dius.gov.uk/docs/home/ScienceInnovation.pdf (accessed 18 January 2012).
20. http://www.microfinancegateway.org (accessed 20 June 2012).
21. For a view of the European context of regulatory structures that impact microfinance, see Expert Group report, 2007, 'The Regulation of Microcredit in Europe'. Online. Available HTTP: http://ec.europa.eu/enterprise/entrepreneurship/financing/publications.htm#microcredit_regulation_2007 (accessed 18 January 2011).
22. Includes limits on the percentage of a loan portfolio that can be lent on an unsecured basis, limits on group guarantee mechanisms, reporting requirements, limits on branch office operations (scheduling and security), and requirements for the contents of loan files.
23. At the time of writing, the level of lending from one bank to another is very low, due to pervasive fears about the security of the assets of other banks. It should be noted, too, that at such a time of crisis various poor practices are exposed and scandals of varying intensity emerge. This makes regulators very wary about supporting new initiatives, as opposed to tightening the supervisory systems whose weaknesses have been revealed.

BIBLIOGRAPHY

Armendáriz de Aghion, B. and Morduch, J. (2000) 'Microfinance beyond Group Lending'. *The Economics of Transition* 8 (2): 401–420.
Armendáriz de Aghion, B. and Morduch, J. (2005) *The Economics of Microfinance*. Cambridge, MA: The MIT Press.
Baron, J. (1993) 'The Small Business Technology Transfer (STRR) Program: Converting Research into Economic Strength'. *Economic Development Review* 11 (4): 63–70.
Bogan, V. (2008) *Microfinance Institutions: Does Capital Structure Matter?* Online. Available HTTP: http://ssrn.com/abstract=1144762 (accessed 18 January 2012).

Bond, S., Harhoff, D. and van-Reenen, J. (2003) *Investment, R&D and Financial Constraints in Britain and Germany.* London: London School of Economics' Centre for Economic Performance, Productivity and Innovation Programme.

Brewer, E., Genay, H., Jackson, W. E. and Worthington, P. (1996) 'How Are Small Firms Financed? Evidence from Small Business Investment Companies'. *Economic Perspectives* 20 (6): 2–18.

Bugamelli, M., Pagano, P., Paterno, F., Pozzolo, A. F., Rossi, S. and Schivardi, F. (2003) 'Ingredients for The New Economy: How Much Does Finance Matter?' EFIC working paper 03–31. Maastricht: The UN University Institute for New Technologies (INTECH).

Burke, J. (2011) 'Impoverished Indian Families Caught in Deadly Spiral of Microfinance Debt'. *The Guardian.* 31 January 2011.

Butler, J., Cox, D., Gagliardi, D., Howells, J. and Nugroho, Y. (eds.) (2006) *Monitoring Industrial Research: The Annual Digest of Industrial R&D 2006.* European Commission: DG Research. Online. Available HTTP: http://iri.jrc.es/research/docs/annual_digest_ird.pdf (accessed 23 January 2012).

Callaghan, I., Gonzalez, H., Maurice, D., Novak, C. and Stanley, M. (2007) 'Microfinance—On the Road to Capital Markets'. *Journal of Applied Corporate Finance.* 19 (1): 115–124.

Canepa, A. and Stoneman, P. (2002) 'Financial Constraints on Innovation: A European Cross Country Study'. EFIC working paper 03–11. Maastricht: The UN University Institute for New Technologies (INTECH).

Canepa, A. and Stoneman, P. (2008) 'Financial Constraints to Innovation in the UK: Evidence from CIS2 and CIS3'. *Oxford Economic Papers* 60 (4): 711–730.

CGAP. (2003) 'Helping to Improve Donor Effectiveness in Microfinance: Regulation and Supervision of Microfinance'. Report. Donor Brief No. 12, CGAP.

Christen, R. P., Rosenberg, R. and Jayadeva, V. (2004) 'Financial Institutions with a Double-Bottom Line: Implications for the Future of Microfinance'. CGAP occasional paper.

Committee for Microfinancing (2007) 'Microfinancing as an Instrument for Stimulating Entrepreneurship in the Netherlands'. Advice from the Committee for Microfinancing in the Netherlands to the State Secretary for Economic Affairs. Committee for Microfinancing in the Netherlands. Online. Available HTTP: http://www.european-microfinance.org/data/file/micro-finance-in-the-netherlands-first-advice-2007-english-version.doc (accessed 20 June 2012)

Corsi, M., Botti, F., Rondinella, T. and Zacchia, G. (2006) 'Women and Microfinance in Mediterranean Countries'. *Development* 49: 67–74.

Cosh, A., Hughes, A., Bullock, A., Fu, X., Lester, R., Milner, I. and Yang, Q. (2005) 'Innovation Benchmarking: Europe and the US'. Presentation at CIS Users Group meeting. 15 July. Mimeo: Centre for Business Research, Cambridge University. Online. Available HTTP: http://www.berr.gov.uk/files/file11028.ppt (accessed 23 January 2012).

Cull, R., Demirgüç-Kunt, A. and Morduch, J. (2005) 'Contract Design and Microfinance Performance: A Global Analysis'. Washington, DC: World Bank. Online. Available HTTP: http://info.worldbank.org/etools/docs/library/232655/Cull-MorduchDemirgucKunt_MicrofinContractsPerformance_5–24.pdf (accessed 23 January 2012).

Curran, L. (2005) 'Financing Microfinance Loan Portfolios'. *Small Enterprise Development* 16 (1): 42–49.

EC (2003a) The EC recommendation C No. 1422 of 6 May 2003. . Online. Available HTTP: http://eur-lex.europa.eu/LexUriServ/LexUriServ.do?uri=CELEX:32003H0361:EN:NOT (accessed 20 June 2012)

EC (2003b) Microcredit for small businesses and businesses creation: bridging a market gap. Report. DG Enterprise, Online. Available HTTP: http://ec.europa.

eu/enterprise/newsroom/cf/_getdocument.cfm?doc_id=1115 (accessed 20 June 12)

EMN/MFC/cdfa (2007) 'From Exclusion to Inclusion through Microfinance—Critical Issues'. April 2007, Paris. Online. Available HTTP: http://www.european-microfinance.org/data/file/14_euro_report.pdf (accessed 14 August 2012).

Estapé-Dubreuil, G. and Torreguitart-Mirada, C. (2011) 'Information Technology and Microfinance in Developed Countries: The Spanish Case, with a Focus on Catalonia'. In *Advanced Technologies for Microfinance: Solutions and Challenges*, 302–322. IGI Global. doi:10.4018/978-1-61520-993-4.ch017. Editor of the volume: Arvind Ashta. City of publication: Vancouver, BC.

Euractiv. (2006a) 'EU's R&D Expenditure Still at Impasse'. 5 September.

Euractiv. (2006b) 'SMEs & Access to R&D Funding'. 3 August. Online. Available HTTP: http://www.euractiv.com/en/science/smes-access-rd-funding/article-143886 (accessed 18 January 2012).

Eurostat. (2004) 'Innovation in Europe: Overview of the Third Community Innovation Survey (CIS3)'. Eurostat Research Unit (B5). Luxembourg: Office for Official Publications of the European Communities.

Evers, J. (2007) 'Status of Microfinance in Western Europe'. EMN issue paper. European Microfinance Network.

Evers, J. and Lahn, S. (2006) 'Promoting Microfinance: Policy Measures Needed'. *Finance & The Common Good* 25 (47): 53.

Gonzalez, A. (2007) 'How Many Borrowers and Microfinance Institutions (MFIs) Exist?' Report. Washington, DC: Microfinance Information Exchange (MIX).

Helms, B. (2006) *Access for All: Building Inclusive Financial Systems*. Washington, DC: CGAP/World Bank.

Hoffman, K., Milady, P., Bessant, J. and Perren, L. (1998) 'Small Firms, R&D, Technology and Innovation in the UK: A Literature Review'. *Technovation* 18: 39–55.

Hogan, T. and Hutson, E. (2005) 'Capital Structure in New Technology-Based Firms. Evidence from the Irish Software Sector' *Global Finance Journal* 15(3):369–387

Hölzl, W. and Janger, J. (2011) 'Innovation Barriers across Firm Types and Countries'. Paper presented at the DIME Final Conference. Maastricht. 6–8 April 2011. Online. Available HTTP: http://final.dime-eu.org/files/hoelzl_janger_E5.pdf (accessed 2 February 2012).

Hulme, D. and Arun, T. G. (2011) 'What's Wrong and Right with Microfinance—Missing an Angle on Responsible Finance?' BWPI working paper 155. Manchester: Brooks World Poverty Institute.

Kyereboah-Coleman, A. (2007) 'The Impact of Capital Structure on the Performance of Microfinance Institutions'. *The Journal of Risk Finance* 8 (1): 56–71.

Ledgerwood, J. (2000) *Microfinance Handbook: An Institutional and Financial Perspective*. Washington, DC: The World Bank.

Mersland, R. (2005) *The Agenda and Relevance of Recent Research in Microfinance*. Kristiansand: Agder University College.

Myers, D. G. and Lamm, H. (1976) 'The Group Polarization Phenomenon'. *Psychological Bulletin* 83 (3): 602–627.

Myers, S. C. (2001) 'Capital Structure'. *The Journal of Economic Perspectives* 15 (2): 81–102.

Rivaud-Danset, D. (2001) 'The Financing of Innovation and the Venture Capital'. The National Financial and Sectoral Systems. ESSY TSER FP4 project (Sectoral Systems in Europe—Innovation, Competitiveness and Growth) ESSY working paper. Mimeo: CREII, Universite de Paris 13.

Sau, L. (2007) 'New Pecking Order Financing for Innovative Firms. An Overview'. Working paper 02/2007. Torino: Università di Torino.

Sika, J. M. and Strasser, B. (2000) 'Tontines in Kamerun: Verknüpfung tradition-eller und semi-formeller Finanzierungssysteme'. *E+Z Entwicklung und Zusamenarbeit* 41 (11): 316–318.

Stiglitz, J. (1993) 'Endogenous Growth and Cycles'. National Bureau of Economic Review (NBER) Working Papers No. 4286.

Tether, B. S., Smith, I. J. and Thwaites, A. T. (1997) 'Smaller Enterprises and Innovation in the UK: The SPRU Innovations Database Revisited'. *Research Policy* 26 (1): 19–32.

Vigenina, D. and Kritiko, A. S. (2004) 'The Individual Micro-lending Contract: Is It a Better Design Than Joint-Liability?: Evidence from Georgia'. *Economic Systems* 28 (2): 155–176.

Viviani, D., Giorgino, M., Minola, T. and Dellarossa, M. (2008) 'Capital Structure and Innovation of SMEs in European Countries'. Paper presented at International Council for Small Business World Conference. Halifax, Nova Scotia. 22–25 June. Online. Available HTTP: http://www.smu.ca/events/icsb/proceedings/creaf4f.html (accessed 18 January 2012).

von Pischke, J. D. (2003) 'The Evolution of Institutional Issues in Rural Finance: Outreach, Risk and Sustainability'. Paper presented at Broadening Access and Strengthening Input Market Systems—Collaborative Research Support Programme (BASIS–CRSP) Conference on Paving the Way Forward for Rural Finance. Washington, DC. 2–4 June.

Part III

The Labor Force and Human Capital and Societal Issues

8 Skills and Innovation

Lawrence Green, Barbara Jones and Ian Miles

The rate, extent and success of innovation in organizations (and in society at large) is linked intimately with the presence and availability of trained and skilled workers. Such individuals generate and apply knowledge, intelligence, techniques and ideas in the creation of novel products and development of new processes, and in so doing, contribute crucially to the efficiency and competitive advantage of the organizations, sectors and regions in which they work. Not surprisingly, a long-term push towards enhancement of the stock of innovation-related skills can be seen across all developed economies, with enhanced linkages between the education and training sector and employer organizations a key priority in the policy environment. In addition, the importance of certain forms of skills—especially problem-solving, technical and collaborative working skills—is acknowledged across the spectrum of industrial and public agencies, and organizations across all sectors have demonstrated an eagerness to build the specialist capabilities that are expected to sustain and grow their operations. Thus, it can be suggested with some confidence that the centrality of a skilled workforce to innovative and competitive enterprise has never been more clear. This assertion is certainly accepted in the policy community, where urgent calls for a swelling of the human capital and skills pools have resonated increasingly loudly in unfolding political discourse.

Despite the current focus on skills and innovation capacity, our current understanding of the relationship between the two remains heavily constrained: differing and broad definitions of the concepts, inadequate attention to the linkages between training systems and the dynamics of the skills base, and difficulties in measuring human capital and innovation outcomes have all implied the persistence (and perhaps expansion) of knowledge gaps. It can be argued strongly that such ignorance cannot be permitted to continue: a lack of understanding implies potentially damaging consequences for managers and policy-makers, and for regional and national economies. Without more adequate and accurate understanding and intelligence, opportunities may be lost, competitive ground ceded, and future planning severely hampered. Where skills are a key determinant of innovation capacity, and such capacity correlates with competitive advantage, sophisticated cognition of the articulation between capabilities and successful innovation becomes an urgent requirement.

It is now recognised universally that human capital and physical capital are the twin and fundamental ingredients in R&D and new product development. Thus, in addition to ensuring the availability of requisite physical resources, attracting and training skilled people is critical to the stimulation of innovation and to the acceleration of productivity growth. The competitiveness of firms, nations and trading blocs is clearly linked to their innovation performance, and to the skills and competences of their workers and citizens. Indeed, the presence of strong innovation-facilitating skills is the factor that confers competitive advantage on specific companies and locations, and where innovation leadership is evident, so too sophisticated education, skills and training regimes are invariably in place, It is clear, however, that some—even developed—regions lag behind others in terms of innovation (for example, Europe lags behind the US and Japan, despite concerted efforts to reverse the situation), and this raises the important question of just what skills and competences are implicated in successful and sustainable innovation. It also raises the question of just what forms of education and training systems are best suited to growing and supporting an innovation culture, and to the diffusion of progressive innovation practices. We may also wish to consider what needs to be done by those firms and regions that aspire to parity with current innovation leaders. Moving still further to a more granular examination, we can also ask 'what skills are needed to deliver success with respect to different forms of innovation', 'what are the skills that are found in the more innovative companies and regions', and 'how can innovation skills be measured'? It is questions of this nature that this chapter sets out to address.

The first section of the chapter deals with some general themes relating to (a) definitions and forms of skills and innovation, and (b) the role of skills in firm-level, regional and national innovation performance. Section two examines the types of skills that are required for different types of innovation processes, and for innovation in different types of organizations. We conclude with a short discussion of the status of existing knowledge with respect to the skills-innovation dynamic, and with a review of current directions (and remaining gaps) in the research and policy agenda.

CONCEPTUALIZING AND DEFINING 'SKILLS FOR INNOVATION'

Human capital (or skills) accumulation and innovation have been described as the 'twin engines of growth' (Lloyd-Ellis and Roberts, 2002). It is argued that these engines act together and combine with other factors[1] to accelerate economic development and growth at firm, regional and national level. In so doing, they both shape the ways in which we nurture and deploy capabilities that are conducive to innovation, and create demand for new forms and combinations of skills. If the articulation between skills and innovation then is increasingly clear, the mechanisms through which they interact remain somewhat opaque. While we will explore the evidence with respect to inter-linkages and combinatorial modes later, first we need to set out what we mean when we use the terms 'skills' and 'innovation'.

Skills, in their most general sense, can be viewed as the abilities of individuals for which there is a demand within the formal economy. Such skills can include management and leadership abilities, technical, scientific and production abilities, and soft/interpersonal abilities. Individuals typically acquire skills that enable them to implement and use existing technologies and to fit in with *current ways of doing things*. However, they also acquire skills that assist them in developing novel products or in organizing work and production processes in new ways. Tether et al. (2005) define a 'skill' as 'an ability or proficiency at a task that is normally acquired through education, training and/or experience'. These authors also indicate that the term 'skill' is sometimes used synonymously with related concepts of 'competence', 'expertise', 'knowledge' or 'human capital'. They suggest that there are many forms of skills and that the term is used in a wide variety of contexts. Here (and at a most basic level) it is useful to distinguish between different *levels* and different *types* of skills. Discussion of level implies that we consider the aptitudes, experience, credentials or abilities that are required of individuals in the performance of a task or function. With respect to types of skill, here we are concerned with various classes such as engineering, technical, organizational, problem-solving, language, relationship-building and communication skills.

Innovation is a complex and contested term that can be used in a variety of contexts.[2] The OECD's Oslo Manual (1995) defines innovation as: 'The implementation of a new or significantly improved (to the user) product (good or service), or process, a new marketing method, or a new organizational method in business practices, workplace organization or external relation'. This definition captures both the meaning of innovation as a *process* (implementation) and as a new *artifact or practice* (product, process, method, etc.). However, a more elaborate definition can be found in *The Oxford Handbook of Innovation* (2004, p.4) where Fagerberg notes that:

> An important distinction is normally made between invention and innovation. Invention is the first occurrence of an idea for a new product or process, while innovation is the first attempt to carry it out into practice. Sometimes, invention and innovation are closely linked, to the extent that it is hard to distinguish one from another . . . In many cases, however, there is a considerable time lag between the two . . . Such lags reflect the different requirements for working out ideas and implementing them. While inventions may be carried out anywhere, for example in universities, innovations occur mostly in firms, though they may also

occur in other types of organizations, such as public hospitals. To be able to turn an invention into an innovation, a firm normally needs to combine several different types of knowledge, capabilities, skills, and resources. For instance, the firm may require production knowledge, skills and facilities, market knowledge, a well functioning distribution system, sufficient financial resources, and so on . . .

Definitions of innovation often stress '*the successful exploitation of new ideas*'[3]—this particular formulation is from the UK government's Department for Business Innovation and Skills (DBIS) but echoes the emphasis on success often found in the management literature. The concept of 'success' is, however, somewhat ambiguous—a technical success may be a commercial disaster!

THE ROLE OF SKILLS IN INNOVATION

The definitions sketched above, and the wider discussions in which they are set, indicate that there are different types of innovation and innovation processes, varying for instance in terms of the following:

- Types of idea and underpinning knowledge (e.g., technological ideas are emphasized to the exclusion of cultural or organizational ones)[4]
- Ways of generating ideas (e.g., research and development are prioritized as compared to innovations developed in practice or on the job)
- Forms of success (e.g., economic return or social benefit and/or acclaim) and
- Levels of novelty—since some new ideas are groundbreaking while others are minor changes in established ways of doing things, there is a classic distinction between *incremental* and *radical* innovation. Many related concepts have been introduced such as 'revolutionary', 'architectural' and 'configurational' innovations. In addition, innovation studies may ask whether an innovation is 'new to the firm, new to the industry, or new to the world'.[5]

Different forms of innovation can be introduced too. For example, the European Commission's Community Innovation Survey (CIS4) deploys four widely used classes:

- *Product innovation* (usually technological)—This is where innovation involves the development of new goods, services, machinery, equipment, components, software (or novel assemblages of these).
- *Process innovation*—Here innovation focuses on development of new systems or routines of production, again with an emphasis on the tools, equipment and software that are to be used in novel processes.

- *Organizational innovation*—Here innovation relates to changing management practices or workflow structures.
- *Marketing innovation*—Here innovation involves new ways of relating to customers and potential customers (including new ways of promoting products). This is closely related to the idea of *delivery innovations*, targeted at transforming the ways in which products or services reach their consumers.

Much discussion centers on research and development (R&D) as the way in which innovations are generated. In practice, however, innovations often come from work on the shop floor or front office, and R&D departments are, anyway, rare other than in high-tech manufacturing (and a few high-tech services) companies. Often, major innovations are organized through project development teams. In some firms and sectors the main influences on innovation are the introduction of new machinery and software from suppliers of such tools; in others, professional associations and industry associations provide an important source of knowledge; in yet more, the clients are a major stimulus for innovative ideas, and so on.

Further, we should note that the innovation process is itself something that changes over time. From the first development of an idea (invention), through its development into a new product or process, the rollout of the idea in the innovating organization (translation), and then the distribution and implementation of this by further users (diffusion), new ideas may be introduced at any stage. In addition, the design of the innovation may be adapted in the light of feedback as to user requirements, technical problems or competitor products.

Two important ideas here are the 'product life cycle' and the 'industry life cycle'. Each refers to a stylized path of development. In the *product life cycle* the picture refers to the development of an innovation from being expensive and hard to use, to being cheap and available for low-skill users (and often mass markets). The focus of innovative effort evolves from one of getting the product to work and to be well adapted to users needs, to one of mass-producing it easily and cheaply. The *industry life cycle* points to the parallel phenomenon, wherein firms rise and decline and production may be moved from highly knowledge-intensive locations to ones characterized by cheap and less skilled labor. These 'life cycles' are useful frameworks for thinking about labor product and industrial change, but there are many cases where the patterns described earlier are not followed with any precision.

Given then that there are many forms of innovation that do not follow a defined set of stages, the relationship between innovation and skills is inevitably complicated. Skills involved in innovation will depend on the following:

(a) The nature of the innovation in question (incremental vs. radical; product, process or organizational)

(b) The nature and distribution of skills within and available to an organization

(c) The possibility of transforming and growing new skills within enterprises and the wider economy

It is possible for an individual enterprise to go through the whole process of innovation without changing its skills set (especially if the innovation is incremental, rather than radical). However, it is also likely that innovation may lead to, or require, a change (possibly of various different kinds) in the skills profile of the business. It is also clear that at both the level of the firm and across the economy, the various stages of innovation in manufacturing and services will at some point impact on the demand for skills and new skill composition, including that relating to management and leadership, technical and scientific work, and soft/interpersonal activities.

Following from the foregoing, it could be expected that different 'types' or classes of innovation will require different types of skills (i.e., skills differing in both form and level). These skills are needed to support development and diffusion. The configuration in Figure 8.1 is not intended to be comprehensive (as there are of course many generic skills involved in innovation of all forms). Rather, it is indicative, offering an overview of the types of core skills frequently associated with different classes of innovation. Data in Figure 8.1 draws upon work by Tether et al. (2005), Tidd et al. (2001) and Utterback (1996).

We can now look in more detail at classes of innovation and the forms of skills that are generally required to ensure their realization (Tether et al., 2005).

Product and technological innovation is commonly understood to concern the development of new goods, equipment and services that generate demand for scientific, technological, design and engineering skills

Class of Innovation	Skills
Product and Technological	Scientific and Technological; Engineering Design; Packaging Design; Market and User Research
Process	Technical; Project Management; Organizational and Workflow Design; Interaction and Relationship Management
Organizational	Opportunity Recognition; Systems Design; Leadership; Communication
Marketing, Delivery and Interface	ICT & Systems Development; Web Design and Content Development; Data Analysis; Language and Communication

Figure 8.1   Classes of innovation and associated core skills.

(especially in the case of innovation associated with the development of tangible goods). Technological innovation in developed economies has been described as skill-biased, insofar as it is perceived to increase demand for higher-level skills and reduce demand for lower-level skills. Market research skills are also necessary for the collection of data relating to the orientations and preferences of potential consumers, as are client interfacing (and communication) skills in the case of new service development and delivery. Given the 'distributed' nature of much contemporary innovation, skills for the management and coordination of team-based working are perceived to be an increasingly necessary ingredient in innovation.

Process innovation involves the development and commercial exploitation of a new way of producing an organization's product(s). Much discussion in the economics of innovation literature focuses on the 'job reducing' character of process innovation: this is because much of this innovation is of the kind where capital—in the form of new machinery or equipment—replaces labor (particularly where such labor is unskilled). However, process innovation can involve the use of more labor relative to capital, or the offsetting of job losses by the creation of jobs elsewhere in a company or the economy (for example, in the upstream production of new machinery). Process innovation itself is complex (and evident in many forms), and usually requires some technical and project management skills to ensure successful specification and implementation (especially where new deployment of technologies is implied). Organizational and management skills will usually be required in order to ensure successful redesign of workflow processes. Interaction and relationship management skills are also frequently necessary where introduction of a new process implies disruption to existing work routines.

Organizational innovation implies change in management practices and organizational structures and can have a variety of effects on the demand for skills. While it is closely related to process innovation (as the latter frequently requires some level of organizational change), at a basic level, the term implies the introduction of new management practices and/or the redesign and reorganization of work practices and routines (i.e., new ways of 'getting the job done', or the introduction of new jobs and methods of working). Skills for the initiation of organizational innovation include an ability to recognize opportunities for (and value to be derived from) the introduction of new systems. They also include an ability to conceive of and design appropriate new systems. The management of organizational innovation frequently involves leadership and communications skills, and an ability to convey a (positive) vision of change to secure the buy-in of workers affected by change.

Marketing, delivery and interface is concerned with the development of new ways of getting products and information to clients and service users. The extraordinary growth in the number and sophistication of commercial and public agency websites over the past decade is clear evidence of the efforts of contemporary organizations to create novel ways of interfacing with their users, partners and customers. Importantly, this growth also highlights the central role of ICTs in the development and realization of interface innovations.[6] New technologies, including mobile telephony and web infrastructure, have made it possible for firms and agencies to evolve novel business models (e.g., around e-business and remote transactions), and to use data captured via interactions with their customers in their innovation activity. Skills involved in the development of delivery and interface innovations are wide-ranging but there is a clear focus on high-level technology skills, such as those associated with systems development and integration, and cyber security. Web design, data analysis, and creative and content development skills are also important, as are language and communication skills where delivery innovations involve the establishment of remote customer service facilities. Enhancing services—or indeed providing these through alternative delivery channels such as by phone or Internet— often requires soft skills including oral communication, customer handling, local problem solving and teamwork. These skills applied through 'emotional labor' are increasingly important for businesses seeking to compete on the basis of enhanced quality of service, rather than price (Becker, 2001; Frenkel et al., 1999).

Incidence of the classes of innovation sketched earlier is liable to vary across the product/industry life cycle, and stages in these life cycles are liable to affect both demand for and supply of various types of skills. Stages of the life cycle and associated skills are presented in Figure 8.2.

With respect to product innovation, Tether et al. (2005) report that businesses can be expected to transit through three stages, each differing in their demand for skills. During an early, 'fluid stage', the product is ill-defined, and the key skills needed are those of entrepreneurism (often combined with scientific or technical specialisms, and skills in marketing). Production skills at this stage tend to be general and adaptable, rather than specific and rigid. At this stage, production workers have to adapt to rapidly changing

Innovation	Fluid Phase Radically new products	Transitional Phase Focus on process to achieve production scale efficiencies	Specific Phase Gradual cumulative improvements in productivity & quality
Key Skills	Entrepreneurial skills, coupled with high-level specialism in technology and/or marketing; also, an adaptive workforce, which develops more specific skills over time	Organized, functional 'scientific management', plus development of specialist workforce skills associated with mechanization of production	Small 'elite' with managerial command & control skills, seeking to maintain control over a workforce with low or non-specific skills

Figure 8.2   Characteristics of innovation and skills over the product/industry life cycle. Source: Tether et al. (2005).

technologies and demands. Subsequently the product tends to become more defined and standardized, and a 'dominant design' emerges. This is a 'transitional stage', in which there is a shift from product to process innovation. The emergence of a clearly defined product denotes entry into a 'specific stage' where firms increasingly compete on costs and price, rather than on product quality and features. During this phase, management skills become more functional and 'scientific', while workforce skills become more specific, and the division of labor more precise.

There is often a tension between how finely honed workers' skills are to a task and their ability to learn and adapt. The introduction of specialist equipment may at first augment the skills of skilled workers. However, in the long run, capital (i.e., machinery, equipment) tends to replace skilled labor. During the mature phase of the industry the remaining labor force becomes increasingly low-skilled. Technologically-based product and process innovations, then, can have different effects on the demand for skills. Process innovation is generally assumed to be of the kind where capital replaces labor, particularly unskilled labor. However, innovation could increase demand for the firm's products, stimulating employment, or jobs can be created elsewhere in the economy (for example, where firms supply capital equipment). Product innovation is broadly expected to generate employment, because it can increase demand for a firm's products.

As we shall discuss later, innovation processes are also increasingly distributed or 'open', requiring clusters of firms and other stakeholders to work together rather than 'going it alone'. These distributed processes require managerial skills in forming and sustaining collaborative arrangements for innovation.

Overall, it is difficult to disentangle the skills that drive innovation from those that are demanded as a result of change brought about by innovation. The skills of the workforce and management will help determine the innovation that takes place within a firm. This will then help determine the changed demand for skills in the firm, and this in turn will influence the innovation that takes place and so on. Understanding the relationships requires modeling that is currently not yet widespread.

Nevertheless, there is enough analysis and evidence available to be able to draw many conclusions about the nature of skills for innovation and their implications for developed economies. Below we will see how far these enable us to address the series of issues that have been posed.

SKILLS, INNOVATION AND PERFORMANCE

We can now turn to how needs for skills and innovation vary across different types of organizations, and the ways in which skills for innovation impact on their performance. Many companies—especially SMEs—are not able to put much effort into thinking about innovation, and so do not have articulated views about their skill needs for innovation. We might conclude that they have a need for management skills associated with maintaining awareness of the challenges and opportunities with which innovation confronts them! More generally, many firms will have difficulty in identifying the broader management and workforce skills required for effective innovation in their sectors and markets, and management capabilities for such strategic skills analysis are highly desirable. We should also note that there is some evidence that innovative SMEs, at least, seem to see the main issue as one of developing skills in their existing workforce, rather than accessing them from external sources.

There is evidence for both national and regional economies that higher skill levels tend to be associated with higher levels of economic performance (e.g., productivity increases and/or ratings on competitiveness indices). One regional analysis concerns the UK; Boddy et al. (2005) conclude that the relative performance of different UK regions has much to do with differences in capital investment and in skill levels. At a cross-national level, the 2002 European Competitiveness Report reviewed studies demonstrating the positive impact of human capital formation on national economic performance. Skill shortages in the EU were seen to be related to the underperformance of most EU economies when compared to the US (especially in terms of productivity growth). The study puts emphasis on the need to match skills with capital investment. Indeed, the literature here typically suggests that human capital cannot be considered in isolation; it is the combination of skills with management, capital investment, and other factors—for example, transport and communications infrastructure—that is necessary for really effective performance.

Shortages of higher-level skills have been reported to have a negative impact on performance insofar as they introduce delays into the innovation process (Mason, 1999; 2000). The UK Technical Graduates Employers Survey in 1998 (reported in Forth and Mason, 2004) in the UK found that two-thirds of employers that had experienced difficulties in recruiting high-level skilled personnel reported the incidence of commercial problems as a result. The most commonly mentioned problem was delays in product development and process improvement projects, impacts that may have no immediate effect on performance but may contribute to weakened performance in the longer term. The link may not be a mechanical one—groups of skilled workers may dig in their heels to protect their jobs, working conditions and status, and resist the introduction of specific innovations. However, there is a wide consensus that innovation is in general more prevalent where there are higher levels of workforce skills. Most of the evidence concerns skills in general, rather than 'skills for innovation' specifically. A line of useful evidence comes from innovation surveys that question firms with respect to their innovative activities and other factors that relate to innovation, including employment of graduates and expenditure on innovation-related training.

An analysis of UK data from the fourth EC Community Innovation Survey (CIS4), conducted by the authors in 2005, points to there being a strong link between skills and innovation. This survey asked managers in firms with more than ten employees a series of questions about innovation-related issues. We analyzed data at firm and at sector level, with similar broad results. There was a positive relationship between the proportion of workers with higher education qualifications at firm or sector level, and the likelihood of firms engaging in product, process or organizational innovation in the previous three years. There was a weaker relationship between innovation propensity and the average amount of expenditure on innovation-associated training per employee—suggesting that greater training expenditure does not automatically result in more innovative ideas being put into practice. We would expect that the cost of training staff to use new technologies may vary considerably across sectors and types of innovations. We also note a positive relation between propensity to innovate and the prevalence of reports that a 'lack of qualified personnel' is a barrier to innovation. The more innovative firms experience this problem most, which suggests that skill shortages are more often a barrier to further innovation and commercialization, than they are something that prevents innovation initiatives altogether.

MEASURING SKILLS FOR INNOVATION

The need to develop improved measures for skills for innovation is a problematic but important area for the development of policy (Hanel, 2008; Toner, 2011). It is also an important issue for those sectors and firms that wish to benchmark their innovation capacity as a component in strategic and competitive positioning. One major obstacle resides in the fact that the definition of skills is not uniform across (or within) Europe, the US and Asia: in addition, qualifications are usually adopted as a proxy and these too are not uniform across countries. As a result we find that different methodological approaches are used. Taking the European case as an example, the most common definition for skills employs both occupational skills and educational attainment components (Ireland, France, the Netherlands, Poland, Finland and Romania). In addition to these common components, the UK uses the term 'qualifications', as well as attempting to build on the generic skills concept by including social and personal skills to expand the definition. Greece also applies diverse skill concepts covering generic, technical and personal skills. In Estonia, Italy and Cyprus, skills are defined mainly in terms of occupations. In the Czech Republic and Germany more emphasis is placed on educational attainment and qualifications. Whatever approaches are apparent, there is little evidence that any European country measures skills for innovation specifically and explicitly. Indeed, in view of the foregoing it would be surprising if there was a consensus on what these might be.

The ideas sketched in Lorenz and Valeyre (2006) go some way towards identifying a set of indicators for skills and innovation. The approach is premised on evidence that suggests that firms that combine science-based learning and skills development with experience-based learning tend to be more innovative than those that are biased towards only one of the forms. However, it is important to recognize that national systems differ in terms of how learning is organized in both of these dimensions. The current confusion calls for a broad definition of skills for innovation, and some progress has been achieved in this regard. Lorenz proposed an STI-mode and DUI-mode characterization of skills development. The STI (science, technology and innovation) mode is characterized by a formal science approach and includes engineering training and skills. The DUI (learning by doing, using and interacting) mode refers to experience-based learning and skills that are tacit, embedded in routines and embodied in people. A Composite Skills for Innovation Index is thus proposed comprising four STI-mode indicators and four DUI-mode indicators, along with a set of skills maintenance, and foundation skills indicators. While this configuration has been helpful in aiding thinking about determining indicators for skills and innovation, there is clearly much space and need for further work to establish a holistic and internationally applicable framework for the measurement of skills for innovation.

CONTEXT-DEPENDENT SKILLS FOR INNOVATION

As outlined earlier, it is clear that different stages of the innovation process will require the application of specific types and combinations of skills. Attempts to 'unpack' and describe innovation activity are many and varied but most identify four or five broad stages in the process (see Zaltman, Duncan and Holbek, 1973; Rogers, 1983; Tidd, Bessant and Pavitt, 2001; Boden and Miles, 2000; Christensen and Raynor, 2003). Though differences in emphasis and delineation exist between commentators and theorists, stages of the innovation process are frequently cast in the following terms:

1. Sourcing and selection of ideas.
2. Development of ideas and experimentation with alternative configurations, assemblages and processes.
3. Testing, stabilization and commercialization.
4. Implementation and/or diffusion.

While this four-stage characterization probably captures the main steps in the innovation process for a majority of firms, it is important to recognize that different organizations and sectors (manufacturing, private services and public services) are likely to demonstrate sometimes sharply differing approaches to the organization and operationalization of innovation. Such differences (or 'specificities') remain a subject of research and debate (Rubalcaba, 2006; INSEE, ZENTRUM, IFS, 2005), but relate closely to the constraints, operating and market conditions, assumptions and routines that are found across different firms and sectors. Differences will clearly impact perceived and actual skills needed for innovation, as will the classes of innovation activities (i.e., product, process, organizational or delivery-oriented) that are pursued within individual firms and organizations.

It is clear that some generic skills are central to the management of innovation throughout and across the various steps of the process sketched above. An ability to coordinate activities, select appropriate (and appropriately skilled) individuals, assemble teams, motivate and inspire, resolve problems and disputes, generate a creative (and protected) environment, communicate up and down the supply/value chain, and provide focus and leadership are just some of the skills that are required of managers and innovation leaders in contemporary organizations (Klein and Sorra, 1996; Deschamps, 2005). Beyond these, management of the innovation process requires the confidence to take 'Go' or 'Kill' decisions with respect to projects, or to identify and pursue more viable alternatives (Danneels and Kleinschmidt, 2001), and an ability to manage and maintain the complex of intra- and inter-organizational relationships that frequently characterize both large and more modest innovation projects (Hagel and Singer, 1999).

'*Stage-specific*' innovation skills are clearly more difficult to identify and delineate than generic skills, and they are to some extent conditioned by sector and 'class' of innovation, as noted earlier. Some recent work has started to grapple with the issue of stage-specific skills (Tether et al., 2005) and we now see the emergence of ideas relating to the competencies and capabilities that are required to drive innovation through the various steps of the emergence of a new product or process. These include sourcing and selection of ideas, where skills requirements are connected centrally with the identification, collection and filtering of ideas for innovation (Sundbo, 1997). Innovation managers—and employees—will ideally have an awareness of existing sources for innovation both within and outside their organizations, and an ability to 'scan the horizon' for (and develop relationships that will lead to) new sources of ideas and stimuli for innovation. An ability to interpret data (from market, consumer and competitor research) and to evaluate the viability of innovation ideas is also crucial. Knowledge of and an ability to apply relevant IP protection mechanisms constitute a further important skill. Once an innovation idea is selected for possible progression to the development stage, skills in arguing for its viability and potential value—often in the face of strong competition from competing projects—become paramount.

The development of ideas for innovation frequently requires skills connected with the assemblage of development teams, allocation and management of budgets and resources, generation of appropriate spaces and conditions for experimentation, sourcing and specifying complementary inputs, and establishment of networks and partnerships. In contemporary environments, the latter factor can be critical: given the distributed and networked nature of much innovation, skills associated with the orchestration of a disparate range of actors and inputs can be central to success. Further, where innovation is focused on the development of new artifacts or technologies, the sourcing of technical and design skills is likely to be a central concern.

In the testing, stabilization and commercialization stage, evaluation of risks and benefits of continued experimentation is an important skill. Cost-effective innovation requires an ability to recognize the optimal point at which to call a halt to prototyping and the comparison of competing alternatives. It also requires a good knowledge of the preferences and requirements of the intended user or consumer base, and an understanding of the ways in (and extent to) which an innovative product or process will meet anticipated needs. An understanding of the ability of potential users to derive benefits from an innovation (i.e., their 'absorptive capacity') is also necessary. Stabilization and commercialization of a novel product require that an innovating company has the skills in place to ensure reproducibility of an artifact or service at an acceptable price (technical, engineering, design and marketing skills are often to the fore here). Commercialization also requires that attention is afforded to 'capturing value' from an innovation—here, skills associated with managing risk and designing appropriate marketing and rollout strategies are highlighted.

The marketization, implementation and diffusion stage is frequently understood to be connected intimately with project management and technology transfer skills. Beyond these, skills in managing and coordinating value and supply-chain relationships, and in evaluating innovation practice and performance are crucial. Reflexivity too is becoming an increasingly important component of innovation practice as firms recognize that collection and evaluation of data (i.e., knowledge management and intelligence generation) can result in the development of improved innovation processes and practices. In a similar vein, skills associated with the evaluation of alliance and partnership working modes can be highly valuable. Given the network-based nature of much innovation activity, companies need to nurture 'valued' partners, and build intelligence with respect to the factors that result in successful co-innovation activities.

REFLEXIVITY IN THE INNOVATION-
SKILLS RELATIONSHIP

Another useful way of thinking about skills for innovation at different stages of the innovation process—and in associated value chains—derives from the study of 'product life cycles'.[7] Introducing the notion of *circularity*, Tether et al. (2005) argue that it is problematic to distinguish between the skills that facilitate and support innovation within an organization and those that are required because of changes brought about by innovation. The authors suggest that the management and workforce skills that are present within an organization will have a major influence on the nature and style of its innovation. The process of 'doing innovation' in the firm will trigger changes in skills demands, and the emergent skills profile of the organization will in turn shape the direction and form of subsequent generations of innovation activity. Tether et al. (2005) link this idea to the notion of product life cycle and indicate that the latter can provide clues with respect to the ways in which innovation involves shifts in demand for skills throughout the development stages of a new product.[8] Employing a three-phase model, Tether argues that in the first phase, 'conception', where product attributes and characteristics are still weakly defined, key skills requirements revolve around entrepreneurism, scientific and technical expertise and market research and development. In the second phase, 'transition', where the shape of a standard or 'dominant product design' has emerged, the skills focus tends to shift from product to process innovation: here, more operational, functional and scientific management skills (and sometimes, specialist workforce skills) are emphasized as firms gear up for production and distribution. In the third phase, 'stabilization and incremental development'—where attention is directed towards reduction of production costs—managerial 'command and control skills' tend to be highlighted alongside relatively low-level and often non-specific workforce skills. Beyond this, however, where firms target product development— or strive to respond to low-cost competition via iterative improvement, movement into markets for higher-quality goods, or product differentiation—technical, design, branding and marketing skills are likely to take on increasing importance.

CLASSES, FORMS AND LOCATIONS OF INNOVATION—IMPLICATIONS FOR SKILLS

It is clear that innovation (a) has many forms, (b) takes place in widely differing sectors and locations, and (c) can be initiated and undertaken by actors across a broad range of roles and functions. This raises important questions about the skills that are necessary with respect to different types of innovation and the skills that are required in different industrial settings. In Figures 8.3, 8.4 and 8.5 we set out three broad innovation dichotomies[9] and contrast the skills that might be required in radical versus incremental innovation environments, technological versus organizational processes, and manufacturing versus services settings. Of course, we cannot hope to provide comprehensive coverage of all the different classes of innovation and their associated skills needs; however, the figures present an outline map of the skills most commonly associated with core and specific classes of innovation activity.

Innovation Type	Features	Associated Skills
Radical	*Radical innovation*, sometimes also described as 'breakthrough', 'revolutionary' or 'disruptive' innovation, is normally associated with major scientific and technological developments that result in highly significant and far-reaching changes across industries, markets and consumption behaviors (Harvard Business School, 2000). Radical innovations are perceived to bring about dramatic shifts, often ushering in whole new classes of products, new methods of production and even new industries or industrial sectors. Radical innovations can be many years in gestation and frequently result from a scientific or technological discovery or breakthrough (for example, steam power, isolation of DNA and development of computers). Radical innovations are relatively sporadic and rare – sometimes the result of long-term effort in R&D and university labs – and often require much complementary effort and innovation before marketable products emerge.	Very high-level science and technology skills (computing, medicine, biology, physics). Synthesizing skills (bringing together ideas and knowledge from disparate disciplines and domains). Knowledge translation and transfer skills. Lobbying and negotiation skills (especially where long-term development funding and social acceptance are required, and licensing agreements are in play). Opportunity recognition skills. Market development skills. Coordination skills (especially where the realization of an innovation or class of innovations requires much distributed and complementary effort).
Incremental	*Incremental innovation* is much more common than its radical counterpart and involves the inception of relatively minor improvements or enhancements to goods, processes and services that are (usually) already in existence in one form or another. Such innovations are often managed and effected by actors who work on an ongoing basis with existing technologies, equipment, methods or processes (von Hippel, 2005). In essence, incremental innovation involves taking steps forward along a recognized technology or organizational trajectory, and such innovation is not likely to result in major changes to business operations, product ranges or markets. Although incremental innovations are targeted at relatively minor upgrading of organizational routines or product characteristics and functionalities, such innovations often require the input of science and technology specialists and are frequently developed within R&D departments. An important characteristic of incremental innovation is that it often relies heavily on feedback and inputs from users or consumers.	Science and technology skills. Engineering skills. Design skills. Process management and technical skills. Coordination skills. Market research and analysis skills (and competitor analysis skills). Business and product positioning skills. Strategic analysis skills. ICT skills (especially in the case of services where the producer-consumer relationship is electronically mediated).

Figure 8.3   Radical versus incremental innovation.

Innovation Type	Features	Associated Skills
Technological	*Technological innovation* – As noted earlier, technological innovation is generally understood to concern the development of new equipment, goods and software. OECD's Oslo Manual (2005, p. 31) describes technological product and process (TPP) innovations as those that 'comprize implemented technologically new products and processes and significant technological improvements in products and processes. A TPP innovation has been implemented if it has been introduced on the market (product innovation) or used within a production process (process innovation). TPP innovations involve a series of scientific, technological, organizational, financial and commercial activities.'	Science and technology skills. Software development skills. Systems development and integration skills (especially in the domain of technological process development). Engineering and ergonomy design skills. Negotiation, coordination and communication skills (especially where licensing, royalties and distribution agreements, production partnerships and outsourcing, and organization of complementary inputs are concerned). Value-chain organization skills. Professional skills (for example, accounting and finance, marketing, sales, IP protection and legal skills).
Organizational	*Organizational innovation* involves the creation of transformation of commercial/business and public sector agency structures, models, routines and practices. Such innovation can embrace business model and marketing innovation and frequently involves the implementation of new production and interfacing processes. Organizational innovation often accompanies business repositioning and strategy development and, in the public sector in particular, has been triggered by government modernization and public service renewal agendas. Organizational innovation is commonly targeted at securing increased efficiency and effectiveness and has been implicated in the major off-shoring and outsourcing programs that have been witnessed in the past decade. While it can be conceived and managed internally, it is not uncommon for major organizational innovation to be designed and implemented by external agencies.	Strategy development and business modeling skills. Procurement and negotiation skills (especially where innovation involves the contracting of external consultants). Communication skills (especially where innovation implies major changes to work practices and impacts on employees). Workflow and job design skills. Professional skills (especially human resources). ICT and systems design skills (where reorganization is reliant on ICTs or involves relocation or off-shoring of work).

Figure 8.4   Technological versus organizational innovation.

Innovation Type	Features	Associated Skills
Manufacturing	*Innovation in the manufacturing sector* concerns the development or improvement of tangible products. Much manufacturing innovation is incremental by nature, involving (a) the gradual replacement of products or product lines, or (b) the introduction of new or enhanced functionalities to existing products and equipment. Though manufacturing innovation goes beyond mere re-styling, design and engineering have an important role. Much manufacturing innovation is triggered by competition: this is especially true in relation to established technologies or goods where attention has been directed increasingly over time towards the reduction of production costs. Iterative product development can assist manufacturers in their efforts to compete with low cost commodity producers and stay ahead of the pack (where this is feasible and desirable).	Engineering and design skills Science and technology skills Market and competitor research skills (and data analysis skills) Customer interfacing skills Process organisation and management skills Business development and positioning skills
Service	*Service innovation* refers to the creation, marketisation and diffusion of service products (e.g, insurance policies or health information programmes). Whilst service innovations are often perceived to be less dependent on scientific and technological knowledge than manufacturing/goods innovations, many are heavily reliant on developments in ICTs (connected as they are with information processing, communication and interaction). However, a key resource for innovation in services is close contact with customers and many service innovators are eager to exploit the detailed data that they derive from on-going interactions with clients, partners and service users. The organisation of innovation in the services sectors rarely resembles that in manufacturing where formalised processes for sourcing and development of new products is common. Service innovation is frequently managed by ad hoc teams rather than specific R&D divisions and dedicated budgets for development activity in services are rare. Service innovation is clearly a concern for service firms and agencies, but much service innovation is also found in manufacturing organisations as the latter increasingly bundle service packages with their goods (for example, finance packages with car sales).	Client interfacing and communication skills ICT skills (especially systems design and integration) Data management and analysis skills Market research and analysis skills Team assembly, co-ordination and management skills Ideas harvesting skills (gathering ideas for innovation from service workers, partners and service users) Procurement and coordination skills (especially where service development involves partnership projects, complementary innovation and technological components) Professional skills (legal, policy analysis and translation, Human Resources)

Figure 8.5 Manufacturing versus Services innovation.

The comparisons shown highlight some useful distinctions between classes of innovations in different sectors and point to the different types and levels of skills that are required in pursuit of innovation. However, it is also important to acknowledge the overlaps that exist across classes. This is particularly true in the case of manufacturing and service sector innovation. Beyond the bundling of services and artifacts in combined packages, it is notable that many manufacturing organizations are home to a range of service functions and service workers (designers, market researchers, sales staff). Thus manufacturers can be important producers of service innovation (so too, they are likely to be important loci of organizational and process innovations).

CONCLUSIONS

As inventions and innovations accumulate and are built upon each other, so the portfolio of knowledge that is required to master the creation of new products and processes grows. The scope of knowledge that is needed to bring a new idea to fruition may be much wider than previously understood, and the forms of knowledge that may be called upon to support the development of each innovation may be different in many respects. So, the range of skills required to facilitate innovation expands rapidly, and the complexity of linkages between actors with specific competencies is intensified. In addition, the increasingly networked nature of innovation calls for the acquisition of new capabilities, as orchestration and management of disparate groups of (sometimes geographically distributed) co-innovators become a common requirement. Given this growing complexity in innovation networks and activities, and the intensified focus on innovation as a driver of competitiveness, the future—at policy, sector and firm levels—is likely to see ever greater attention afforded to efforts to nurture human capital and build skills for innovation. As we have seen, however, current understanding of the articulation between innovation performance and skills remains somewhat fragile, and vigorous efforts are required if we are to be able to map connections, and work towards (internationally) standardized definitions and measures for innovation skills.

As we suggested in the introduction, this chapter set out to address a number of questions with respect to skills for innovation and, on the basis of existing evidence and theory, has provided a provisional answer to some. Importantly, we see the emergence of a better understanding of the types of skills that are needed to enable (a) different forms of innovation, and (b) innovation at different stages of the product development life cycle. So too, we have hinted at the factors and characteristics that can support improved innovation performance at sector and firm level. We have also noted the problems that confront efforts to develop appropriate metrics for skills for innovation, though it is clear that adequate remedies are not yet within our grasp. With respect to the improvement of regional competitiveness via human capital development, again, we have flagged the key issues without providing comprehensive recommendations (though policymakers in Europe may wish to cast an inquisitive eye both east and west). Indeed, there remains much to be done at policy and research level if we are to both understand the linkages between skills and innovation more comprehensively, and devise supports for the accelerated acquisition or development of innovation capabilities. Perhaps beyond policy too, there is an urgent need to stimulate increased attention and action. At firm and sector level, while it might be difficult to disentangle the skills that drive innovation from those demanded as a result of innovation, greater effort to map and nurture skills (and to plot future skills needs) is likely to pay significant dividends.

NOTES

1. Other factors include the impacts of international trade, labor market institutions (including the minimum wage and trade unions), the domestic competitive environment, education and training and their institutional structures, public expenditure and public policy more generally.
2. While this short passage cannot hope to review the different perspectives that have been brought to bear on the notion of innovation, it is important to recognize the complex, nuanced and contested nature of the concept.
3. See online. Available HTTP: http://www.bis.gov.uk/ (accessed 3 February 2012).
4. Though 'invention' is more commonly applied to technologies than to organizational or artistic ideas.
5. Note that Fagerberg's 'first occurrence' does not necessarily mean the 'first occurrence' anywhere at any time of the innovation. Indeed, often the first example of an innovation does not achieve wide uptake. The diffusion process involves many users effecting their first use of the innovation.
6. The rise of the 'call center' phenomenon is another example of the ways in which organizations are using technologies to enhance and streamline the delivery of public and private services. It is worth noting here too that ICTs have provided organizations with an opportunity to outsource or offshore many services, and to exploit the skills of workers in remote locations.
7. We should note here that Product Life Cycle theory derives principally from the study of manufacturing innovation and is normally applied at industry rather than firm level. See Cawson et al. (1995).
8. In essence, Tether recommends that we consider the ways in which skills for successful innovation change over the product life cycle.
9. Binary distinctions appear frequently in the innovation literature. These constitute a useful heuristic but frequently conceal the significant overlaps that exist between classes.

BIBLIOGRAPHY

Becker, M. C. (2001) 'Managing Dispersed Knowledge: Organizational Problems, Managerial Strategies and Their Effectiveness'. *Journal of Management Studies* 38 (7): 1037–1051.

Boden, M. and Miles, I. (eds.) (2000) *Services and the Knowledge-Based Economy*. London: Routledge.

Boddy, M., Hudson, J., Plumridge, A. and Webber, D. (2005) 'Regional Productivity Differentials: Explaining the Gap'. Discussion papers. University of the West of England, Department of Economics.

Cawson, A., Haddon, L. and Miles, I. (1995) *Shape of Things to Consume*. Brookfield, VT: Ashgate Publishing.

Christensen, C. and Raynor, M. (2003) *The Innovator's Solution: Creating and Sustaining Successful Growth*. Boston: Harvard Business School Press.

Danneels, E. and Kleinschmidt, E. (2001) 'Product Innovativeness from the Firm's Perspective: Its Dimensions and Their Relation with Project Selection and Performance'. *Journal of Product Innovation Management* 18 (6): 357–373.

Deschamps, J. P. (2005) 'Different Leadership Skills for Different Innovation Strategies'. *Strategy and Leadership* 33 (5): 31–38.

EC. (2002–2004) 'European Commission's Community Innovation Survey (CIS4)'. Online. Available HTTP: http://www.bis.gov.uk/policies/science/science-innovation-analysis/cis/cis4_questionnaire (accessed 3 February 2012).

EC. (2002) 'European Competitiveness Report 2002: Commission Staff Working Document' (sec(2002) 528). Online. Available HTTP: http://bookshop.europa.eu/en/european-competitiveness-report-2002-pbN-BAK02001/ (accessed 3 February 2012).

Fagerberg, J., Mowery, D. and Nelson, R. (eds.) (2004) *The Oxford Handbook of Innovation*. Oxford: Oxford University Press.

Forth, J. and Mason, G. (2004) 'The Impact of High-level Skill Shortages on Firm-Level Performance: Evidence from the UK Technical Graduates Employers Survey'. NIESR discussion paper no. 235. National Institute for Economic and Social Research, London.

Frenkel, S., Korczynski, M., Shire, K. A. and Tam, M. (1999) *On the Front Line: Organization of Work in the information Economy*. Ithaca, NY: Cornell University Press.

Hagel, J. and Singer, M. (1999) 'Unbundling the Corporation'. *Harvard Business Review* 77 (2): 133–141.

Hanel, P. (2008) 'Skills Required for Innovation: A Review of the Literature'. Report for CIRST, Quebec, Canada.

INSEE, ZENTRUM, IFS. (2005) 'Innovation and Employment in European Firms: Microeconometric Evidence' (Final report on project HPSE CT2001–00047 to EC DG Research).

Klein, K. and Sorra, J. S. (1996) 'The Challenge of Innovation Implementation'. *The Academy of Management Review* 21 (4): 1055–1080.

Lloyd-Ellis, H. and Roberts, J. (2002) 'Twin Engines of Growth: Skills and Technology as Equal Partners in Balanced Growth'. *Journal of Economic Growth* 7 (2): 87–115.

Lorenz, E. and Valeyre, A. (2006) 'Organizational Forms and Innovative Performance: A Comparison of the EU15'. In Lorenz, E. and Lundvall, A-B. (eds.), *How Europe's Economies Learn: Coordinating Competing Models*, 140–161. Oxford: Oxford University Press. .

Mason, G. (1999) 'The Labour Market for Engineering, Science and IT Graduates: Are There Mismatches between Supply And Demand?' DfEE research report no. 112. London: National Institute of Economic and Social Research.

Mason, G. (2000) 'Key Issues in IT Skills Research in the UK'. DfEE research report. London: National Institute of Economic and Social Research.

Miles, I. (2000) 'Services Innovation: Coming of Age in the Knowledge-Based Economy'. *International Journal of Innovation Management* 4 (4): 371–389.

Miles, I. (2004) 'Innovation in Services'. In Fagerberg, J., Mowery, D. and Nelson, R. (eds.), *The Oxford Handbook of Innovation*, 433–458. Oxford: Oxford University Press.

OECD. (1995) 'The Measurement of Scientific and Technological Activities. Proposed Guidelines for Collecting and Interpreting Technological Innovation Data'. Oslo Manual, 2nd ed. European Commission (EC) Eurostat, Paris. Online. Available HTTP: http://www.oecd.org/dataoecd/35/61/2367580.pdf (accessed 12 January 2012).

OECD. (2005) 'Oslo Manual'. European Commission (EC). Online. Available HTTP:http://epp.eurostat.ec.europa.eu/cache/ITY_PUBLIC/OSLO/EN/OSLO-EN.PDF (accessed 6 February 2012).

Rogers, E. (1983) *Diffusion of Innovations*. 3rd ed. New York: Macmillan.

Rubalcaba, L. (2006) 'Which Policy for Innovation in Services?' *Science and Public Policy* 33 (10): 745–756.

Sundbo, J. (1997) 'Management of Innovation in Services'. *The Services Industry Journal* 17 (3): 432–455.

Tether, B., Mina, A., Consoli, D. and Gagliardi, D. (2005) 'A Literature Review on Skills and Innovation: How Does Successful Innovation Impact on the Demand for Skills and How Do Skills Drive Innovation?' CRIC report for the Department of Trade and Industry (DTI).

Tidd, J., Bessant, J. and Pavitt, K. (2001) *Managing Innovation: Integrating Technological, Market and Organizational Change*. Chichester: John Wiley & Sons.

Toner, P. (2011) 'Workforce Skills and Innovation: An Overview of Major Themes in the Literature'. OECD Directorate for Science, Technology and Industry (STI), Centre for Educational Research and Innovation (CERI). Working Paper Series. Paris. Online. Available HTTP: http://www.oecd.org/dataoecd/19/10/46970941.pdf (accessed 12 January 2012).

Utterback, J. M. (1996) *Mastering the Dynamics of Innovation*. Boston: Harvard Business School Press.

von Hippel, E. (2005) *Democratizing Innovation*. Boston: MIT Press.

Zaltman, G., Duncan, R. and Holbek, J. (1973) *Innovations and Organizations*. New York: John Wiley & Sons.

9 Innovation and Demographic Change

Jennifer Hayden and Barbara Jones

INTRODUCTION

Major demographic shifts affect every aspect of society; the current global trend of population ageing is no exception. Currently about 700 million or 10 percent of the global population are in the sixty-plus age group and the projections are that this will rise by 2050 to two billion, or 20 percent of projected global figures (Vos et al., 2007). These long-term demographic trends of population ageing are most pronounced across high income OECD countries, albeit at differing rates of advance. Within the European Union, some 36 percent of the current population are over fifty years old with projections set for this to rise to 50 percent over the next twenty-five years. How such trends will affect future capacities to *enhance or stifle innovation* is difficult to decipher. Innovation is a complex amalgam of cultural, political and organizational forces at play with individual and group *dynamics* in ways that may be more, or less, affected by a change in the age structure of society. The shift towards an older demography raises some fundamental issues, not least of which are culturally specific notions of what it means to be old in the early part of the new millennium. These notions are contested and in flux, as the constituents of this new demography challenge conventional and *stereotypical* notions of 'ageing'. Innovations that assist in creating a society that is good to grow old in will become increasingly marketable as populations age. New approaches to workforce management, social care systems and public services will be necessary if the quality and costs of such services are to be maintained within sustainable boundaries.

This chapter looks briefly at innovative opportunities that may emerge from demographic shift.

AGEING AND DEPENDENCY

Ageing, a biological fact located within real parameters of life expectancy rates, is difficult to define. The concept has different meanings and connotations across a wide range of cultural groups within and across societal and geographical borders. Ageing as a topic is, of course not new, but little is to be found under discussion in the innovation literature. Generally, the literature has focused on macroeconomic implications, such as burdens on pensions and health care financing, and on the development and forecasting of science and medicine to mitigate age-associated disability.

Many commentators (Bhagat and Unisa, 2006; Schultz and Binstock, 2008) have suggested that the evidential support that the ageing demographic will necessarily create a burden on welfare systems is not definitive. Demographic projections for future population growth and the widely cited dependence ratios rest on assumptions made about complex drivers such as fertility and morbidity, and therefore the results vary across organizations producing these figures. The statistical projections for dependency ratios are always in flux and so need to be viewed skeptically: for example, 'projections of the size of the American population aged 65 and over in 2040 range from 92 million (high variant) to 59 million (low variant)—a difference of 33 million people. These substantial differences are rarely reported and we are led to believe that there is real certainty about how many older people there will be in the future' (Gee, 2002, p. 751). Room must be made then to exercise the idea that dependency as a result of population ageing will not be the drain that many projections and interpretations would suggest.

Demographers have defined 'dependence' as a label applicable to any person who falls outside of the work-age range—those younger than eighteen and older than sixty-four years. Conceptualizing society in these terms creates a dichotomization of cohorts—the dependent versus independent, 'which may obscure the interdependent nature of social life and sets the backdrop for an intergenerational equity debate based on fictive assumptions that homogenize people on the basis of age' (Gee, 2002 p. 752). It should not necessarily be assumed that older adults are dependent or non-creative, as many remain mentally and physically active well beyond retirement age, either formally in full- or part-time work positions, or informally as caregivers, volunteers and social activists (Bhagat and Unisa, 2006). Recognizing the uncertainty around this debate is useful as it helps to temper fears that the ageing population will be both a societal financial drain and constraint on creativity. An ageing demographic is not an abstract conglomerate but rather a compilation of unique individuals who define quality of life through very different personal calculations and through very different contributions to societal well-being.

OPPORTUNITIES FOR NEW MARKETS, NOVEL PRODUCTS AND SERVICES

Demographic shifts, in fact, open up new opportunities and paradigms in terms of economic, social and technological developments. There may well be an increasing demand for products and services geared to the needs of older people. Products that support an active ageing process give rise to a higher level of social benefits (merit goods). Innovative solutions in the market, including new technologies, products and services, emerge through understanding and by taking account of the specific needs of older people (Bachofner and Bossart, 2006). New technologies (Coughlin, Pope and Leedle, 2006) will be able to transform the delivery of care, in care systems that engage and empower patients and their families, directly connecting patients to caregivers, and personalizing services in response to patients' unique needs, preferences and values. Leveraging a synthesis of technology, disease management and home health may more efficiently and effectively meet the needs of a rapidly ageing society.

A new consumer segment demanding innovative products and services customized to the specific needs of older adults is expected to grow in response to the new demographics. This segment has been defined as the 'silver economy' and is well established in Japan, from which examples can be drawn (Kohlbacher and Herstatt, 2008). In addition to novel products in robotics, smart homes and other assistive technologies, there have been adaptations of well-developed consumer products, such as mobile phones, to enhance usability for older adults and other users who desire stream-lined technology (Kohlbacher and Herstatt, 2008; Kurniawan, Nugroho and Mahmud, 2006). Older adults with greater disposable incomes have also opened up growth in the leisure and financial management service sectors. We will look at some trends and emerging developments.

THE SILVER ECONOMY

Among one of the consequences of population ageing is the potential to stimulate innovation in products and services that are tailored to the specific needs of older citizens. The advent of the term 'silver economy' and its potentialities highlights the benefits inherent in the opportunities of the demographic shift. Japanese businesses are leading in this market, and may serve well as case studies for future innovations for the European market. Kohlbacher (2008) identifies three important areas for new market growth and innovation in products and services: easy-to-use products and technologies; general and luxury products and services for the wealthy; and gerontechnologies and supportive care devices and services.

The market segments opening up to the wealthy older adult market in particular include niche leisure travel and financial management services (Kohlbacher, 2008). The leisure travel industry is harnessing the benefits of an increase in older travelers by offering more experiential travel packages. These cater to the profile of retired travelers, who are often looking for an active or educational experience over a longer period of time than work-age travelers (Lehr, 2007). There is the potential here to offer creative courses, trips tailored to single older adults, and trips coordinated with nursing or assisted living communities. In the area of new financial products for this market, there is an increasing need for skilled financial personnel who are competent in dealing with issues unique to retirees' financial well-being. In response to this, the UK Financial Services Skills Council, an industry group, in consultation with civil society groups and NGOs such as Age Concern, has developed the novel 'Later Life Adviser Accreditation' to address the needs of older adults.

According to the Silver Economy Network of European Regions, or SEN@ER (a cross-Europe initiative to create, identify and support economic growth based on the projected increases of older adult consumers in society), the positive growth possibilities in this consumer sector are formidable: 'calculations for Germany as a whole predict more than 900,000 new jobs in the Silver Economy within the next two decades. There are no other sectors or businesses with a higher growth potential. These calculations should be comparable to other regions and countries in Europe' (Laschet, 2006:1).

RESPONSIVE ORGANIZATIONAL STRATEGY

Some organizations have already responded and adopted strategies based on 'silver' market segmentation, while others are adopting a more inclusive approach. Such strategies adopted by companies seeking opportunities presented by the new demographics are broadly analyzed in Figure 9.1.

The relevance of firm strategy is dependent on the organization's activities whereas age profile appears not to be a relevant marker for segmentation. Segmentation based on functionality—on specific customer needs—is applicable across age cohorts and so can be customized to specific user groups. Following from this, Kohlbacher and Herstatt (2008) proposed an organized

No specific age-related strategy	Opportunities of demographic change *not perceived* OR Perceived through the ageing lens, as *possibly harmful for the company's brand, image*, especially in terms of design, marketing, communication.
'Silver market' strategy	Development of products and services *specifically targeted* at elderly people ('third age' travels) OR *Adaptation* of products and services to fit the elderly (easy to use cell phone with optional, progressive functions)
Age-neutral / Inter-generational strategy	Voluntary development of *age neutral* products (luxury goods and services) OR Development of products that are *accessible to all*, possibly even with the aim of connecting generations together (Wii games)

Figure 9.1 Firm strategy for the silver economy. Source: Kohlbacher (2008).

		NO **AGE SPECIFIC** YES (explicitly)	
Technology Solution	**NEW**	UNIVERSAL DESIGN • Not disabled • Physical/cognitive disability	SILVER PRODUCT DESIGN • Not disabled • Physical/cognitive disability
	EXISTING	PRODUCT ADAPTATION Not disabled	MODIFICATION Physical/cognitive disability

'Universal design is the design of products and environments to be usable by all people, to the greatest extent possible, without the need for adaptation or specialized design'. Architect Ron L. Mace.

Figure 9.2 Addressing age in product development. Source: Kohlbacher (2008).

approach in addressing age in product development that is dependent on the needs of either all or specific user groups (see Figure 9.2).

Innovative approaches will depend on the identified needs and on each company's activity and strategy. The outcomes may take several forms: *radical* innovation to create new solutions to specific situations (e.g., new medical devices) that moderate the effects of declining health to sustain independence; *disruptive* innovation to provide adapted solutions to consumers and thereby enlarge the group of potential customers for the concerned products. The latter may encompass low-end innovation and new market disruptions—for example, simplified cell phones for people who could not use these technologies before.

Innovative approaches are needed to address product developments in any emerging market, but as (2004, p. 13) points out, opening up new trajectories to enable new products is often more difficult on the ground than thought in the boardroom: 'even radical innovations . . . are not usually isolated events, nor are they mainly the replacement of obsolete products or processes . . . (they) come in clusters . . . [and] are not disconnected random agglomerations of new things'. Importantly, production and financial capital is attracted by future high returns to the investment and innovation opportunities that new products and/or new markets are seen to offer, and therefore these resources must be expended to ensure capital is available to make any new system, product or service viable.

UNIVERSAL DESIGN

Universal design (UD) is defined as 'the design of products and environments to be usable by all people, to the greatest extent possible, without the need for adaptation or specialized design', (Centre for Universal Design, 2006, p. 1) and as such does not encourage the creation of products exclusively for older user groups or those with disabilities (Mace, 1998; Macdonald, 2007). Adopting universal design in planning or product creation means that spaces, services and products can be accessed and enjoyed by everyone while concomitantly creating a good society to grow old in. As a leader in this arena, Japan is actively engaged with the UD philosophy through policy measures such as the Heartful Building Law of 1994, Transportation Barrier-Free of 2000, general principles of UD Policy of 2005 and the u-Japan strategy for 2010. Japanese business culture has quickly adopted these principles, as evidenced by the recently formed International Association of UD.

Japan is not alone in its use of UD as there are significant lobbying efforts taking place in countries, such as the US, to have UD principles included in building standards for new homes. Universal design of homes would enable environments conducive to the needs of an ageing population, as well as others with chronic conditions or disabilities, while also providing indoor spaces that are pleasing and easy to live in for all people. This is an innovative approach to maintaining independent living for more people regardless of age or ability (Kose, 2006). The list of considerations for designing a home that is good to grow old in is comprehensive; as such the time and thought that must go into the creation of such a usable space are considerable when compared to standard design practice (Crews and Zavotka, 2006). In view of this, guidelines are readily, inexpensively available to the building trades, and there is considerable research being carried out to further investigate specific design elements that will be most conducive to improving the liveability of homes for all ages. While the movement for universal design in homes came out of earlier movements such as barrier-free design, which was specifically targeted at disabled people, the current form aims to create homes for everyone and may therefore garner more widespread uptake than previous proposals.

Universal design principles are being applied outside of home building as well, to consumer products, services and the outdoor, built environment. An interesting example of a very successful product innovation using UD is the Nintendo Wii gaming system. The system has created a new market where older adults, who had not previously been consumers of video games, are now able to engage in a trans-generational social game that has been shown to improve quality of life (Kohlbacher and Hang, 2007). The phenomenon of Wii uptake in residential care facilities for older adults with disabilities has been cited in the popular press since the system's introduction in 2007. Wii has been well received in nursing homes because many of the residents enjoy virtually playing sports, such as bowling or tennis, that they are no longer able to play in reality (Suttie, 2009). In a recent New Zealand study of the effects of video gaming in residential homes, researchers concluded that, overall, they are beneficial. For instance, some residents have made new friends when they most likely would not have if the Wii was not present (Vickers, 2009). The gaming system has made residents more sociable not only with one another but also with younger visitors, as Wii is able to bridge a once impassable divide. The system has even found its way into hospital-led rehabilitation regimes for older adults, disabled veterans and the like, resulting in the term Wiihab (Associated Press, 2009). Wii is a universally designed product that is user-friendly, physically stimulating and fun while encouraging socialization. It is therefore a good example of the kinds of UD innovation that have broad appeal while improving the lives of older adults. However, it must be noted that UD principles can be problematic in that they homogenize very disparate groups of people and needs, especially when applied to products with global reach.

ASSISTIVE TECHNOLOGIES

The use of assistive technologies, particularly in the home, is increasing. These range from low-end tech, such as an ergonomically curved spoon or entry ramp, to higher-end functions, such as Internet-ready computers and a range of ambient technologies in smart homes. Some EU member states provide or subsidize services to modify homes for the disabled through government programs. These modifications range from threshold leveling to modifying kitchens and bathrooms and installing stair lifts (Purdam and Norman, 2010; Johansson, Josephsson and Lilja, 2009; Smith, Bange and Hall, 2000). More innovative assistive technologies are likely to become available to older adults in the near future. Among these are developments in the new interdisciplinary field of 'gerontechnology', which has emerged in response to the perceived needs and aspirations of older people coupled with recent significant advances in technology. Gerontechnology has so far made use of robotic technologies to deliver physical and cognitive therapy and to extend traditionally clinic-based therapy into the home through tele-health solutions. The field is opening up and promises to deliver more innovative products and services for an ageing population in the years to come.

Some types of personal robots are also classed as assistive technologies and are already available on the market. They are designed to provide potentially useful, everyday services such as cooking, heavy lifting and bathroom cleaning. In this field there is also the recent advent of animaloid or pet-like robotics that have multiple sensing capabilities. Some also provide mental stimulation in the form of cognitive games, which may serve to slow or reverse certain forms of dementia (Wada et al., 2008). The field of robotics research is excited about the potential use of such systems in the future. They envisage that 'humanoid robots will become more and more common in the house helping the elders to satisfy their needs. 'In this case, the humanoid assistant will be able (as a nice old friend) to anticipate the needs of the user and to help him/her only when necessary and disappearing otherwise' (Micera, Bonato and Tamura, 2008, p.13). However, it may be the case that the positive outlook of those driving this innovation should be tempered as consumer uptake of such robots has been lackluster. Foulk (2007[1]), reporting for Reuters from Japan, describes how older adults in institutional care did not appreciate the robotic 'friends' that had been purchased for their home: 'Among the most high-profile failures was Hopis, a furry pink dog-like robot capable of monitoring blood sugar, blood pressure and body temperature'.

The development of technologies to counter cognitive decline is a very promising field. Cognitive impairment due to ageing and age-related diseases, such as dementia, is increasing in incidence, rendering more people unable to navigate their daily life independently. Current trends point towards increased prevalence of dementia, linked to the increasing median age of the population. People exhibiting cognitive impairment symptoms require the presence of a carer to help with performing daily activities. Given this trend, more people will seek support, and providing this kind of continuous support is costly and could strain the health care system of many states. Various institutions are increasingly seeking solutions to mitigate this problem, by enabling those with dementia to lead an independent life at home for as long as possible, thus postponing the need to move to a residential care facility. These technologies can be deployed at home, and range from simple, low-cost sensors up to smart assistive robots and interfaces, as mentioned earlier. They also include video analysis to detect patient behavior, memory aids and other cognitive prosthetics.

TELE-HEALTH SOLUTIONS

Tele-medicine, such as the use of wireless technology within the home to assist in physical rehabilitation, is another nascent field of innovation created to address the needs of the disabled. The technology links wireless remote sensors on a patient's body to a distant physical therapist, enabling the therapist to guide the patient through a therapy session without physically being in the same location (Hamel, Fontaine and Boissy, 2008). This kind of teleconferencing means that the patient does not have the hassle of travelling to a remote center to receive individualized therapy. Developments in wireless infrastructure, such as body-area networks or pervasive health-monitoring systems, have proved beneficial to deliver tele-medicine services regardless of a patient's physical location. Wireless applications for this kind of health care are an emerging cross-disciplinary activity, and recent advances in hardware design and wireless communications along with the evolution of new generations of embedded wireless devices facilitating reliable, comprehensive and high-standard health care have potential for creating entirely new products and services.

Remote monitoring is another tele-health solution; it works by remotely sensing a person's activities in the home, providing alarm and status reports to distant caregivers. Such systems can include motion detectors to determine a person's location, contact switches on cabinets and refrigerator doors to indicate whether they have been opened, pressure sensors that indicate whether a person is sitting in a bed or chair and thermometers that indicate whether a stove has been turned on. Biosensor monitors measure vital signs such as heart rate and body temperature, with the resultant data regularly transmitted to authorized carers (Pollack, 2005). One such biosensor system is used by the US Veterans Administration and allows care coordinators to remotely monitor an older veteran's chronic illness, such as diabetes or high blood pressure. The monitoring is complemented by education and self-management strategies and has been producing beneficial results, including an increase in care-coordinator initiated clinic visits and a concomitant decrease in hospitalizations as a result of vigorous monitoring enabling early intervention (Bendixen et al., 2009). There is an additional class of systems under development that are designed to proactively assist with cognitive impairments. These more advanced systems are envisaged as offering navigational support, aid in remembering daily schedules or multi-step tasks, assistance in recognizing faces and help in locating misplaced objects.

As touched upon earlier, tele-care has several different functions: facilitating access to existing services; expanding services to encompass health promotion and maintenance; and creating and delivering new services (Barlow, 2003). Telecare is thus a *package of care* to individuals in the community, which may include domiciliary visiting, assistive technologies (including home adaptations and 'smart' homes), medication and therapy, among other things. Appropriate business models capable of delivering tele-care have yet to be developed to encourage financial viability. Business and service delivery models for tele-care to be sustainable must fit into the more general political and economic environment of health and social care delivery. This implies the need for close collaboration between public and private sectors, a change in roles of existing actors and the emergence of new players.

While not strictly classed as a tele-health solution, much of the literature addressing innovation—for example, Europe's ageing demographic—discusses the potential benefits of the new field of 'smart home' technologies. These homes would harness the benefits of ICT discussed earlier to create living spaces where older adults could remain independent for longer (Hilbert and Fretschner, 2008). A 'smart home' is defined as 'a residence equipped with technology that facilitates monitoring of residents and/or promotes independence and increases residents' quality of life. The technology is integrated into the infrastructure of the residence and does not in principle require training of, or operation by, the resident' (Demiris and Hensel, 2008, p.33). Smart homes offer individuals of any age the ability to remain in place through changing health care needs. Demiris and Hensel (2008) have completed an exhaustive literature review of existing smart home projects, where the emphasis is on health-related technologies, as opposed to energy efficiency. The European Commission is currently funding a large-scale pilot project of smart homes called SOPRANO. The goal of this project is to 'design the next generation of systems for ambient assisted living in Europe: highly innovative context-aware, smart home environment services, built to an innovative and integrative standards and service-orientated architecture and supporting a uniquely broad set of natural and comfortable interfaces for older people at affordable cost, so elderly people can live independently in their preferred environment' (SOPRANO, 2007, p.1). The kinds of technologies intended for smart homes are extensive, encompassing most of those aforementioned. Ultimately of course, the design of such homes and the use of such technologies have to be based on the needs of end users rather than novel or cutting-edge technologies.

SOCIAL NETWORKS

Social and community networks provide important support for ageing adults. Many such networks are intergenerational and are increasingly being seen as arenas to provide opportunities for collective and collaborative knowledge exchange. The resultant intergenerational solidarity improves social cohesion, cooperation and mutual respect. The creation and support of these intergenerational social networks provide a conduit for the tacit knowledge of older adults to be relayed to younger generations, thus ensuring the continuity of society's amassed knowledge. The Madrid Action Plan (UN, 2002, p. 16) has noted mentoring, mediating and advising through such networks as a means to achieve the goal of 'full utilization of the potential and expertize of persons of all ages, recognizing the benefits of increased experience with age'.

Face-to-Face Social Networks

Older adults engage in a wide range of activities organized by religious, political, trade union, charitable and recreational networking organizations. Fostering wider growth of such informal activities is perceived as a virtuous policy aim adding to and enhancing societal creativity. Overall, however, the proportion of older people participating in such activities is not very high—around one-quarter in church and religious activities, 3 percent in political parties and trade unions and around 20 percent in recreational groups (EC, 2008). The Survey of Health, Ageing and Retirement in Europe (SHARE) provides detail about the informal activities of the over-fifties in some EU member states. Hank and Stuck (2008), using results from SHARE, found that one of the most common activities, far removed from the aforementioned recreation or political involvement, was regular caring for grandchildren. The survey identified significant country differences in volunteering rates, informal helping, caring for other adults and civic or social organization involvement. Older people most involved in these activities (and especially in the 65–74 age group) were to be found in the Netherlands, Sweden and Denmark, with the lowest participation rates in Southern and Central Europe. These figures highlight different cultural constructs concerning attitudes to social participation, but they may also reflect differing social welfare regimes, including health care regimes and pension disparities across EU member states (Hank and Stuck, 2007). The trend towards more involvement, while contingent on cultural conditions, has the possibility to create societies that are good to grow old in, as older adults continue to be contributing members of a socially inclusive community, and feeling useful in this way is positively correlated with longevity and health (Gruenewald et al., 2007).

Internet Access and Virtual Networks

New Internet learning environments can offer positive arenas for facilitating creative social exchange in and between age groups. The ability to access and utilize information technology, particularly the Internet, has become important for many people in maintaining or creating social networks, accessing health care information, entertainment or other forms of information that can contribute to an increased quality of life (Seals et al., 2008). For most older adults today, the Internet is simply not a part of their lives. However, the baby boom generation that is now entering retirement will perhaps begin a trend of increasingly computer- and technology-savvy older adults. There are issues of physical, social and cognitive barriers to some older adults' uptake of the Internet, which must be considered in light of any discussion around the potential benefits it may offer this cohort (Harley and Fitzpatrick, 2009). Certainly, the Internet is not a necessary component to living a rich life, and perhaps in some cases the resultant information overload can be overwhelming. However, it is clear that access and ability to utilize select services would be beneficial if extended out across the digital divide regardless of physical or financial capacity.

Virtual social networks can overlap and reinforce traditional ones for older adults, especially given the increasing prevalence of geographical dissolution in familial structures. The ability to use the Internet for communication can provide a vital means for staying connected and staving off loneliness or isolation for both older adults and their distant kin. Innovations, such as the video conferencing solution Skype, are now widespread in Internet-using parts of society. There is much anecdotal evidence in the popular press to suggest that older adults are using such Internet services to communicate with geographically distant friends and family. When interviewed about her video conference use, an eighty-eight-year-old grandmother in the US spoke about keeping in touch with her great-grandchildren in Germany: 'With the little ones, it's so important—I just feel so blessed . . . Some people say, "I don't want a computer", How can they live without a computer?' (Kurz, 2009[2]) Local governments and service organizations can play a role in providing access to and instruction on how to use computers equipped for Internet conferencing through institutions such as libraries and community centers.

Recent work in the UK developing and assessing an innovative IT network has identified new potentials for social networking and e-information accessing for and by older adults (Godfrey and Johnson, 2009). In this pilot program researchers worked with older adults and their existing circles of support to develop a Web-based portal for accessing community and social information that was previously scattered and difficult to obtain. The first hurdle encountered was in developing a platform that would be easy to use for both older adults and their carers. Through iterations and user feedback, the research team was able to arrive at notions underpinning a suitable design which focused on universal usability when providing software. The key finding of this project was the importance of utilizing an older adult's circle of support to act as technology literate intermediaries for those older adults who cannot or do not wish to use computers.

Another interesting potential for virtual networking is the development of Web 2.0 systems which are designed specifically for over-fifties. Sites, such as Saga Zone and Eons, provide a social networking interface specifically designed for older adults to socialize among themselves. Another Web 2.0 application, YouTube, has been hosting intergenerational discussions for some time and there may be an emergent trend in which older users socialize with younger users through video blogging on this popular website. Harley and Fitzpatrick (2009) offer a case study of this phenomenon where an eighty-plus-year-old man has been active on the video networking site since 2006 posting stories of his life. Several younger users posted video comments about these stories resulting in a regular following of thousands to whom he offers solicited advice.

Lifelong Learning and Exchange

Innovations built using the Internet can play a role in knowledge transfer. Older adults necessarily have a wealth of life experience and tacit knowledge that can provide positive grounds for rich intergenerational exchange and the retention of knowledge in society. The university has an important role to play in facilitating this knowledge transfer, especially of the more tacit and experiential knowledge of older skilled and educated adults who are no longer allowed participation in the workforce. Once these adults leave work, many would like to contribute to their communities but perhaps not in traditional voluntary roles of caregiver or charity workers. There is thus the need to offer diverse and meaningful ways for retirees and partial retirees to continue contributing to society if they choose. Innovations in education delivery, such as the Open University model and online short courses, offer a good starting point to enable this kind of knowledge transfer. However, to support older adult participation in such arenas, technology infrastructure, most notably broadband access, must first be rolled out to the often fringe geographical areas where retirees tend to congregate (Garlick and Soar, 2007).

It is evident that ICT, and Internet access in particular, can already offer a host of benefits to older adults and their support networks. The onus of bridging the digital divide, especially for low-income older adults, lies with governments (Coughlin, 2008).[3] The European Commission has addressed the potential of ICT in supporting 'active ageing' and ageing well by concluding that, 'Holistic policies are needed to support learning opportunities in ageing societies' (Ala-Mutka et al., 2008, p. 5). Such policies include supporting local communities in providing accessible ICT facilities, encouraging ICT-based networking to involve older adults in communities, virtual or otherwise, promoting ICT-related learning opportunities, funding relevant R&D projects, and developing appropriate IT literacy courses.

The older adults of tomorrow promise to be increasingly technology savvy and demanding participants in virtual networks and communities. Multi-level policy response—at local, regional, national and supra-national levels—involving all social partners is thus necessary to harness the benefits of virtual networking for older adults now and in the future. Policy should be focused on issues of fair access to ICT and appropiate education and training to enable the use of such access. Policy can also aid in enabling ICT-assisted intergenerational knowledge exchange by supporting the creation of novel platforms for such networking. In this area, as in all others regarding ageing, the challenge is to develop innovative policy instruments and modes of communication that can be disseminated widely and adapted to local circumstances.

CONCLUSIONS

It is, as yet, generally unclear how demographic ageing will influence the processes of innovation. Novel fields encompassing diverse services and products are emerging in response to the needs of new and enlarged groups of older consumers, whereas other sectors may suffer due to burdens on social care networks and productivity levels in organizations. What appears most evident is that a population shift such as that projected will touch many areas of social and working life in ways that are not truly foreseeable. Innovation is a complex construct that often coalesces in unexpected places: an ageing population will not *necessarily* be either a boon or drag on a society's capacity and ability to create and market innovations.

Changes in familial and social structures mean that growing numbers of people will spend more years living alone as they age. Such trends challenge social cohesion and will require significant adaptations in our family, social and work lives and in devising adequate methods for social protection. Minimizing the threats posed and the opportunities available from the new demographics is complex (see Figure 9.3).

High standards of state-sponsored welfare provision in many OECD countries in the latter half of the twentieth century have, in great measure, protected large numbers of vulnerable older adults and have contributed to reducing generational disparities in longevity. However, against a continuing background of global economic shocks) there is now a degree of disengagement by public authorities and an increasing competitive commercialization of welfare services. This, combined with changing family structures, has in some areas exacerbated exclusion, damaged social cohesion and may have as yet a poorly understood impact on innovative capacity.

Products and services geared toward older adults of all ability levels and wealth are needed as the population ages. Innovation in areas such as home design, products for disability and health delivery and financial and travel services will undoubtedly be developed to meet the needs of this expanding niche market. At the level of the state, policy can be targeted at aiding start-ups in fields geared toward the silver market economy, as well

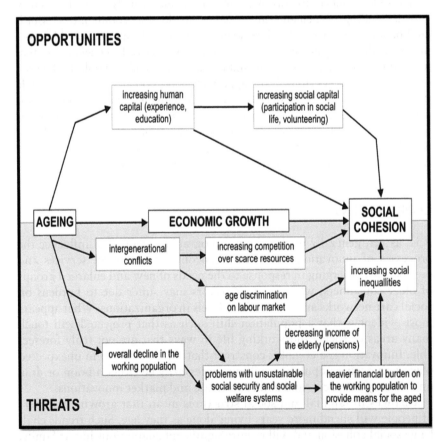

Figure 9.3   Threats and opportunities in the new demographics. Source: Kupiszewski et al. (2006).

as offering support to innovative outcomes of established fields of service provision, such as the tele-health revolution in health care services.

Innovation, in the context of demographic change—and because it is bound to be responsive to social developments—will be a crucial vector not just in terms of medical and scientific advance, but also within public services and the private sector. Demographic shift will create opportunities associated with the active participation of increasing numbers of older adults in the economy and society at large. But there are also important challenges, especially those related to the financial viability of pension systems, the costs of health care systems and the full integration of older people as active agents in social life. Prospering and thriving in fast-changing societies in an increasingly interconnected and competitive world will require vital mental and material resources from all citizens to ensure the future prosperity and well-being of all.

NOTES

1. http://www.reuters.com/article/2007/08/06/idUSSP1709620070806
2. http://www.telegram.com/article/20090215/NEWS/902150391

BIBLIOGRAPHY

Ala-Mutka, K., Malanowski, N., Punie, Y. and Cabrera, M. (2008) 'Active Ageing and the Potential of ICT for Learning'. JRC Scientific and Technical Reports. Luxembourg: European Commission

AP (The Associated Press). (2009) 'Hospitals Discover the Power of "Wiihab'. Online. Available HTTP: http://www.cbsnews.com/stories/2008/02/08/tech/main3810739.shtml (accessed 25 October 2011).

Bachofner, T. and Bossart, M. (2006). *Innovation for Successful Ageing (ISA)* (Aspekte aus Seniorenoptik). Bern: Federal Office for Professional Education and Technology.

Barlow, J (2003). 'Mainstreaming Telecare in the UK. Overcoming the Barriers'. Paper presented at the Southern Institute for Health Informatics Conference. University of Portsmouth. June 2003.

Bendixen, R. M., Levy, C. E., Olive, E. S., Kobb, R. F. and Mann, W. C. (2009) 'Cost Effectiveness of a Telerehabilitation Program to Support Chronically Ill and Disabled Elders in Their Homes'. *Telemed J E Health* 15 (1): 31–38.

Bhagat, R. B. and Unisa, S. (2006) 'Ageing and Dependency in India: A New Measurement'. *Asian Population Studies* 2 (2): 201–214.

Center for Universal Design. (2006) 'Universal Design in Housing'. Raleigh: North Carolina State University. Online. Available HTTP: http://mdhousing.org/website/Documents/UniversalDesigninHousing.pdf (accessed 4 July 2012).

Coughlin. J. (2008) 'Ageing, Innovation and Policy'. Paper presented at the Symposium conducted at Civil Service College: Centre for Governance and Leadership. Singapore. January 2008.

Coughlin, J., Pope, J. and Leedle, B. (2006) 'Old Age, New Technology, and Future Innovations in Disease Management and Home Health Care'. *Home Health Care Management & Practice* 18 (3): 196–207.

Crews, D. E. and Zavotka, S. (2006) 'Aging, Disability, and Frailty: Implications for Universal Design'. *Journal of Physiological Anthropology* 25 (1): 113–118.
Demiris, G. and Hensel, B. K. (2008) 'Technologies for an Aging Society: A Systematic Review of "Smart Home" Applications'. *IMIA Yearbook of Medical Informatics* 2008: 33–40.
European Commission. (2008) 'Commission Staff Working Document: Demography Report 2008: Meeting Social Needs in an Ageing Society'. Full report plus annexes. SEC (2008) 2911. Brussels: European Commission.
Foulk, E. (2007) 'Robots Turn Off Senior Citizens in Aging Japan'. Online. Available HTTP: http://uk.reuters.com/article/2007/09/20/tech-japan-ageing-gadgets-dc-idUKT29547120070920 (accessed 25 October 2011).
Garlick, S. and Soar, J. (2007) 'Human Capital, Innovation and the Productive Ageing: Growth and Senior Aged Health in the Regional Community through Engaged Higher Education'. Paper presented at the 4th Annual AUCEA Conference. Alice Springs, AU. 2–4 July. Online. Available HTTP: http://eprints. usq.edu.au/3799/1/Garlick_Soar_AUCEA_2007_Conf.pdf (accessed 25 October 2011).
Gee, E. M. (2002) 'Misconceptions and Misapprehensions about Population Ageing'. *International Journal of Epidemiology* 31 (4): 750–753.
Godfrey, M. and Johnson, O. (2009) 'Digital Circles of Support: Meeting the Information Needs of Older People'. *Computers in Human Behavior* 25: 633–642.
Gruenewald, T. L., Karlamangla, A. S., Greendale, G. A., Singer, B. H. and Seeman, T. E. (2007) 'Feelings of Usefulness to Others, Disability, and Mortality in Older Adults: The "MacArthur Studies of Successful Aging"'. *Journal of Gerontology: Psychological Sciences* 62B (1): 28–37.
Hamel, M., Fontaine, R. and Boissy, P. (2008) 'In-Home Telerehabilitation for Geriatric Patients'. *Engineering in Medicine and Biology Magazine, IEEE* 27 (4): 29–37.
Hank, K. and Stuck, S. (2007) *Gesellschaftliche Determinanten Producktiven Aletrns in Europa (Societal Determinants of Productive Aging in Europe)*. Manheim: Manheim Research Institute for the Economics of Aging.
Hank, K. and Stuck, S. (2008) 'Volunteer Work, Informal Help and Care among the 50+ in Europe: Further Evidence for 'Linked' Productive Activities at Older Ages'. *Social Science Research* 37 (4): 1280–1291.
Harley, D. and Fitzpatrick, G. (2009) 'Creating a Conversational Context through Video Blogging: A Case Study of Geriatric1927'. *Computers in Human Behaviour* 25 (3): 679–689.
Hilbert, J. and Fretschner, R. (2008) *Meeting the Needs of Older People: Adaptations Required in the Provision of Public and Private Services and New Market Opportunities*. Gelsenkirchen: University of Applied Sciences.
Johansson, K., Josephsson, S. and Lilja, M. (2009) 'Creating Possibilities for Action in the Presence of Environmental Barriers in the Process of "Ageing in Place"'. *Ageing and Society* 29 (1): 49–70.
Kohlbacher, F. (2008). 'Innovation Strategies for the Silver Market'. Paper presented at the INNO GRIPS Innovation Policy Workshop 'Innovation in an Ageing Society. Brussels. 18 December. Online. (accessed 4 July 2012)
Kohlbacher, F. and Hang, C. C. (2007) 'Disruptive Innovations and the Greying Market'. Paper presented at the IEEE International Conference on Industrial Engineering and Engineering Management. Singapore. Online. Available HTTP: http://ieeexplore.ieee.org/stamp/stamp.jsp?tp=&arnumber=4419525 (accessed 25 October 2011).
Kohlbacher, F. and Herstatt, C. (2008) 'The Silver Market Phenomenon: The Aging and Shrinking Society Has Huge Implications for Businesses in Japan'.

J@pan.Inc, September, 22–23. Online. Available HTTP: http://www.dijtokyo. org/articles/J_inc0809_Silvermarket.pdf (accessed 25 October 2011).

Kose, S. (2006) 'Universal Design for the Ageing'. In Karwowski, W. (ed.), *International Encyclopaedia of Ergonomics and Human Factors*, 227–230. London: CRC Press.

Kupiszewski, M., Bijak, J. and Nowok, B. (2006) 'Impact of Future Demographic Changes in Europe'. CEFMR working paper 6/2006.

Kurniawan, S., Nugroho, Y. and Mahmud, M. (2006) 'A Study of the Use of Mobile Phones by Older Persons'. Paper presented at the 'Interact. Inform. Inspire' Conference on Human Factors in Computing Systems. Montreal. 22–27 April. Online. Available HTTP: http://dl.acm.org/citation.cfm?id=1125451.1125641 (accessed 25 October 2011).

Kurz, J. (2009) 'Tech-Savvy Elders Keep Family Close: Seniors Communicate via Internet'. Online. Available HTTP: http://www.telegram.com/article/20090215/NEWS/902150391 (accessed 28 October 2011).

Laschet, A. (2006) SEN@ER external newsletter. January, no. 1. Bonn: Silver Economy Network of European Regions.

Lehr, U. (2007) 'Demographic Change and Its Consequences for the Tourism Branch': Paper presented at the Third Silver Economy Conference. Seville. November 2007.

Macdonald, A. (2007) 'The UD Phenomenon in Japan: Product Innovation through Universal Design'. In Stephanidis, C. (ed.), *Universal Access in HCI, Part I, HCII*, 224–233. Berlin: Springer.

Mace, R. (1998) 'Universal Design: Housing for the Lifespan of All People'. Washington, DC: US Department of Housing and Urban Development.

Micera, S., Bonato, P. and Tamura, T. (2008) 'Gerontechnology'. *IEEE Engineering in Medicine and Biology Magazine* 27 (4): 10–14.

Perez, C (2011) 'Finance and Technical Change: A Long-term View'. *African Journal of Science, Technology, Innovation and Development* 3 (1): 10–35

Pollack, M. E. (2005) 'Intelligent Technology for an Aging Population: The Use of AI to Assist Elders with Cognitive Impairment'. *AI Magazine* 26 (2): 9–24.

Purdam, K. and Norman, P. (2010) 'Geographical and Social Variations in Unpaid Caring within and outside the Household in England and Wales'. CCSR Working Paper 2010–03 Online. Available HTTP: http://www.ccsr.ac.uk/publications/working/2010–03.pdf (accessed 25 October 2011)

Schulz, J. H and Robert H. Binstock (2008) *Aging Nation The Economics and Politics of Growing Older in America*. Baltimore Md: John Hopkins University Press.

Seals, C. D., Clanton, K., Agarwal, R., Doswell, F. and Thomas, C. M. (2008) 'Lifelong Learning: Becoming Computer Savvy at a Later Age'. *Educational Gerontology* 34 (12): 1055–1069.

Smith, R. O., Bange, M., & Hall, M. (2000). Using assistive technologies to enable self-care and daily living. In C. Christiansen (Ed.), *Ways of living*, 2nd ed. 333–361. Bethesda, MD: American Occupational Therapy Association.

SOPRANO. (2007) 'Service-Oriented Programmable Smart Environments for Older Europeans'. Online. Available HTTP: http://cordis.europa.eu/search/index.cfm?fuseaction=proj.document&PJ_RCN=9076856 (accessed 3 February 2012).

Survey of Health, Ageing and Retirement in Europe (SHARE). Online. Available HTTP: http://share-dev.mpisoc.mpg.de/ (accessed 9 January 2012).

Suttie, A. (2009) 'Scottish Care Home Group Provides Nintendo Therapy'. Online. Available HTTP: http://www.communitycare.co.uk/Articles/03/03/2009/110886/Care-home-residents-use-Nintendo-Wii-to-relive-their-sporting.htm (accessed 25 October 2011).

224 *Jennifer Hayden and Barbara Jones*

UN. (2002) 'Report of the Second World Assembly on Ageing'. New York: United Nations. Online. Available HTTP: http://www.c-fam.org/docLib/20080625_Madrid_Ageing_Conference.pdf (accessed 25 October 2011)
Vickers, L. (2009) 'Wii Love the Sports'. Online. Available HTTP: http://www.stuff.co.nz/auckland/1997647/Wii-love-the-sports (accessed 25 October 2011)
Vos, R., Kozul-Wright, R., Cortez, A., Cunningham, S. and Kawamura, H. (2007) 'Managing Health Care in an Ageing World'. UN-DESA policy brief no. 2. New York: United Nations.
Wada, K., Shibata, T., Musha, T. and Kimura, S. (2008) 'Robot Therapy for Elders Affected by Dementia'. *Engineering in Medicine and Biology Magazine, IEEE* 27 (4): 53–60.

Part IV

Broadening and Deepening
Innovation Policy

10 Innovation and Creative Places

Ian Miles and Sally Gee

INTRODUCTION

This chapter focuses on how innovation relates to the spatial contexts in which it is located. A later chapter considers 'cultures and innovation'. Economists and geographers have long studied the propensity of similar activities to be grouped together in space. This is known as agglomeration. In the 20th century, cities were widely seen as the most important and visible units of economic agglomeration. Moving beyond the basic idea of economies of agglomeration, cities were seen as supporting economic growth by leveraging localization and urbanization (Fujita and Thisse, 2002). They are implicated in innovation in various ways. Many observers argue that the level of the nation-state is typically too large to give adequate grasp of innovation dynamics. Cities are complex networks of institutions that, according to de la Mothe (2004), enable firms and households to deal with uncertainties and changing contingencies in a complex and dynamic environment. They constitute pools of human capital in which social and intellectual diversity can foster creativity and innovation (Florida, 2002). With a critical mass for specialized activities and being the base for a great diversity of such activities, there is opportunity for innovative cross-fertilization (Castells, 2001). Individual cities work within global networks, while being 'brands' in their own right, sites of economic and cultural activity and symbolic significance. They are also nodes in internationally connected economies and international city networks (Scott, 2006). This is of particular relevance for innovations that embody widely distributed knowledge, and whose generation requires 'open innovation'–type (Chesbrough, 2006) processes. There has been an explosion of interest in these themes in the 21st century. A survey of literature on cities and innovation from Athey et al. (2005) outlines some major lines of debate here. We should acknowledge that there are traditions of sophisticated analysis going back for several decades, including notably the work of the GREMI group on 'creative milieu';[1] and at the turn of the century Hall (2000) reviewed much earlier work on creative cities. But there is also a powerful argument that location does not matter so much, indeed that it is practically obsolescent. We begin with this point of view.

THE PREMATURE ANNOUNCEMENT
OF THE DEATH OF DISTANCE

The World Is Flat

For several decades at least, commentators have been arguing that new tele-communications technologies strongly reduce the significance of spatial location and distance. Indeed, de Sola Pool (1977) reports forecasts from the 1890s that telephony would reduce the number of personal meetings and from the first decades of the 20th century that we would see business being conducted at a distance and traffic congestion being alleviated. Pool pointed out that the impact of telephones and telegraphy on travel and transport was a complex one, as relationships could be developed and maintained between more remote people, leading to new patterns of social life and commerce. But this did not stop a good deal of excitement in the last quarter of the 20th century as new information technology (IT) offered many new means of communication, including emails, video conferences and web services of many kinds. The idea of the 'telecommunications/travel trade-off', which Pool had done much to demystify, again became popular.

The prefix 'tele-' was attached to many words, to indicate that the activities involved could be carried out at a great distance from their traditional geographical bases (e.g., telework, teleshopping, tele-health, teleconference). It is interesting that other prefixes have come to the fore in the 21st century (e.g., 'e-' and 'mobile' being prominent at the time of writing). Expectations of a rapid shift to new ways of organizing activities—so that telecommunications would increasingly displace travel, telecommuters would repopulate rural areas, for example—failed to materialize anything like as rapidly as many commentators had expected. However, facilities such as email became very widely used. First pagers and then mobile phones enabled workforces to stay connected, and there was enough visible development of 'e-work'[2] to sustain the sense that a great change actually is underway. It is just that such a large-scale reorganization of economy and society takes decades rather than years.

It is in this context that Thomas Friedman achieved a bestselling and prize-winning success with his 2005 book, *The World Is Flat: A Brief History of the Twenty-First Century*. Going beyond the focus on new IT, though this of course plays an important role, he points to the effects of globalization and the fall of the Berlin Wall on creating a more level playing field for international trade and one in which supply chains extend over vast distances, linking together actors in all world regions; and to the growth of the knowledge society as creating economies that are more reliant on potentially mobile, intellectual labor. The book identifies a major innovation challenge for the 21st century and is largely aimed at providing a wake-up call to the US about its need to create a more skilled workforce in order to remain globally competitive, but it does make a few points concerning innovation and location.

The developments in new IT and international relations have enabled the creation of:

a global, Web-enabled platform for multiple forms of collaboration . . . [that] enables individuals, groups, companies and universities anywhere in the world to collaborate—for the purposes of innovation, production, education, research, entertainment, and, alas, war-making—like no creative platform ever before. This platform operates without regard to geography, distance, time, and, in the near future, even language. . . . Wealth and power will increasingly accrue to those countries, companies, individuals, universities and groups who get three basic things right: the infrastructure to connect with this flat-world platform (especially broadband Internet access), the education to get more of their people innovating on, working off of, and tapping into this platform, and, finally, the governance to get the best out of this platform and cushion its worst side effects. (Friedman, 2006, p. 205)[3]

It is this triple convergence—of new players, on a new playing field, developing new processes and habits for horizontal collaboration—that I believe is the most important force shaping global economics and politics in the early twenty-first century. Giving so many people access to all these tools of collaboration, along with the ability through search engines and the Web to access billions of pages of raw information, ensures that the next generation of innovations will come from all over Planet Flat. The scale of the global community that is soon going to be able to participate in all sorts of discovery and innovation is something the world has simply never seen before . . . True, maybe only 10 per cent of this new 1.5 billion-strong workforce entering the global economy have the education and connectivity to collaborate and compete at a meaningful level. But that is still 150 million people, roughly the size of the entire US workforce. (Friedman, 2006, pp. 212–213)

The stress on collaboration, putting aside language and cultural differences that are supposed to be diminishing in the flat world, is offset by the argument that innovation is happening at an increasing rate, and that those who do not innovate will have innovation imposed on them by others. Thus it is vital to remain abreast of developments across the world, and Friedman has argued that it is especially important for individuals to have capabilities in two or more areas of specialism that they can join together to create new things. What Castells saw as taking place in cities, where there is convergence of information flows, Friedman sees more as a matter of individual imaginations transcending space and place.

LOCATION, LOCATION, LOCATION!

Many commentators have criticized Friedman's analysis, notably Richard Florida, who also happens to be one of the main proponents of the idea of cities as hubs in the innovation economy. He argued that, contrary to the view that the 'world is flat', it is actually 'spiky'. Improved transport and telecommunications may reduce the significance of distance, but have not necessarily eroded the importance of place. Not all areas have become equal:

> In terms of both sheer economic horsepower and cutting-edge innovation, surprisingly few regions truly matter in today's global economy. What's more, the tallest peaks—the cities and regions that drive the world economy—are growing ever higher, while the valleys mostly languish. The most obvious challenge to the flat-world hypothesis is the explosive growth of cities worldwide. More and more people are clustering in urban areas, the world's demographic mountain ranges, so to speak. The share of the world's population living in urban areas, just three percent in 1800, was nearly 30 percent by 1950. Today it stands at about 50 per cent; in advanced countries three out of four people live in urban areas . . . [yet] differences in population density vastly understate the spikiness of the global economy; the continuing dominance of the world's most productive urban areas is astounding. When it comes to actual economic output, the ten largest US metropolitan areas combined are behind only the US as a whole and Japan. New York's economy alone is about the size of Russia's or Brazil's and Chicago's is on a par with Sweden's. Together New York, Los Angeles, Chicago, and Boston have a bigger economy than all of China. If US metropolitan areas were countries, they'd make up forty-seven of the biggest 100 economies in the world. (Florida, 2005, pp. 48–49)

The main difference between now and even a couple of decades ago is not that the world has become flatter but that the world's peaks have become slightly more dispersed and that the world's hills, the industrial and service centers that produce mature products and support innovation centers, have proliferated and shifted. For the better part of the twentieth century the US claimed the lion's share of the global economy's innovation peaks, leaving a few outposts in Europe and Japan. But America has since lost some of those peaks, as such industrial-age powerhouses as Pittsburgh, St. Louis and Cleveland have eroded. At the same time, a number of regions in Europe, Scandinavia, Canada, and the Pacific Rim have moved up. The world today looks flat to some because the economic and social distances between peaks worldwide have gotten smaller . . . (Florida, 2005, p. 50)

Florida's 2005 *Atlantic Monthly* critique of Friedman created a stir partly because of the presentation of maps depicting this spikiness. He used an image of the nighttime world as a proxy indicator for cities' economic activity, where the peaks represent the light emissions and thus (crudely) the energy use and associated economic activity. On this map, America had large mountains or 'Himalayas', Europe a smaller mountain range while Asia displayed occasional peaks. Isolated hills are scattered elsewhere. A second map measuring innovation,[4] using the even more problematic indicator of patents, showed acute spikiness. Florida notes that the University of California generated more patents than either India or China, while IBM accounted for five times as many patents as the two countries manage together. He also went on to plot where in the world the 1,200 most heavily cited scientists in key fields lived, and found that such scientific leadership to be even more concentrated than patenting activity and not always based in the same places.

Thus Florida suggested that several commercially innovative East Asian cities display little scientific excellence, while some other cities are specialized in the reverse direction. Relatively few places lead in both respects, and those that do are particularly well positioned in the global economy. The particular indicators used by Florida will of course affect how we assess performance in science and commercialization; quite possibly other approaches, less focused on patenting and citation, would lead to different conclusions about cities' capabilities. But the underlying message about spikiness is unlikely to be affected substantially.

Elaborating the argument, Florida distinguishes between three types of places:

- *The tallest peaks.* The relatively few cities that generate innovations, new products, new industries. They are connected to one another by communication networks and human mobility. Exemplars of open innovation at a city scale, perhaps the world is paradoxically 'flattest' for those at its peaks! Attracting global talent, Florida sees these peaks as difficult to topple, even as growing higher.
- *The economic 'hills'.* Prosperous but insecure cities. They typically perform much less innovative manufacturing and provide services like call centers. Some are losing position; some are themselves on the way to becoming peaks. Florida mentions Dublin and Seoul. It would be interesting to know if this characterization would apply now.
- *The vast valleys.* Large tracts of the world that are showing little dynamism and ability to shape global technology and economic affairs. These have mainly local connections. Indeed, much telecommunications traffic is actually contained within quite limited geographical areas, as several critics of Friedman point out.

The implication, then, is that the forces that Friedman sees as leading to a flatter world are often leading to more concentration of innovative effort in certain cities, even if there is change over time in just which cities are most effective.[5] Florida, like Friedman, argues that we are in a new phase of economic development. But he stresses that the driving forces of this phase of economic development are human factors rather than simply technological and organizational parameters. This is not so different from Friedman's emphasis on individual imagination and the capacity to combine ideas from different fields of specialism. Florida emphasizes the role of place and is less immediately concerned with the capacity to combine different types of knowledge. He links levels of creativity and innovation to the openness and tolerance of the environment in which people live and work, to features of the city (or region) that go beyond simple measures of inputs to innovation:

> Given that creativity has emerged as the single most important source of economic growth, the best route to continued prosperity is by investing in our stock of creativity in all its forms, across the board. This entails more than just pumping up R&D spending or improving education, though both are important. It requires increasing investment in the multidimensional and varied forms of creativity—arts, music, culture, design and related fields—because all are linked and flourish together. It also means investing in the related infrastructure and communities that attract creative people from around the world and that broadly foment creativity. (Florida, 2002, p. 320)

This leads us to the debates about the creative class and the creative city, where Florida has made very influential, if controversial, contributions. The topic of innovation often comes to the fore in these discussions, though the frequent stress on artistic, entertainment and cultural issues means that this body of work makes more frequent reference to creativity in the first instance. Openness to outside ideas and tolerance of diversity are cultural dimensions that may have a significant impact on innovation, and the relationship between innovation and culture is discussed in more detail in the following chapter of this book.

CREATIVITY SQUARED: CLASSES AND CITIES

The Creation of the Creative Class

In 2002, Richard Florida's *The Rise of the Creative Class* was published, and rapidly, thanks to a marketing campaign similar to that surrounding *The World Is Flat* a few years later, reached a wide audience.[6] It proposed that the traditional grand socioeconomic classes—blue-collar workers, middle-class white-collar workers, small entrepreneurs and wealthy managers and owners—have been in many ways overhauled by a new class. While earlier commentators have identified a new 'service class', or new classes of 'information workers' and/or 'knowledge workers', Florida argues that 'the economic need for creativity' has led to the emergence of a 'creative class':

> Some 38 million Americans, 30 per cent of all employed people, belong to this class. I define the core of the Creative Class to include people in science and engineering, architecture and design, education, arts, music and entertainment, whose economic function is to create new ideas, new technology and/or new creative content. Around the core, the Creative Class also includes a broader group of creative professionals in business and finance, law, healthcare and related fields. These people engage in complex problem solving that involves a great deal of independent judgment and requires high levels of education or human capital. In addition, all members of the Creative Class—whether they are artists or engineers, musicians or computer scientists, writers or entrepreneurs—share a common creative ethos that values creativity, individuality, difference and merit. For the members of the Creative Class, every aspect and every manifestation of creativity—technological, cultural and economic—is interlinked and inseparable . . . (Florida, 2002, p. 8)

He differentiated between three subgroups of this class:

- The *Creative Core*. Specialized in technical creativity, such as researchers, engineers, doctors, characterized by high skills and educational attainment, accounting for much of the economic value produced.
- *Creative Professionals*. The largest subgroup, with managerial and professional skills, such as managers and professional service workers.[7]
- *Bohemians*. With more aesthetic and cultural creativity, such as artists, writers, designers, usually constituting fewer creative workers than the other groups, but possibly a key set of what were called earlier 'omnivorous consumers', and important consumers of urban services and producers of urban culture whose presence is attractive to other technical, economic and social creatives.

These ideas can be applied to various sorts of comparisons. Thus Florida and Tinagli (2004) concluded that creative class workers outnumber blue-collar workers in the Netherlands, Belgium and Finland (where they are around 30 percent of the workforce) and in the United Kingdom, Ireland and Denmark, while Italy and Portugal have fewer than 15 percent of the workforce in the creative class. These authors go on to argue that within Europe, competitive advantage is shifting from the traditional big powers to a cluster of Scandinavian, Nordic and northern European countries, where the creative class is prominent. Developing or accessing creative workers could be described as a key innovation challenge for the 21st century.

Florida's ideas have attracted much criticism, to the extent that there is even a group in Canada, where Florida has had much influence, that calls itself *Creative Class Struggle*.[8] For instance, Peck (2005) challenges the analysis over a wide range of points, while Markusen (2006) takes issue with the supposed coherence of the creative class. However, the thesis has exerted a considerable attraction for policymakers, especially at the urban level providing clear policy recommendations for political innovation challenges, and there is a corresponding wave of research employing various elements of Florida's concepts.

For instance, Lorenzen and Andersen (2007—see also Lorenzen and Andersen, 2009) analyzed the geographical distribution of Florida's 'creative class' among 445 European cities. They explore various arguments as to what makes cities attractive to creative individuals. In general, larger cities attract more creatives, but the pattern is not linear. There is some evidence that the smallest cities (below 70,000 inhabitants) show strong relationships between size and the share of creatives. This may mean that there are minimum scales for supporting creative industries or cultures, creative product and labor markets.[9] Cities with more than 1.2 million inhabitants, in contrast, show a weaker relationship between increasing size and share of the creative class, possibly reflecting increasing unattractiveness due to urban congestion and similar features (see Figures 10.1, 10.2 and 10.3). Bohemians were especially attracted to large cities. The authors showed that the 'cultural offer' of European cities (as indicated by a measure of the number employed within cultural services) was strongly related to city size. For cities smaller than 80,000 inhabitants, there seemed to be a strong decline in cultural services with decreasing size, and the creatives and especially bohemians could be seen as responding to this, though there may be some circularity in the argument here, since bohemians are likely to work in cultural services.

ATTRACTING THE CREATIVE CLASS: THE CREATIVE CITY

Florida argues that creatives are drawn to cities with particular features, and that their presence helps these cities become innovation hubs. He suggested thinking in terms of three 'T's—that is, *technological capacity* is a prerequisite for innovation; *talent* is also vital, with flows of talented individuals into the region being essential; *tolerance* is seen as the cultural foundation for creative clusters to be built. Florida refers to creatives' 'common creative ethos', attributing a shared set of values to them,[10] something that Markusen (2006) strongly challenges, and going on to argue that they are attracted to, and try to develop, places where these values can be expressed.

Florida courted controversy and achieved considerable media coverage by combining measures of such environmental features with more conventional measures of innovative outcomes, such as the number of patent registrations, to provide an overall creative city rating. In his initial work on US cities he combined the following statistics:

- High-Tech Index: Measure of high-tech industries.
- Innovation Index: Measure of numbers of patented innovations per capita.
- Gay Index: Measure of same sex couples living in region.
- Bohemian Index: Measure of artistically creative people.
- Talent Index: Based on numbers of people with bachelor degrees and above.
- Melting Pot Index: Measure of foreign-born people living in region.

These yield composite indicators such as the following:

- Composite Diversity Index: Composite of gay, Bohemian and melting pot indices.
- Creativity Index: Composite measure of the innovation, high-tech, gay and creative class indices.

Florida presented evidence showing correlations between the importance of the creative class (as indexed by the numbers in particular occupations as a share of the population or labor force) in US cities and the extent to which these cities offer cultural facilities and displayed ethnic diversity and 'tolerance' towards alternative lifestyles (which has been one of the more controversial aspects of his analysis, with a positive connotation for gayness outraging most varieties of homophobe). The causality is supposed to

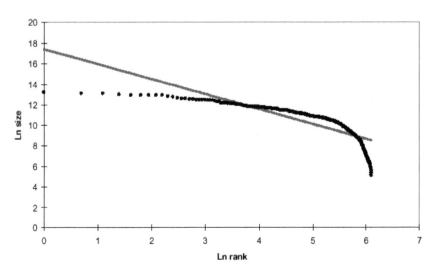

Figure 10.1   The rank-size distribution of the European creative class (2000). Source: Lorenzen and Andersen (2007, Figure 1) (Ln is an abbreviation for logarithm).

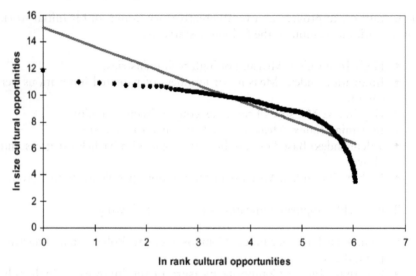

Figure 10.2   The rank-size distribution of European cities' cultural offer (2000). Source: Lorenzen and Andersen (2007, Figure 5) (ln is an abbreviation for logarithm).

be that the creative class prefers particular sorts of work and cultural environments as captured in the three 'T's—thus the interest in developing city-level indicators, as in the Lorenzen and Andersen study discussed earlier.

Much of the literature on *creative* cities deals with places that are well known for their being sites of *innovation* (e.g., Silicon Valley is home to

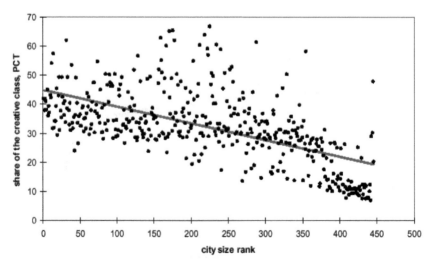

Figure 10.3   European city population rank and share of creative class (2000). Source: Lorenzen and Andersen (2007, Figure 7)

much IT hardware, software and services innovation). The idea is that creative contexts are ones that tolerate and indeed reward new ideas and practices, displays of creativity and practical applications of new ideas. So the link to innovation is clear. There should be creativity in the generation of new combinations and new ideas and also in the willingness to adopt new routines—that is, in funding innovation as well as in business practice and work organization. As places where diverse skills are available, they make it possible to establish teams to work on new projects and thus to react more rapidly to changing market and technological conditions.[11]

Some urban environments are more welcoming to this sort of cooperative flux than others. One policy implication is that supply-side efforts in training and retaining graduates and attracting 'star' scientists should be complemented with policies addressing more challenging cultural issues. City governments have ways in which they can foster a thriving artistic scene or at least reduce their negative impacts on such scenes. This may help improve the attractiveness of a place to immigrants (and to qualified graduates looking for a permanent base). A mixture of vibrant cultural spaces and more relaxed parks and suburbs can be built over the long term, and these factors may also be attractors. But whether such policy moves support the sorts of city or organizational culture that (as we discuss in the next chapter) nurture innovation is harder to assess.

The approach has caused much controversy. Even before Florida's book put the creative cities thesis on the map, research results suggesting similar conclusions were being picked up by urban policymakers. One analyst,[12] comparing twenty American cities with high levels of high-technology industries and patent activities, concluded that the 'Cities of Ideas' were more open to new ideas and other cultures, were more likely to engage in individualistic activities, were more optimistic, and had a higher percentage of artists, musicians and writers than did 'Traditional Cities'. The work of William Frey, a demographer with the Milken Institute and a professor at the University of Michigan,[13] was seen as providing evidence that cities with robust migration are in ascendance while those that cannot attract immigrants are in decline (Lisheron and Bishop, 2002).

Florida clearly struck a chord in that many of the cities he identified as diverse and creative are recognizable as centers of high-tech innovation. His approach has allowed for a simple statistical representation of creativity or at least of critical success factors for nurturing it. However, he has been criticized for stressing narrow measures and types of innovation,[14] and for confounding by-products of a highly creative professional population with factors that might attract such a population.[15] As with much other discussion of creative and innovative clusters, his work has been attacked as being misleading in being 'voluntaristic', suggesting that policies can readily engineer innovative environments, while most of the cases depicted are more a product of serendipity and/or market forces. For example, Malanga (2004), and in a related argument Nathan (2005), argues that the model that seems to work for US cities may be less valid for a European context. Factors such as low tax environments and 'business friendly' administrations have been held up as the real issue, rather than cultural diversity and openness. Left-wing critics focus on the failure to take into account intra-urban inequalities and the growth of an underclass in cities where there is inflation in property prices and few opportunities for upward mobility on the part of people lacking the right sort of creativity. On the other hand, many urbanists point to success stories in regeneration, where the goal of a creative city does seem to have been at least brought closer by the activities of local and sometimes national political authorities.[16] Probably the most rigorous comparative study of cities and regions to date was undertaken in the project 'Technology, Talent and Tolerance in European Cities: A Comparative Analysis'. The Lorenzen and Andersen (2007) study is one of its outputs.[17]

The concept of a 'creative city' is often attributed not to Richard Florida, but to Charles Landry, who was using the phrase in the 1980s. Landry had set out to document good practice, as a result of which he generated a list of initiatives that appear to work together so as to create, or at least underpin, more creative cities. Many of his themes relate to technological and other innovation.[18]

A convenient summary is provided by Landry and Bianchini (1995) and we summarize (and occasionally augment) their proposals on 'how to become a creative city':

- Make the most of creative individuals. Positively sanction 'creative deviance', e.g. through experiment-encouraging grants for innovation and pilot projects; encourage entry of 'outside' attitudes and skills to encourage more critical and imaginative views and approaches.
- Recognize the contribution of immigrants. Settled immigrants, simultaneously outsiders and insiders, have different ways of looking at problems and different priorities; a balance has to be struck between maintaining a separate identity and integrating into the majority community.
- Use catalysts. These may be events, organizations and spaces that create opportunities for people with different perspectives to come together and share ideas, create mutual understanding of the city's problems and possibilities, develop leadership groups.
- Balance cosmopolitanism and locality. Encourage, host and participate in national and international competitions, exhibitions, trade fairs, the membership of international networks of cities, cultural and educational exchanges, twinning, staff exchanges, and cooperation between research centers. These initiatives can enhance the receptiveness, open-mindedness and international orientation of a city. Again, there is a balance to be struck, this time between cosmopolitanism and the local roots that underpin confidence and sense of direction. Thus international initiatives should co-exist with festivals and other celebrations and events strengthening local identity.

- Move from multiculturalism to interculturalism. Cultural hybrids matter. Creativity arises more from interculturalism than multiculturalism. The latter here meaning the strengthening of separate cultural identities of ethnic minorities, but with the risk of poor communication between cultures. Creativity may be encouraged by fragmentation, but not by marginalization. Ethnic ghettoes are unlikely to contribute to solving the wider problems of cities. Intercultural projects build bridges between the fragments and produce something new out of the urban multicultural patchwork. Successful new ideas can be generated through cultural crossovers.
- Treat participation as more than a slogan. It creates 'ownership' since people are more likely to become stakeholders in projects they have participated in. So encourage it through means such as citizen audits and juries. Landry and Bianchini suggest using these for such things as the design and management of their housing estates and assessment of public sector organizations, but there is also scope for citizens to be involved in the development of R&D priorities and the design of innovative technology-related programs.[19]
- Develop creative spaces. Land and buildings at affordable prices and preferably close to other cultural amenities need to be made available, where lower financial risk encourages experimentation. There is scope for new types of science parks and cultural industries quarters, for instance, as well as more market-driven occupation of particular sites—for example, areas near city centers that are undergoing change, such as old ports and areas of declining industries.
- Identify early winners and staging posts. Start with easier projects that become 'early winners', helping to build momentum. Establish intermediate goals or staging posts to make visible how the city is moving and to generate confidence and enthusiasm. As well as events such as festivals, the authors suggest that other possibilities include new regulations and subsidy schemes. We could add that there might be successful innovation-related actions such as the creation of a city-level wireless network or e-payment system.
- Rethink urban management. City management needs to concentrate on strategic oversight and the things it does best and contract out or delegate inappropriate tasks to private, voluntary or semi-public organizations. For such delegation, city stakeholders need vision and leadership, bringing together leaders from local politics, business and the voluntary sector.

CONCLUSIONS

There is plenty to take issue with in the particular analyses and indicators used by Florida. But there is substantial evidence that much innovation is localized in particular cities and regions, albeit places that are particularly well connected, or 'open'. Creative places can be regarded as ideal spaces for open innovation, grounded, yet tolerant and diverse. It is of great interest to identify the factors that account for this and to explore how far it might be possible to exert benign influence upon these.

As always, policy action may well have unclear consequences and by-products. One such, conceded by Florida himself, is the possible impact on social inclusion/exclusion of the soaring property prices associated with desirable milieux. But, at least, following the sorts of prescriptions that are developed in the creative cities debates should take us away from the 'race to the bottom'. This race has been apparent in so much of regional policymakers' competing to attract inward investment by means of offering docile and low-wage workforces, tolerance of environmental degradation and the like. By putting innovation (creativity) and quality of life into the same frame, the debates reviewed here point towards more progressive approaches.

This is not to say that everything will be plain sailing. There are bound to be some conflicts between demands to create more innovative milieu and desires to establish more rewarding and sustainable environments. Better understanding of how and when such conflicts arise and of the strategies for confronting them is important. Seeing urban and regional policies as needing to address the multiple challenges of innovation and sustainability, and creativity and social cohesion in the 21st century can only be a good thing. Likewise, the debates here relay significant messages to those concerned with innovation management and policy, not least that we should look beyond the financial bottom line and consider the wider range of factors motivating and mobilizing creative individuals.

NOTES

1. GREMI stands for Groupe de Recherche Européen sur les Milieux Innovateurs, and its results have been discussed in many publications, including Aydalot (1986) and Camagni (1999).
2. The EMERGENCE project tracked e-work development in Europe over a number of years, with its reports having a considerable impact. Online. Available HTTP: http://www.emergence.nu (accessed 18 July 2011).
3. The quotations are taken from the 2006 edition and there have been revisions subsequent to this.
4. From use of data from the World Intellectual Property Organization and the US Patent and Trademark Office.
5. For a detailed comparison of the Florida and Friedman approaches, see Feiock et al., 2008.
6. *The Rise of the Creative Class* has been described 'as the most popular book on regional economies in the past decade' (Glaeser, 2004, p. 1).
7. We suspect that in some financial centers it is this group that yields the most added value, at least as conventionally defined.
8. Online. Available HTTP: http://creativeclassstruggle.wordpress.com (accessed 18 July 2011).

9. For the technically minded, they are using ranked data, and testing Zipf's 'rank-size' Law.
10. This is rather reminiscent of the 'postmaterialist values' we discuss in a later chapter.
11. This account clearly resonates with analyses of the changing dynamics of science (the 'Mode 1' versus 'Mode 2' thesis of Gibbons et al., 1994) and those of innovation (i.e., distributed innovation processes, user involvement in innovation) and with analysis of 'projects' and the organization of creative industries.
12. Cushing, R. (2002) Online. Available HTTP: http://www.statesman.com/specialreports/content/specialreports/citiesofideas/0428lists.html (accessed 18 July 2011).
13. An extensive collection of his work, spanning more than a decade. Online. Available HTTP: http://www.frey-demographer.org/briefs.html (accessed 18 July 2011).
14. A rapid and interesting response to Florida's article came in a blog from John Hagel. Online. Available HTTP: http://edgeperspectives.typepad.com/edge_perspectives/2005/10/the_world_is_sp.htm (accessed 18 July 2011). Hagel argues that Florida defines innovation too narrowly and thus overlooks the scope for 'new agglomerations of creative talent to come together and connect into the global economy'. Patents and scientific leadership may focus our attention on product innovation and fundamental science. But 'hills' can be extraordinarily innovative in terms of rapid incremental process innovation, which can underpin rapid economic growth. 'Companies in some of the rapidly growing urban areas like Shenzhen and Bangalore are pursuing a powerful form of innovation bootstrapping that starts with relatively modest incremental innovations pursued in rapid iterations and amplified by rich interactions with dense local business ecosystems. This . . . accelerates learning and capability building and ultimately bridges into more fundamental product and technology innovation, as is already happening in areas like wireless technology in both China and India. With aggressive use of bootstrapping, even the most modest hills have the opportunity to become formidable peaks'.
15. See Musterd et al. (2007) for a detailed review of arguments from Florida and his predecessors as well as followers and a critical exposition of what secure conclusions can be drawn and what research questions remain open.
16. Thus Hospers (2003) accepts that local governments cannot simply create local knowledge, creativity and innovation 'from scratch'. However, he concludes the experiences of creative cities—e.g., Austin and Barcelona—demonstrate that local policymakers can help increase the scope for the emergence of urban creativity, by providing the appropriate underlying framework conditions.
17. The project, supervised by Professors Bjorn Asheim and Meric Gertler, is reported most fully in Asheim (2009), though many other reports are scattered over the Web. The studies present many nuanced interpretations of a large set of results, suggesting, among other things, that different components of the creative class have very different patterns of values and behavior and that this is not merely of academic interest. The UK part of the study was led by Phil Cooke at Cardiff and reported in Cooke (2007). For a detailed study of England and Wales in terms of these data, see Clifton (2008).
18. Musterd et al. (2007) point out two lines of critique of these approaches. First, it is by no means clear whether it is the city, city-region, or some other unit of analysis that is best targeted in particular instances. Second, the creative city may be characterized by underclasses, geographical segmentation (leafy suburbs versus squalid centers) and other social problems.

19. Cf. Irwin (1995) and Den Hertog et al. (1995).

BIBLIOGRAPHY

Asheim, B. (2009) 'Introduction to the Creative Class in European City Regions'. *Economic Geography* 85 (4): 355–362.
Athey, G., Nathan, M. and Webber, C. (2005) 'What Role Do Cities Play in Innovation, and to What Extent Do We Need City-Based Innovation Policies and Approaches?' NESTA working paper, 1 June 2007. Centre for Cities, NESTA Cities and Innovation Project. Online. Available HTTP: http://www.centreforcities.org/assets/files/cities_and_innovation_working_paper_NESTA.pdf (accessed 27 September 2011).
Aydalot, P. (1986) *Milieux Innovateurs en Europe*. Paris: GREMI.
Camagni, R. (1999) 'The City as a Milieu: Applying GREMI's Approach to Urban Evolution'. *Revue d'Economie Régionale et Urbaine* 3: 591–606.
Castells, M. (2001) *The Internet Galaxy: Reflections on the Internet, Business and Society*. Oxford: Oxford University Press.
Chesbrough, H. (2006) *Open Innovation*. Boston, Mass.: Harvard Business School Press.
Clifton, N. (2008) 'The "Creative Class" in the UK: An Initial Analysis'. Geografiska Annaler: Series B, *Human Geography* 90 (1): 63–82.
Cooke, P. (2007) 'Technology, Talent and Tolerance in European Cities: A Comparative Analysis: Full Research Report, ESRC End of Award Report'. RES-000–23–0467. Swindon: ESRC. Online. Available HTTP: http://www.esrcsocietytoday.ac.uk/search/search-page.aspx?q=Technology%2C+Talent+and+tolerance (accessed 27 September 2011).
Cushing, R. (2002) 'A Look at the Creative Class'. *The Statesman*. 28 April. Online. Available HTTP: http://www.statesman.com/specialreports/content/specialreports/citiesofideas/0428lists.html (accessed 4 October 2011).
de la Mothe, J. (2004) 'The Institutional Governance of Technology, Society, and Innovation'. *Technology in Society* 26 (2–3): 523–536.
de Sola Pool, I. (1977) 'The Communications/Transportation Tradeoff'. *Policy Studies Journal* 6 (1): 74–83.
Den Hertog, P., Stein, J. A., Schot, J. and Gritzalis, D. (1996) 'User Involvement in RTD: Concepts, Practices and Policy Lessons'. TNO Report STB/96/011. Apeldorn: TNO Centre for Technology and Policy Studies.
Feiock, R. C., Jae Moon, M. and Park, H. J. (2008) 'Is the World "Flat" or "Spiky"? Rethinking the Governance Implications of Globalization for Economic Development'. *Public Administration Review* 68: 24–35.
Florida, R. (2002) *The Rise of the Creative Class: And How It's Transforming Work, Leisure, Community, and Everyday Life*. New York: Basic Books.
Florida, R. (2005) 'The World Is Spiky'. *The Atlantic Monthly Review* 296 (3): 48–51.
Florida, R. and Tinagli, I. (2004) *Europe in the Creative Age*. London: Demos and the Carnegie-Mellon Software Industry Center.
Friedman, T. L. (2005) *The World Is Flat: A Brief History of the Twenty-First Century*. New York: Farrar, Straus & Giroux.
Friedman, T. L. (2006) *The World Is Flat: [Updated and Expanded] A Brief History of the Twenty-First Century*. 2nd ed. New York: Farrar, Straus & Giroux.
Fujita, M. and Thisse, J. (2002) *Economics of Agglomeration: Cities, Industrial Location, and Regional Growth*. Cambridge: Cambridge University Press.

Gibbons, M., Limoges, C., Nowotny, H., Schwartzman, S., Scott, P. and Trow, M. (1994) *The New Production of Knowledge: The Dynamics of Science and Research in Contemporary Society.* London: Sage.

Glaeser, E. L. (2004) 'Review of Richard Florida's The Rise of the Creative Class'. Online. Available HTTP: http://www.creativeclass.com/rfcgdb/articles/Glaeser-Review.pdf (accessed 27 September 2011).

Hall, P. (2000) 'Creative Cities and Economic Development'. *Urban Studies* 37 (4): 639–649.

Hospers, G. J. (2003) 'Creative Cities: Breeding Places in the Knowledge Economy'. *Knowledge, Technology, and Policy* 16 (3): 143–162.

Irwin, A. (1995) *Citizen Science: A Study of People, Expertise and Sustainable Development.* London: Routledge.

Landry, C. and Bianchini, F. (1995) 'The Creative City'. London: Demos. Online. Available HTTP: http://www.demos.co.uk/publications/thecreativecity (accessed 27 September 2011).

Lisheron, M. and Bishop, B. (2002) 'Austin's Fast-Growing Immigrant Community Is Source of Wealth'. *The Statesman.* 9 June. Online. Available HTTP: http://www.statesman.com/specialreports/content/specialreports/citiesofideas/0609immigration.html (accessed 4 October 2011).

Lorenzen, M. and Andersen, K. V. (2007) 'The Geography of the European Creative Class: A Rank-Size Analysis.' DRUID Working Paper No. 07–17, Aalborg and Copenhagen: Danish Research Unit for Industrial Dynamics. Online. Available HTTP: http://www3.druid.dk/wp/20070017.pdf (accessed 17 June 2012).

Lorenzen, M. and Andersen, K. V. (2009) 'Centrality and Creativity: Does Richard Florida's Creative Class Offer New Insights into Urban Hierarchy?' *Economic Geography* 85 (4): 363–390.

Malanga, S. (2004) 'The Curse of the Creative Class'. *City Journal* Winter: 36–45. Online. Available HTTP: http://www.city-journal.org/html/14_1_the_curse.html (accessed 27 September 2011).

Markusen, A. (2006) 'Urban Development and the Politics of a Creative Class: Evidence from the Study of Artists'. *Environment and Planning A* 38: 1921–1940.

Musterd, S., Bontje, M., Chapain, C., Kovács, Z. and Murie, A. (2007) 'Accommodating Creative Knowledge: A Literature Review from a European Perspective'. ACRE report no. 1. Amsterdam: AMIDSt, University of Amsterdam. Online. Available HTTP: http://dare.uva.nl/document/123534 (accessed 27 September 2011).

Nathan, M. (2005) 'The Wrong Stuff'. Centre for Cities discussion paper 1. London: Centre for Cities. Online. Available HTTP: http://www.centreforcities.org/assets/files/pdfs/the_wrong_stuff_discussion_paper_1.pdf (accessed 27 September 2011).

Peck, J. (2005) 'Struggling with the Creative Class'. *International Journal of Urban and Regional Research* 29: 740–770.

Scott, A. J. (2006) 'Creative Cities: Conceptual Issues and Policy Questions'. *Journal of Urban Affairs* 28 (1): 1–17.

11 Cultures and Innovation

Sally Gee and Ian Miles

INTRODUCTION

In this chapter we explore the cultural dimensions of innovation, particularly the ways in which culture shapes and creates the preconditions for creativity, innovation and diffusion. 'Culture' can be understood and approached in many ways. In this chapter we understand culture as the system of shared beliefs, values, customs, behaviors and artifacts that the members of society use to cope with their world and with one another, and that are transmitted from generation to generation through learning (Bates and Plog, 1990). Following on from the previous chapter, we distinguish between values, attitudes and practices, which are elements of culture, choosing to focus on cultural differences at the national and organizational levels (Kroeber and Kluckhohn, 1952). Attitudes to risk and entrepreneurship, novelty and tradition, and conformity and transgression are among the features of culture that will obviously bear upon innovation in the 21st century. 'Attitudes', and the related idea of 'values' that may be thought of as the deeper symbolic structures from which attitudes about more immediate experiences are generated, are often thought of as matters of individual psychology. Nevertheless, the ways in which attitudes are formed and communicated, and values and cultural judgments are embodied in material artifacts and in rules and regulations, are inherently social and transpersonal, providing a cultural context to innovation and innovative activity.

In this chapter, we examine firstly attitudes and values among members of nations and organizations—for example, their willingness to take one or another sort of risk. Secondly, we consider institutional arrangements and practices—for example, financial markets and predispositions for debt or equity finance. Regulatory regimes are identified as one form of embedded interaction between cultures at the national and organizational level.

Two interesting ideas, 'risk society' and 'postmaterialism', are identified, and the implications of these ideas for innovation are discussed. Several points of distinction are made in this context: attitudes to specific innovations may vary dramatically; culture may better be seen as *shaping* innovation rather than just accelerating or slowing it; and innovation *processes* are shaped as well as specific innovations and their adoption. National differences in attitudes towards technology development, risk and perceptions of trust influence inventive, innovative and diffusive activities, reflecting values such as environmentalism.

On a different tack, attitudes and values are expressed and instituted in heterogeneous structures, processes, rules and regulations. One tool for analyzing national differences in structures and innovative capacity is the 'national systems of innovation framework'. Culture is implicit in this approach and social norms and values are embodied and reproduced at the institutional level—for example, within the education system, providing one mechanism through which institutional structures stabilize. We explore the institutional expression of culture and the complex interaction between culture and innovation. Representatives of national culture influence the design and implementation of regulations, having a direct impact on the selection of innovation at the national level as well as the direction and momentum of those activities. Public attitudes towards a technology are shown to impact the uptake and diffusion of the innovation, for example, attitudes towards biotechnology or information communication technologies.

At the organizational level we note that organizational and management researchers have approached firms in much the same way to the creative cities approach discussed in the previous chapter, arguing that the culture of firms can be more or less conducive to innovation and that it is possible to identify enabling factors and strategies that managers can follow to build such cultures. As with the other topics considered in this book, the issue of culture emerges as a multifaceted one, where many dimensions play a role, including firm size, sector and age. There will rarely be a one-to-one relationship between any one element of culture and the innovative outcomes for organizations.

ATTITUDES AND VALUES

The 'Risk Society'

A sociological approach that has considerable relevance to innovation was introduced by Ulrich Beck in 1992, using the term 'risk society'. In the past, he argued, dangers were largely seen as beyond human control, as being the product of forces of nature or the will of God. But in contemporary societies, risk is, or at least is seen as, increasingly created by human activities—including technological innovations. Risk is also managed, so that those in power are seen as responsible for foreseeing, averting and dealing with the consequences of natural and human-made hazards. Modern risks are thus seen as a matter of human agency–decisions and choices—rather than one of chance or matters beyond our influence. This analysis helps to explain the rise of litigation, the 'blame culture' (for example, somebody must be held responsible when things go wrong or somebody should have been aware of the dangerous consequences of actions), the 'audit culture' (necessitating the creation of audit trails showing that due diligence has been exercised) and risk management philosophies and practices (Powers, 1997).

The approach is potentially very relevant to studies of innovation. On the one hand, we might expect awareness of these trends to influence innovators' propensity to take risks, at least those risks that might lead to others blaming them for bad consequences that they are experiencing. The response may not be just to reduce risk-taking; it may lead to (a) decisions to take some sorts of risks rather than others—for example, less visible risks, those affecting less powerful and vocal groups; (b) effort going into risk management systems, and related research and design efforts that minimize those risks that have been identified; (c) investment in public relations and legal services that can reduce the likelihood of regulatory action or successful litigation against the innovator. It is interesting to note in this context that the US is simultaneously held to be a highly litigious country and one that accepts a great deal of technological innovation.[1]

On the other hand, the analysis is also liable to be relevant to consumption decisions and thus to the uptake of innovations. The analysis would suggest that there should be greater awareness that there are consequences of our consumption decisions, and governments have been keen to promote this awareness in at least the health domain for many years now. The case here—that as major epidemic diseases have been curtailed, many of the main sources of mortality reflect individual consumption decisions—accords with the risk society account quite neatly. Certainly a proportion of the population is highly interested in personal and sometimes broader social and environmental consequences of their consumption decisions, though the continual need for strong government and pressure group campaigns suggests that this is a minority position. There does not yet seem to be a great deal of analysis of variations in attitudes to risk across societies and regions, conducted within the Beck framework. The next subsection will, however, introduce some related ideas that have been studied extensively on a geographical basis.[2]

Risk has been at the heart of some analyses that are not completely aligned with the Beck work. The UK Foresight Programme, for example, has commissioned major analyses of the social psychology of risk (one good publication here is Eiser, 2004). More generally, innovation and other researchers have noted that some technologies are more controversial than others; the degree of controversy is related to the perceived risks associated with the technology, and how these risks are being addressed.[3] A key innovation challenge for the 21st century is managing risk, whether perceived or actual.

'POSTMATERIALISM'

Perhaps the best-known and most influential approach to understanding the evolution and spatial variations in values and attitudes derives from the work of Ronald Inglehart. For several decades, he has been elaborating a theory of intergenerational value change and accumulating evidence on this process on a cross-national basis. He draws upon Maslow's very well-known theory of a hierarchy of needs, which argues that basic needs have to be satisfied before more sophisticated needs are pursued. Inglehart suggests that as Western societies (and several others) experienced a long period of increasing affluence and relief from the effects of war and natural disasters, cohorts have grown up with their basic 'materialist' needs being largely securely satisfied. In consequence, they have put more priority on 'postmaterialist' needs. Eurobarometer surveys have incorporated simple Inglehart indicators for surveys across the European Union from the early 1970s. Many other countries, including the US and Japan, have been included in studies using similar indicators. Current European surveys suggest that postmaterialists and materialists are roughly equally balanced in Western countries, while in the early 1970s only one-quarter were postmaterialists (Abramson and Inglehart, 1994). Thus, as threats to basic welfare have declined, so a shift of values across generations has followed. Inglehart termed this the 'Silent Revolution'. This could be related to the 'risk society' argument, in that the sorts of risk encountered have been less to do with one's basic material circumstances, and have become more to do with threats to self-esteem and self-realization.

WHAT ABOUT INNOVATION?

First, consider Inglehart as compared to Beck. Though neither Beck nor Inglehart spells it out in quite this way, we could suggest that the trend would be such that threats to basic welfare will increasingly be seen (a) as threats to one's self-esteem and status as well as purely material deprivations and (b) as the products of human agency and thus as threats that have to be responded to accordingly. Delving deeper, though, there might appear to be a contradiction in a simple reading of what the Beck and Inglehart theses say about innovation. Might not 'risk society' approaches lead us to expect that risk-averse people would be more cautious about innovation? Might not 'postmaterialist' approaches imply a growth of people prepared to experiment with ways of self-expression and self-realization? The situation is more complex. 'Risk society' does not necessarily mean more 'risk averse', but more 'risk-oriented' when it comes to making decisions and reflecting on routines. This may mean embracing innovations that offer, for example, longer lives (dietary supplements to reduce cholesterol or stave off the effects of ageing), and greater security (mobile phones to stay in contact with emergency services and family members). It will be the type of innovation, the risks it addresses and the risks it raises that will be the issue. 'Postmaterialists' may be concerned about certain types and trajectory of innovation on account of the risks to their cherished values. Thus some analysts have suggested that the Eurobarometer surveys indicate that countries where there are higher levels of postmaterialistic individuals tend to express more pessimistic views of technology, while countries with higher levels of materialistic values tend to be more optimistic (Durant, Bauer and Gaskell, 1998), reflected in a desire for technological 'progress' and innovation. We shall consider some of the cross-national comparative work later.

Values such as environmentalism, together with concerns over the directions of technological change, appear to be associated with postmaterialism. Commentators in the Inglehart tradition see the shift towards postmaterialism as a major driver of environmental concerns and movements, for instance.[4] Postmaterialists tend to place higher priority on protecting the environment than materialists. They are markedly more likely to join environmentalist groups.[5] More recent birth cohorts generally have stronger environmentalist values than do cohorts born earlier.[6] Given the deep-seated environmental problems that are associated with the development paths of Western societies (and increasingly, the whole industrialized and industrializing world), it is not surprising that postmaterialists have some reservations about the technological development that has been intrinsic to these paths. They might be expected to be sympathetic to technological solutions of the clean and clean-up varieties, but not necessarily to 'macroengineering' answers to climate change (large-scale and largely untried projects with their own risks and unintended consequences) and to processes of technology choice in general that involve centralized and non-participative decisions and systems.

Attitudes to innovations and the way that the innovation process is governed are liable to reflect both increased interest in 'postmaterial' goals and increased concern with how various types of risks are being addressed. We also will need to consider specific types of innovation and perhaps even types of innovation processes. Furthermore, the risk and postmaterialism arguments both stress the long-term development towards societies dominated by new types of value. Inglehart argues that the generational values he assesses are very stable ones, so that there is little hope for rapid results from policy interventions aimed at changing these elements of culture. However, the way in which these 'deep' values are expressed is affected by opportunities and by perceptions. Attitudes and behavior towards specific innovations may be influenced by whether these are seen as favoring or acting against certain key values. This understanding underpins much effort by marketing experts to persuade consumers that new (or established) products really can help them fulfill one or another life goal. It might also be relevant to policymakers thinking about how to position and describe their innovation choices and programs.

ATTITUDES AND VALUES IN SPATIAL CONTEXTS

The Postmaterialist Shift and National Differences

As for cross-national differences, in addition to the economic development process that increases individual resources, Inglehart (1997) and others cluster nations into larger 'cultural zones' that tend to share similar world-views, institutions and ways of life. Inglehart follows a relatively common

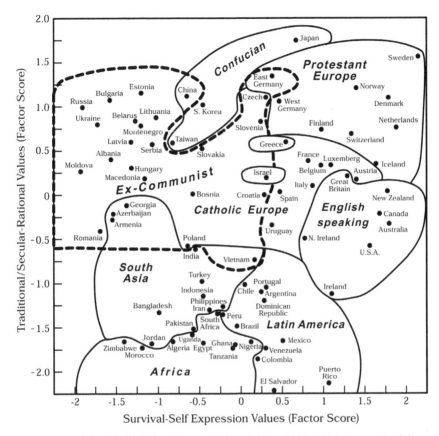

Figure 11.1 The World Value Survey Cultural Map 1999-2004 Source: Inglehart & Welzel. (2005).

approach of classification according to common religious roots, as displayed in Figure 11.1, where clusters based largely on measures of values in the population are interpreted in terms of mainly religious traditions. This is of course interesting in the context of the huge and long-lasting impact of Max Weber's thesis as to the impact of the Protestant ethic on the growth of capitalism. But it is striking that there is no obvious immediate correlation between location on this map and innovativeness. It would perhaps be aesthetically pleasing if movement towards the top right-hand corner were tied to innovativeness (note that Finland is in this area). But neither the US nor Japan is here, and they are in fact quite distant from one another.

In one respect this may be reassuring; a country is not necessarily bound by its long-standing religious/cultural traditions to be less innovative than might be desired. Matters are more complicated, and in other work, Inglehart shows that Catholic France and Protestant Britain are much more alike in terms of (weak) religious observance than are Catholic Ireland and Italy and the Protestant US (Norris and Inglehart, 2004). Religious and other aspects of cultural institutions may mediate between the sorts of values implied in the postindustrialism thesis (and in work on risk, omnivorousness and other values) and their manifestation in behavior. But the underlying value shifts may still be underway, and they may impact upon the cultural institutions themselves in due course. We may see defensive traditionalist/fundamentalist reactions, or more tolerant and liberal adaptations, for example.

Another important issue here is that there is considerable variation within countries, despite the supposed homogenizing effects of mass media. Norris and Inglehart, indeed, show that religious practices vary dramatically within countries, and these variations seem to be fairly closely related to social dimensions such as class. This might suggest that we should drop a territorial focus, and instead consider social groups independently of space. There may be some merits in doing so.

But let us briefly consider a few more straws in the wind relating (national) culture to innovation. Rusanen (2002) examined the question of how it is that Finland, a society that would be expected to feature a high level of postmaterialism, is innovative, and not only in respect to information technology.[7] There is also a high level of support for biotechnology applications in both agriculture and industry, unlike in many European countries and contrary to some expectations that might be derived from risk society and postmaterialist analyses. Though, as we suggested earlier these deductions do not rest on very solid foundations, even if we were completely behind one or both of these lines of analysis. Rusanen argues that other sorts of cultural phenomena can and do play important roles. In the Finnish case, the climate and geography have led to distinctive agricultural history in terms of reliance on technological innovation and probably popular sentiment about farming and nature too. The information technology success story is seen as having helped rescue the country from an economic impasse and thus innovation is regarded as beneficial. Again we could gloss Rusanen by suggesting that this story is also felt to be rather tenuous; what happens if Nokia leaves, or makes costly mistakes? And thus pinning hopes on other foci of innovation is a reasonable strategy.

Studies emphasize the complexity and interdependency of innovative activity and sociocultural factors. It looks as if there are different responses to broad classes of innovation related to the sorts of knowledge and interventions in the natural and social orders that they imply. Furthermore, there are suggestions that responses will also vary according to the types of applications involved. Military-related innovations are liable to be less popular than health-related ones, for instance. Particular innovations may meet with different reactions in different cultures. The obvious example is the US resistance, at least from the national government, to stem cell technology (based on embryonic tissues), as compared to the supposed openness of US culture to innovation in general.

Institutions, Rules and Regulations in Spatial Contexts

Reflecting this complexity and interdependency, attitudes and values are expressed and instituted in heterogeneous structures, processes, rules and regulations. Aspects of national culture contribute to the cognitive framework through which individuals perceive the world and influence how we attempt to organize it. Attitudes towards risk are embodied in institutional norms—for example, a strong health and safety culture, readiness to engage in complex contractual arrangements, or predispositions for different forms of corporate governance. Similarly, postmaterialism values can be embedded in political, organizational or regulatory structures. The relationship between institutions, rules, regulations and innovation has been a topic of global debate, clearly demonstrated, for example, by the reaction of policymakers in Europe and North America to the emergence of a highly successful and innovative Japanese economy in the 1980s. The perceived competitive advantage of Japan was partly understood as a cultural phenomenon and analytical attention centered on understanding the relationship between culture and institutional structures, as well as the organization of work.

National Innovation Systems

A well-developed tool for analyzing national differences in institutional structures and innovative capacity is the national innovation systems approach (Freeman, 1987; Lundvall, 1992; and Nelson, 1993). Literature in this tradition has tended to examine formal institutional arrangements. Culture is often not explicitly discussed. Implicitly, however, the variety of institutional arrangements and heterogeneity of elements involved in the innovation system are understood to be subject to a variety of evolutionary processes, both path-dependent and unpredictable. The emergence of the institutions, rules and regulations that make up a national innovation system, including firms, the education system, the regulatory environment, the legislative environment and the financial system, are influenced by the cultural context of a space. As emphasized, they may develop and interact in a complex manner.

Social norms and values are reproduced by the education system. For example, the degree of egalitarianism or elitism in the system affects the capacity of the whole workforce to contribute to innovation. Historical features of countries are reflected in a heritage of educational structures, such as which subjects are given more or less emphasis in curricula and whether the focus is on vocational or academic education. For example, some analysts relate the UK's long-term poor economic performance to factors stemming from the imperial past directing education towards running an empire, not managing and working in modern institutions and enterprises. The relative status of subjects clearly influences the direction of innovation in a nation over the medium term, perhaps offset by immigration policies and skilled migrant workers. The current preoccupation with professional services in the UK reflects a cultural shift that was instituted by deregulation and reform in the 1980s. Related to this, the status of engineering in the UK is relatively low, while US engineering schools are high-status and French polytechnics and mining schools are elite institutions, reflecting industrial strengths and priorities, all of which have an impact on innovation in the 21st century.

Likewise, there are cultural dimensions to the functioning of the financial system that might well impact the innovative climate of a country, such as long-term debt finance, available, for example, in Germany and Japan, as opposed to the relatively short-term financial support found on the capital markets in the UK (Tylecote, 2007). Attitudes to risk will have an impact on the type of innovative activity that is funded through financial institutions as well as the structure of the finance. Mechanisms such as reducing individual risk through limited partnerships and developing positive mechanisms for bankruptcy reflect general attitudes and values, and are likely to impact behavior at the individual and organizational level. Similarly, the availability of venture capital and private money more generally, in the US is often cited as an important facilitator of innovative activity (Florida and Kenney, 1988). Perspectives that link the availability of venture capital with innovative activity often focus on a national predisposition for entrepreneurialism attributed to attitudes and values—that is, culture. However, a positive relationship between entrepreneurship and innovative capacity does not necessary mean there is a negative relationship between low levels of entrepreneurship and innovation. This is something that we touch on later in this chapter.

We cannot discuss institutional arrangements without stressing the connections and linkages of the national system. Large bodies of research, notably at the regional level, have emphasized interdependency, co-generation and learning. Often particular types of linkages are the focus of study. For example, university-academy relations and the commercialization of knowledge are prominent research fields in innovation studies. Conflicting cultures between the (often) public university and the private firm are identified as a potential barrier to the co-generation process. However, the different cultures and contexts of the university and industry support complementary economic functions and phases of innovative activity. The ability to connect potentially disparate elements of the economy is widely agreed to provide significant advantage. For example, spatial constraints may be overcome through networks; though the small size of Nordic countries could be seen as a disadvantage in terms of market size and absolute numbers of innovative people, the connections that exist between institutions have been seen to confer an advantage to innovative activity (Walsh, 1988).

Similarly, institutional arrangements, rules and regulations interact and may complement or conflict with each other influencing the nature, direction and rate of innovative activity. Legal institutions can influence innovative activity in a variety of ways. The Japanese Intellectual Property Rights (IPR) system encourages reverse engineering and modifications rather than radical innovations, compared to both France and the US (Maskus and McDaniel, 1999). Thus the combination of the US IPR system and the availability of venture capital provides a supportive environment for radical innovation. We must be careful when correlating these institutional features. The US experienced significant growth in the micro-processor and biotechnology sectors and both industries benefited from significant federal funding, political support, science and engineering capabilities and a high propensity to patent. Replicating a venture capital market and a strong IPR system in another country, aside from proving very difficult, is unlikely to have a similar effect. It is naive to assume that institutional structures or cultural conventions can be successfully 'transplanted'.

REGULATION

Representatives of the national 'culture', such as trade unions and non-government organizations (NGOs), directly influence the design and implementation (as well as the content) of regulations. One line of research has examined cross-national variations in acceptance and implementation of major (usually controversial) new technologies (e.g., studies in Bauer, 1995). Among these are studies of GMOs and food biotechnology (for a sophisticated analysis of the GM tomato debate, see Harvey et al., 2002). Jasanoff (2005) also examines food biotechnology. She argues that US debate and regulation focus narrowly on risk, with a more 'technocratic' regulation process. In Europe, Germany in particular, a much more important role is played by broader value- and worldview-related dimensions. Outcomes may be similar across these different systems (Jasanoff, 1995), or may diverge, and a 'messy' political process is involved. Jasanoff goes on to argue that the difficulties of harmonizing standards across countries and cultures requires seeing harmonization as 'reciprocal commentary' rather than a process that can be reduced to purely scientific and technical analysis. Reciprocal commentary means the exchange among partners of qualitative and not only quantitative information about prior practices. Feedback mechanisms are required to enable appreciation of successes or failures across countries, to promote mutual learning and shared understanding of each other's institutions, culture and history.

Gaskell and colleagues have considered the relationships between public perceptions of technology and regulation, conducting fascinating research on cross-national and within-country differences (e.g., Gaskell, 2004; Gaskell et al., 2005; Gaskell et al., 2006). One example of these results on differences in public attitudes to biotechnology is demonstrated by Figure 11.2, suggesting that Europeans[8] were less optimistic about biotechnology than either Canadians or Americans between 1995 and 2002.

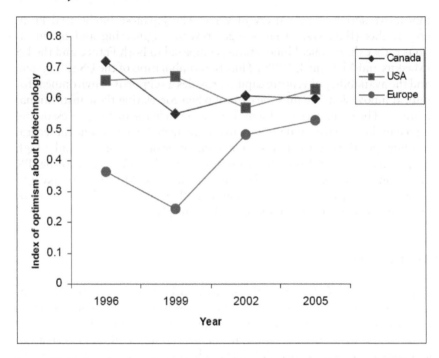

Figure 11.2   Levels of optimism towards biotechnology in Canada, the US and Europe. Source: Gaskell et al. (2006).

However, Gaskell et al. (2006) have found that levels of trust across European countries have significantly increased over the past six years. The suggestion is that prior to 1999 'biotechnology' and 'industry' were associated with agrobio technologies, such as GM crops, but other applications (e.g., health) have since come to the fore. Perhaps this analysis supports the risk society and postmaterialism perspective. It certainly serves to emphasize that different forms of innovation will receive different responses from consumers and the public more generally, making it difficult to draw conclusions about public or market attitudes to innovation generally. Figure 11.3 emphasizes how different technologies elicit different levels of optimism, noting the increasing levels of optimism about biotechnology.

It is evident that there are many complicated relations between culture, specific institutions and institutional arrangements, and innovation processes, around the world. Regulatory regimes at the national and sectoral level are the outcome of negotiated processes between government, firms and other stakeholders. Consultation and conflict epitomize the emergence and evolution of regulation instituting cultural norms, as well as changing attitudes and values. These characteristics are also observed at the organizational level.

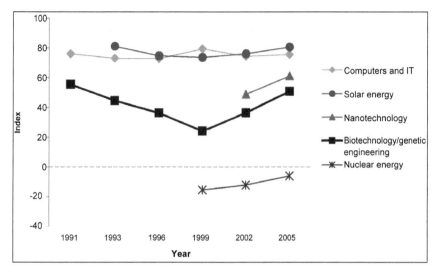

Figure 11.3   Index of optimism at the European level towards five technologies.
Source: Gaskell et al. (2006).

ORGANIZATIONAL CULTURE AND INNOVATION

A diverse range of organizations participate in innovative activity. Firms are generally perceived to be the most important economic agents in the innovation process. However, there is a body of literature emphasizing the role of non-governmental and public service organizations. Cultures vary wildly within and across these categories, and general wisdom perceives large firms as the source of most incremental innovation, small entrepreneurial firms as the primary source of radical innovation and the public sector as broadly non-innovative. Attitudes, values, rules and procedures are identified as influencing the level, direction and pace of innovative activity at the organizational level. As one might expect, the identification of an archetypal culture that fosters innovation has been the subject of extensive research in the organization and management sciences. Much of this literature relies on case studies of exemplar organizations (usually firms), though there are some attempts to provide systemic evidence on the relationships between culture and innovation.

Attitudes and Values in Organizations

Although many authors, including Schein (2010), argue that culture is the most difficult organizational attribute to change, there is no shortage of frameworks to characterize particular organizational cultures (e.g., Hofstede, 1980; Deal and Kennedy, 1982) or of mechanisms to change it (e.g., Senge, 1990). As the Creative Cities approach has been popular with policymakers, similarly practitioners turn to the management literature for ways to create a culture that fosters innovation. A number of attitudes and values have been identified as having a positive relationship with innovative activity, perhaps the most significant being attitudes to risk and tolerance of failure, which are widely agreed to influence individuals', and ultimately organizations', propensity to innovate. Fear of failure, or a rampant blame culture, may stifle creativity and reduce opportunities for learning, a key feature of innovation. Public sector organizations are often characterized by their risk awareness, an issue related to Beck's risk society, as discussed earlier. The emphasis on audit trails, accountability and transparency coupled with a prominent 'blame culture'; hierarchical structure and high levels of employee risk aversion all contribute to the image of public organizations as non-innovative.[9] See Potts (2009) for a compelling argument that the 'efficiency' agenda in public services inhibits the experimentation necessary for innovation and ultimately for providing effective service provision. Organizational attitudes to risk may also influence the type of innovative activity undertaken. As risk of failure increases when innovation is more radical than incremental, highly risk-averse cultures may concentrate on incremental innovation. This finding can be related to the organization of work (see discussion on Arundel et al., 2007, ahead) as high autonomy, tolerance of mistakes and acceptance of risk are embodied by firm practices. Van der Meer (2007) argues that managing innovation is about managing paradoxes; creativity and inventive activity are different from commercialization and innovative activity. Other authors have demonstrated that individuals have the ability to be both creative and pay attention to detail (Miron, Erez and Naveh, 2004) necessary for commercialization. As many organizations, particularly larger ones, have clear divisions of labor between functions, we could expect to see different values and attitudes within the same structure.

Successful innovative organizations have been identified as engaging in supportive open and transparent communication that is based on trust, and 'connectedness' between employees (Kohli and Jaworski, 1990; Rose and Shoham 2002). Similarly perceptions of fairness and justice have been found to have substantial impacts on the organizational climate (Shoham et al., 2003). Team-building activities are employed in order to establish a localized culture of cooperation in an organization. One of the authors encountered such methods being used in a chemicals firm that was forced to accelerate its innovation processes and combine new sorts of knowledge in order to cope with the challenge of developing and commercializing alternatives to CFCs, for instance. In emerging fields such as biotechnology and nanotechnology, scientists from different disciplines often struggle to overcome very different disciplinary backgrounds. An increase in multidisciplinary working practices is an important innovation challenge for the 21st century and Florida identifies tolerance of diversity as an attractive characteristic of highly creative spaces, one that encourages creative people to live and work in them. The analysis could clearly apply to organizations as well as to cities, and their ability to recruit creative people as well as their ability to use them well. Tolerance of differences allows diversity to exist and flourish (e.g., Scott and Bruce, 1994) and intolerant organizations inhibit innovations by restricting employees to uniform menus of expected behaviors (Zaltman, Duncan and Holbek, 1973; King, 1990). Perhaps this last issue is of particular relevance for public sector organizations that are often characterized by high degrees of bureaucracy. Issues of immigration have also been raised in policy and organizational research, and the mobility of labor, particularly highly skilled and entrepreneurial individuals, is cited as a contributing factor to the dominance of the US economy in many technological and creative industries (e.g., Saxenian, 2006).

Much of the debate about variations in innovative performance in the US and Europe is constructed around the notion that the US is characterized by high levels of entrepreneurialism. The assumption behind this notion is that countries with high levels of entrepreneurs are more innovative and this assumption is often supported with case studies of highly innovative start-ups. Entrepreneurs *are* doing new things, starting new firms, in particular. Whether they are innovative in terms of introducing new products and processes to the world, or to the national or local industry or market, is less clear. A major source of information on cross-national variations in entrepreneurship is the Global Entrepreneurship Monitor (GEM), which presents many reports and publications.[10] A particularly useful resource is GEM's Annual Summary Results. Figure 11.4 reproduces some telling results from recent GEM analyses, relating early-stage entrepreneurship to the level of economic development indexed by per capita GDP levels.

There is a striking relationship between the two variables. At low levels of economic development it is typical to find a large share of very small enterprises in the structure of the economy. Industrialization tends to see the rise of larger and longer-established firms, catering to growing markets, and providing more employment opportunities. Perhaps we also see the effect of the demographic transition here, too, with fewer young people coming into the labor market and pursuing the jobs there available. But at higher levels of income still, the entrepreneurial sector begins to increase its share once more. There are several likely factors for this, including a shift from mass consumption to differentiated consumer needs; a growing demand for services (including new technology activities and others with lower capital entry barriers); the resources to risk going into business and perhaps the reassurance of social welfare provision should they fail; and political support for new small firms.[11]

Beyond these large trends, a range of what the GEM authors call 'the demographic, cultural and institutional characteristics of each country' presumably affect entrepreneurialism, accounting for the scatter of countries around the trend line. While it is likely that variations in national culture encourage or discourage entrepreneurship,[12] these studies[13] offer only

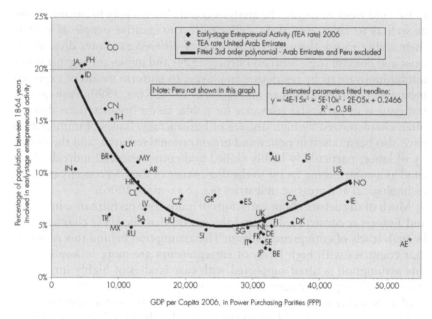

Figure 11.4   Early-stage entrepreneurial activity rates and GDP per capita, 2006. Source: Bosma and Harding (2006).
Note: Fitted 3rd order polynomial—Arab Emirates and Peru excluded; PPP-corrected GDP levels are taken from the IMF's World Economic Outlook Database (October 2006). Permission to use a figure from the Global Entrepreneurship Monitor (GEM) 2006 Global Report, which appears here, has been granted by the copyright holders. The GEM is an international consortium and this report was produced from data collected in, and received from, forty-two countries in 2006. Our thanks go to the authors, national teams, researchers, funding bodies and other contributors who have made this possible.

tantalizing glimpses as to what these key variations might be. It is interesting to note that both Japan and Finland have low levels of entrepreneurial activity, yet both countries are widely perceived to be highly innovative. This suggests that although entrepreneurial behavior may be a useful indicator of some sorts of innovative activity, other types of innovative activity matter, so that countries with relatively low numbers of entrepreneurs can be engaging in successful innovative behavior. Indeed, were this not the case, we would not find any significant innovation in public services, which can actually be rather active here (see Halvorsen et al., 2005).

Though there is a fascinating body of research on small, high-tech firms, there is limited evidence on trends in the propensity of entrepreneurs to be innovators (and vice versa) and what sorts of innovators they might be. However, the GEM 2006 study did go on to enquire as to the relationship between entrepreneurial activities and innovation. Just over half of the early-stage entrepreneurs in high-income and low-income countries alike did not consider that they were responsible for products that were new to their customers, and less than 20 percent thought they were introducing a product new to all consumers or 'new to market'. Most entrepreneurs do not see themselves as using new technology and small proportions consider themselves to be using the latest technology. Despite some vocal advocates of the clear link between entrepreneurial culture and innovation, the situation appears more complex.

Structures and Practices in Organizations

'Intrapreneurship' is discussed as a key facilitator of innovative activity within firms. Many authors agree that when work is organized to promote learning and problem-solving, innovation is supported (Arad, Hanson and Schneider, 1997; Lock and Kirkpatrick, 1995; Samaha, 1996). A large body of literature attempts to identify the structures and practices that are associated with successful (usually large) innovative firms. Much has been made of flat structures, autonomy and work teams as opposed to specialization, formal and standardized practices and central control (Arad, Hanson and Schneider, 1997; CIMA Study Text, 1996). Attempts have been made to replicate smaller, flatter working environments within large organizations, in an attempt to increase their innovative capacity—for example, the recent internal restructuring within major electronics and pharmaceutical companies.[14] The perceived disadvantages of large and overly bureaucratic organizations in terms of innovative ability have implications for public sector organizations (Parker and Bradley, 2000), which are often characterized by their scale and complexity.

However, there is very little quantitative, survey-based research exploring what organizational environments promote learning and innovation on a global basis. Arundel et al. (2007) used the 3rd European Survey of working conditions and the CIS-3 to develop an EU-wide mapping of the adoption of organizational practices and policies associated with innovative activity. They argue that the structure of how people work and learn may be deeply rooted in the national innovation system. This would imply that attempts to benchmark innovation 'best practice' may present only the 'tip of the iceberg',[15] neglecting institutional and cultural contexts.

The authors selected indicators on the basis of points raised in the literature on high performance work and on the relation between organizational design and innovation. They analyzed the survey data to identify four basic systems of work organization.

1) Discretionary Learning—Associated with high autonomy, learning, and task complexity.
2) Lean Production—Associated with low employee discretion, job rotation, team work, quality rules, bureaucracy.
3) Flexible Taylorism—Core work practices, low discretion, low problem-solving.

4) Traditional—Machine bureaucracies, low employee discretion.

Figure 11.5 presents some basic results. The researchers found that the discretionary learning system was most widely diffused in the Nordic countries and Netherlands. In comparison, the lean production model was found to be most widely diffused in the UK, Ireland and Spain. Conversely the Taylorist model was most frequently found in Southern Europe, Ireland and Italy. The traditional model was found in Greece and Italy. As the discretionary learning model is generally positively correlated with innovative behavior (endogenous, adoption and radical) then these findings support the perception of the Nordic countries as successful innovators. In comparison Southern European countries, the UK, Italy, Greece, Belgium and Portugal are generally perceived as being less innovative.

The UK case warrants further discussion. In Arundel et al.'s (2007) study, the UK is identified as the only country within the group of European high-training nations where the lean form of work organization, usually associated with the Japanese J-form firm, is more widely diffused than the discretionary learning model, associated with high autonomy, learning and task complexity and (not insignificantly) in-house innovation of a more radical nature. This leads the authors to consider what 'unexplained' factors (e.g., firm size, industry structure and occupation) influence organizational practices. The authors find a positive relationship between the relative frequency of discretionary learning and a measure of the level of generalized trust that is commonly used in the literature on social capital and productivity growth. The measure of trust is based on a question in the World Values Survey: 'Generally speaking would you say that most people can be trusted, or that you can't be too careful in dealing with people?' For the EU 15, the percentage of the respondents saying that most people can be trusted ranged from a low of 12.3 percent for Portugal to a high of 66.5 percent for Denmark. One way to interpret these results is that high levels of trust support high levels of autonomy in work; whereas low levels of trust tend to give rise to relatively rule-bound and hierarchical forms of organization.

The authors suggest that the position of the UK as a high-training nation that does not use the discretionary learning model reflects the low levels of generalized trust in comparison to the Nordic countries, where discretionary learning is the most widely diffused organizational form. Additionally, although organizations in the UK have adopted best practice models of work organization associated with lean production and incremental innovation, there is a tendency towards bureaucratic and rule-based organizational structures and an extremely high level of non-innovating firms in the economy. It is suggested that the low levels of generalized trust in the British culture have impacted on employees' discretion to organize work and problem-solve, either because they are averse to the risk (due to lack of trust) or because managers are unwilling to allow discretion (due to lack of

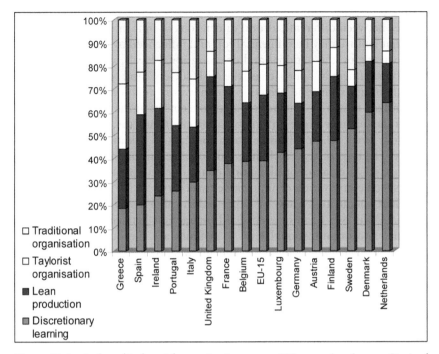

Figure 11.5 Styles of industrial organization across EU countries. Source: Derived from data presented in Arundel et al. (2007).

trust). As a result, the lean production methods in use in the UK are not as 'effective' as when employed within the Japanese culture.

It should be noted that multiple forms of work organization can be used in the same organization. Studies like this are likely to pick up mainly the dominant model. It is also not straightforward to relate organizational forms to innovation, but Arundel et al. (2007) draw on earlier work on the propensities for different national economies to display one or the other style of innovation (strategic innovators, intermittent innovators, technology modifiers and technology adopters). Countries seem to show related patterns of organizational culture and innovative style.[16]

CONCLUSIONS

There is a large body of literature, from different analytical perspectives, on culture, innovation and the relationship between culture and innovative activity. We have not attempted to provide an exhaustive review of this literature. Instead we have drawn on ideas that we feel are particularly interesting and relevant to scholars and practitioners of innovation in the 21st century. We have approached this topic in a reflective and systemic way, hoping to capture some of the complexity of relationships and interdependencies between different cultural dimensions of innovation, as well as the way that culture may be influential for, and influenced by, innovative activity. Focusing on the national and organizational levels, we have discussed how two influential approaches, the 'risk society' and 'post-materialism', provide insights into the behavior of innovators and consumers. We have emphasized how 'risk-orientation' and concepts of agency help explain the rise of the 'blame culture' in Anglo-Saxon environments, but warn against inferring direct relationships between concepts of risk and innovative outcomes. The type of risk (including risk to values) an innovation addresses, and raises, is crucial to the likelihood of any one group pursuing or embracing a specific innovation or innovative trajectory.

Values and attitudes may be expressed through institutional structures. Regulation is one form of embedded interaction between cultures at the national and organizational level as regimes are the outcome of negotiated processes between government, firms and other stakeholders. Cultural norms, and changing attitudes and values, are instituted through these interactions. For example, Europeans have been described as less optimistic about biotechnology than Americans, and these values are reflected in their respective regulatory regimes. The US regulatory system has a greater emphasis on scientific possibilities, and a narrower perception of risk. In Europe, a more important role is given to broader social views, as represented by the adoption of the 'precautionary principle' for genetically modified (GM) crops in the region. These different responses cannot be reduced to technophilic or technophobic values and attitudes. The acceptance of GM crops, as opposed to embryonic stem cells in the US, and vice versa in Europe, emphasizes how different types of innovations will provoke different responses in different contexts. Similarly, values, attitudes and practices change over time. The lifting of the moratorium on GM crops in Europe and proposed changes to National Institute of Health (NIH) guidelines on stem cell research in the US reflect shifts in broader social values.

A major conclusion that we draw from this literature is the need to be attentive to the complexity of the relationships that are encountered. The links between attitudes and values; institutions and regulations; responses to innovative ideas and products; entrepreneurship and risk-taking; and creativity and innovation are all relevant. These linkages provide the context within which we can talk about the relationships between 'cultures and innovation'. It is because of the many elements of this complex that we have to be wary of the assumption that there are direct links. One-to-one mapping is unlikely to be the rule. Neither is it likely that practices once transferred from one setting to another will have a similar outcome, as emphasized by research on the adoption of organizational practices. Discretionary learning models are less diffused in the UK than the lean form of work organization due to relatively low levels of generalized trust, and presumably related to a relatively high degree of 'risk-orientation'.

But, equally, there are important reasons to consider the wider set of linkages that constitute the relationships between cultures and innovation. For example, while entrepreneurship and new firms may not be the main sources of some classes of innovation, and while some highly innovative countries may not feature high levels of entrepreneurial activity; this does not mean that entrepreneurship and innovation are not linked in important ways. Clearly they are, and we have to be sensitive to the way in which these relationships are mediated through different contexts. It is worthwhile to examine cases of what appears to be good practice, to establish what practices and policies for fostering supportive relationships between cultural dimensions and innovation have developed (spontaneously or by design) in these cases. This is not 'benchmarking' in the sense of identifying approaches that can be transplanted in a 'me-too' way. The many elements of the cultural context mean that this may often result in failure. Rather, it is 'learning by comparing' to use a phrase from Lundvall. It is learning about how the relations between cultures and innovation are operating in one context as compared to another.

NOTES

1. Litigation around the effects of pharmaceuticals may yet have a major impact, and arguably already has impacted decisions about where trials of new drugs are carried out.
2. Lash et al. (1996) explore some of these themes.
3. Risk frameworks emphasize the importance of moving beyond the specific characteristics of the products and processes to the social system of information surrounding the technology (Einsiedel, 1998).
4. But it is unwise to assume that postmaterialists are somehow 'beyond' wanting more material goods—their material aspirations may be high ones (Miles, 1975). Advanced sports training and audiovisual equipment can have a high material component!
5. Inglehart (1990); Kanagy et al. (1994).
6. This appears to be more stable and consistent than the relationship between environmentalism and, say, gender and occupational status.
7. Note the apparent contradiction here with the Eurobarometer results displayed earlier.
8. For an intra-European comparison refer to Gaskell et al. (2006).
9. Paradoxically, many public organizations are highly innovative—for example, the National Health Service in the UK. Additionally, public bodies through procurement practices may offer niche markets for the development of alternative or radical innovative solutions.
10. Online. Available HTTP: http://www.gemconsortium.org/ (accessed 2 February 2012).
11. Political factors may also foster the emergence of new small firms, as governments promote this sector either as a more or less short-term way of reducing unemployment, or as a longer-term solution to problems of job creation (MacDonald and Coffield, 1991).
12. Some studies also address regional variations in culture within countries, even finding it in countries with relative homogeneity and shared values.

Examining new firm formation across regions in Sweden, Davidsson and Wiklund (1995) concluded that regional variations in the levels of entrepreneurship are influenced by the prevalent cultural values, even though they found a rather limited range of cultural values across the regions. They surveyed people as to their change orientation, need for autonomy, acceptance of capitalism, competitiveness and valuation of money. Variations in achievement, motivation and Jante-mentality (the attitude that one shouldn't try to stand out from the crowd) were not found to be important, though this does not mean that they would not play an important role if a wider range of cultures were sampled. The precise causality is an interesting question. Are people less prone to develop entrepreneurial orientations, or are they less able to actualize them in hostile environments and are thus being forced to migrate to other regions? What is the causality—are the values being shaped by experience of entrepreneurship, or vice versa? Life being complicated, it is quite possible that all of these possibilities have some truth.

13. The GEM results were supported by a cross-national survey by EOS Gallup Europe (2004), where respondents expressed their preference for self-employed or employee status.
14. See the European Restructuring Monitor. Online. Available HTTP: http://www.eurofound.europa.eu/emcc/erm/index.htm (accessed 14 September 2011).
15. There is a large body of literature that warns against attempts to transfer best practice from one organizational (or national) setting to another.
16. Arundel et al. (2007) also display suggestive relationships between their measures of organizational culture and measures of trust—for example, in this case being drawn from the same World Value Survey data that Inglehart uses. Perhaps there are more overlaps between these lines of analysis than explored so far.

BIBLIOGRAPHY

Abramson, P. R. and Inglehart, R. (1994) 'Education, Security, and Postmaterialism: A Comment on Duch and Taylor's "Postmaterialism and the Economic Condition"'. *American Journal of Political Science* 38 (3): 797–814.
Arad, S., Hanson, M. A. and Schneider, R. J. (1997) 'A Framework for the Study of Relationships between Organisational Characteristics and Organisational Behaviour'. *The Journal of Creative Behaviour* 31 (1): 42–58.
Arundel, A., Lorenz, E., Lundvall, B-A. and Valeyre, A. (2007) 'How Europe's Economies Learn: A Comparison of Work Organisation and Innovation Mode for the EU-15'. *Industrial and Corporate Change* 16 (6): 1175–1210.
Bates, D. and Plog, F. (1990) *Cultural Anthropology.* 3rd ed. New York: McGrawHill.
Bauer, M. (ed.) (1995) *Resistance to New Technology.* Cambridge: Cambridge University Press.
Beck, U. (1992) *Risk Society: Towards a New Modernity.* London: Sage Publications.
Bosma, N. and Harding, R. (2006) 'Global Entrepreneurship Monitor 2006 Results'. Babson College, MA, and London Business School, London. Online. Available HTTP: http://www.gemconsortium.org/about.aspx?page=global_reports_2006 (accessed 12 September 2011).
CIMA Study Text. (1996) 'Organizational Management and Development'. Stage 3, paper 11, 3rd ed. London: BPP Publishing.
Davidsson, P. and Wiklund, J. (1995) 'Cultural Values and Regional Variations in New Firm Foundation'. Frontiers of Entrepreneurship Research. Online.

Available HTTP: http://www.babson.edu/entrep/fer/papers95/per.htm (accessed 12 September 2011).

Deal, T. E. and Kennedy, A. A. (1982) *Corporate Cultures: The Rites and Rituals of Corporate Life*. Harmondsworth: Penguin Books.

Directorate-General Enterprise. (2005) 'Population Innovation Readiness'. Special Eurobarometer 236 (authors: TNS Opinion & Social). Luxembourg: European Commission. Online. Available HTTP: http://ec.europa.eu/public_opinion/archives/ebs/ebs_236_en.pdf (accessed 12 September 2011).

Durant, J., Bauer, M. W. and Gaskell, G. (eds.) (1998) *Biotechnology in the Public Sphere: A European Source Book*. London: Science Museum.

Einsiedel, E. F. (1998) 'The Market for Credible Information in Biotechnology'. *Journal of Consumer Policy* 21: 405–444.

Eiser, J. R. (2004) 'Public Perception of Risk'. Report. London: Foresight Office of Science and Technology. Online. Available HTTP: http://www.bis.gov.uk/assets/bispartners/foresight/docs/intelligent-infrastructure-systems/long-paper.pdf (accessed 12 September 2011).

EOS Gallup Europe. (2004) 'Entrepreneurship'. Flash Eurobarometer 160. Luxembourg: European Commission. Online. Available HTTP: http://ec.europa.eu/public_opinion/flash/fl160_en.pdf (accessed 12 September 2011).

Florida, R. and Kenney, M. (1988) 'Venture Capital-Financed Innovation and Technological Change in the USA'. *Research Policy* 17 (3): 119–137.

Freeman, C. (1987) *Technology Policy and Economic Performance*. London: Pinter.

Gaskell, G. (2004) 'Policy Making and Public Consultation'. PowerPoint presented at Genomics Symposium. Ottawa. 24 March. Online. Available HTTP: http://policyresearch.gc.ca/doclib/Gen_GeorgeGaskell_e.pdf (accessed 13 September 2011).

Gaskell, G., Allansdottir, A., Allum, N., Corchero, C., Fischler, C., Hampel, J., Jackson, J., Kronberger, N., Mejlgaard, N., Revuelta, G., Schreiner, C., Stares, S., Torgersen, H. and Wagner, W. (2006) 'Europeans and Biotechnology in 2005: Patterns and Trends'. Eurobarometer 64.3. A report to the European Commission's Directorate-General for Research. Online. Available HTTP: http://www.ec.europa.eu/research/press/2006/pdf/pr1906_eb_64_3_final_report-may2006_en.pdf (accessed 13 September 2011).

Gaskell, G., Einsidel, E., Hallman, W., Hornig Priest, S., Jackson, J. and Olsthoorn, J. (2005) 'Social Values and the Governance of Science'. *Science* 310: 1908–1909.

Halvorsen, T., Hauknes, J., Miles, I. and Røste, R. (2005) 'On the Differences between Public and Private Sector Innovation'. PUBLIN Report Project No. D9, Innovation in the Public Sector. Oslo: NIFU STEP.

Harvey, M., Quilley, S. and Beynon, H. (2002) *Exploring the Tomato: Transformations of Nature, Society and Economy*. Cheltenham, U.K., and Northampton, Mass.: Edward Elgar Publishing.

Hofstede, G. H. (1980) *Cultural Consequences: International Differences in Work-Related Values*. London: Sage Publications.

Inglehart, R. (1990) *Culture Shift in Advanced Industrial Society*. Princeton: Princeton University Press.

Inglehart, R. (1997) *Modernization and Postmodernization*. Princeton: Princeton University Press.

Inglehart, R., Welzel, C. (2005) *Modernization, Cultural Change and Democracy*. New York: Cambridge University Press.

Jasanoff, S. (1995) 'Product, Process or Programme: Three Cultures and the Regulation of Biotechnology'. In Bauer, M. (ed.), *Resistance to New Technology*. Cambridge: Cambridge University Press, p311–331

Jasanoff, S. (2005) *Designs on Nature: Biotechnology Regulation in America and Europe*. Princeton: Princeton University Press.

Kanagy, C. L., Humphrey, C. R. and Firebaugh, G. (1994) 'Surging Environmentalism: Changing Public Opinion or Changing Publics'. *Social Science Quarterly* 75: 804–19.

King, N. (1990) 'Innovation at Work: The Research Literature'. In West, M. A. and Farr, J. L. (eds.), *Innovation and Creativity at Work; Psychological and Organisational Strategies*, Chichester: Wiley, p15–59.

Kohli, A. K. and Jaworski, B. J. (1990) 'Market Orientation: The Construct, Research Propositions and Managerial Implications'. *Journal of Marketing* 52 (2): 1–18.

Kroeber, A. and Kluckhohn, C. (1952) 'Culture: A Critical Review of Concepts and Definitions'. Harvard University Peabody Museum of American Archaeology and Ethnology Papers, 47.

Lash, S., Szerszynski, B. and Wynne, B. (eds.) (1996) *Risk, Environment and Modernity: Towards a New Ecology*. London: Sage Publications.

Lock, E. A. and Kirkpatrick, S. A. (1995) 'Promoting Creativity in Organizations'. In Ford, C. M. and Gioia, D. A. (eds.), *Creative Action in Organizations: Ivory Tower Visions and Real World Voices*. London: Sage, p115–120.

Lundvall, A. E. (ed.) (1992) *National Innovation Systems: Towards a Theory of Innovation and Interactive Learning*. London: Pinter.

MacDonald, R. and Coffield, F. (1991) *Risky Business? Youth and the Enterprise Culture*. Basingstoke: Falmer Press.

Maskus, K. and McDaniel, E. C. (1999) 'Impacts of the Japanese Patent System on Productivity Growth'. *Japan and the World Economy* 11 (4): 557–574.

Miles, I. (1975) *The Poverty of Prediction*. Farnborough: Saxon House/Lexington Books.

Miron, E., Erez, M. and Naveh, E. (2004) 'Do Personal Characteristics and Cultural Values That Promote Innovation, Quality, and Efficiency Compete or Complement Each Other?' *Journal of Organizational Behaviour* 25: 175–199.

Nelson, R. (1993) *National Innovation Systems*. New York: Oxford University Press.

Norris, P. and Ingelhart, R. (2004) *Sacred and Secular: Politics and Religion Worldwide*. New York: Cambridge University Press.

Parker, R. and Bradley, L. (2000) 'Organizational Culture in the Public Sector: Evidence from Six Organizations'. *The International Journal of Public Sector Management* 13 (2): 125–141.

Potts, J. (2009) 'The Innovation Deficit in Public Services: The Curious Problem of Too Much Efficiency and Not Enough Waste and Failure'. *Innovation: Management, Policy and Practice* 11 (1): 34–43.

Powers, M. (1997) *The Audit Society: Rituals of Verification*. Oxford University Press, Oxford

Rose, G. M. and Shoham, A. (2002) 'Export Performance and Market Orientation: Establishing an Empirical Link'. *Journal of Business Research* 55 (3): 217–225.

Rusanen, T. (2002) 'Challenging the Risk Society: The Case of Finland'. *Science Communication* 24: 198.

Samaha, H. E. (1996) 'Overcoming the TQM Barrier to Innovation'. *HR Magazine* 6: 145–149.

Saxenian, A. (2006) *The New Argonauts: Regional Advantage in the Global Economy*. Cambridge, MA, Harvard University Press.

Schein, E. H. (2010) *Organizational Culture and Leadership*. 4th ed. San Francisco, CA: Jossey-Bass.

Scott, S. G. and Bruce, R. A. (1994) 'Determinates of Innovative Behaviour: A Path Model of Individual Innovation in the Workplace'. *Academy of Management Journal* 37 (3): 580–607.

Senge, P. M. (1990) *The Fifth Discipline: The Art and Practice of the Learning Organization*. London: Random House.

Shoham, A., Ruvio, A., Vigoda, E. and Schwabsky, N. (2003) 'Organizational Innovativeness in the Public Sector: Towards a Nomological Network'. Paper presented at the EGPA meeting. Oeiras, Portugal. 4–6 September. Part of the PUBLIN project EC 5FP.

Tylecote, A. (2007) 'The Role of Finance and Corporate Governance in National Systems of Innovation'. *Organizational Studies* 28 (10): 1461–1481.

van der Meer, H. (2007) 'Open Innovation—The Dutch Treat: Challenges in Thinking in Business Models'. *Creativity and Innovation Management* 16 (2): 192–202.

Walsh, V. (1988) 'Technology and the Competition of Small Countries: A Review'. In Freeman, C. and Lundvall, B-A. (eds.), *Small Countries Facing the Technological Revolution*. London: Pinter, p37–66.

Zaltman, G., Duncan, R. and Holbek, J. (1973) *Innovations and Organizations*. New York: John Wiley and Sons.

12 Innovation Policy and Design
Design as a Tool for Innovation

*Lawrence Green, Deborah Cox
and Pierre Bitard*

INTRODUCTION

While the fundamental role of design in innovation and new product development is now firmly acknowledged within the practitioner, policy and academic communities, the situation has not always been thus. Prior to the pioneering work in the late 1980s of Bruce, Roy and Walsh in the UK, and Clark and Chew in the US, design had been associated only weakly with innovation. Perceived essentially as a discretionary input, design was connected primarily with peripheral issues of styling, aesthetics, ergonomics or packaging. Drawing attention to the range and importance of the inputs of designers to the innovation process, Bruce, Clark et al. laid the foundations for a program of research that has recently exposed more fully the ambit, extent and value of design activities. The impact of investment in design on the bottom line for innovating companies is now much more apparent, as is the role of design in understanding and planning for future markets. So too, the deployment of design methods in the solution of technological, commercial and social problems is widely recognized, alongside the role of designers in mapping and visualizing future trends, consumption patterns and drivers. Of perhaps greatest significance, the application of design methodologies in the development of organizational strategy has gained acceptance, with some leading global companies weaving 'design thinking' (Brown, 2008) and a 'design attitude' into both strategic decision-making and new product development processes.

Over the past three decades there has been increased attention to design issues and activities in the domain of policy, alongside increased recognition of the value and role of design across a range of commercial functions and activities. As product and industrial design has been identified as an input with high value-adding potential and as a key contributor to strategic planning and futures-oriented work at firm level, supports for the development of design capability and the wider use of designer inputs across a range of commercial activities have been instituted in both developed and developing economies. Such supports have taken the form of educational initiatives, promotional programs, the rollout of incentives to suppliers and

users of design services, and initiation of projects designed to trigger partnership between designers and potential customers. Many such programs
have been delivered primarily via state agencies, but many too have been
operationalized in the form of partnerships involving, variously, public
agencies, private companies, trade and professional associations and promotional bodies in the design sector.

It is perhaps possible to identify a symbiotic relationship between the
evolution of policy supports and the development of the design industry.
Policy initiatives have demonstrated some success in broadening the use of
design services and in developing the reputation of design as a core input
to business development processes. In turn, design has become established
as a major component in product development and its utility has raised its
profile. Design has also been perceived increasingly as a potentially valuable input in a broader set of processes in industrial, commercial and public
sector settings including strategic development, market analysis, planning
and trend mapping. Acknowledging this trajectory, revised policies and
supports have been required in order to ensure that the full potential value
of design activities might be recognized and realized across the range of
commercial activities. Indeed, one of the key challenges for policy has been
to obviate the view of design as a mere commodity input and to substitute
this with an understanding that design can play a fundamental role in strategic business development, the establishment of new markets, and support
for social and community development goals.

This chapter will begin by unpacking the range of activities that are
involved in design, and by examining the role of professional designers. Here
we will also explore the relationship between design and innovation as this
has been theorized in the existing literature. The chapter will then move on to
examine the importance of design within contemporary economies. We will
consider the historical development of product design in the international
context and the emergence of professional design organizations and support
agencies at national level. The chapter will outline the emergence of policy supports for design and consider the international spectrum of support
models and their associated objectives and outcomes. In later sections, we
will examine the very significant and relatively recent evolution of the design
industry, and the expansion in the ways in which design services are deployed
within client industries. Here we will survey trends in design support initiatives and address some of the challenges that confront the policy community
with respect to the promotion of design activities. In essence then, the chapter will examine the role of design in innovation and explore the evolution of
the design industry and related design support policies. It will also take a forward look, plotting contemporary developments in the application of design,
in sites for application and in setting out future challenges and options for
support policies where governments and industry bodies are eager to exploit
design as a major contributor to both national and sectoral competitiveness
and social and community development.

DESIGN AND DESIGNERS IN THE INNOVATION
AND PRODUCT DEVELOPMENT PROCESS[1]

What is design? It is important to begin by examining the concept of design, and to set out the roles and tasks that are undertaken by designers. Design can have a multitude of meanings in different settings, and considerable effort has been applied (and controversy sparked) in the search for universal descriptors and definitions (Ulrich, 2011). To complicate the picture, there are many different varieties of design, from furniture, fashion and graphics, through to product, industrial and service and many locations in which design activities can take place. For the purposes of this chapter, we focus in the main on product and industrial design. This is the form that is most routinely associated with innovation and the form that has attracted, or demanded, the attention of policymakers in recent decades.

While it is neither possible nor desirable to review the spectrum of definitions that circulate around product design, it is worth noting some of the more influential and informative variants. One popular configuration is that from Ulrich (2011, p.394), who writes of the design process as one that is built around *'conceiving and giving form to goods and services that address needs'*. Similarly, Krippendorff and Butter (1984, p.4) define design as the *'conscious creation of forms to service human needs'*. Adding a strategic component, and hinting at the potential role of design in market positioning and development, Kotler and Rath (1984) argue that design permits producer organizations to match customer requirements to product performance, fitness for purpose, quality, durability and price. In a similar vein, but leaning towards the articulation of design with innovation, OECD acknowledges that design involves both the creation of concept and the process of translating concepts into physical products—that is, the marriage of design and development. For OECD (1982) (cited in Walsh et. al.,1992: 18), design is perceived to lie at the heart of the creation of any physical product, *'[it] is the very core of innovation, the moment when a new object is managed, devised and shaped in prototype form'*. For observers from within the design community, design is sometimes perceived as a cognitive activity rather than a function or professional status. Here, for example, Visser (2009) alludes to the problem-solving nature of design activities and the requirement placed upon the designer to develop particular and context-specific solutions to sometimes weakly defined problems. In his approach, Visser draws upon the ideas of Simon, perhaps the preeminent figure in 20th-century design scholarship. According to Simon (1981, p.129), *'Everyone designs who devises courses of action aimed at changing existing situations into preferred ones'*. We can see then that definitions range from the general to the specialized and from the practical to the philosophical. Further, it is perhaps useful to perceive of the term design as an elastic one that can be used to reference activities, actors, functions and even aspirations and frames of mind. Perhaps underlying all approaches, however, is the notion that design involves the targeted application of creativity with the deliberate intention of bringing about positive change or novelty.

The role(s) and activities of designers. In the effort to unpack and specify both the higher order and day-to-day contributions of the design community, in its many guises and locations, a simple description may be apposite. In basic and perhaps traditional terms, it can be suggested that designers are responsible for undertaking research and applying specialized creative skills to generate products that are functional, useable, reliable, safe, technologically efficient, ergonomic, stylish and suited to the cultural preferences of target users. In essence according to Miles and Green (2008, p. 28) designers create the '*artefacts, tangible goods, devices, equipment and gadgets etc., that we use in our daily lives as consumers and workers*'. While this is a useful working description, it is one that is arguably diminishing in its adequacy. As the range of activities and sphere of influence of designers have grown, the role for some at least has implied greater involvement in the strategic components of clients' activities and enhanced engagement with the market and competitive positioning of partner firms. In this shift, we see progression from the traditional persona of technical designer to that of design-driven product and brand consultant (Green and Bolton, 2008).

CONNECTING DESIGN AND INNOVATION

Why is design important to the study of innovation? Until relatively recently the issue of design has not received great attention from the innovation research community. Apart from the early work of the Design Innovation Group (DIG), a 1980s collaborative venture involving UMIST and the Open University in the UK, design as a topic remained largely the preserve of product development managers and engineers. The work undertaken by DIG and the evolution of its research themes illustrate increased understanding of design and its long-time status as a major but inadequately understood component of the innovation process (Green, Miles and Rutter, 2007). The need for a better understanding of the role of design in innovation is set out by Le Masson et al. (2006). The core assumption of these authors is that understanding design is a crucial step towards a better understanding of innovation itself. For Le Masson a contemporary emphasis on R&D investments and improved metrics for innovation misses an important point. While economic aggregates have a role and measurement of the inputs and outputs with respect to innovation is an important activity for governments and firms, understanding innovation involves the creation of a detailed description of the activities and capabilities of the actors involved and the identification of the specific and situated features of the creative design act. It is through detailed analysis of the work of designers in interaction with clients, suppliers, artists, specialist engineers, scientists and technologists, and collaborating partners that we can start to understand better the total process of innovation. Le Masson conceives of design (for innovation) as a collective process that develops gradually. At the outset neither the whole set of ideas nor the whole set of actors can be known. Design is a complex and uncertain learning process that requires mapping and framing as it evolves. It is also an activity wherein uncertainty and risk are inevitable and the key challenges for designers frequently pertain to the solution of ill-structured, complex and emergent problems. Progression towards better understanding and management of the design process entails identifying and analyzing the specifics of the organization of the activities that lie behind innovation—activities that are often labeled design 'models' or 'modes'. An improved understanding also requires a greater acknowledgment and investigation of the role of users, customers, supply-chain partners and knowledge intermediaries in the design and innovation process. It is ever more apparent that in an array of industries, producer-centered innovation is being eclipsed by more networked and user-centered forms (von Hippel, 2007).

Taking a less philosophical, and more pragmatic and commercially focused line, the UK 'Cox Review' (Cox, 2005) sets out to anoint design as the pivotal factor in the innovation process. According to Cox (p.2), '[design] *links creativity and innovation. It shapes ideas to become practical and attractive propositions for users or customers. Design may be described as creativity deployed to a specific end*'. Here we see the emergence of an increasingly popular perspective, and the affordance of an elevated role to the design profession. For Cox, wherever we see successful innovation, we find evidence of the skills of the designer in creative and intelligence-driven manipulation of both tangible and intangible product features. Without design and designers, innovation becomes impossible and invention will rot on the vine. Though a somewhat dramatic representation (a core aim of the Cox report was to stimulate greater government support), the central thesis of the study carries significant credibility. If nations are to prosper via the exploitation of ideas, the flowering of variety and differentiation, and the perpetual creation and diffusion of innovative products and processes, then the role of design in making possible such prosperity cannot be ignored.

Design and the economy. Product design lies at the heart of the creative industries, a sector that includes broadcasting, advertising, the performing arts, architecture, software and publishing. In Europe as a whole, the creative industries generate around 3 percent of total annual GDP, approximately €500 billion, and employ almost six million workers. According to the Department for Culture, Media and Sport (DCMS) (2008), some two million people are employed in creative jobs in the UK, and the sector contributes more than £60 billion per annum to the British economy. Over the past decade in the UK, the creative sector has grown at twice the rate of the economy in general, and continued growth is predicted as demand for creative content increases. In other countries too, the creative industries, and design in particular, are being recognized as highly significant economic players. Further, these industries are acknowledged as ones with high growth and high value-adding potential.

Addressing the design industry specifically, we can see that the sector is highly significant in terms of both employment and revenue, although definitions are contested and data is not always comparable or available. The UK is home to more than 4,000 design firms, a quarter of which are situated in the product and industrial design sector. UK Design as a whole has an annual gross income of approximately €5 billion, a figure that includes €600 million from overseas earnings (Design Council, 2005). Italy employs almost 1.5 million people in its design industry, which is dominated by fashion and garments, and the sector contributes more than €4 billion in annual GVA. The Netherlands has more than 4,000 independent industrial designers working across 2,000 firms, and an annual turnover of more than €670 million. In Germany, more than 130,000 workers are employed across 40,000 design agencies in an independent design sector that boasts an annual turnover of more than €16 billion. Notably, many more design workers are to be found in the in-house design teams of Germany's world-leading manufacturing firms.

Design is clearly big business, and the important and growing contribution of design to the economies of Europe and beyond renders it a topic of significant interest to policymakers. Not surprisingly, there is increasing eagerness to better understand the articulation of design within the economy as a whole and this has resulted in the launch of major research and promotional initiatives. The European Design Innovation Initiative, announced in 2011, is one such program that aims to strengthen connections between design, innovation and competitiveness, and ensure optimal exploitation of the potential of design. Implicit in this initiative is the recognition that, beyond the headline contribution of design to national economies, it is crucial to acknowledge and build the role of design in supporting innovation in adjacent sectors of the economy, including services, public services, manufacturing firms, infrastructure and utilities. Without design inputs, provided either in-house or as contracted services, all organizations are likely to find their growth aspirations either severely circumscribed or curtailed entirely.

Design and the firm. Various levels of intensity and variety in the use of design can be identified (Hertenstein, Platt and Veryzer, 2005), and recent studies have demonstrated that firm size is an important factor in the attitude of its management to design. In a major UK study, the Design Council (2007) discovered that recognition of the contribution of design to a company grows with increasing size of business: 44 percent of small businesses, 56 percent of medium-sized and 77 percent of large businesses were reported to perceive design as a contributory factor in competitiveness in the previous decade. The larger the company, the greater the likelihood that it would use or buy design services and the greater its degree of design maturity, accumulated experience and precedent with respect to the use of design services. There is sound reasoning among those firms that consider design to have contributed to the fortunes of their business. The UK Design Council's research also established a link between design and improved business performance. In this work, analysts isolated design from other business factors, and built statistical models to identify relationships between design and businesses' performance. They measured a number of indicators that characterize business growth, turnover, profit and employment growth and then assessed the effect that businesses perceived design to have had on growth. Businesses that had increased their investment in design over the previous three years were found to have increased their chances of turnover growth and businesses that perceived design as integral to their activities were more than twice as likely as others to see rapid growth. The authors concluded that design can have a positive effect on all business performance indicators, from turnover and profit to market share and competitiveness.

Design and innovation—the need for policy and improved measures. Given the central role of design in driving and supporting innovation and the importance of the latter in national and firm-level competitiveness, it is not surprising that governments have awoken recently to the need to promote improvements in both the design infrastructure and environment. New initiatives have emerged at national and supra-national level, some with the aim of growing the market for design services, some targeted at increasing the profile of the design industry, yet more created to explore new roles for design agencies in addressing social, sustainability and community development themes. Underpinning promotion and growth support programs, efforts have been directed towards improvement of the measurement of design activities and means of more accurately representing the contribution of the design sector to the performance of client industries and to economic development as a whole. Certainly measurement and the development of data collection and statistical tools are a thorny issue. National innovation policy agencies have struggled to define design and have tended to use imprecise terminology and widely varying descriptors that have hampered standardization, and thus the production of broadly comparable international data. It is clear that better measurement is crucial. Without a clear, operational definition of design activity, one that translates into an effective official measurement and reporting system, policies in support of design will remain fundamentally flawed. It is arguable that even the harmonized European Community Innovation Survey questionnaire fails to adequately acknowledge the place of design in innovation and R&D activities. Indeed, perhaps only the UK has so far progressed towards the establishment of a data collection system, within the British Community Innovation Survey, that adequately addresses design as a specific and core function within the innovation milieu. Clearly, the need for improved and standardized benchmarks and measures and efforts to evaluate the contribution of design to a broader set of industrial and service innovation activities remains an important challenge for contemporary innovation policymakers.

THE EVOLUTION OF DESIGN INSTITUTIONS AND THE INSTITUTION OF DESIGN POLICY

The ascendance and global growth of the design industry. The professional organizations formed around the arts and crafts industries around the turn of the 20th century—for example, the Swedish Society for Industrial Design—were the first to raise the issue of design as an economic asset. At this time, the main objective of such associations was to provide a legal framework for protection of the interests and intellectual property assets of designers and design firms. By the middle of the 20th century, industrial design had started to flourish with postwar reconstruction, increasing affluence, the spread of mass production and consumption systems in the US and Europe; the opportunities for product designers had grown rapidly. In the 1960s and 1970s, factors such as increasing spending power, the growing shoots of Post-Fordist consumption and greater sophistication in marketing techniques ensured that design might become embedded as a core component in product development and differentiation activities. Now, design was no longer limited to the industrial context and designers benefitted progressively from increasing consumer interest in styling, detailing, feature bundling, ergonomics, aesthetics and differentiation, factors that could be manipulated by producers in the fulfillment and generation of consumer preferences and the creation of brands. Design itself became a focus for celebration and national pride, and some individual product designers started to achieve celebrity status. The late 1960s saw the opening of public spaces and galleries dedicated to design, and the launch of promotional campaigns and educational initiatives targeted at raising its profile. Reinvigoration and renewal of design associations followed, with, for example, the creation of the Norwegian Design Council, and the re-naming of the British Council of Industrial Design to the current 'Design Council'. At the same time design was recognized as an essential skill and lever for competitive advantage in the East—here, South Korea and Japan entered the industrial design scene rapidly, with neighboring Asian countries such as Taiwan, Singapore, Thailand and Hong Kong following in their wake.

The evolution of the design industry was paralleled by the development of design and innovation policies across the globe. However, significant lags and divergence in developmental pathways are evident. Indeed, it was not until the 1990s that the emergence of the first comprehensive, integrated and dedicated innovation-design policies were seen (in South Korea and Denmark in 1993 and 1997 respectively). By the early years of the

21st century, most European countries had embarked on the path of developing new design-innovation policies. In the main these policies consider design primarily as an economic asset, from which competitiveness can be derived. However, in some, there is explicit acknowledgment that the value of design resides in its ability to improve quality of life. Here we see design connected not just with economic development aims, but also with progression towards sustainability, improved resource use, and human and community development goals.

Policy initiatives in support of design. The development of design-oriented polices has its roots in Europe and diffusion can be traced from here to the US and the rest of the world. Although few countries have developed fully integrated and dedicated design policies, an increasing number have considered the issue and are developing support and promotion programs. The main players in the field are located in Europe (including Eastern Europe), North America, South East Asia and Australasia. Countries in these regions have identified design as a tool to leverage economic progress through innovation leadership, though many different flavors are evident and individual countries tend to adopt a specific focus and orientation for their support programs. For example, design has been identified variously as a tool to improve quality of life, a means of providing uplift in health outcomes and experiences and a route to improved sustainability, energy efficiency and urban renewal.

DESIGN SUPPORT MODELS

While there is evidence of variety at national level, design support models tend to exhibit a number of common features in terms of their operation, content and objectives. Designium's Global Design Watch report (2010) contains a listing of national design policy initiatives in a selection of twenty-two countries.[2] In countries where dedicated design policies have been implemented, initiatives or programs tend to be rolled out at a national or regional level, depending on the institutional arrangements of the host. Programs are generally characterized by a set of strategic plans, well-defined objectives and a means of achieving the latter within a set time frame. Countries that have implemented dedicated policies are to be found in Europe, South East Asia, Australasia and North America. Within the category of 'design policy' countries, a distinction can be made between those in which the entire process is conceptualized, orchestrated and managed by public sector actors and those in which a public-private partnership is created to lead the policy initiative. Many Asian countries appear to follow an 'all public' model in which government initiates, finances and controls the scheme, perhaps reflecting the centralized administration mode that is common in the region. In most other countries, private actors are incorporated at some stage in the process of conception or delivery. Here, notionally state-operated initiatives are co-conceived with private design sector actors and others, including regional development agencies, sustained by mixed funding, and operationalized via a consortium of industry, third sector and public stakeholders.

While examples of dedicated design policies have been somewhat scarce, there is evidence that the incidence and magnitude of new initiatives are increasing. This perhaps reflects the enhanced importance afforded to the design sector and its impact on economic performance. At one extreme, we see the policy-inspired establishment of supra-national programs such as the European Design Innovation Initiative and the European Creative Industries Alliance. At the other we see the rollout of a plethora of regionally administered, highly targeted, issue-driven projects that are configured to address very specifically the concerns and challenges confronted by design industry players. In the case of such actions, public or mixed funding is commonly used for implementation and the intended target is design sector firms and their actual or potential clients. Often the aim is to promote or demonstrate the value-adding benefits of design, or to stimulate regional business development and growth via the sponsorship of design-business collaborations. Many examples of these forms of projects can be found, for example, in the UK, Germany and Italy.

Although design policy actions in some countries are still founded on the notion of product design as a contributor to aesthetics, ergonomics or marketability, or to competitiveness at best, most countries have now adopted a broader and more nuanced view of the value of design. While competitiveness remains as a central interest, the role of design in building social equity and in contributing to quality of life and social and community development goals is also recognized. Indeed, it is increasingly clear that in some regions (Scandinavia in particular), competitiveness and social development goals are perceived to be strongly linked and the use of design to support cross-fertilization is strongly encouraged.

In general, public and government agencies have focused specifically on either competitiveness or life improvement objectives. Approaches tend to reflect a combination of the cultural background of the country or region, features of the local economy, political priorities and available budgets, and the actions that are undertaken are frequently an expression of political and cultural preferences and economic needs and constraints. While the content of public actions in support of design can be highly varied, past and current programs have included features such as the delivery of general information on design, provision of technical support to concerned actors, initiation of financial incentives, creation of frameworks for discussion and future actions, promotion of a 'design culture' among the populace, supports for design education and training, and provision of a platform for regional or local design at a national or international level. An elaboration of some of these measures follows.

Policy measures for improved competitiveness. A linkage between the use of design and increased competitiveness has been acknowledged in many studies. According to research from the New Zealand Institute of Economic Research (NZIER), there is a clear linear relationship between the overall competitiveness of a country and its effective use of design (Designium World Design Series, 2003). Given that most major developed countries have acquired comparable technical capacities, the comparative advantage of regions is perceived to derive in large measure from their stock of value-adding expertise and capabilities. Here, design skills are perceived as a key asset, and one that can deliver enhanced innovation and competitiveness. Anticipating the needs of end users and creating products that are differentiated and more adapted to preferences are increasingly crucial in crowded and intensely competitive markets.

Supportive actions are often directed towards areas of national or regional comparative advantage. This draws attention to the specific role and use of design and the content of design policies in particular locations. Given the labor market characteristics of their home markets, Western European and North American companies tend to experience difficulty in competing on price and are pressured to build competitive advantage on the basis of product quality and non-price factors or intangibles. Support policy for design in these territories is frequently targeted at brand-building, collaborative innovation, client-management, and smart generation and application of intellectual property. Asian economies still have a comparative (labor) cost advantage that favors export strategies. This hints strongly at the reasons for a focus in many Asian countries on support for product design as an input to original equipment manufacturing (OEM) operations and the manufacture of fast-moving consumer goods.

Policy measures for improved quality of life. There are numerous examples of policy actions that have been employed to try to deploy design as a means of tackling social and human challenges. For example, designers have been involved in 'ageing society' projects, those designed to increase participation in democratic processes and those targeted at 'designing-out' crime from urban spaces. The types of actions selected in relation to particular problems depend on context and invariably reflect regional cultures and social and political priorities.

While many actions have been launched in response to recognized and long-standing issues, others have targeted more recent and emerging challenges. Indeed, the deployment of design as a means of addressing contemporary concerns has led to the creation of new subbranches and concept sets within the design sector. For example, *eco-design* has evolved as an approach—and methodology—that seeks to limit potential environmental degradation by building into the product design process consideration of the environmental impacts of a new good or service at every stage in its life cycle. Similarly, *universal design* and *design for all* are citizen- and user-centered approaches that require that accessibility and usability issues for all potential users of a new good or service are taken into account at each step in the product development and rollout process. Universal design approaches are predicated on the notion that it is possible to 'design-in' inclusivity features as new products and spaces are brought into being.

Several countries are now moving towards the development of design policies that feature a focus on both competitiveness and quality of life themes. While economic development retains central importance, there is recognition that growth must not be achieved at the cost of social and environmental standards. Some recent policy actions embody these twin concerns and target sustainable and environmentally responsible development. A good example of one such action is the initiation of the Ecodesign Centre in Wales, which was established in 2006 as a part of the Welsh Assembly's commitment to sustainable development. The aim was to build capacity and capabilities in industry, public sector organizations and higher education institutions with a view to facilitating effective eco-design in Wales.

National models, national flavors. Strategies and policies for design are invariably closely aligned with national economic and industrial profiles, and with fundamental aims and priorities. In Germany, regional design councils have been responsible for the development of engineering-oriented design policies that accord with a national focus on high-quality, engineering-based manufacturing. Support actions are designed to address directly the needs of engineering companies, which are, essentially, improved performance and competitiveness and are developed in partnership with a range of business stakeholders. The actions are also constructed around the aim of securing medium- and longer-term national competitiveness via provision of support to core German industrial sectors.

Implementation of design policy in the US also reflects national conventions and arrangements. The support model is one in which policy is translated into actions by private sector organizations. The latter provide technical assistance and networking services to design agencies, delivering business support functions, raising profiles, promoting the value of design, and facilitating the development of partnerships between design companies and clients. Support for the use of design as a strategic tool in corporate development is an important feature, as is promotion of the role of design in styling, brand reinforcement and progression of social projects (Designium, 2010). In Italy, too, traditional governance arrangements are reflected in design policy implementation—support is organized at the local level and targeted at specific, priority economic sectors such as automobiles, architecture and fine art. As might be expected, policy is focused on building an Italian brand in which 'style' is an important component.

DESIGN SUPPORTS: FORMS AND FEATURES

Pursuit of competitiveness and 'quality of life' goals, in whatever mix, via the application of design can involve the implementation of one or many from a broad spectrum of instruments. As noted earlier, the creation of initiatives and selection of approaches will depend on contexts, priorities, aims and resources at national or local level. While it is not possible to survey here the full range of support instruments that have been, or might in future be, applied in promoting the design, it is useful to outline some key categories.

Awareness. Given that design is to many an abstract concept, awareness raising, information dissemination, and promotion are common first steps in encouraging a perception of design as a key and actionable economic and social asset. Most countries that have aimed to increase the utilization of design services in business and elsewhere have considered awareness-raising to constitute a priority action. The targets for promotional activity can vary, but frequently involve a mix of business, education, research and public service actors, and the general public.

Design centers. The establishment of national and regional design centers has been an important means of generating familiarity among the general public with various approaches to and features of design. Such centers permit visitors to experience and build an understanding of design at first hand. They also ensure that design is accessible, and in so doing promulgate an appreciation of design that might sow the seeds of a widespread national 'design culture'. Some design centers—for example, those in Denmark—also aim to establish themselves as 'knowledge centers' and have initiated repositories for design literature, databases and artifacts in effect, evolving a design reference and cataloguing function.

Events. In addition to 'making design public', design events possess a strong promotional component. Policy-driven actions have included the organization of exhibitions and fairs intended to promote a country's or region's design brand on the local or international stage. Some cross-national events have also been launched. In 'Design Year 2005', Norway, Sweden, Finland and Denmark came together to organize a range of platform events created to promote Scandinavian design excellence. Other promotional events have included seminars, conferences and shows aimed at encouraging networking within and across specific design and design-user communities. Competitions and awards are also common, especially in Europe. The aim here is to identify and celebrate both younger and more well-established designers, and, in so doing, raise the profile of the design industry as a whole, cementing its reputation as a contributor to commercial success.

Education. Actions in the realm of education are frequently built from the notion that school students should be introduced to the principles of design and further encouraged to recognize both the breadth of its application and potential value. Some initiatives have focused on encouraging school students to consider the application of design as a tool for tackling both societal and commercial challenges. Singapore's 'Many Ways of Seeing' project, which is essentially a design appreciation scheme, encouraged participants to absorb design principles and to scale these and transfer them to all areas of their educational and social development. The aim was to inculcate a 'design attitude' that would equip students to tackle challenges in a structured but creative and multi-perspectival manner.

Higher education and training. Actions in higher education have focused largely on equipping design graduates for successful progression into professional practice. In many design-intensive countries, it is common to see high levels of interaction between design schools and design agencies. There has also been policy-led encouragement for the establishment of fully fledged 'in-house' design agencies within universities and colleges, to provide students with first-hand experience of design practice and client interaction and to provide revenue-generation opportunities for university departments (Miles and Green, 2008).[3] Some recent policy-inspired initiatives have seen the establishment of dedicated 'innovation universities', designed to foster collaborations between economists, artists, designers and technologists, such as the Aalto University, established in Helsinki in 2010. The university's mission is to underpin Finnish export success via the delivery of transdisciplinary teaching and research in the fields of computation, materials, ICTs and media.

Linked to the establishment of innovation universities is the rollout of strategic design centers. Such centers are focused on encouraging the emergence of a research community in design, and activities involve international exchange, networking and the development of joint actions between academic and business actors. An important aim in strategic design is the transfer of knowledge and methodologies from the domain of design to that of business (and vice versa) (Bolton and Green, 2008).

Brokering services. One of the more commonly observed forms of design support is the delivery of brokering services that pair design providers with potential users. SMEs are most frequently the target in such programs. The risk aversion of many such companies implies that they are less likely to experiment with the use of design inputs than their larger counterparts (in almost all industrial sectors). To counter this tendency, support projects are configured to inform potential design-user companies with respect to the strategic value of design, assist them in the first steps towards engagement and encourage continuing interaction.

Design grants. Grants constitute a form of public intervention that target both students or researchers and commercial enterprises. Within grant schemes, the researchers are offered scholarships and research bursaries with the aim of encouraging development of the knowledge base with respect to design issues. On the other side of the coin, companies receive grants to support the integration of design into strategic activities and product development. Business design grants are designed specifically to fund either initial investments in design or original design projects.

Tax credits. It is not easy to generate a picture of all of the tax credits that are linked with design across different fiscal systems and national frameworks. Too often, the picture is obscured by a complex of R&D credits and those relating to design specifically are hidden or bundled in with more general allowances. However, it is clear that some countries have offered incentives to investment in design by distinguishing design tax credits from those associated with more general research and development activities. Further, some countries with highly evolved credit systems—for example, Canada—are moving to distinguish between different forms of design for the purposes of creating fiscal incentives.

Voucher schemes. Piloted in the UK, with considerable success, design voucher schemes represent an extension of brokering programs that are well established across Europe and the US. Voucher programs frequently involve competitive bidding and often matched funding arrangements. SMEs are invited to set out a case for support with a project that involves a significant design component. If the bid is successful, the firm will be awarded a voucher that it can then redeem to purchase design services from a design agency of its choice.

Effectiveness of design support—the evidence? While there is clear evidence of the rollout of a broad range of policy actions and initiatives relating to design, evidence of their success, or otherwise, is much more difficult to find. While program evaluation has been built into some national schemes, only limited evidence has appeared in the public domain. Where major and rigorous reviews of policy and outcomes have been conducted, notably in Korea, Sweden, Finland, the UK and the US, the results have been promising. Awareness-raising, tax incentives, voucher schemes and educational initiatives have all demonstrated some success when judged against original objectives, and design grants and provision of design-focused business services, such as brokering, have been popular with both design companies and their clients (NESTA, 2011). Commercial examinations too have given rise to optimism. Where policy actions have resulted in increased uptake of design services and, more specifically, strategic deployment of design across business functions, the impacts on profitability can be dramatic (Boston Consulting, 2006). Despite these encouraging signs, there is little doubt that much more rigorous research is required with respect to the effectiveness of design policy and related actions. Moreover, standardization in the classification and characterization of promotional initiatives represents a crucial precursor to any efforts to establish international comparisons.

NEW DIRECTIONS IN DESIGN, NEW DIRECTIONS IN POLICY

As suggested throughout this chapter, the role of design in business and the position of designers in the innovation and market development process have shifted significantly in the past decade (Borja de Mozota, 2003). While some designers have bemoaned the 'commoditization' of design and the pressures faced by design practices in globalizing and increasingly competitive markets, others have identified opportunities for repositioning and have expanded their practice to include brand consultancy, brand development, service design, trend analysis and end-to-end design-to-manufacture services (Miles and Green, 2008). Many leading and smaller but dynamic design agencies are working to offer a broad range of creative services linked to the business growth and market development needs of their clients. Given the insight-generation techniques and operational methodologies that are in use in the design sector and the expertise, knowledge and intelligence of consumer and market trends accrued by designers in the course of their work, it is not surprising that some from among the latter have carved for themselves an increasingly important strategic and developmental role within client organizations. It is not now unusual to find designers and design engineers involved in decision-making at board level in some of the world's most influential and progressive companies, although the value of design as a strategic tool is not recognized universally!

In this section we explore briefly some key movements in the design industry and some of the emergent trajectories in the business-design relationship. To conclude, we also discuss a number of emergent and prospective design-innovation policy responses.

Strategic design. The emergence of *strategic design* centers, noted earlier, represents an initiative that brings together ideas nurtured within the design world with a policy action targeted at delivering business growth. Within strategic design partnerships, higher education design research groups are working with commercial actors to co-create opportunities for knowledge generation and sharing, collaborative innovation, and hybrid skills building—that is, the creation of capabilities that combine elements of business management with creative problem-solving and risk-taking. Such centers are at present few,[4] though early successes are leading to replication and an enhanced reputation in the policy community, especially that in the European Union.

Design thinking. The concept of design thinking is associated primarily with the ideas of Tim Brown and his work with leading international brand and design consultancy IDEO. Brown (2008) describes design thinking as the ability to combine empathy, creativity and rationality to meet user needs and drive business succes'. In many respects, Brown's work represents a formalization of the processes and methodologies deployed by product designers in the prosecution of their craft and an effort to demonstrate the power of systematized creativity in delivering strategic renewal and commercial growth. In effect, design thinking offers a toolkit to business, one designed to aid managers in developing and capturing latent creativity and deploying this in both product development and organizational positioning processes. The concept of design thinking—in its least sophisticated configuration—is built around a seven-step process that includes: issue definition; research and stakeholder engagement; ideation and brainstorming; experimentation, prototyping and formalization of ideas; review and selection; realization and delivery; and evaluation, learning and improvement.

These seven steps are perceived to be those that underpin the design enterprise and for Brown represent a set of principles that can be applied with equal success across a range of functions from product development to organizational reconfiguration, strategic positioning and market development. Clearly, several of the world's major corporations agree—for example, General Electric, P&G and Phillips—and the influence of design thinking approaches is apparent in the strategizing and planning programs of many leading consumer and business-to-business brands (Business Week, 2009).

Design-driven innovation. The notion of 'design-driven innovation' (DDI), the core principles of which have been elaborated with greatest authority by Verganti (2009), is one that has received increased attention. The influence of DDI in the world of business is growing, and the adoption of the ideas and methods that underpin it is evident in some of the contemporary success stories reported by firms including Alessi, Artemide, WL Gore and Apple. As the title suggests, DDI is founded on the principle that design can be used to *lead* the innovation process, rather than constituting a mere component within it.

Essentially, DDI embarks from the premise that some of the most successful ideas for innovations are sparked by visionary designers with a capacity to recognize latent consumer needs, to anticipate and interpret evolution in cultural landscapes and to capture shifts in cognitive and symbolic frames. For Verganti, such designers are often 'outsiders', not bounded by organizational rationales or history, or tied to user research or consumer observation. As a result, they are able to generate breakthrough concepts based on visions of 'what could be' rather than on existing products or user feedback.[5] For the proponents of DDI, designers with an ability to envision and realize radical alternatives, or to create game-changing future products, provide a means for progressive firms to move beyond satisfying known need, into the generation of innovations that facilitate for consumers an opportunity to construct new experiences, attachments, applications and emotional responses. For companies that have applied DDI, the aim is to move away from a user-pull orientation towards a vision-driven 'push' approach, in which consumer experience and engagement are redefined.[6] In effect, rather than chasing user need, design-driven organizations aim to present entirely novel alternatives and deliver breakthrough and class-redefining products.

Service design. While the ideas behind service design have been in circulation in the academic community for more than thirty years (see, for example, Shostack, 1982 on the 'service blueprint'), it is only since 2000 that this branch of design has gained significant momentum. Even now, according to Pinhanez (2009), industrial design plays only a minor role in the planning and management of most service businesses and activities. With this caveat in mind, it is possible to identify a growing number of instances in which designers have been contracted to lead or assist the (re-)configuration of major service products in both the public and private sectors.

At its core, service design involves the planning and coordination of physical and intangible factors, including spaces, infrastructure, personnel, intelligence, plant and equipment, information and communication systems, in order to deliver enhanced service experience to the user, and optimal allocation of resources for the provider. Given the capabilities that characterize the design sector, it is clear that designers might beneficially occupy a central role in the creation of new services and the configuration of the services encounter. For Morelli (2006), industrial designers are able to transfer readily into the services domain common design methodologies and deploy these in a core set of service design activities that include 'actor identification', 'definition of service scenarios' and 'service mapping, sequencing and representation'. Many instances of such transfer are now evident in Europe and the US, and product design agencies have taken a prominent role in the redesign of hospital, school, welfare, transport and leisure services. For example, in the UK, designers have been involved in the re-configuration of the 'patient journey' in hospital settings, and in planning the 'consumer encounter' for various experience industry operators, including Disney, Virgin and Bluewater (Voss, Roth and Chase, 2008). In Denmark, design agencies have been contracted to work on service projects as diverse as youth road safety campaigns and the creation of internal communications systems for employment support agencies. The results from such projects have been highly promising, and although service design remains in relative infancy, its potential has been recognized and the prospects for further growth are strong, especially in those economies where public service reform is a priority and services in general are a major contributor to GVA.

DESIGN POLICY FUTURES—SOME CONCLUDING REMARKS

We discussed earlier the dialectical relationship between design trajectories and support policy. Sometimes and in some locations, designers have forged ahead. At other times and in other locations, policymakers have provided the impetus for development. Whatever the direction of 'push', reactions and responses in the opposite camp have usually resulted in mutual forward movement. The current phase of development is a rich one indeed. In design-intensive territories, the evolution of new approaches and movements (notably, those outlined earlier) has witnessed the ascension of designers into the boardrooms of many powerful corporations. In such territories, policy too has largely kept pace. There is a clear recognition among policymakers of the value of design (for innovation) at firm, national and societal level, and thus the need to support continued development and diffusion.

Despite some promising progress and the emergence of more enlightened attitudes, it is clear that (a) important challenges remain, and (b) more can be done to increase the utilization of design in business and beyond. Swann

(2010) provides a comprehensive review of current and emerging policy options and lists five core vectors in which future policy actions are likely to deliver benefits for designers and innovators in the public, third sector and private arenas. These include: strengthening the design profession via education, training and network-building; creation of national design assets;[7] increasing public expenditure on design, especially with respect to the provision of stronger IP regimes and enhanced tax credits; establishing standards for design; and enhancing the profile and visibility and thus business and public perceptions of the design industry. While Swann stops short of setting a detailed policy agenda, his work and that of design commentators more generally suggests that for design to realize its full potential as a tool for strategic innovation, attention is required with respect to three core policy challenges. These are firstly, ensuring greater alignment between the visions, goals and mindsets of business practitioners and their counterparts in the design world where education in business and design schools has a fundamental part to play; secondly, reinforcement of the role of design in tackling community, societal and sustainability issues, where there is an important need to improve the interface between designers and community, environmental and social business entrepreneurs and thirdly, development and application of robust tools and metrics, both quantitative and qualitative, that demonstrate the true value of design inputs across the spectrum of public and private sector activities.

It is evident that there remains much to be achieved, and that significant political will is required. However, it is also evident that with an appropriate mix of policies, initiatives and supports, the continued and mutually beneficial embedding of design in both commercial organizations and social institutions might reasonably be assured.

NOTES

1. The authors would like to express their gratitude to Professor Simon Bolton of Cranfield University (UK) for inputs and commentary in relation to this and other sections of the chapter.
2. The Designium report is the fourth in a series that has plotted developments in design policy in selected design-intensive nations for the past decade.
3. This is a practice that has met with some resistance from the professional design community. Accusations of 'unfair competitive advantage' have been aired with some ferocity (BDI, 2009).
4. Important examples can be found at Aalto and Cranfield Universities in Finland and the UK respectively.
5. In many ways the approach provides a counterpoint to user-centered forms of innovation, and one that is appropriate where more radical or alternative solutions are sought.
6. The Apple iPad is a useful example here. For many, the reintroduction—in highly revised form—of an ostensibly defunct concept (the tablet computer) has revolutionized the computing, entertainment and communications experience.

7. For example, museums, festivals and councils to celebrate the contribution of design.

BIBLIOGRAPHY

BDI. (2009) *Delivering the Innovation Dream.* London: British Design Innovation.

Bolton, S. and Green, L. (2008) 'Common Ground'. *New Design Journal* July: 47–49.

Borja de Mozota, B. (2003) *Design Management: Using Design to Build Brand Value and Corporate Innovation.* New York: Allworth Press.

Boston Consulting. (2006) 'Innovation Survey 2006'. Boston Consulting Group.

Brown, T. (2008) 'Design Thinking'. *Harvard Business Review* June 86 (6): 84–92

Business Week. (2009) 'How Business Is Adopting Design Thinking'. *Business Week.* November. Online. Available HTTP: http://www.businessweek.com/innovate/content/sep2009/id20090930_853305.htm (accessed 6 March 2012).

Cox, C. (2005) 'Cox Review of Creativity in Business: Building on the UK's Strengths'. HM Treasury.

DCMS. (2008) 'Creative Britain, New Talents for the New Economy'. UK Government white paper. Department for Culture, Media and Sport.

Design Council. (2005) *The Business of Design.* London: Design Council.

Design Council. (2007) 'The Value of Design Factfinder Report'. London: Design Council. Online. Available HTTP: http://www.designfactfinder.co.uk:8080/design-council/pdf/TheValueOfDesignFactfinder.pdf (accessed 6 March 2012).

Designium World Design Series. (2003) 'Design Policy and Promotion Programmes in Selected Countries and Regions'. Survey prepared at Designium, the New Centre of Innovation in Design, in the University of Art and Design in Helsinki. October. Online. Available HTTP: http://arts.aalto.fi/fi/research/designium/publications/design_policy_rep/ (accessed 6 March 2012).

Designium World Design Series. (2010) 'Global Design Watch 2010'. Online. Available HTTP: http://www.seeproject.org/docs/Global%20Design%20Watch%20-%202010.pdf (accessed 6 March 2012).

Green, L. and Bolton, S. (2008) 'Into the Light'. *New Design Journal* September: 24–27.

Green, L., Miles, I. and Rutter, J. (2007) 'Hidden Innovation in the Creative Sectors'. Interim report and working paper for NESTA.

Hertenstein, J. H., Platt, M. B. and Veryzer, R. W. (2005) 'The Impact of Industrial Design Effectiveness on Corporate Financial Performance'. *Journal of Product Innovation Management* 22: 3–21.

Kotler, P. and Rath, G. A. (1984) 'Design: A Powerful but Neglected Strategic Tool'. *Journal of Business Strategy* 5 (2): 16–21.

Krippendorff, K. and Butter, R. (1984) 'Product Semantics: Exploring the Symbolic Qualities of Form'. *Innovation* 3 (2): 4–9.

Le Masson, P., Weil, B. and Hatchuel, A. (2010), *Strategic Management of Innovation and Design.* Cambridge University Press

Miles, I. and Green, L. (2008) 'Hidden Innovation in the Creative Industries'. Final report for NESTA.

Morelli, N. (2006) 'Developing New PSS, Methodologies and Operational Tools'. *Journal of Cleaner Production* 14 (17): 1495–1501.

NESTA. (2011) 'Creating Innovation in Small and Medium-Sized Enterprises: Evaluating the Short-Term Effects of the Creative Credits Pilot'. NESTA working paper. London.

OECD. (1982) 'Innovation in Small and Medium Firms'. Paris: Organization for Economic Cooperation and Development.

Pinhanez, C. (2009) 'A Service Science Perspective on Human-Computer Interface Issues on Online Service Applications'. *International Journal of Information Systems in the Service Sector* 1 (2): 17–35.

Shostack, L. G. (1982) 'How to Design a Service'. *European Journal of Marketing* 16 (1): 49–63.

Simon, H. A. (1981) *The Sciences of the Artificial.* 2nd ed. Cambridge, MA: MIT Press.

Swann, G. M. P. (2010) 'The Economic Rationale for a National Design Policy'. BIS occasional paper no. 2. UK Government, Department for Business Innovation and Skills.

Ulrich, K. T. (2011) 'Design Is Everything?' *Journal of Product Innovation Management* 28: 394–398.

Verganti, R. (2009) *Design-Driven Innovation: Changing the Rules of Competition by Radically Innovating What Things Mean.* Boston MA: Harvard Business Press.

Visser, F. S. (2009) 'A Framework for Empathy in Design: Stepping into and out of the User's Life'. *Journal of Engineering Design* 20 (5): 437–448.

Von Hippel, E. (2007) 'An Emerging Hotbed of User-Centered Innovation'. *Harvard Business Review* 85 (2): 43–45.

Voss, C. A., Roth, A. V. and Chase, R. B. (2008) 'Experience, Service Operations Strategy, and Services as Destinations: Foundations and Exploratory Investigation'. *Production and Operations Management* 17 (3): 247–266.

Walsh V, Roy R, Bruce M, Potter S. (1992) *Winning by Design: Technology, Product Design and International Competitiveness.* Oxford, UK: Wiley-Blackwell

Conclusion
Challenges or Opportunities?

Paul Cunningham

As the title of this book suggests, the authors of the component chapters have sought to write about or identify the particular challenges facing those engaged, at various levels and in various ways, with the process of innovation. While it is not possible to say that the authors are able to provide answers to these challenges, the chapters raise issues that shed some new light on how these challenges may be viewed and, hopefully, offer some insights to those who are tasked with designing policies to support and facilitate innovation, in its more desirable forms.

The introductory chapter, untypically for a book about innovation, does not commence with a formal, policy-centered definition of the process of innovation, many of which typically derive from the academic literature, but rather it offers the reader a worldlier, individual-oriented view. Innovation, it states, 'involves a connection between our innate creativity on the one hand and our roles in economic life on the other'. As the chapters in this book demonstrate, innovation is a highly individualistic phenomenon, rarely undertaken for its own sake and frequently undertaken in order to create new ways of doing things or to transform the world in some way or to solve problems. Innovation, thus, may be seen as a way of dealing with challenges. However, as the opening chapter alludes, innovation may also be the originator of some of these problems. Here the challenge is how to avoid the unwanted and unforeseen consequences of innovation and how to ensure that policies aimed at stimulating innovation do not themselves create new problems.

The first section deals with the challenge of identifying who is driving innovation and how it can be controlled for the greater public good. Whatever the individual motives for innovation, it is clear that governments see innovation as 'a good thing'—a driver for economic growth and improved quality of life. Thus, it is a process that governments seek to promote and sustain. However, as a process that derives from human creativity and that is often stimulated by the desire to create wealth, can governments really influence innovation or are they mere bystanders—can 'creative destruction' be harnessed and shaped? Hence the first section of this book approaches this question from a variety of perspectives: government as a driver of innovation; government as a user of innovation; and government itself as an innovator.

Chapter 1 focuses on the role of government as a driver of innovation in some detail. In their chapter, Rigby et al. provide a typology that examines the roles that various actors in the innovation system (citizens, government, firms and universities) may play in the overall innovation process. Concluding that government should play a key role in driving innovation, they then identify four approaches that it may adopt. These approaches are all predicated on the assumption that the forms of innovation to be driven are all aimed at the general improvement of social and or environmental conditions, typically goals that form the basis of 'strategic research' directly funded by public sources and often performed in public laboratories or universities. In reality, the target of much government policy for innovation is more often than not indigenous sources or users of innovation (i.e., firms) whose economic performance can be linked to economic spillovers that improve the prosperity of the country and hence the quality of life of its population. Nevertheless, whatever the approach that may be adopted, it becomes clear that government alone cannot drive innovation without developing a clear understanding of the roles that all other actors in the process must play. An additional challenge—particularly at the European level—is, once having identified the key actors, to 'create coherent networks of actors, to align incentives and to create mutual confidence' while ensuring that the risks and uncertainties are shared among government, business and the market.

Clearly, governments have several 'policy levers' that enable them to play various roles, in addition to undertaking innovation-related activities themselves, such as through the provision of support, by facilitation and by offering an environment within which innovation might be expected to flourish. The abiding challenge here, as Rigby et al. note, is to be able to assess and select which of these levers are the most effective and appropriate in delivering innovation. This challenge forms the basis of the second chapter, in which Ian Miles and John Rigby examine one particular route towards fostering innovation open to government—the topic of demand-led innovation. This topic has become the focus of increasing policy attention over recent years and has faced the challenge of a lack of truly convincing evidence (although this is growing, particularly at the individual project level) to substantiate the assertions that the public sector can use the considerable resources at its disposal for the procurement of public sector goods and services in order to stimulate innovation. Nevertheless, Miles and Rigby conclude that in order to foster successful industrial innovation and for innovation to assist in confronting the so-called Grand Challenges, there is a major imperative to take demand into account in the formulation of policy in advance of 'scholarly clarification of the complex and evolving links between demand and innovation'—a message that implies policymakers should go with what they know works, and seek to understand precisely how it works later, perhaps the best form of evidence-based policy-making. However, they also note that policymakers have not waited for the rumination of academics and a number of policy instruments that harness demand for the furtherance of innovation are already in play. It appears that the challenge will be to learn the lessons of what factors are necessary for the success of these policies—a task made more difficult by the plethora of instruments and the unique nature of the successful projects and their outcomes. Obtaining evidence in order to derive generic lessons that can be applied in coordinated and broader-based approaches will pose a challenge to policymakers until a substantial evidence base has evolved.

In the final chapter in this section, Hugo Thénint and Ian Miles look within government itself in order to see whether it is possible to meet the challenge of innovation from within—can the public sector act as a source of innovation? In order to address this challenge, Thénint and Miles highlight the need to recognize that our understanding of innovation in the public sector context requires a broader, more encompassing interpretation of innovation, one that includes non-technological processes and services. Innovation in the public sector shares some characteristics with more 'traditional' forms of innovation. For example, it often stems from individual creativity and insights but requires an environment that is conducive to such ideas, which can recognize their value, foster them and allow them to flourish in order to reach their transformative potential. The implications of such innovation, dealing with social and environmental problems, for instance, are also likely to be more complex than those arising from businesses. Numerous studies, some of which are documented in this chapter, have mapped the various shaping factors that impinge upon public sector innovation. Although significant progress has been made towards gaining a better understanding of the role of the public sector in society, the ways in which it may foster and implement innovations and how those innovations eventually impact across society require further attention. The opportunities for public sector innovation are potentially enormous, not only in the delivery of improved public services, but also in making them more cost-effective in the face of increasingly constrained public budgets and the financial austerity measures demanded by the economic downturn. Accordingly, Thénint and Miles argue, policymakers should focus on public sector innovation that addresses the Grand Challenges and which fosters social democracy and equity.

The second section of the book shifts the focus to the principal actors involved with innovation, examining more closely the roles of government and industry and, in particular, how they may interact. As recognized in the first chapter, if the challenge of driving innovation is to be successfully met, the relationship between government and business (and between businesses) must be one that fosters mutual trust and recognition, and that shares the burden of risk inherent in innovation. Thus, John Rigby and Jennifer Hayden select the key policy topic of financing Europe's innovative

SMEs through the means of public-private partnerships. The challenge, they state, is not just to enable early-stage SMEs with the potential for high growth to better access sufficient capital from the private sector to fund their development, but also to get the conditions by which hybrid venture capital is delivered in a form that is of greatest benefit to the recipients. Several policy lessons may be learned from examples from across Europe (and beyond). The first is to strike the correct balance between a positive rate of return for the private investor and ensure the government's policy goals are met. The authors suggest the use of an EU-wide fund-of-funds approach (possibly based on an expansion of the CIP GIF initiative) dedicated to innovation, operated over a predetermined time frame. However, they do note that the existence of a finance gap for innovative SMEs remains open to debate or, if one does exist, whether it is the sole determinant for market failure. Regardless of whether they are correct, it is clear that the implications of the credit squeeze and continuing economic uncertainty in Europe cannot be anything other than disadvantageous to Europe's SMEs and that a policy response is required.

SMEs continue to form the focus of the next chapter, where Mercedes Bleda, Kathryn Morrison and John Rigby analyze the role and relevance of small, high-growth firms, or 'gazelles', in terms of innovation and competitiveness. The importance of such firms to economic growth and performance is widely documented and policymakers have identified them as a key target for policy attention—the challenge lies in the design of effective policy interventions to foster and support them. A key issue is that their dynamic and innovative characteristics make it difficult to provide a widely accepted definition of what a gazelle actually is and, at the same time, make them difficult to study. This highly specific nature calls for the formulation and implementation of equally specific policies that depart from the more traditional forms of support. Consequently, examples of policies dedicated to the support of gazelles have until quite recently been rare, in turn making it difficult for policymakers to learn about their effects. In addition, there is still debate over whether it is better to have policies that lead to an increase in the numbers of gazelles (targeting SMEs that are what might be termed 'proto-gazelles') or to target the gazelles themselves; it could be argued that in order to be a gazelle, an SME already has the characteristics necessary for growth. In short, while there is widespread agreement over the economic significance of gazelles, consensus over how, and indeed if, they should be supported has yet to be achieved.

Mutual trust and the mechanisms by which this may be affected form the subject of John Rigby and Jennifer Hayden's examination of the notions of firm-to-firm collaboration, open innovation and the role played by IPR. In this chapter they examine the use of IPR regimes as a potential policy tool for enhancing inter-firm and inter-sectoral knowledge transfer through collaboration, with a particular focus on the phenomenon of open innovation. Leaving aside the disputed novelty of open innovation, the authors note that, at the least, the term forms a useful reminder that the nature of collaborative innovation activities and knowledge production has changed dramatically over recent years as have the policy levers by which they may be supported. Several 'push' and 'pull' factors are identified that may explain this shift towards 'open' innovation. Of the former, there is a clear divergence between the increased complexities of knowledge, whether technological or market-oriented, and the capacity of firms to deal with this in-house, while the latter indicate a greater complexity in terms of the mechanisms and actors involved in collaboration. Whether there is a greater willingness (as opposed to necessity) to collaborate on the part of firms is open to discussion but it is evident that significant pressures and incentives exist for the sharing of knowledge. Rigby and Hayden also note ways in which IPR systems (including their weaknesses) may themselves contribute to this propensity to collaborate and hence promote open innovation. Although a number of patent strategies are highlighted that tend to diminish this propensity, patents are generally viewed as a tacit means to support the establishment of mutual trust upon which successful collaboration depends, and a number of alternative approaches to IPR also appear to offer promising incentives for collaboration in an open innovation context. Thus, the challenge for policymakers is to better understand the ways in which IP arrangements are used to foster mutual trust and hence to develop policy tools that facilitate such arrangements in order to promote increased levels of innovation. Here, Rigby and Hayden conclude that a case study approach would offer such valuable lessons.

In the final chapter in this section, Ian Miles and Yanuar Nugroho examine the issue of finance for innovation. They note the evidence from exercises such as the Community Innovation Survey (CIS), which identifies the lack of finance as a major barrier to innovation, and the crucial role that sources such as venture capital may play, particularly for small firms that wish to innovate. However, they choose to focus down to the level of microfinance, a set of financing mechanisms that has hitherto been typically associated with the support of entrepreneurship (often as a means of alleviating poverty) in developing economies but that, particularly in the light of the 2008 financial crisis and its ensuing ramifications, notably the drying up of credit streams, appears to have increasing relevance for policymakers in more developed economies. This potential seems particularly strong where support is needed for peripheral regions or for the alleviation of social exclusion. Unfortunately, Miles and Nugroho find that while there is empirical evidence on both microfinance *as* innovation (i.e., as a novel source of financial support) and innovation *for* microfinance (i.e., technologies that facilitate its use), little work has been done on microfinance *for* innovation (i.e., as another potential policy tool for the support of innovation). Nevertheless, their first conclusion is that microfinance appears to be highly applicable to some of the innovation financing issues encountered by small firms but that these issues are likely to exhibit extensive variation across regions, sectors and types of enterprises. The initial challenge they identify is the need for more detailed data on the specific financing requirements of firms, particularly those at the small and micro-levels. Greater exploration of existing data (such as that from the CIS) might offer insights as would more tailored studies of financing issues. They consider the scope for microfinancing support to be potentially quite broad, able to address a range of innovation activities, not just R&D but technology acquisition, diffusion and adoption, IPR and market development and others. Certainly its potential applications at the regional and local levels and in supporting social inclusion are worthy of further exploration.

The human element is critical to innovation but is no longer the domain of the lone inventor; better understanding of the innovation process, including the development of the idea of networked innovation, has broadened the spotlight onto the skills and capacities required, and the policies needed to enhance and develop these, in order that innovation may proceed. As Lawrence Green, Barbara Jones and Ian Miles point out in their opening chapter to the third section of the book, 'innovation depends on people who are able to generate and apply knowledge and ideas in the workplace and in society at large'. Particular skills are crucial to the generation and diffusion of innovation, such as problem-solving, technical, communication and interpersonal skills and collaborative working. One could also add that this is true both at the level of the individual and collectively— teaching skills to individuals is only half of the solution; the organization of individual skills sets in a way to maximize innovation potential is also required. The authors argue that the challenge here is to improve the current understanding of the relationship between skills and innovative capacity through developing clearer definitions of skills and innovation, and improving the measurement of human capital and innovation outcomes. Thus, while survey results, for example, clearly point to lack of skills as a barrier to innovation, identification of the skills necessary for innovation is far more problematic. Examining the 'twin engines of growth'—that is, the combination of skills development (or human capital accumulation) with innovation—the authors review the ways in which these act together with other variables to affect both the demand for skills and the ways in which skills that are conducive to innovation can be nurtured. A recurring problem appears to be how to reconcile the linear process through which skill sets develop and change as an innovation matures with the cyclical nature and requirements of the broader innovation process—one solution may be through the greater use of distributed skill sets, something that could be delivered through the process of 'open' innovation. Another challenge for policymakers is the continuing demand from business that education policies fail to deliver the skilled individuals they require—although the distinction between skills for innovation and training for a job or set of tasks may need clarification in this context. Although the chapter concludes with the recognition that any attempt to disentangle the skills that drive innovation from those that are demanded as a result of change brought about by innovation is far from straightforward, the authors go some way to casting some light on how this problem may be approached.

In their chapter, Jennifer Hayden and Barbara Jones take the examination of the human factor in innovation a step further by raising the question 'what are the implications of demographic change for the skills supply and for innovation?' They note that even the conventional and stereotypical notions of ageing are being challenged by the new demography and that this has profound implications for innovation, not least through the opportunities that might be created. They place these implications into two broad categories: the 'market opportunities' offered by an ageing population in its demand for novel services and products and the requirement for innovative solutions to alleviate the various burdens posed by an increasingly ageing population. However, as they also note, this dichotomy over-simplifies the complex interplay of social, health, work and other factors that a shifting demographic entails; innovation and an ageing population are not independent phenomena—each is driven and influenced by the other. The challenge for policymakers and others is to harness each in a way that optimizes the benefits that may ensue and that minimizes the risks posed by an accelerating pace of societal change.

The final section of the book shifts to the broader context of innovation, examining first the spatial and cultural milieu within which innovation can occur before considering the role of creativity in the innovation process. In the first of two offerings, Ian Miles and Sally Gee focus on the spatial context of innovation and the notion of agglomeration. Looking at a scale larger than that of the much visited 'innovation cluster', in their discussion, they contrast the large body of literature that supports the notion of 'creative cities'—loci for creativity and innovativeness, where the critical mass and diversity for these activities can arise and, in turn, lead to innovative cross-fertilization—with the countervailing argument that location no longer matters. They conclude that the evidence to suggest that much innovation is localized in particular cities and regions is substantial. Several factors may contribute to this, the key among which are the size and the composition of the population—particularly the presence of a 'creative class' and the willingness to accept and adopt new procedures and new approaches to established routines. The attractiveness (a feature that can encompass aesthetic, economic, infrastructural, regulatory and other considerations) of specific locations is also crucial in attracting and supporting creative and innovative activities. As in previous chapters, the challenge is addressed to policymakers—how they may shape these factors in ways that promote both quality of life and innovation, yet preserve environmental and social diversity and avoid social exclusion. Thus, Miles and Gee propose a combination of innovation policy with urban and regional policies that consider sustainability and social cohesion as a useful way forward towards the creation of desirable, innovative milieus.

In their next chapter, Gee and Miles examine the ways in which culture (rather than location) shapes and creates the preconditions for creativity, innovation and diffusion. Their discussion takes in values, attitudes and practices and focuses on cultural differences at the national and organizational levels. The idea of creativity and innovation as applied to geographic locales (in the previous chapter) is extended to the development of innovation culture at the firm level. At each level, however, the discussion is based on comparisons of how the influence of culture on innovation varies between nations, systems of innovation and firms. Noting the complexity of the interplay of cultural influences on innovation, Gee and Miles first examine the cultural influence of risk (perception and attitudes) upon innovation and, what may be seen as its counterbalance, regulation. Indeed, regulation is viewed as a form of embedded interaction between cultures—in this case the cultures of government, firms and other stakeholders, not least the public. A clear lesson is that similar forms of innovation can and do provoke different reactions and responses in different cultural situations: the complexity of the links between attitudes and values; institutions and regulations; responses to innovative ideas and products; entrepreneurship and risk-taking; and creativity and innovation all represent a challenge to policymakers, not least because there are rarely any direct links. This has several consequences, but perhaps the most relevant in the context of this book is that practices and policies for fostering innovation are rarely transposable across differing cultural contexts. Until there is a better understanding of how the relations between cultures and innovation operate across a range of contexts, policymakers must be wary of making assumptions that what works best in one nation, system or organization will do so in others.

In the final chapter Lawrence Green, Deborah Cox and Pierre Bitard consider the role of design and creativity—linked aspects of innovation that clearly mark a departure from the traditional view of innovation as a process that concerns the translation of inventions to the marketplace. They note that the issue of design as a topic of innovation research is quite novel, yet it is a major, albeit poorly understood element of the innovation process: improving our understanding of design is essential for developing a better understanding of the process of innovation and of how that process may be supported. The importance of design is now apparent to most consumers—witness the success of Apple and its 'i-' brand, where product design assumes as much, if not greater, significance than product functionality. Design aspects, more than ever before, confer high levels of added value to a whole range of consumer goods, from cars to furnishings to electrical goods and appliances and more. Design activities are now applied across a range of commercial functions and processes and have led to the development of various forms of design support and services, in which the public sector has sought to intervene through a variety of policy mechanisms. Our particular interest lies in the authors' examination of trends in design support initiatives and their identification of the key challenges that are faced by policymakers in the, admittedly still developing, efforts to promote the significance of design activities. It is clear that, through a range of initiatives, policymakers have been successful in their efforts to raise awareness of the importance of design and hence in its more widespread application as a facet of innovation within business practice and, more widely, in addressing societal needs. However, challenges remain, particularly in the need to develop improved and standardized benchmarks, measures and tools (not least to assist in evaluating 'the contribution of design to a broader set of industrial and service innovation activities' across the public and private sectors). Greater efforts, notably through education in business and design schools, are also needed to increase the alignment between the 'visions, goals and mindsets of business practitioners, and their counterparts in the design world'. Lastly, the role of design in tackling community, societal and sustainability issues requires further reinforcement and better articulation.

So, where does this leave us in terms of policies for innovation? Firstly, it is clear that an increasing understanding of the process of innovation has not provided policymakers with a series of 'magic bullets' that may be used to effectively support innovation in all its diverse forms. Rather, with increased understanding has come recognition of the ever more complex nature of innovation and a requirement to develop increasingly sophisticated policies through which it may be supported and promoted. Thus, having moved beyond the direct funding of R&D projects in businesses and the placement of graduate students to undertake R&D–related research studies in firms, to give two examples of 'traditional' innovation support measures, policymakers are now confronted with a range of instruments that, variously, influence collaboration through the regulation of IP, promote the will-o'-the-wisp notion of entrepreneurship, encourage firms to undertake R&D in order to offset tax payments, harness the intangible benefits of design in carving out new markets and driving competitiveness and a host of other indirect routes, to induce and encourage innovative behaviors.

Moreover, we are now using a new policy mode that does not rely on simply addressing market failures, although this is frequently used as a fallback rationale for guiding policy intervention; the need to address system failures has become the new yardstick for policy design. Unfortunately, as this book has effectively shown, innovation systems are complex entities as are the behaviors of the actors (firms, governments, markets and other stakeholders) within them—and it seems the further we investigate them, the more complex they become. They also inhabit complex environments in which factors such as skills, cultures, location, demographics and design, among others, have both discernible and (as yet) indiscernible influences. Whether we have the right set of policy tools to deal with these complexities (as is asked in the introduction to this book) is not clear—as many of the authors conclude, we need further evidence both of the influence of these factors and of the appropriateness of the currently available policy toolkit. For the time being, however, it seems that we are heading in the right direction.

The introductory chapter also posed the question of whether policy-making was following a consistent approach or if it was more a scattergun approach. One would conclude from the contents of this book that there are two elements to the answer. First, policy design and implementation are increasingly adopting a consistent approach along what has been termed evidence-based policy-making. This is in large part due to the efforts of individual governments and pan-governmental organizations, such as the OECD and the European Commission, in disseminating good practice for policy design and management—not least through their recognition of the importance of policy evaluation and its associated governance practices. Learning from the policy experience of others has become an adopted routine. However, we have also seen that context is critical—that which works in one location, region, country or cultural setting may not be replicable in others. Thus, a diversity of policy approaches is also desirable and provides a rich, global policy mix from which lessons may be learned about what elements of policy design work where and how. Policymakers are also cautious—this is taxpayers' money after all and resources are finite. Hence there is a tendency to experiment with new forms of policy instruments—for example, at the regional level or through limited pilot schemes in order that their degree of success may be assessed before scaling up. As in the educational field, any learning regimes must be appropriate to the context in which they are employed. In the innovation policy field this implies the need for robust and comparable sets of metrics and evaluative tools that will ensure that lessons learned in one context are equally applicable (or comparable) to those learned elsewhere.

The next question was 'if innovation is so unpredictable and takes place at so many levels, can effective policies to support it be developed?' A response might be to counter that innovation is not unpredictable—it will occur, but the route and time of its fruition are subject to such a range of influences that the challenge to policy is to attempt to identify the means by which it may be achieved in the most effective and efficient manner. Clearly, policies cannot address every level at which innovation may occur (or at which the process of innovation may be facilitated)—thus the task is to identify those levels (or nodes) at which policy levers may be effectively applied. This is not the same as the 'traditional' innovation policy objective of dealing with 'bottlenecks'—the process of innovation is not canalized but can be viewed more as a delta where multiple channels lead to a range of opportunities. This book has provided evidence that policymakers are indeed becoming better at identifying where and how policy efforts should be implemented albeit with varying degrees of success.

This leads us to the final question posed in the introductory chapter: which policy areas, not covered within the scope of this book, could also be relevant for the stimulation of innovation? Obvious candidates that come immediately to mind would perhaps include competition law, broader forms of regulation and standards, pricing and taxation—to name but a few. Such a question ignores the central conclusion of the book, that innovation is a multifaceted and context-specific phenomenon, which cannot easily be directed by a set of neatly compartmentalized policy fields. Rather, since itself it is a product of a complex array of interrelated and interacting factors, it requires an equally complex set of complementary policies for its facilitation—the environment in its entirety must be conducive to innovation. The challenge for the future, then, would appear to be the need to address the design of balanced innovation policy mixes that include not only direct and complementary stimuli for innovation, but also broader framework conditions, including social, geo-spatial and design considerations.

Contributors

Pierre Bitard is a researcher at the National Agency of Telecommunication Regulation (ANRT), where he is responsible for 'innovation and foresight'. He is involved in expertise and animation of permanent working groups on R&D and fiscal policy (R&D tax credit), valorization of public research and innovation in services. He has a PhD in economics of innovation (2001), the fieldwork for which was carried out at Renault 'Technocentre' as an internal consultant on organization matters. He started his career in 1995 as a project manager in a technology transfer organization before moving to applied economic research (innovation, spatial and industrial dynamics). He then moved to being a research fellow at the Division of Innovation at the University of Lund and has also worked as a senior consultant at Technopolis.

Mercedes Bleda is a research fellow at the Manchester Institute of Innovation Research (MIoIR). She has a first degree in economics and an MPhil in dynamic economics (Dept. of Quantitative Methods, University of Murcia, Spain), and a PhD in economics from CRIC (ESRC Centre for Research on Innovation and Competition Centre) at The University of Manchester in the UK. Her research interests are mainly focused on the use of complex evolutionary explanations and simulation modeling techniques for the analysis of the dynamics of socioeconomic systems. A substantial part of her work is centered on the study of processes of technological change and evolutionary innovation policy in the environmental realm.

Deborah Cox is a research fellow at the Manchester Institute of Innovation Research, Manchester Business School, in The University of Manchester, UK. Her academic qualifications are in social sciences and information management. She has published, with colleagues, in *Science and Public Policy, Foresight, Technology Analysis and Strategic Management, Accounting, Auditing & Accountability Journal* and *Journal of Documentation* and is a co-author on the monograph *Scrutinizing Science: The Changing UK Government of Science*, published by Palgrave

MacMillan. Her current research is in the field of STI policy research and has recently been concerned with public sector research systems and asset sharing in universities.

Paul Cunningham (PhD, BSc) is a senior research fellow and director in the Manchester Institute of Innovation Research (MIoIR) at Manchester Business School, The University of Manchester. Originally trained as a marine ecologist, he now has over twenty-five years' experience in the field of science, technology and innovation policy studies. During this time his research interests have expanded to cover a wide range of science and innovation policy-related fields, including: the study and practice of innovation and R&D evaluation methodologies, investigations of HEI-industry collaboration mechanisms, studies of quantitative measures of R&D performance and the development of science and technology indicators, and studies of international scientific collaboration.

Sally Gee is a researcher at the Manchester Institute of Innovation Research (MIoIR) and the Sustainable Consumption Institute (SCI) at The University of Manchester. She has a BSc in international management, an MSc in technology management from UMIST, and a PhD in distributed (open) innovation from the ESRC Centre for Research on Innovation and Competition (CRIC). She uses case studies to follow innovation processes over time and analyze system emergence and evolution, particularly focusing on the creation of knowledge and shifting patterns of industrial organization. Her recent work explores the potential of large public and private purchasers to steer system transformation.

Lawrence Green has been involved in teaching and research in connection with innovation for more than fifteen years. Following employment with Manchester Business School, Cranfield University, Oxford University and Central St. Martins College of Art and Design, he is currently a senior research fellow at the Centre for International Business and Innovation at Manchester Metropolitan University Business School. His research interests are focused firmly on the field of innovation studies and, in particular, relate to innovation in the service sector. His most recent work has examined the formation of multi-sector innovation networks, and innovation in the creative and cultural industries.

Jennifer Hayden is a research assistant and doctoral student in the department of Agricultural Economics and Rural Sociology at Penn State University. She has an MSc in nature, society and environmental policy from the Oxford University Centre for the Environment. Her research interests focus on the sociology of agriculture, including sustainability in the US food system, alternative food networks, gender and inequality, human health and soil management decision-making.

Dr. Barbara Jones is an associate researcher of the Manchester Institute of Innovation Research (MIoIR) at The University of Manchester. Her research interests include the political economy of technological change and innovation and the relationship between work, education and training in new technology areas. Recent publications include *Innovation Diffusion in the New Economy: The Tacit Dimension* (Routledge 2008).

Ian Miles is a professor of technological innovation and social change at Manchester Institute of Innovation Research (MIoIR) and co-director of the Centre for Service Research at Manchester Business School. He graduated in psychology from The University of Manchester in 1969, and received a higher doctorate in social science from the same university in 2011. Professor Miles is also head of the Laboratory of Economics of Innovation at ISSEK, Higher School of Economics, Moscow. In addition to research on service innovation and knowledge-intensive business services, his work has encompassed foresight and futures studies, information technology innovation and social indicators.

Kathryn Morrison has a first degree in geography and English from the University of Liverpool. She also holds an MA in development studies from the University of Manchester (2004) and a master's in education from Manchester Metropolitan University (2012). She worked as a research assistant at the Manchester Institute of Innovation Research, where her work included research on innovation for development and drivers of innovation. Her most recent research has focused on developments in education.

Yanuar Nugroho is a research fellow at Manchester Institute of Innovation Research (MIoIR) and a core staff member of the Centre for Development Informatics (CDI), Manchester Business School. He graduated in industrial engineering from the Institute of Technology Bandung (ITB) Indonesia in 1994, received an MSc in information systems engineering from UMIST in 2001 and a PhD in innovation studies from The University of Manchester in 2007. He was awarded the Hallsworth Fellowship in Political Economy of Innovations and Social Change (2010–2012). His research interests and publications are concerned with technological innovation and social change, in particular the adoption and diffusion of innovations in the third sector; innovation, development and sustainability; new communication media and social change; and knowledge and science dynamics.

John Rigby read history at Cambridge and then worked in IT before completing a PhD at The University of Manchester, studying under Professor Luke Georghiou and Dr. Mark Boden of PREST, and Dr. Sue Tindal of the Building Research Establishment, and writing his thesis on the rationale, rhetoric and impact of an information and advice dissemination program for energy efficiency. He works in the Manchester Institute of Innovation Research (of which PREST is now a part), the University's main research center in science and technology policy. He is a member of the Council of the Manchester Statistical Society.

Hugo Thénint is a senior consultant in a private company. He has a master's degree in economic policy analysis and an MA in European policy studies. His research fields respectively deal with international trade, economic geography and European regional policy. Hugo Thénint worked as the research coordinator for the European Commission–sponsored INNO-GRIPS project in the framework of the European initiative PRO-INNO. He has contributed to several studies on regional strategies for innovation, research and higher education, information society, entrepreneurship and cluster support policy. He was also involved in the European Foresight Monitoring Network, a network of policy professionals, foresight experts and analysts of science and technology carrying out a continuous monitoring of foresight initiatives and policies, at global, national and regional levels.

Index

For Product Safety Concerns and Information please contact our
EU representative GPSR@taylorandfrancis.com Taylor & Francis
Verlag GmbH, Kaufingerstraße 24, 80331 München, Germany